Statistical Analysis with R

by Joseph Schmuller, PhD

Statistical Analysis with R For Dummies®

Published by: **John Wiley & Sons, Inc.,** 111 River Street, Hoboken, NJ 07030-5774, www.wiley.com

Copyright © 2017 by John Wiley & Sons, Inc., Hoboken, New Jersey

Published simultaneously in Canada

For general information on our other products and services, please contact our Customer Care Department within the U.S. at 877-762-2974, outside the U.S. at 317-572-3993, or fax 317-572-4002. For technical support, please visit https://hub.wiley.com/community/support/dummies.

Wiley publishes in a variety of print and electronic formats and by print-on-demand. Some material included with standard print versions of this book may not be included in e-books or in print-on-demand. If this book refers to media such as a CD or DVD that is not included in the version you purchased, you may download this material at http://booksupport.wiley.com. For more information about Wiley products, visit www.wiley.com.

Library of Congress Control Number: 2017932881

ISBN: 978-1-119-33706-5; 978-1-119-33726-3 (ebk); 978-1-119-33709-6 (ebk)

Manufactured in the United States of America

10 9 8 7 6 5 4 3 2 1

Contents at a Glance

Table of Contents

Introduction

So you're holding a statistics book. In my humble (and absolutely biased) opinion, it's not just another statistics book. It's also not just another R book. I say this for two reasons.

First, many statistics books teach you the concepts but don't give you an easy way to apply them. That often leads to a lack of understanding. Because R is ready-made for statistics, it's a tool for applying (and learning) statistics concepts.

Second, let's look at it from the opposite direction: Before I tell you about one of R's features, I give you the statistical foundation it's based on. That way, you understand that feature when you use it — and you use it more effectively.

I didn't want to write a book that only covers the details of R and introduces some clever coding techniques. Some of that is necessary, of course, in any book that shows you how to use a software tool like R. My goal was to go way beyond that.

Neither did I want to write a statistics "cookbook": when-faced-with-problem-category-#152-use-statistical-procedure-#346. My goal was to go way beyond that, too.

Bottom line: This book isn't just about statistics or just about R — it's firmly at the intersection of the two. In the proper context, R can be a great tool for teaching and learning statistics, and I've tried to supply the proper context.

About This Book

Although the field of statistics proceeds in a logical way, I've organized this book so that you can open it up in any chapter and start reading. The idea is for you to find the information you're looking for in a hurry and use it immediately — whether it's a statistical concept or an R-related one.

On the other hand, reading from cover to cover is okay if you're so inclined. If you're a statistics newbie and you have to use R to analyze data, I recommend that you begin at the beginning.

Similarity with This Other For Dummies Book

You might be aware that I've written another book: *Statistical Analysis with Excel For Dummies* (Wiley). This is not a shameless plug for that book. (I do that elsewhere.)

I'm just letting you know that the sections in this book that explain statistical concepts are much like the corresponding sections in that one. I use (mostly) the same examples and, in many cases, the same words. I've developed that material during decades of teaching statistics and found it to be very effective. (Reviewers seem to like it, too.) Also, if you happen to have read the other book and you're transitioning to R, the common material might just help you make the switch.

And, you know: If it ain't broke. . . .

What You Can Safely Skip

Any reference book throws a lot of information at you, and this one is no exception. I intended for it all to be useful, but I didn't aim it all at the same level. So if you're not deeply into the subject matter, you can avoid paragraphs marked with the Technical Stuff icon.

As you read, you'll run into sidebars. They provide information that elaborates on a topic, but they're not part of the main path. If you're in a hurry, you can breeze past them.

Foolish Assumptions

I'm assuming this much about you:

» You know how to work with Windows or the Mac. I don't describe the details of pointing, clicking, selecting, and other actions.

» You're able to install R and RStudio (I show you how in Chapter 2) and follow along with the examples. I use the Windows version of RStudio, but you should have no problem if you're working on a Mac.

How This Book Is Organized

I've organized this book into five parts and three appendixes (which you can find on this book's companion website at www.dummies.com/go/statistical analysiswithr).

Part 1: Getting Started with Statistical Analysis with R

In Part 1, I provide a general introduction to statistics and to R. I discuss important statistical concepts and describe useful R techniques. If it's been a long time since your last course in statistics or if you've never even had a statistics course, start with Part 1. If you have never worked with R, *definitely* start with Part 1.

Part 2: Describing Data

Part of working with statistics is to summarize data in meaningful ways. In Part 2, you find out how to do that. Most people know about averages and how to compute them. But that's not the whole story. In Part 2, I tell you about additional statistics that fill in the gaps, and I show you how to use R to work with those statistics. I also introduce R graphics in this part.

Part 3: Drawing Conclusions from Data

Part 3 addresses the fundamental aim of statistical analysis: to go beyond the data and help you make decisions. Usually, the data are measurements of a sample taken from a large population. The goal is to use these data to figure out what's going on in the population.

This opens a wide range of questions: What does an average mean? What does the difference between two averages mean? Are two things associated? These are only a few of the questions I address in Part 3, and I discuss the R functions that help you answer them.

Part 4: Working with Probability

Probability is the basis for statistical analysis and decision-making. In Part 4, I tell you all about it. I show you how to apply probability, particularly in the area of modeling. R provides a rich set of capabilities that deal with probability. Here's where you find them.

Part 5: The Part of Tens

Part V has two chapters. In the first, I give Excel users ten tips for moving to R. In the second, I cover ten statistical- and R-related topics that wouldn't fit in any other chapter.

Online Appendix A: More on Probability

This online appendix continues what I start in Part 4. The material is a bit on the esoteric side, so I've stashed it in an appendix.

Online Appendix B: Non-Parametric Statistics

Non-parametric statistics are based on concepts that differ somewhat from most of the rest of the book. In this appendix, you learn these concepts and see how to use R to apply them.

Online Appendix C: Ten Topics That Just Didn't Fit in Any Other Chapter

This is the Grab Bag appendix, where I cover ten statistical- and R-related topics that wouldn't fit in any other chapter.

Icons Used in This Book

Icons appear all over *For Dummies* books, and this one is no exception. Each one is a little picture in the margin that lets you know something special about the paragraph it sits next to.

TIP

This icon points out a hint or a shortcut that can help you in your work (and perhaps make you a finer, kinder, and more insightful human being).

REMEMBER

This one points out timeless wisdom to take with you on your continuing quest for statistics knowledge.

WARNING

Pay attention to the information accompanied by this icon. It's a reminder to avoid something that might gum up the works for you.

TECHNICAL STUFF

As I mention in the earlier section "What You Can Safely Skip," this icon indicates material you can blow past if it's just too technical. (I've kept this to a minimum.)

Where to Go from Here

You can start reading this book anywhere, but here are a couple of hints. Want to learn the foundations of statistics? Turn the page. Introduce yourself to R? That's Chapter 2. Want to start with graphics? Hit Chapter 3. For anything else, find it in the table of contents or the index and go for it.

In addition to what you're reading right now, this product comes with a free access-anywhere Cheat Sheet that presents a selected list of R functions and describes what they do. To get this Cheat Sheet, visit www.dummies.com and type **Statistical Analysis with R For Dummies Cheat Sheet** in the search box.

1
Getting Started with Statistical Analysis with R

IN THIS CHAPTER

» **Introducing statistical concepts**

» **Generalizing from samples to populations**

» **Getting into probability**

» **Testing hypotheses**

» **Two types of error**

Chapter **1**

Data, Statistics, and Decisions

S tatistics? That's all about crunching numbers into arcane-looking formulas, right? Not really. Statistics, first and foremost, is about *decision-making*. Some number-crunching is involved, of course, but the primary goal is to use numbers to make decisions. Statisticians look at data and wonder what the numbers are saying. What kinds of trends are in the data? What kinds of predictions are possible? What conclusions can we make?

To make sense of data and answer these questions, statisticians have developed a wide variety of analytical tools.

About the number-crunching part: If you had to do it via pencil-and-paper (or with the aid of a pocket calculator), you'd soon get discouraged with the amount of computation involved and the errors that might creep in. Software like R helps you crunch the data and compute the numbers. As a bonus, R can also help you comprehend statistical concepts.

Developed specifically for statistical analysis, R is a computer language that implements many of the analytical tools statisticians have developed for decision-making. I wrote this book to show how to use these tools in your work.

The Statistical (and Related) Notions You Just Have to Know

The analytical tools that that R provides are based on statistical concepts I help you explore in the remainder of this chapter. As you'll see, these concepts are based on common sense.

Samples and populations

If you watch TV on election night, you know that one of the main events is the prediction of the outcome immediately after the polls close (and before all the votes are counted). How is it that pundits almost always get it right?

The idea is to talk to a *sample* of voters right after they vote. If they're truthful about how they marked their ballots, and if the sample is representative of the *population* of voters, analysts can use the sample data to draw conclusions about the population.

That, in a nutshell, is what statistics is all about — using the data from samples to draw conclusions about populations.

Here's another example. Imagine that your job is to find the average height of 10-year-old children in the United States. Because you probably wouldn't have the time or the resources to measure every child, you'd measure the heights of a representative sample. Then you'd average those heights and use that average as the estimate of the population average.

Estimating the population average is one kind of *inference* that statisticians make from sample data. I discuss inference in more detail in the upcoming section "Inferential Statistics: Testing Hypotheses."

REMEMBER

Here's some important terminology: Properties of a population (like the population average) are called *parameters*, and properties of a sample (like the sample average) are called *statistics*. If your only concern is the sample properties (like the heights of the children in your sample), the statistics you calculate are *descriptive*. If you're concerned about estimating the population properties, your statistics are *inferential*.

REMEMBER

Now for an important convention about notation: Statisticians use Greek letters (μ, σ, ρ) to stand for parameters, and English letters $(\bar{X}, s, r)$ to stand for statistics. Figure 1-1 summarizes the relationship between populations and samples, and between parameters and statistics.

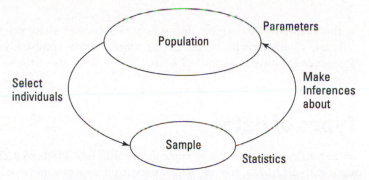

FIGURE 1-1:
The relationship
between
populations,
samples,
parameters, and
statistics.

Variables: Dependent and independent

A *variable* is something that can take on more than one value — like your age, the value of the dollar against other currencies, or the number of games your favorite sports team wins. Something that can have only one value is a *constant*. Scientists tell us that the speed of light is a constant, and we use the constant π to calculate the area of a circle.

Statisticians work with *independent* variables and *dependent* variables. In any study or experiment, you'll find both kinds. Statisticians assess the relationship between them.

For example, imagine a computerized training method designed to increase a person's IQ. How would a researcher find out if this method does what it's supposed to do? First, he would randomly assign a sample of people to one of two groups. One group would receive the training method, and the other would complete another kind of computer-based activity — like reading text on a website. Before and after each group completes its activities, the researcher measures each person's IQ. What happens next? I discuss that topic in the upcoming section "Inferential Statistics: Testing Hypotheses."

For now, understand that the independent variable here is Type of Activity. The two possible values of this variable are IQ Training and Reading Text. The dependent variable is the change in IQ from Before to After.

REMEMBER

A dependent variable is what a researcher *measures*. In an experiment, an independent variable is what a researcher *manipulates*. In other contexts, a researcher can't manipulate an independent variable. Instead, he notes naturally occurring values of the independent variable and how they affect a dependent variable.

REMEMBER

In general, the objective is to find out whether changes in an independent variable are associated with changes in a dependent variable.

In the examples that appear throughout this book, I show you how to use R to calculate characteristics of groups of scores, or to compare groups of scores. Whenever I show you a group of scores, I'm talking about the values of a dependent variable.

Types of data

When you do statistical work, you can run into four kinds of data. And when you work with a variable, the way you work with it depends on what kind of data it is. The first kind is *nominal* data. If a set of numbers happens to be nominal data, the numbers are labels – their values don't signify anything. On a sports team, the jersey numbers are nominal. They just identify the players.

The next kind is *ordinal* data. In this data-type, the numbers are more than just labels. As the name "ordinal" might tell you, the order of the numbers is important. If I ask you to rank ten foods from the one you like best (one), to the one you like least (ten), we'd have a set of ordinal data.

But the difference between your third-favorite food and your fourth-favorite food might not be the same as the difference between your ninth-favorite and your tenth-favorite. So this type of data lacks equal intervals and equal differences.

Interval data gives us equal differences. The Fahrenheit scale of temperature is a good example. The difference between 30° and 40° is the same as the difference between 90° and 100°. So each degree is an interval.

People are sometimes surprised to find out that on the Fahrenheit scale, a temperature of 80° is not twice as hot as 40°. For ratio statements ("twice as much as", "half as much as") to make sense, "zero" has to mean the complete absence of the thing you're measuring. A temperature of 0° F doesn't mean the complete absence of heat – it's just an arbitrary point on the Fahrenheit scale. (The same holds true for Celsius.)

The fourth kind of data, *ratio*, provides a meaningful zero point. On the Kelvin Scale of temperature, zero means "absolute zero," where all molecular motion (the basis of heat) stops. So 200° Kelvin is twice as hot as 100° Kelvin. Another example is length. Eight inches is twice as long as four inches. "Zero inches" means "a complete absence of length."

An independent variable or a dependent variable can be either nominal, ordinal, interval, or ratio. The analytical tools you use depend on the type of data you work with.

A little probability

When statisticians make decisions, they use probability to express their confidence about those decisions. They can never be absolutely certain about what they decide. They can only tell you how probable their conclusions are.

What do we mean by probability? Mathematicians and philosophers might give you complex definitions. In my experience, however, the best way to understand probability is in terms of examples.

Here's a simple example: If you toss a coin, what's the probability that it turns up heads? If the coin is fair, you might figure that you have a 50-50 chance of heads and a 50-50 chance of tails. And you'd be right. In terms of the kinds of numbers associated with probability, that's $\frac{1}{2}$.

Think about rolling a fair die (one member of a pair of dice). What's the probability that you roll a 4? Well, a die has six faces and one of them is 4, so that's $\frac{1}{6}$. Still another example: Select one card at random from a standard deck of 52 cards. What's the probability that it's a diamond? A deck of cards has four suits, so that's $\frac{1}{4}$.

These examples tell you that if you want to know the probability that an event occurs, count how many ways that event can happen and divide by the total number of events that can happen. In the first two examples (heads, 4), the event you're interested in happens only one way. For the coin, we divide one by two. For the die, we divide one by six. In the third example (diamond), the event can happen 13 ways (Ace through King), so we divide 13 by 52 (to get $\frac{1}{4}$).

Now for a slightly more complicated example. Toss a coin and roll a die at the same time. What's the probability of tails and a 4? Think about all the possible events that can happen when you toss a coin and roll a die at the same time. You could have tails and 1 through 6, or heads and 1 through 6. That adds up to 12 possibilities. The tails-and-4 combination can happen only one way. So the probability is $\frac{1}{12}$.

In general, the formula for the probability that a particular event occurs is

$$\text{Pr(event)} = \frac{\text{Number of ways the event can occur}}{\text{Total number of possible events}}$$

At the beginning of this section, I say that statisticians express their confidence about their conclusions in terms of probability, which is why I brought all this up in the first place. This line of thinking leads to *conditional* probability — the probability that an event occurs given that some other event occurs. Suppose that I roll a die, look at it (so that you don't see it), and tell you that I rolled an odd number. What's the probability that I've rolled a 5? Ordinarily, the probability of a 5 is $\frac{1}{6}$, but "I rolled an odd number" narrows it down. That piece of information eliminates the three even numbers (2, 4, 6) as possibilities. Only the three odd numbers (1,3, 5) are possible, so the probability is $\frac{1}{3}$.

What's the big deal about conditional probability? What role does it play in statistical analysis? Read on.

Inferential Statistics: Testing Hypotheses

Before a statistician does a study, he draws up a tentative explanation — a *hypothesis* that tells why the data might come out a certain way. After gathering all the data, the statistician has to decide whether or not to reject the hypothesis.

That decision is the answer to a conditional probability question — what's the probability of obtaining the data, given that this hypothesis is correct? Statisticians have tools that calculate the probability. If the probability turns out to be low, the statistician rejects the hypothesis.

Back to coin-tossing for an example: Imagine that you're interested in whether a particular coin is fair — whether it has an equal chance of heads or tails on any toss. Let's start with "The coin is fair" as the hypothesis.

To test the hypothesis, you'd toss the coin a number of times — let's say, a hundred. These 100 tosses are the sample data. If the coin is fair (as per the hypothesis), you'd expect 50 heads and 50 tails.

If it's 99 heads and 1 tail, you'd surely reject the fair-coin hypothesis: The conditional probability of 99 heads and 1 tail given a fair coin is very low. Of course, the coin could still be fair and you could, quite by chance, get a 99–1 split, right? Sure. You never really know. You have to gather the sample data (the 100 toss-results) and then decide. Your decision might be right, or it might not.

Juries make these types of decisions. In the United States, the starting hypothesis is that the defendant is not guilty ("innocent until proven guilty"). Think of the evidence as "data." Jury-members consider the evidence and answer a conditional probability question: What's the probability of the evidence, given that the defendant is not guilty? Their answer determines the verdict.

Null and alternative hypotheses

Think again about that coin-tossing study I just mentioned. The sample data are the results from the 100 tosses. I said that we can start with the hypothesis that the coin is fair. This starting point is called the *null hypothesis*. The statistical notation for the null hypothesis is H_o. According to this hypothesis, any heads-tails split in the data is consistent with a fair coin. Think of it as the idea that nothing in the sample data is out of the ordinary.

An alternative hypothesis is possible — that the coin isn't a fair one and it's loaded to produce an unequal number of heads and tails. This hypothesis says that any heads-tails split is consistent with an unfair coin. This alternative hypothesis is called, believe it or not, the *alternative hypothesis.* The statistical notation for the alternative hypothesis is H_1.

Now toss the coin 100 times and note the number of heads and tails. If the results are something like 90 heads and 10 tails, it's a good idea to reject H_o. If the results are around 50 heads and 50 tails, don't reject H_o.

Similar ideas apply to the IQ example I gave earlier. One sample receives the computer-based IQ training method, and the other participates in a different computer-based activity — like reading text on a website. Before and after each group completes its activities, the researcher measures each person's IQ. The null hypothesis, H_o, is that one group's improvement isn't different from the other. If the improvements are greater with the IQ training than with the other activity — so much greater that it's unlikely that the two aren't different from one another — reject H_o. If they're not, don't reject H_o.

REMEMBER

Notice that I did *not* say "accept H_o." The way the logic works, you *never* accept a hypothesis. You either reject H_o or don't reject H_o. In a jury trial, the verdict is either "guilty" (reject the null hypothesis of "not guilty") or "not guilty" (don't reject H_o). "Innocent" (acceptance of the null hypothesis) is not a possible verdict.

Notice also that in the coin-tossing example I said "around 50 heads and 50 tails." What does *around* mean? Also, I said that if it's 90-10, reject H_o. What about 85-15? 80-20? 70-30? Exactly how much different from 50-50 does the split have to be for you to reject H_o? In the IQ training example, how much greater does the IQ improvement have to be to reject H_o?

I won't answer these questions now. Statisticians have formulated decision rules for situations like this, and we'll explore those rules throughout the book.

Two types of error

Whenever you evaluate data and decide to reject H_o or to not reject H_o, you can never be absolutely sure. You never really know the "true" state of the world. In the coin-tossing example, that means you can't be certain if the coin is fair or not.

All you can do is make a decision based on the sample data. If you want to know for sure about the coin, you have to have the data for the entire population of tosses — which means you have to keep tossing the coin until the end of time.

Because you're never certain about your decisions, you can make an error either way you decide. As I mention earlier, the coin could be fair and you just happen to get 99 heads in 100 tosses. That's not likely, and that's why you reject H_o if that happens. It's also possible that the coin is biased, yet you just happen to toss 50 heads in 100 tosses. Again, that's not likely and you don't reject H_o in that case.

Although those errors are not likely, they are possible. They lurk in every study that involves inferential statistics. Statisticians have named them *Type I* errors and *Type II* errors.

If you reject H_o and you shouldn't, that's a Type I error. In the coin example, that's rejecting the hypothesis that the coin is fair, when in reality it is a fair coin.

If you don't reject H_o and you should have, that's a Type II error. It happens if you don't reject the hypothesis that the coin is fair, and in reality it's biased.

How do you know if you've made either type of error? You don't — at least not right after you make the decision to reject or not reject H_o. (If it's possible to know, you wouldn't make the error in the first place!) All you can do is gather more data and see if the additional data is consistent with your decision.

If you think of H_o as a tendency to maintain the status quo and not interpret anything as being out of the ordinary (no matter how it looks), a Type II error means you've missed out on something big. In fact, some iconic mistakes are Type II errors.

Here's what I mean. On New Year's day in 1962, a rock group consisting of three guitarists and a drummer auditioned in the London studio of a major recording company. Legend has it that the recording executives didn't like what they heard, didn't like what they saw, and believed that guitar groups were on the way out. Although the musicians played their hearts out, the group failed the audition.

Who was that group? The Beatles!

And *that's* a Type II error.

Chapter **2**

R: What It Does and How It Does It

R is a computer language. It's a tool for doing the computation and number-crunching that set the stage for statistical analysis and decision-making. An important aspect of statistical analysis is to present the results in a comprehensible way. For this reason, graphics is a major component of R.

Ross Ihaka and Robert Gentleman developed R in the 1990s at the University of Auckland, New Zealand. Supported by the Foundation for Statistical Computing, R is getting more and more popular by the day.

RStudio is an open source integrated development environment (IDE) for creating and running R code. It's available in versions for Windows, Mac, and Linux. Although you don't need an IDE in order to work with R, RStudio makes life a *lot* easier.

Downloading R and RStudio

First things first. Download R from the Comprehensive R Archive Network (CRAN). In your browser, type this address if you work in Windows:

```
cran.r-project.org/bin/windows/base/
```

Type this one if you work on the Mac:

```
cran.r-project.org/bin/macosx/
```

Click the link to download R. This puts the `win.exe` file in your Windows computer, or the `.pkg` file in your Mac. In either case, follow the usual installation procedures. When installation is complete, Windows users see an R icon on their desktop, Mac users see it in their Application folder.

Both URLs provides helpful links to FAQs. The Windows-related URL also links to "Installation and other instructions."

Now for RStudio. Here's the URL:

```
www.rstudio.com/products/rstudio/download
```

Click the link for the installer for your computer, and again follow the usual installation procedures.

After the RStudio installation is finished, click the RStudio icon to open the window shown in Figure 2-1.

If you already have an older version of RStudio and you go through this installation procedure, the install updates to the latest version (and you don't have to uninstall the older version).

The large Console pane on the left runs R code. One way to run R code is to type it directly into the Console pane. I show you another way in a moment.

The other two panes provide helpful information as you work with R. The Environment and History pane is in the upper right. The Environment tab keeps track of the things you create (which R calls *objects*) as you work with R. The History tab tracks R code that you enter.

Get used to the word *object.* Everything in R is an object.

The Files, Plots, Packages, and Help tabs are in the pane in the lower right. The Files tab shows files you create. The Plots tab holds graphs you create from your data. The Packages tab shows add-ons (called *packages*) you downloaded as part of the R installation. Bear in mind that "downloaded" doesn't mean "ready to use." To use a package's capabilities, one more step is necessary – and believe me – you'll want to use packages.

Figure 2-2 shows the Packages tab. The packages are in either the user library (which you can see in the figure) or the system library (which you have to scroll down to). I discuss packages later in this chapter.

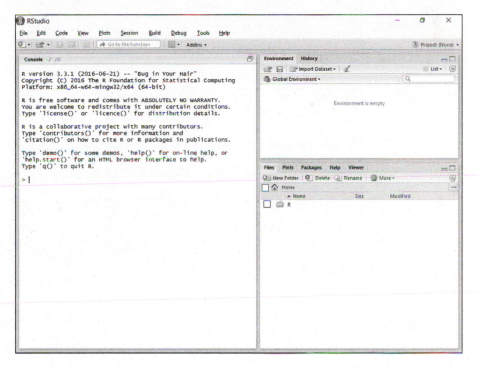

FIGURE 2-1:
RStudio, immediately after you install it and click on its icon.

The Help tab, shown in Figure 2-3, provides links to a wealth of information about R and RStudio.

To tap into the full power of RStudio as an IDE, click the larger of the two icons in the upper right corner of the Console pane. That changes the appearance of RStudio so that it looks like Figure 2-4.

FIGURE 2-2:
The RStudio
Packages tab.

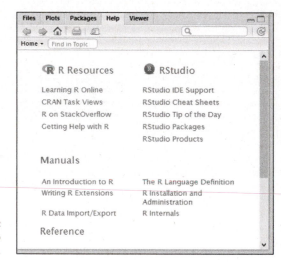

FIGURE 2-3:
The RStudio
Help tab.

The top of the Console pane relocates to the lower left. The new pane in the upper left is the Scripts pane. You type and edit code in the Scripts pane and press Ctrl+R (Command+Enter on the Mac), and then the code executes in the Console pane.

TIP

Ctrl+Enter works just like Ctrl+R. You can also select

Code ⇨ Run Selected Line(s)

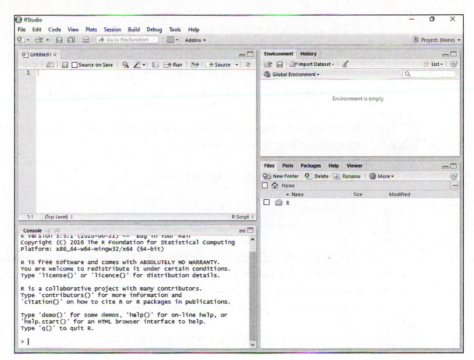

A Session with R

Before you start working, select

> File ⇨ Save As . . .

and then save as My First R Session. This relabels the tab in the Scripts pane with the name of the file and adds the `.R` extension. This also causes the filename (along with the `.R` extension) to appear on the Files tab.

The working directory

What exactly does R save, and where does R save it? What R saves is called the *workspace*, which is the environment you're working in. R saves the workspace in the *working directory*. In Windows, the default working directory is

```
C:\Users\<User Name>\Documents
```

If you ever forget the path to your working directory, type

```
> getwd()
```

in the Console pane, and R returns the path onscreen.

In the Console pane, you don't type the right-pointing arrowhead at the beginning of the line. That's a prompt.

My working directory looks like this:

```
> getwd()
[1] "C:/Users/Joseph Schmuller/Documents
```

Note which way the slashes are slanted. They're opposite to what you typically see in Windows file paths. This is because R uses \ as an *escape character*, meaning that whatever follows the \ means something different from what it usually means. For example, \t in R means *Tab key*.

You can also write a Windows file path in R as

```
C:\\Users\\<User Name>\\Documents
```

If you like, you can change the working directory:

```
> setwd(<file path>)
```

Another way to change the working directory is to select

```
Session⇨ Set Working Directory⇨ Choose Directory
```

So let's get started, already

And now for some R! In the Script window, type

```
x <- c(3,4,5)
```

and then Ctrl+R.

That puts the following line into the Console pane:

```
> x <- c(3,4,5)
```

As I mention in an earlier Tip, the right-pointing arrowhead (the greater-than sign) is a prompt that R supplies in the Console pane. You don't see it in the Scripts pane.

What did R just do? The arrow sign says that x gets assigned whatever is to the right of the arrow sign. So the arrow-sign is R's *assignment operator*.

To the right of the arrow sign, the *c* stands for *concatenate*, a fancy way of saying "Take whatever items are in the parentheses and put them together." So the set of numbers 3, 4, 5 is now assigned to x.

REMEMBER

R refers to a set of numbers like this as a *vector*. (I tell you more on this in the later "R Structures" section.)

You can read that line of R code as "x gets the vector 3, 4, 5."

Type **x** into the Scripts pane and press Ctrl+R, and here's what you see in the Console pane:

```
> x
[1] 3 4 5
```

The 1 in square brackets is the label for the first value in the line of output. Here you have only one value, of course. What happens when R outputs many values over many lines? Each line gets a bracketed numeric label, and the number corresponds to the first value in the line. For example, if the output consists of 21 values and the 18th value is the first one on the second line, the second line begins with [18].

Creating the vector x causes the Environment tab to look like Figure 2-5.

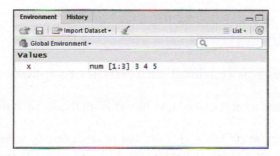

FIGURE 2-5:
The RStudio Environment tab, after creating the vector x.

TIP

Another way to see the objects in the environment is to type

```
> ls()
```

Now you can work with x. First, add all numbers in the vector. Typing

```
sum(x)
```

in the Scripts pane (remember to follow with Ctrl+R) executes the following line in the Console pane:

```
> sum(x)
[1] 12
```

How about the average of the numbers in the vector x?

That's

```
mean(x)
```

in the Scripts pane, which (when followed by Ctrl+R) executes to

```
>  mean(x)
[1] 4
```

in the Console pane.

TIP

As you type in the Scripts pane or in the Console pane, you'll notice that helpful information pops up. As you gain experience with RStudio, you'll learn how to use that information.

As I show you in Chapter 5, *variance* is a measure of how much a set of numbers differs from their mean. What exactly is variance, and how do you calculate it? I'll leave that for Chapter 5. For now, here's how you use R to calculate variance:

```
> var(x)
[1] 1
```

In each case, you type a command and R evaluates it and displays the result.

Figure 2-6 shows what RStudio looks like after all these commands.

To end a session, select File ⇨ Quit Session or press Ctrl+Q. As Figure 2-7 shows, a dialog box opens and asks what you want to save from the session. Saving the selections enables you to reopen the session where you left off the next time you open RStudio (although the Console pane doesn't save your work).

Pretty helpful, this RStudio.

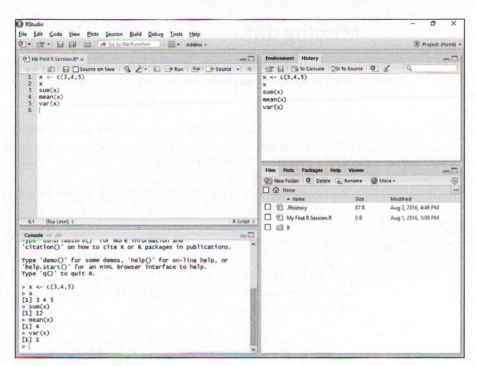

FIGURE 2-6:
RStudio after creating and working with a vector.

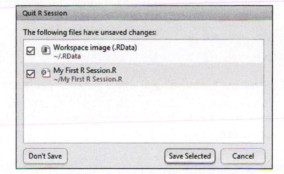

FIGURE 2-7:
The Quit R Session dialog box.

REMEMBER

Moving forward, most of the time I don't say "Type this R code into the Scripts pane and press Ctrl+Enter" whenever I take you through an example. I just show you the code and its output, as in the var() example.

REMEMBER

Also, sometimes I show code with the > prompt, and sometimes without. Generally, I show the prompt when I want you to see R code and its results. I don't show the prompt when I just want you to see R code that I create in the Scripts pane.

Missing data

In the statistical analysis examples I provide, I typically deal with best-case scenarios in which the data sets are in good shape and have all the data they're supposed to have.

In the real world, however, things don't always go so smoothly. Oftentimes, you encounter data sets that have values missing for one reason or another. R denotes a missing value as NA (for Not Available).

For example, here is some data (from a much larger data set) on the luggage capacity, in cubic feet, of nine vehicles:

```
capacity <- c(14,13,14,13,16,NA,NA,20,NA)
```

Three of the vehicles are vans, and the term *luggage capacity* doesn't apply to them — hence, the three instances of NA. Here's what happens when you try to find the average of this group:

```
> mean(capacity)
[1] NA
```

To find the mean, you have to remove the NAs before you calculate:

```
> mean(capacity, na.rm=TRUE)
[1] 15
```

So the rm in na.rm means "remove" and =TRUE means "get it done."

TIP

Just in case you ever have to check a set of scores for missing data, the is,na() function does that for you:

```
> is.na(capacity)
[1] FALSE FALSE FALSE FALSE FALSE  TRUE   TRUE FALSE   TRUE
```

R Functions

In the preceding section, I use c(), sum(), mean(), and var(). These are examples of *functions* built into R. Each one consists of a function name immediately followed by parentheses. Inside the parentheses are the *arguments*. In this context, "argument" doesn't mean "disagreement," "confrontation," or anything like that. It's just the math term for whatever a function operates on.

REMEMBER

Even if a function takes no arguments, you still include the parentheses.

The four R functions I've shown you are pretty simple in terms of their arguments and their output. As you work with R, however, you encounter functions that take more than one argument.

R provides a couple of ways for you to deal with multiargument functions. One way is to list the arguments in the order in which they appear in the function's definition. R calls this *positional matching*.

Here's what I mean. The function substr() takes three arguments. The first is a string of characters like "abcdefg", which R refers to as a *character vector*. The second argument is a *start* position within the string (1 is the first position, 2 is the second position, and so on). The third is a *stop* position within the string (a number greater than or equal to the start position). In fact, if you type **substr** into the Scripts pane, you see a helpful pop-up message that looks like this:

```
substr(x, start, stop)
 Extract or replace substrings in a character vector
```

where x stands for the character vector.

This function returns the substring, which consists of the characters between the start and stop positions.

Here's an example:

```
> substr("abcdefg",2,4)
[1] "bcd"
```

What happens if you interchange the 2 and the 4?

```
> substr("abcdefg",4,2)
[1] ""
```

This result is completely understandable: No substring can start at the fourth position and stop at the second position.

But if you *name* the arguments, it doesn't matter how you order them:

```
> substr("abcdefg",stop=4,start=2)
[1] "bcd"
```

Even this works:

```
> substr(stop=4, start=2,"abcdefg")
[1] "bcd"
```

So when you use a function, you can place its arguments out of order, if you name them. R calls this *keyword matching*, which comes in handy when you use an R function that has many arguments. If you can't remember their order, just use their names and the function works.

TIP

If you ever need help for a particular function — substr(), for example — type **?substr** and watch helpful information appear on the Help tab.

User-Defined Functions

Strictly speaking, this is not a book on R programming. For completeness, though, I thought I'd at least let you know that you can create your own functions in R, and show you the fundamentals of creating one.

The form of an R function is

```
myfunction <- function(argument1, argument2, ...){
           statements
           return(object)
           }
```

Here's a simple function for computing the sum of the squares of three numbers:

```
sumofsquares <- function(x,y,z){
  sumsq <- sum(c(x^2,y^2,z^2))
  return(sumsq)
}
```

Type that snippet into the Scripts pane and highlight it. Then press Ctrl+R. The following snippet appears in the Console pane:

```
> sumofsquares <- function(x,y,z ){
+    sumsq <- sum(c(x^2,y^2,z^2))
+    return(sumsq)
+ }
```

Each plus-sign is a *continuation prompt*. It just indicates that a line continues from the preceding line.

And here's how to use the function:

```
> sumofsquares(3,4,5)
[1] 50
```

Comments

A *comment* is a way of annotating code. Begin a comment with the # symbol, which of course is an *octothorpe*. (What's that you say? "Hashtag"? Surely you jest.) This symbol tells R to ignore everything to the right of it.

Comments are very helpful for someone who has to read code that you've written. For example:

```
sumofsquares <- function(x,y,z){  # list the arguments
  sumsq <- sum(c(x^2,y^2,z^2))   # perform the operations
  return(sumsq)    # return the value
}
```

Just a heads-up: I don't add comments to lines of code in this book. Instead, I provide detailed descriptions. In a book like this, I feel that's the most effective way to get the message across.

TIP

As you might imagine, writing R functions can encompass WAY more than I've laid out here. To learn more, check out *R For Dummies*, by Andrie de Vries and Joris Meys (John Wiley & Sons).

R Structures

I mention in the "R Functions" section, earlier in this chapter, that an R function can have many arguments. It's also the case that an R function can have many outputs. To understand the possible outputs (and inputs, too), you must understand the structures that R works with.

Vectors

The *vector* is R's fundamental structure, and I showed it to you in earlier examples. It's an array of data elements of the same type. The data elements in a vector are called *components*. To create a vector, use the function c(), as I did in the earlier example:

```
> x <- c(3,4,5)
```

Here, of course, the components are numbers.

In a character vector, the components are quoted text strings ("Moe," "Larry," "Curly"):

```
> stooges <- c("Moe","Larry", "Curly")
```

TECHNICAL STUFF

Strictly speaking, in the substr() example, "abcdefg" is a character vector with one element.

It's also possible to have a *logical* vector, whose elements are TRUE and FALSE, or the abbreviations T and F:

```
> z <- c(T,F,T,F,T,T)
```

To refer to a specific component of a vector, follow the vector name with a bracketed number:

```
> stooges[2]
[1] "Larry"
```

Numerical vectors

In addition to c(), R provides seq() and rep() for shortcut numerical vector creation.

Suppose you want to create a vector of numbers from 10 to 30 but you don't feel like typing all those numbers. Here's how to do it:

```
> y <- seq(10,30)
> y
 [1] 10 11 12 13 14 15 16 17 18 19 20 21 22 23 24 25 26
[18] 27 28 29 30
```

On my screen, and probably on yours too, all the elements in y appear on one line. The printed page, however, is not as wide as the Console pane. Accordingly, I separated the output into two lines. I do that throughout the book, where necessary.

R has a special syntax for a numerical vector whose elements increase by 1:

```
> y <- 10:30
> y
 [1] 10 11 12 13 14 15 16 17 18 19 20 21 22 23 24 25 26
[18] 27 28 29 30
```

If you want the elements to increase in steps of 2, use seq like this:

```
> w <- seq(10,30,2)
> w
 [1] 10 12 14 16 18 20 22 24 26 28 30
```

You might want to create a vector of repeating values. If so, rep() is the function to use:

```
> trifecta <- c(6,8,2)
> repeated_trifecta <- rep(trifecta,4)
> repeated_trifecta
 [1] 6 8 2 6 8 2 6 8 2 6 8 2
```

Another way to use rep() is to supply a vector as the second argument. Remember from the earlier example that x is the vector (3,4,5) What happens if you supply x as the second argument for rep()?

```
> repeated_trifecta <- rep(trifecta,x)
> repeated_trifecta
 [1] 6 6 6 8 8 8 8 2 2 2 2 2
```

The first element repeats three times; the second element, four times; and the third element, five times.

Matrices

A *matrix* is a 2-dimensional array of data elements of the same type. In statistics, matrices are useful as tables that hold data. (Advanced statistics has other applications for matrices, but that's beyond the scope of this book.)

You can have a matrix of numbers:

5	30	55	80
10	35	60	85
15	40	65	90
20	45	70	95
25	50	75	100

or a matrix of character strings:

"Moe"	"Larry"	"Curly"	"Shemp"
"Groucho"	"Harpo"	"Chico"	"Zeppo"
"Ace"	"King"	"Queen"	"Jack"

The numbers constitute a 5 (rows) X 4 (columns) matrix; the character strings matrix is 3 X 4.

To create the 5 X 4 numerical matrix, first you create the vector of numbers from 5 to 100 in steps of 5:

```
> num_matrix <- seq(5,100,5)
```

Then you use the dim() function to turn the vector into a 2-dimensional matrix:

```
> dim(num_matrix) <-c(5,4)
> num_matrix
     [,1] [,2] [,3] [,4]
[1,]    5   30   55   80
[2,]   10   35   60   85
[3,]   15   40   65   90
[4,]   20   45   70   95
[5,]   25   50   75  100
```

Note how R displays the bracketed row numbers along the side, and the bracketed column numbers along the top.

Transposing a matrix interchanges the rows with the columns. In R, the t() function takes care of that:

```
> t(num_matrix)
     [,1] [,2] [,3] [,4] [,5]
```

```
[1,]     5    10    15    20    25
[2,]    30    35    40    45    50
[3,]    55    60    65    70    75
[4,]    80    85    90    95   100
```

The function `matrix()` provides another way to create matrices:

```
> num_matrix <- matrix(seq(5,100,5),nrow=5)
> num_matrix
      [,1] [,2] [,3] [,4]
[1,]     5   30   55   80
[2,]    10   35   60   85
[3,]    15   40   65   90
[4,]    20   45   70   95
[5,]    25   50   75  100
```

If you add the argument `byrow=T`, R fills the matrix by rows, like this:

```
> num_matrix <- matrix(seq(5,100,5),nrow=5,byrow=T)
> num_matrix
      [,1] [,2] [,3] [,4]
[1,]     5   10   15   20
[2,]    25   30   35   40
[3,]    45   50   55   60
[4,]    65   70   75   80
[5,]    85   90   95  100
```

How do you refer to a particular matrix component? you type the matrix name and then, in brackets, the row number, a comma, and the column number:

```
> num_matrix[5,4]
[1] 100
```

Factors

In Chapter 1, I describe four types of data: nominal, ordinal, interval, and ratio. In nominal data, numbers are just labels, and their magnitude has no significance.

Suppose you're doing a survey of people's eye color. As you record a person's eye color, you record a number: 1 = amber, 2 = blue, 3 = brown, 4 = gray, 5 = green, and 6 = hazel. One way to think of this process is that eye color is a *factor*, and each color is a *level* of that factor. So in this case, the factor eye-color has six levels.

Factor is R's term for a nominal variable (also known as *categorical variable*).

Now imagine that you've used the numeric code to tabulate the eye colors of 14 people and then turned those codes into a vector:

```
> eye_color <- c(2,2,4,1,5,5,5,6,1,3,6,3,1,4)
```

Next, you use the `factor()` function to turn `eye_color` into a factor:

```
> feye_color <- factor(eye_color)
```

Finally, you assign the levels of the factor:

```
> levels(feye_color) <- c("amber","blue", "brown","gray","green",
  "hazel")
```

Now, if you examine the eye color data in terms of the factor levels, it looks like this:

```
> feye_color
 [1] blue  blue  gray  amber green green green hazel amber
[10] brown hazel brown amber gray
Levels: amber blue brown gray green hazel
```

Lists

In R, a *list* is a collection of objects that aren't necessarily of the same type. Suppose that in addition to the eye color of each person in the example in the preceding section, you collect an "empathy score" based on a personality test. The scale runs from 0 (least empathy) to 100 (most empathy). Here's the vector for these people's empathy data:

```
> empathy_score <- c(15,21,45,32,61,74,53,92,83,22,67,55,42,44)
```

You want to combine the eye color vector in coded form, the eye color vector in factor form, and the empathy score vector into one collection named `eyes_and_empathy`. You use the `list()` function for this task:

```
> eyes_and_empathy <- list(eyes_code=eye_color, eyes=feye_color,
  empathy=empathy_score)
```

Note that you name each argument (`eyes_code`, `eyes`, and `empathy`). This causes R to use those names as the names of the list components.

Here's what the list looks like:

```
> eyes_and_empathy
$eyes_code
 [1] 2 2 4 1 5 5 5 6 1 3 6 3 1 4

$eyes
 [1] blue  blue  gray  amber green green green hazel amber
[10] brown hazel brown amber gray
Levels: amber blue brown gray green hazel

$empathy
 [1] 15 21 45 32 61 74 53 92 83 22 67 55 42 44
```

As you can see, R uses the dollar sign ($) to indicate each component of the list. So, if you want to refer to a list component, you type the name of the list, the dollar sign, and the component-name:

```
> eyes_and_empathy$empathy
 [1] 15 21 45 32 61 74 53 92 83 22 67 55 42 44
```

How about zeroing in on a particular score, like the fourth one? I think you can see where this is headed:

```
> eyes_and_empathy$empathy[4]
[1] 32
```

Lists and statistics

Lists are important because numerous statistical functions return lists of objects. One statistical function is t.test(). In Chapter 10, I explain this test and the theory behind it. For now, just concentrate on its output.

I use this test to see if the mean of the empathy scores differs from an arbitrary number — 30, for example. Here's the test:

```
> t.result <- t.test(eyes_and_empathy$empathy, mu = 30)
```

Let's examine the output:

```
> t.result

        One Sample t-test
```

```
data:   eyes_and_empathy$empathy
t = 3.2549, df = 13, p-value = 0.006269
alternative hypothesis: true mean is not equal to 30
95 percent confidence interval:
 36.86936 63.98778
sample estimates:
mean of x
 50.42857
```

Without getting into the details, understand that this output, t.result, is a list. To show this, you use $ to focus on some of the components:

```
> t.result$data.name
[1] "eyes_and_empathy$empathy"
> t.result$p.value
[1] 0.006269396
> t.result$statistic
       t
3.254853
```

Data frames

A list is a good way to collect data. A data frame is even better. Why? When you think of data for a group of individuals — like the 14 people in the example in the earlier section — you typically think in terms of columns that represent the data variables (like eyes_code, eyes, and empathy) and rows that represent the individuals. And that's a data frame. If the terms *data set* or *data matrix* come to mind, you've pretty much got it.

The function data.frame() works with the existing vectors to get the job done:

```
> e <- data.frame(eye_color,feye_color,empathy_score)
> e
  eye_color feye_color empathy_score
1         2       blue            15
2         2       blue            21
3         4       gray            45
4         1      amber            32
5         5      green            61
6         5      green            74
7         5      green            53
8         6      hazel            92
9         1      amber            83
```

```
10          3          brown              22
11          6          hazel              67
12          3          brown              55
13          1          amber              42
14          4          gray               44
```

Want the empathy score for the seventh person? That's

```
> e[7,3]
[1] 53
```

How about all the information for the seventh person:

```
> e[7,]
  eye_color feye_color empathy_score
7         5      green            53
```

Editing a data frame: Looks like a spreadsheet (but isn't)

R provides a way to quickly modify a data frame. The edit() function opens a Data Editor window that looks much like a spreadsheet, and you can make changes in the cells. Figure 2-8 shows what happens when you type

```
> edit(e)
```

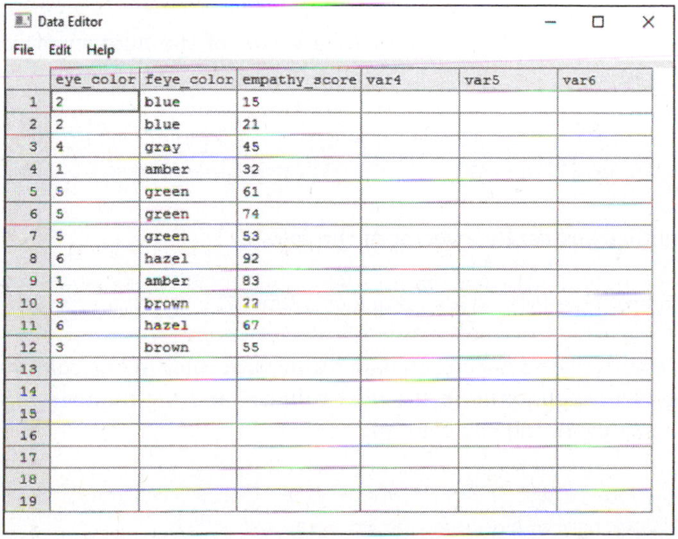

	eye_color	feye_color	empathy_score	var4	var5	var6
1	2	blue	15			
2	2	blue	21			
3	4	gray	45			
4	1	amber	32			
5	5	green	61			
6	5	green	74			
7	5	green	53			
8	6	hazel	92			
9	1	amber	83			
10	3	brown	22			
11	6	hazel	67			
12	3	brown	55			
13						
14						
15						
16						
17						
18						
19						

FIGURE 2-8: The edit() function opens a spreadsheet-like view of a data frame.

You have to close the Data Editor window in order to proceed.

WARNING

For Mac users: The Mac version of RStudio requires the X Window system for some functions, like `edit()`, to work. Apple used to include this capability with the Mac, but not any more. Nowadays, you have to download and install XQuartz.

Extracting data from a data frame

Suppose you want to do a quick check on the average empathy scores for people with blue eyes versus people with green eyes versus people with hazel eyes.

The first task is to extract the empathy scores for each eye color and create vectors:

```
> e.blue <- e$empathy_score[e$feye_color=="blue"]
> e.green <- e$empathy_score[e$feye_color=="green"]
> e.hazel <- e$empathy_score[e$feye_color=="hazel"]
```

Note the double equal-sign (==) in brackets. This is a *logical operator*. Think of it as "if e$feye_color is equal to 'blue.'"

REMEMBER

The double equal-sign (a==b) distinguishes the logical operator ("if a equals b") from the assignment operator (a=b; "set a equal to b").

Next, you create a vector of the averages:

```
> e.averages <- c(mean(e.blue),mean(e.green),mean(e.hazel))
```

Then you use `length()` to create a vector of the number of scores in each eye-color group:

```
> e.amounts <- c(length(e.blue), length(e.green),
    length(e.hazel))
```

And then you create a vector of the colors:

```
> colors <- c("blue","green","hazel")
```

Now you create a 3-column data frame with color in one column, the corresponding average empathy in the next column, and the number of scores in each eye color group in the last column:

```
> e.averages.frame <- data.frame(color=colors,
    average=e.averages, n=e.amounts)
```

As was the case with lists, naming the arguments assigns the argument names to the data frame components (the vectors, which appear onscreen as columns).

And here's what it all looks like:

```
> e.averages.frame
  color  average n
1  blue 18.00000 2
2 green 62.66667 3
3 hazel 79.50000 2
```

Packages

A *package* is a collection of functions and data that augments R. If you're an aspiring data scientist and you're looking for data to work with, you'll find data frames galore in R packages. If you're looking for a specialized statistical function that's not in the basic R installation, you can probably find it in a package.

R stores packages in a directory called the *library*. How do you get a package into the library? Click the Packages tab in the Files, Plots, Packages, and Help pane. (Refer to Figure 2-2.) In the upcoming example, I use the well-known MASS package, which contains over 150 data frames from a variety of fields.

If you want to see what's in the MASS package, click on MASS in the Packages tab. (It's in the System Library section of this tab.) That opens a page on the Help tab, which appears in Figure 2-9.

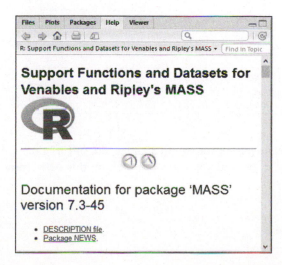

FIGURE 2-9:
The Help tab, showing information about the MASS package.

Scrolling down shows the names of the data frames and functions. Clicking on the name of a data frame opens up a page of information about it.

Back on the Packages tab, you click the check box next to MASS to install the package. That causes this line to appear in the Console window:

```
> library("MASS", lib.loc="C:/Program Files/R/R-3.3.1/library")
```

And the MASS package is installed.

One of the data frames in MASS is named anorexia. It contains weight data for 72 young female anorexia patients. Each patient completed one of three types of therapy. What does the data frame look like? You type this line into the Console pane:

```
> edit(anorexia)
```

to open the Data Editor window, shown in Figure 2-10.

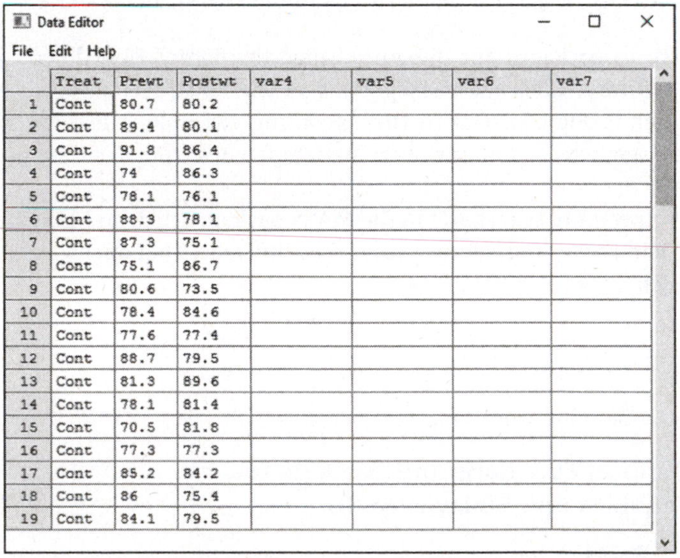

	Treat	Prewt	Postwt	var4	var5	var6	var7
1	Cont	80.7	80.2				
2	Cont	89.4	80.1				
3	Cont	91.8	86.4				
4	Cont	74	86.3				
5	Cont	78.1	76.1				
6	Cont	88.3	78.1				
7	Cont	87.3	75.1				
8	Cont	75.1	86.7				
9	Cont	80.6	73.5				
10	Cont	78.4	84.6				
11	Cont	77.6	77.4				
12	Cont	88.7	79.5				
13	Cont	81.3	89.6				
14	Cont	78.1	81.4				
15	Cont	70.5	81.8				
16	Cont	77.3	77.3				
17	Cont	85.2	84.2				
18	Cont	86	75.4				
19	Cont	84.1	79.5				

FIGURE 2-10: The anorexia data frame in the MASS package.

Looks like it's just waiting for you to analyze, doesn't it? I haven't discussed any statistical analysis yet, but you can work a bit on this data frame with what I've already shown you.

The data frame provides the pre-therapy weight (Prewt) and post-therapy weight (Postwt) for each patient. What about the weight change? Can R calculate that for each patient? Of course!

```
> anorexia$Postwt-anorexia$Prewt
 [1]  -0.5  -9.3  -5.4  12.3  -2.0 -10.2 -12.2  11.6  -7.1
[10]   6.2  -0.2  -9.2   8.3   3.3  11.3   0.0  -1.0 -10.6
[19]  -4.6  -6.7   2.8   0.3   1.8   3.7  15.9 -10.2   1.7
[28]   0.7  -0.1  -0.7  -3.5  14.9   3.5  17.1  -7.6   1.6
[37]  11.7   6.1   1.1  -4.0  20.9  -9.1   2.1  -1.4   1.4
[46]  -0.3  -3.7  -0.8   2.4  12.6   1.9   3.9   0.1  15.4
[55]  -0.7  11.4  11.0   5.5   9.4  13.6  -2.9  -0.1   7.4
[64]  21.5  -5.3  -3.8  13.4  13.1   9.0   3.9   5.7  10.7
```

Hmmm. . . . Remember that t-test I showed you earlier in this chapter? I use it here to see whether the pre-therapy/post-therapy weight change is different from 0. You would hope that, on average, the change is positive. Here's the t-test:

```
> t.test(anorexia$Postwt-anorexia$Prewt, mu=0)

    One Sample t-test

data:  anorexia$Postwt&#x00A0;- anorexia$Prewt
t = 2.9376, df = 71, p-value = 0.004458
alternative hypothesis: true mean is not equal to 0
95 percent confidence interval:
 0.8878354 4.6399424
sample estimates:
mean of x
 2.763889
```

The *t*-test output shows that the average weight change was positive (2.763889 lbs). The high value of t (2.9376), along with the low value of p (0.004458), indicates that this change is statistically significant. (What does *that* mean?) If I tell you any more, I'll be getting ahead of myself. (See Chapter 10 for the details.)

Here's something else: I said that each patient completed one of three types of therapy. Was one therapy more effective than the others? Or were they about the same? Now I'd *really* be getting ahead of myself! (That explanation is in Chapter 12, but see the section "R Formulas," a little later in this chapter.)

More Packages

The R community is extremely active. Its members create and contribute useful new packages all the time to CRAN (the Comprehensive R Archive Network). So it's not the case that every R package is on the RStudio Packages tab.

When you find out about a new package that you think might be helpful, it's easy to install it into your library. I illustrate by installing ggplot2, a useful package that extends R's graphics capabilities.

One way to install it is via the Packages tab. (Refer to Figure 2-2.) Click on the Install icon in the upper left corner of the tab. This opens the Install Packages dialog box, shown in Figure 2-11.

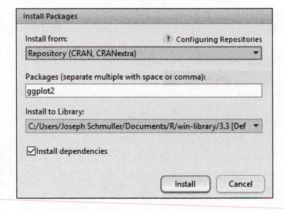

FIGURE 2-11:
The Install Packages dialog box.

TIP

Another way to open the Install Packages dialog box is to select Install Packages from the Tools menu in the menu bar at the top of RStudio.

In the Packages field, I've typed ggplot2. Click Install, and the following line appears in the Console pane:

```
> install.packages("ggplot2")
```

It's difficult to see this line, however, because lots of other things happen immediately in the Console pane and in onscreen status bars. When all that has finished, ggplot2 is on the Packages tab. The final step is to click the check box next to ggplot2 in order to put it in the library. Then you can use the package. Figure 2-12 shows the Packages tab with ggplot2 and the checked box.

Clicking the check box puts the following line in the Console pane:

```
> library("ggplot2", lib.loc="~/R/win-library/3.3")
```

Name	Description	Version
User Library		
☐ colorspace	Color Space Manipulation	1.2-6
☐ dichromat	Color Schemes for Dichromats	2.0-0
☐ digest	Create Compact Hash Digests of R Objects	0.6.10
☑ ggplot2	An Implementation of the Grammar of Graphics	2.1.0
☐ gtable	Arrange 'Grobs' in Tables	0.2.0
☐ labeling	Axis Labeling	0.3
☐ magrittr	A Forward-Pipe Operator for R	1.5
☐ munsell	Utilities for Using Munsell Colours	0.4.3
☐ plyr	Tools for Splitting, Applying and Combining Data	1.8.4
☐ RColorBrewer	ColorBrewer Palettes	1.1-2
☐ Rcpp	Seamless R and C++ Integration	0.12.6
☐ reshape2	Flexibly Reshape Data: A Reboot of the Reshape Package.	1.4.1
☐ scales	Scale Functions for Visualization	0.4.0

FIGURE 2-12: The Packages tab after installing ggplot2 and putting it in the library.

TIP Another way to start the installation process is to type

```
> install.packages("ggplot2")
```

directly into the Console pane.

R Formulas

In Chapter 1, I discuss independent variables and dependent variables. I point out that, in an experiment, an independent variable is what a researcher manipulates and a dependent variable is what a researcher measures. In the earlier anorexia example, Treat (type of therapy) is the independent variable, and Postwt-Prewt (post-therapy weight minus pre-therapy weight) is the dependent variable. In practical terms, "manipulate" means that the researcher randomly assigned each anorexia patient to one of the three therapies.

In other kinds of studies, the researcher can't manipulate an independent variable. Instead, she notes naturally occurring values of the independent variable and assesses their effects on a dependent variable. In the earlier eye color and empathy example, eye color is the independent variable and empathy score is the dependent variable.

The R *formula* incorporates these concepts and is the basis of many of R's statistical functions and graphing functions. This is the basic structure of an R formula:

```
function(dependent_var ~ independent_var, data=data_frame)
```

Read the tilde operator (~) as "is dependent on."

The anorexia data frame provides an example. To analyze the difference in the effectiveness of the three therapies for anorexia, I would use a technique called *analysis of variance*. (Here I go, getting ahead of myself!) The R function for this is named aov( ), and here's how to use it:

```
> aov(Postwt-Prewt ~ Treat, data=anorexia)
```

But this is just the beginning of the analysis. Chapter 12 has all the details, as well as the statistical thinking behind it.

Reading and Writing

Before I close out this chapter on R's capabilities, I have to let you know how to import data from other formats as well as how to export data to those formats.

The general form of an R function for reading a file is

```
> read.<format>("File Name", arg1, arg2, ...)
```

The general form of an R function for writing data to a file is

```
> write.<format>(dataframe, "File Name", arg1, arg2, ...)
```

In this section, I cover spreadsheets, CSV (comma-separated values) files, and text files. The <format> is either xlsx, csv, or table. The arguments after "File Name" are optional arguments that vary for the different formats.

Spreadsheets

The information in this section will be important to you if you've read my timeless classic, *Statistical Analysis with Excel For Dummies* (John Wiley & Sons). (Okay, so that was a shameless plug for my timeless classic.) If you have data on spreadsheets and you want to analyze with R, pay close attention.

The first order of business is to download the xlsx package and put it in the library. Check out the section "More Packages," earlier in this chapter, for more on how to do this.

On my drive C, I have a spreadsheet called Scores in a folder called Spreadsheets. It's on Sheet1 of the worksheet. It holds math quiz scores and science quiz scores for ten students.

To read that spreadsheet into R, the code is

```
> scores_frame <- read.xlsx("C:/Spreadsheets/Scores.xlsx",
    sheetName="Sheet1")
```

Here's that data frame:

```
> scores_frame
   Student Math_Score Science_Score
1        1         85            90
2        2         91            87
3        3         78            75
4        4         88            78
5        5         93            99
6        6         82            89
7        7         67            71
8        8         79            84
9        9         89            88
10      10         98            97
```

As is the case with any data frame, if you want the math score for the fourth student, it's just

```
> scores_frame$Math_Score[4]
[1] 88
```

The xlsx package enables writing to a spreadsheet, too. So, if you want your Excel-centric friends to look at the anorexia data frame, here's what you do:

```
> write.xlsx(anorexia,"C:/Spreadsheets/anorexia.xlsx")
```

This line puts the data frame into a spreadsheet in the indicated folder on drive C. In case you don't believe me, Figure 2-13 shows what the spreadsheet looks like.

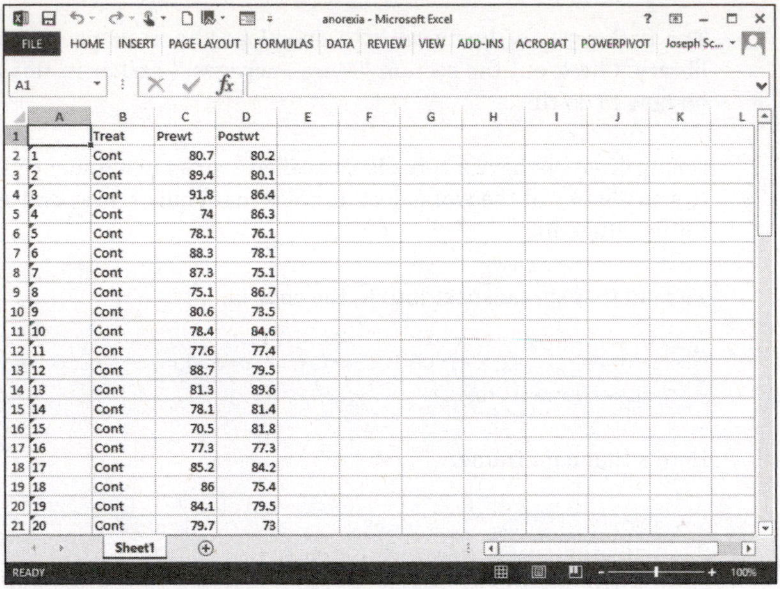

FIGURE 2-13: The anorexia data frame, exported to an Excel spreadsheet.

CSV files

The functions for reading and writing CSV files and text files are in the R installation, so no additional packages are necessary. A CSV file looks just like a spreadsheet when you open it in Excel. In fact, I created a CSV file for the Scores spreadsheet by saving the spreadsheet as a CSV file in the folder CSVFiles on drive C. (To see all the commas, you have to open it in a text editor, like Notepad++.)

Here's how to read that CSV file into R:

```
> read.csv("C:/CSVFiles/Scores.csv")
   Student Math_Score Science_Score
1        1         85            90
2        2         91            87
3        3         78            75
4        4         88            78
5        5         93            99
6        6         82            89
7        7         67            71
8        8         79            84
9        9         89            88
10      10         98            97
```

To write the anorexia data frame to a CSV file,

```
> write.csv(anorexia,"C:/CSVFiles/anorexia.csv")
```

Text files

If you have some data stored in text files, R can import them into data frames. The read.table() function gets it done. I stored the Scores data as a text file in a directory called TextFiles. Here's how R turns it into a data frame:

```
> read.table("C:/TextFiles/ScoresText.txt", header=TRUE)
   Student Math_Score Science_Score
1        1         85            90
2        2         91            87
3        3         78            75
4        4         88            78
5        5         93            99
6        6         82            89
7        7         67            71
8        8         79            84
9        9         89            88
10      10         98            97
```

The second argument (header=TRUE) lets R know that the first row of the file contains column headers.

You use write.table() to write the anorexia data frame to a text file:

```
> write.table(anorexia, "C:/TextFiles/anorexia.txt", quote =
  FALSE, sep = "\t")
```

This puts the file anorexia.txt in the TextFiles folder on the drive C. The second argument (quote = FALSE) ensures that no quotes appear, and the third argument (sep = "\t") makes the file tab-delimited.

Figure 2-14 shows how the text file looks in Notepad. Full disclosure: In the first line of the text file, you have to press the Tab key once to position the headers correctly.

FIGURE 2-14:
The anorexia
data frame
as a tab-delimited
text file.

```
anorexia - Notepad                                                  —   □   ×
File  Edit  Format  View  Help
        Treat    Prewt   Postwt
1       Cont     80.7    80.2
2       Cont     89.4    80.1
3       Cont     91.8    86.4
4       Cont     74      86.3
5       Cont     78.1    76.1
6       Cont     88.3    78.1
7       Cont     87.3    75.1
8       Cont     75.1    86.7
9       Cont     80.6    73.5
10      Cont     78.4    84.6
11      Cont     77.6    77.4
12      Cont     88.7    79.5
13      Cont     81.3    89.6
14      Cont     78.1    81.4
15      Cont     70.5    81.8
16      Cont     77.3    77.3
17      Cont     85.2    84.2
18      Cont     86      75.4
19      Cont     84.1    79.5
20      Cont     79.7    73
21      Cont     85.5    88.3
22      Cont     84.4    84.7
23      Cont     79.6    81.4
24      Cont     77.5    81.2
25      Cont     72.3    88.2
26      Cont     89      78.8
27      CBT      80.5    82.2
28      CBT      84.9    85.6
29      CBT      81.5    81.4
30      CBT      82.6    81.9
```

REMEMBER

In each of these examples, you use the full file path for each file. That's not necessary if the files are in the working directory. If, for example, you put the Scores spreadsheet in the working directory, here's all you have to do to read it into R:

```
> read.xlsx("Scores.xlsx","Sheet1")
```

2

Describing Data

Chapter **3**

Getting Graphic

D ata visualization is an important part of statistics. A good graph enables you to spot trends and relationships you might otherwise miss if you look only at numbers. Graphics are valuable for another reason: They help you present your ideas to groups.

This is especially important in the field of data science. Organizations rely on data scientists to make sense of huge amounts of data so that decision-makers can formulate strategy. Graphics enable data scientists to explain patterns in the data to managers and to nontechnical personnel.

Finding Patterns

Data often resides in long, complex tables. Often, you have to visualize only a portion of the table to find a pattern or a trend. A good example is the `Cars93` data frame, which resides in the MASS package. (In Chapter 2, I show you how to put this package into your R library.) This data frame holds data on 27 variables for 93 car models that were available in 1993.

Figure 3-1 shows part of the data frame in the Data Editor window that opens after you type

```
> edit(Cars93)
```

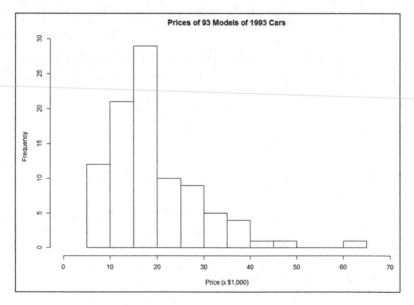

Data Editor — File Edit Help

	Manufacturer	Model	Type	Min.Price	Price	Max.Price	MPG.city	MPG.highway	AirBags	DriveTrain
1	Acura	Integra	Small	12.9	15.9	18.8	25	31	None	Front
2	Acura	Legend	Midsize	29.2	33.9	38.7	18	25	Driver & Passenger	Front
3	Audi	90	Compact	25.9	29.1	32.3	20	26	Driver only	Front
4	Audi	100	Midsize	30.8	37.7	44.6	19	26	Driver & Passenger	Front
5	BMW	535i	Midsize	23.7	30	36.2	22	30	Driver only	Rear
6	Buick	Century	Midsize	14.2	15.7	17.3	22	31	Driver only	Front
7	Buick	LeSabre	Large	19.9	20.8	21.7	19	28	Driver only	Front
8	Buick	Roadmaster	Large	22.6	23.7	24.9	16	25	Driver only	Rear
9	Buick	Riviera	Midsize	26.3	26.3	26.3	19	27	Driver only	Front
10	Cadillac	DeVille	Large	33	34.7	36.3	16	25	Driver only	Front
11	Cadillac	Seville	Midsize	37.5	40.1	42.7	16	25	Driver & Passenger	Front
12	Chevrolet	Cavalier	Compact	8.5	13.4	18.3	25	36	None	Front
13	Chevrolet	Corsica	Compact	11.4	11.4	11.4	25	34	Driver only	Front
14	Chevrolet	Camaro	Sporty	13.4	15.1	16.8	19	28	Driver & Passenger	Rear
15	Chevrolet	Lumina	Midsize	13.4	15.9	18.4	21	29	None	Front
16	Chevrolet	Lumina APV	Van	14.7	16.3	18	18	23	None	Front
17	Chevrolet	Astro	Van	14.7	16.6	18.6	15	20	None	4WD
18	Chevrolet	Caprice	Large	18	18.8	19.6	17	26	Driver only	Rear
19	Chevrolet	Corvette	Sporty	34.6	38	41.5	17	25	Driver only	Rear

FIGURE 3-1: Part of the Cars93 data frame.

Graphing a distribution

One pattern that might be of interest is the distribution of the prices of all the cars listed in the Cars93 data frame. If you had to examine the entire data frame to determine this, it would be a tedious task. A graph, however, provides the information immediately. Figure 3-2, a *histogram*, shows what I mean.

FIGURE 3-2: Histogram of prices of cars in the Cars93 data frame.

The histogram is appropriate when the variable on the x-axis is an interval variable or a ratio variable. (See Chapter 1.) With these types of variables, the numbers have meaning.

In Chapter 1, I distinguish between independent variables and dependent variables. Here, Price is the independent variable, and Frequency is the dependent variable. In most (but not all) graphs, the independent variable is on the x-axis, and the dependent variable is on the y-axis.

Bar-hopping

For nominal variables (again, see Chapter 1), numbers are just labels. In fact, the levels of a nominal variable (also called a *factor* — see Chapter 2) can be names. Case in point: Another possible point of interest is the frequencies of the different types of cars (sporty, midsize, van, and so on) in the data frame. So, "Type" is a nominal variable. If you looked at every entry in the data frame and created a table of these frequencies, it would look like Table 3-1.

TABLE 3-1

Types and Frequencies of Cars in the Cars93 data frame

Type	Frequency
Compact	16
Large	11
Midsize	22
Small	21
Sporty	14
Van	9

The table shows some trends — more midsize and small car models than large cars and vans. Compact cars and sporty cars are in the middle.

Figure 3-3 shows this information in graphical form. This type of graph is a *bar graph*. The spaces between the bars emphasize that Type, on the x-axis, is a nominal variable.

Although the table is pretty straightforward, I think we'd agree that an audience would prefer to see the picture. As I'm fond of saying, eyes that glaze over when looking at numbers often shine brighter when looking at pictures.

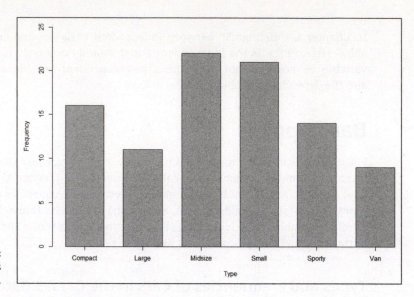

FIGURE 3-3:
Table 3-1 as
a bar graph.

Slicing the pie

The *pie graph* is another type of picture that shows the same data in a slightly different way. Each frequency appears as a slice of a pie. Figure 3-4 shows what I mean. In a pie graph, the area of the slice represents the frequency.

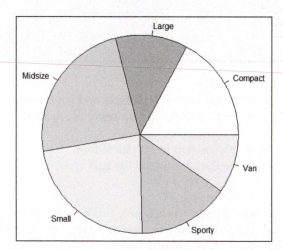

FIGURE 3-4:
Table 3-1 as
a pie graph.

The plot of scatter

Another potential pattern of interest is the relationship between miles per gallon for city driving and horsepower. This type of graph is a *scatter plot*. Figure 3-5 shows the scatter plot for these two variables.

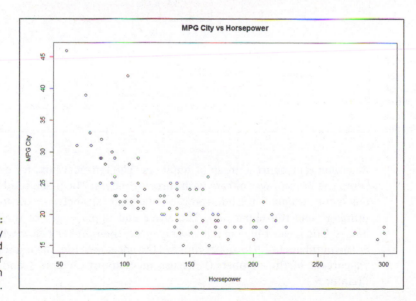

FIGURE 3-5: MPG in city driving and horsepower for the data in Cars93.

Each small circle represents one of the 93 cars. A circle's position along the x-axis (its *x-coordinate*) is its horsepower, and its position along the y-axis (its *y-coordinate*) is its MPG for city driving.

A quick look at the shape of the scatter plot suggests a relationship: As horsepower increases, MPG-city seems to decrease. (Statisticians would say "MPG-city decreases with horsepower.") Is it possible to use statistics to analyze this relationship and perhaps make predictions? Absolutely! (See Chapter 14.)

Of boxes and whiskers

What about the relationship between horsepower and the number of cylinders in a car's engine? You would expect horsepower to increase with cylinders, and Figure 3-6 shows that this is indeed the case. Invented by famed statistician John Tukey, this type of graph is called a *box plot*, and it's a nice, quick way to visualize data.

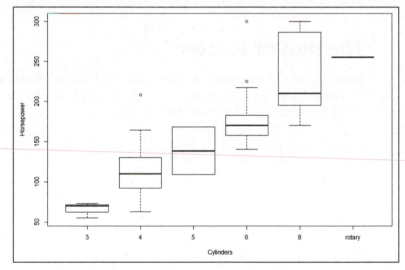

FIGURE 3-6: Box plot of horsepower versus number of cylinders in the Cars93 data frame.

Each box represents a group of numbers. The leftmost box, for example, represents the horsepower of cars with three cylinders. The black solid line inside the box is the *median* — the horsepower-value that falls between the lower half of the numbers and the upper half. The lower and upper edges of the box are called *hinges*. The lower hinge is the *lower quartile*, the number below which 25 percent of the numbers fall. The upper hinge is the *upper* quartile, the number that exceeds 75 percent of the numbers. (I discuss medians in Chapter 4 and percentiles in Chapter 6.)

The elements sticking out of the hinges are called *whiskers* (so you sometimes see this type of graph referred to as a *box-and-whiskers* plot). The whiskers include data values outside the hinges. The upper whisker boundary is either the maximum value or the upper hinge plus 1.5 times the length of the box, whichever is *smaller*. The lower whisker boundary is either the minimum value or the lower hinge minus 1.5 times the length of the box, whichever is *larger*. Data points outside the whiskers are *outliers*. The box plot shows that the data for four cylinders and for six cylinders have outliers.

Note that the graph shows only a solid line for "rotary," an engine type that occurs just once in the data.

Base R Graphics

The capability to create the graphs like the ones I show you in earlier sections comes with your R installation, which makes these graphs part of base R graphics. I start with that. Then in the next section I show you the very useful ggplot2 package.

In base R, the general format for creating graphics is

```
graphics_function(data, arg1, arg2, ...)
```

TIP

After you create a graph in RStudio, click Zoom on the RStudio Plots tab to open the graph in a larger window. The graph is clearer in the Zoom window than it is on the Plots tab.

Histograms

Time to take another look at that Cars93 data frame I introduce in the "Finding Patterns" section, earlier in this chapter. To create a histogram of the distribution of prices in that data frame, you'd enter:

```
> hist(Cars93$Price)
```

which produces Figure 3-7.

You'll note that this isn't quite as spiffy-looking as Figure 3-2. How do you spruce it up? By adding arguments.

One often-used argument in base R graphics changes the label of the x-axis from R's default into something more meaningful. It's called xlab. For the x-axis in Figure 3-2, I added

```
xlab= "Price (x $1,000)"
```

to the arguments. You can use ylab to change the y-axis label, but I left that alone here.

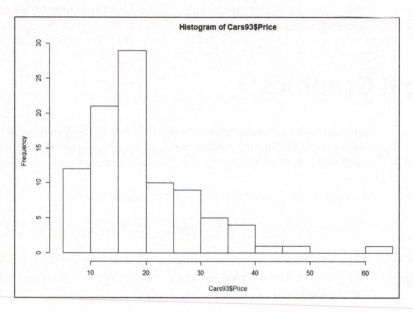

FIGURE 3-7:
Initial histogram
of the distribution
of prices in
Cars93.

I wanted the x-axis to extend from a lower limit of 0 to an upper limit of 70, and that's the province of the argument xlim. Because this argument works with a vector, I added

```
xlim = c(0,70)
```

I also wanted a different title, and for that I used main:

```
main = "Prices of 93 Models of 1993 Cars"
```

To produce the histogram in Figure 3-2, the whole megillah is

```
> hist(Cars93$Price, xlab="Price (x $1,000)", xlim = c(0,70),
            main = "Prices of 93 Models of 1993 Cars")
```

TIP

When creating a histogram, R figures out the best number of columns for a nice-looking appearance. Here, R decided that 12 is a pretty good number. You can vary the number of columns by adding an argument called breaks and setting its value. R doesn't always give you the value you set. Instead, it provides something close to that value and tries to maintain a nice-looking appearance. Add this argument, set its value (breaks =4, for example), and you'll see what I mean.

Adding graph features

An important aspect of base R graphics is the ability to add features to a graph after you create it. To show you what I mean, I have to start with a slightly different type of graph.

Another way of showing histogram information is to think of the data as *probabilities* rather than frequencies. So instead of the frequency of a particular price range, you graph the probability that a car selected from the data is in that price range. To do this, you add

```
probability = True
```

to the arguments. Now the R code looks like this:

```
> hist(Cars93$Price, xlab="Price (x $1,000)", xlim = c(0,70),
        main = "Prices of 93 Models of 1993 Cars",probability
        = TRUE)
```

The result appears in Figure 3-8. The y-axis measures *Density* — a concept related to probability, which I discuss in Chapter 8. The graph is called a *density plot*.

The point of all this is what you do next. After you create the graph, you can use an additional function called lines() to add a line to the density plot:

```
> lines(density(Cars93$Price))
```

The graph now looks like Figure 3-9.

So in base R graphics, you can create a graph and then start adding to it after you see what the initial graph looks like. It's something like painting a picture of a lake and then adding mountains and trees as you see fit.

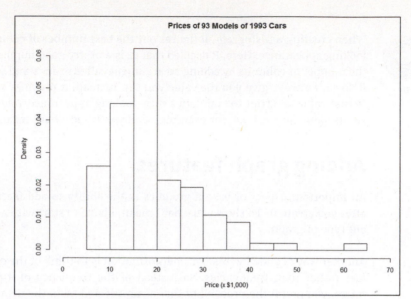

FIGURE 3-8:
Density plot of the distribution of prices in Cars93.

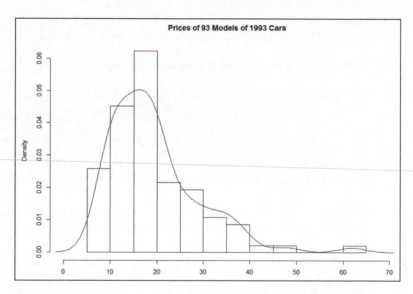

FIGURE 3-9:
Density plot with an added line.

Bar plots

Back in the "Finding Patterns" section, earlier in the chapter, I showed you a bar graph illustrating the types and frequencies of cars, I also showed you Table 3-1. As it turns out, you have to make this kind of a table before you can use barplot() to create the bar graph.

To put Table 3-1 together, the R code is (appropriately enough)

```
> table(Cars93$Type)
```

```
Compact   Large Midsize   Small  Sporty     Van
     16      11      22      21      14       9
```

For the bar graph, then, it's

```
> barplot(table(Cars93$Type))
```

which creates the graph in Figure 3-10.

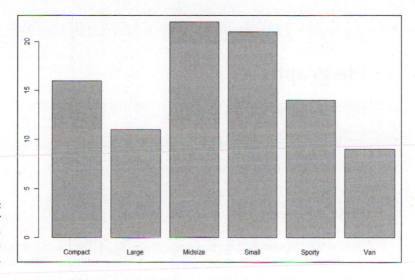

FIGURE 3-10:
The initial bar
plot of table
(Cars93
$Type).

Again, not as jazzy as the final product shown in Figure 3-3. Additional arguments do the trick. To put 0 through 25 on the y-axis, you use `ylim`, which, like `xlim`, works with a vector:

```
ylim = c(0,25)
```

For the x-axis label and y-axis label, you use

```
xlab = "Type"
ylab = "Frequency"
```

To draw a solid axis, you work with `axis.lty`. Think of this as "axis linetype" which you set to `solid` by typing

```
axis.lty = "solid"
```

The values `dashed` and `dotted` for `axis.lty` result in different looks for the x-axis.

Finally, you use `space` to increase the spacing between bars:

```
space = .05
```

Here's the entire function for producing the graph in Figure 3-3:

```
> barplot(table(Cars93$Type),ylim=c(0,25), xlab="Type",
          ylab="Frequency", axis.lty = "solid", space = .05)
```

Pie graphs

This type of graph couldn't be more straightforward. The line

```
> pie(table(Cars93$Type))
```

takes you right to Figure 3-4.

Dot charts

Wait. What? Where did this one come from? This is yet another way of visualizing the data in Table 3-1. Noted graphics honcho William Cleveland believes that people perceive values along a common scale (as in a bar plot) better than they perceive areas (as in a pie graph). So he came up with the *dot chart*, which I show you in Figure 3-11.

Looks a little like an abacus laid on its side, doesn't it? This is one of those infrequent cases where the independent variable is on the y-axis and the dependent variable is on the x-axis.

The format for the function that creates a dot chart is

```
> dotchart(x, labels, arg1, arg2 ...)
```

The first two arguments are vectors, and the others are optional arguments for modifying the appearance of the dot chart. The first vector is the vector of values (the frequencies). The second is pretty self-explanatory — in this case, it's labels for the types of vehicles.

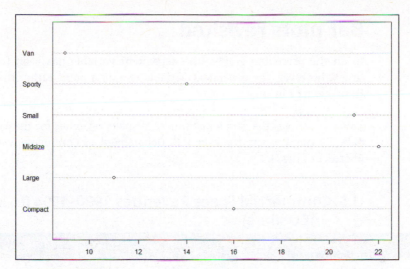

FIGURE 3-11:
Dot chart for the data in Table 3-1.

To create the necessary vectors, you turn the table into a data frame:

```
> type.frame <- data.frame(table(Cars93$Type))
> type.frame
      Var1 Freq
1 Compact   16
2    Large   11
3 Midsize   22
4    Small   21
5 Sporty    14
6      Van    9
```

After you have the data frame, this line produces the dot chart:

```
> dotchart(type.frame$Freq,type.frame$Var1)
```

The `type.frame$Freq` specifies that the Frequency column in the data frame is the x-axis, and `type.frame$Var1` specifies that the Var1 column (which holds the car-types) is the y-axis.

This line works, too:

```
> dotchart(type.frame[,2],type.frame[,1])
```

Remember from Chapter 2 that `[,2]` means "column 2" and `[,1]` means "column 1."

Bar plots revisited

In all the preceding graphs, the dependent variable has been frequency. Many times, however, the dependent variable is a data point rather than a frequency. Here's what I mean.

Table 3-2 shows the data for commercial space revenues for the early 1990s. (The data, by the way, are from the U.S. Department of Commerce, via the Statistical Abstract of the U.S.)

TABLE 3-2   **U.S. Commercial Space Revenues 1990–1994 (In Millions of Dollars)**

Industry	1990	1991	1992	1993	1994
Commercial Satellites Delivered	1,000	1,300	1,300	1,100	1,400
Satellite Services	800	1,200	1,500	1,850	2,330
Satellite Ground Equipment	860	1,300	1,400	1,600	1,970
Commercial Launches	570	380	450	465	580
Remote Sensing Data	155	190	210	250	300

The data are the numbers in the cells, which represent revenue in thousands of dollars. A base R bar plot of the data in this table appears in Figure 3-12.

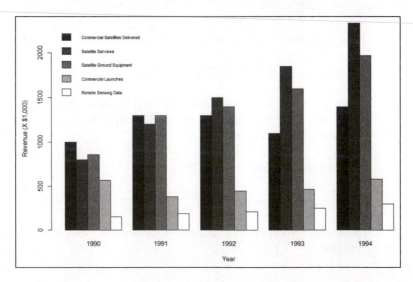

FIGURE 3-12: Bar plot of the data in Table 3-2.

If you had to make a presentation about these data, I think you'd agree that your audience would prefer the graph to the table. Although the table is informative, it doesn't hold people's attention. It's easier to see trends in the graph — Satellite Services rose fastest while Commercial Launches stayed fairly level, for example.

This graph is called a *grouped bar plot*. How do you create a plot like this one in base R?

The first thing to do is create a vector of the values in the cells:

```
rev.values <-
        c(1000,1300,1300,1100,1400,800,1200,1500,1850,
        2330,860,1300,1400,1600,1970,570,380,450,465,580,
        155,190,210,250,300)
```

WARNING

Although commas appear in the values in the table (for values greater than a thousand), you can't have commas in the values in the vector! (For the obvious reason: Commas separate consecutive values in the vector.)

Next, you turn this vector into a matrix. You have to let R know how many rows (or columns) will be in the matrix, and that the values load into the matrix row-by-row:

```
space.rev <- matrix(rev.values,nrow=5,byrow = T)
```

Finally, you supply column names and row names to the matrix:

```
colnames(space.rev) <-
        c("1990","1991","1992","1993","1994")
rownames(space.rev) <- c("Commercial Satellites
        Delivered","Satellite Services","Satellite Ground
        Equipment","Commercial Launches","Remote Sensing Data")
```

Let's have a look at the matrix:

```
> space.rev
                                1990 1991 1992 1993 1994
Commercial Satellites Delivered 1000 1300 1300 1100 1400
Satellite Services               800 1200 1500 1850 2330
Satellite Ground Equipment       860 1300 1400 1600 1970
Commercial Launches              570  380  450  465  580
Remote Sensing Data              155  190  210  250  300
```

Perfect. It looks just like Table 3-2.

With the data in hand, you move on to the bar plot. You create a vector of colors for the bars:

```
color.names = c("black","grey25","grey50","grey75","white")
```

TIP

A word about those color names: You can join any number from 0 to 100 with "grey" and get a color: "grey0" is equivalent to "black" and "grey100" is equivalent to "white". (Far more than fifty shades, if you know what I mean . . .)

And now for the plot:

```
> barplot(space.rev, beside = T, xlab= "Year",ylab= "Revenue
        (X $1,000)", col=color.names)
```

beside = T means the bars will be, well, beside each other. (You ought to try this without that argument and see what happens.) The col = color.names argument supplies the colors you specified in the vector.

The resulting plot is shown in Figure 3-13.

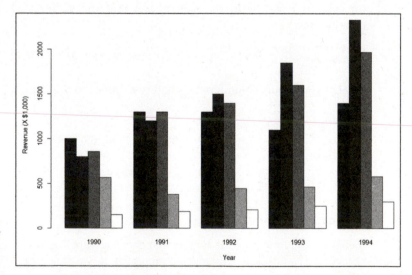

FIGURE 3-13:
Initial bar plot of
the data in
Table 3-2.

What's missing, of course, is the legend. You add that with the legend() function to produce Figure 3-12:

```
> legend(1,2300,rownames(space.rev), cex=0.7, fill = color.
  names, bty = "n")
```

The first two values are the x- and y-coordinates for locating the legend. (That took a *lot* of tinkering!). The next argument shows what goes into the legend (the names of the industries). The cex argument specifies the size of the characters in the legend. The value, 0.7, indicates that you want the characters to be 70 percent of the size they would normally be. That's the only way to fit the legend on the graph. (Think of "cex" as "character expansion," although in this case it's "character contraction.") fill = color.names puts the color swatches in the legend, next to the row names. Setting bty (the "border type") to "n" ("none") is another little trick to fit the legend into the graph.

Scatter plots

To visualize the relationship between horsepower and MPG for city driving (as shown in Figure 3-5), you use the plot() function:

```
> plot(Cars93$Horsepower, Cars93$MPG.city,
        xlab="Horsepower",ylab="MPG City", main ="MPG City vs
        Horsepower")
```

As you can see, I added the arguments for labeling the axes, and for the title.

Another way to do this is to use the formula notation I show you in Chapter 2. So if you want the R code to show that MPG-city depends on horsepower, you type

```
> plot(Cars93$MPG.city ~ Cars93$Horsepower,
        xlab="Horsepower",ylab="MPG City", main ="MPG City vs
        Horsepower")
```

to produce the same scatter plot.

REMEMBER

The tilde operator (~) means "depends on."

A plot twist

R enables you to change the symbol that depicts the points in the graph. Figure 3-5 shows that the default symbol is an empty circle. To change the symbol, which is called the *plotting character*, set the argument pch. R has a set of built-in numerical values (0–25) for pch that correspond to a set of symbols. The values 0–15 correspond to unfilled shapes, and 16–25 are filled.

The default value is 1. To change the plotting character to squares, set pch to 0. For triangles, it's 2, and for filled circles it's 16:

```
> plot(Cars93$Horsepower,Cars93$MPG.city, xlab="Horsepower",
        ylab="MPG City", main = "MPG City vs Horsepower",pch=16)
```

Figure 3-14 shows the plot with the filled circles.

You can also set the argument col to change the color from "black" to "blue" or to a variety of other colors (which wouldn't show up well on the black-and-white page you're looking at).

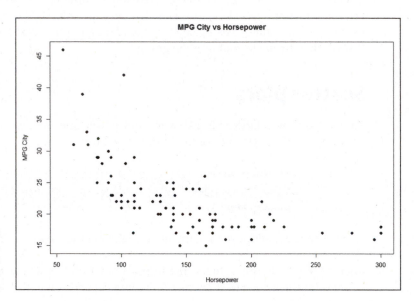

FIGURE 3-14:
MPG City vs. Horsepower with filled-in circles (pch = 16).

You're not limited to the built-in numerical values for pch. Here, for example, is an interesting touch: To help find patterns in the data, you can draw each point in the plot as the number of cylinders in the corresponding car, rather than as a symbol.

To do that, you have to be careful about how you set pch. You can't just assign Cars93$.Cylinders as the value. You have to make sure that what you pass to pch is a character (like "3", "4" or "8") rather than a number (like 3, 4, or 8). Another complication is that the data contains "rotary" as one value for Cylinders. To force the Cylinders-value to be a character, you apply as.character() to Cars93$Cylinders:

```
pch = as.character(Cars93$Cylinders)
```

and the plot() function is

```
> plot(Cars93$Horsepower,Cars93$MPG.city, xlab="Horsepower",
         ylab="MPG City", main = "MPG City vs Horsepower", pch
         = as.character(Cars93$Cylinders))
```

The result is the scatter plot in Figure 3-15. Interestingly, as.character() passes "rotary" as "r".

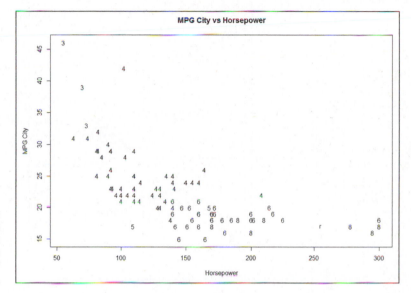

FIGURE 3-15:
MPG City vs Horsepower with points plotted as number of cylinders.

In line with our intuitions about cars, this plot clearly shows that lower numbers of cylinders associate with lower horsepower and higher gas mileage, and that higher numbers of cylinders associate with higher horsepower and lower gas mileage. You can also quickly see where the rotary engine fits into all this (low gas mileage, high horsepower).

Scatter plot matrix

Base R provides a nice way of visualizing relationships among more than two variables. If you add price into the mix and you want to show all the pairwise relationships among MPG-city, price, and horsepower, you'd need multiple scatter plots. R can plot them all together in a matrix, as Figure 3-16 shows.

The names of the variables are in the cells of the main diagonal. Each off-diagonal cell shows the scatter plot for its row variable (on the y-axis) and its column variable (on the x-axis). For example, the scatter plot in the first row, second column shows MPG-city on the y-axis and price on the x-axis. In the second row, first column, the axes are reversed: MPG city is on the x-axis, and price is on the y-axis.

The R function for plotting this matrix is pairs(). To calculate the coordinates for all scatter plots, this function works with numerical columns from a matrix or a data frame.

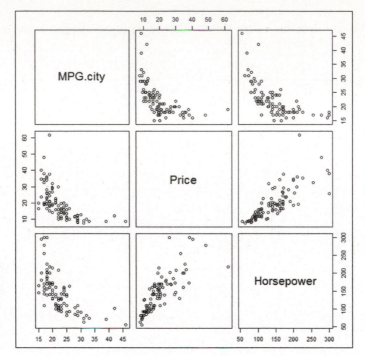

FIGURE 3-16:
Multiple scatter plots for the relationships among MPG-city, price, and horsepower.

For convenience, you create a data frame that's a subset of the `Cars93` data frame. This new data frame consists of just the three variables to plot. The function `subset()` handles that nicely:

```
> cars.subset <- subset(Cars93, select = c(MPG.
      city,Price,Horsepower))
```

The second argument to `subset` creates a vector of exactly what to select out of `Cars93`. Just to make sure the new data frame is the way you want it, use the `head()` function to take a look at the first six rows:

```
> head(cars.subset)
  MPG.city Price Horsepower
1       25  15.9        140
2       18  33.9        200
3       20  29.1        172
4       19  37.7        172
5       22  30.0        208
6       22  15.7        110
```

And now,

```
> pairs(cars.subset)
```

creates the plot in Figure 3-16.

This capability isn't limited to three variables, nor to continuous ones. To see what happens with a different type of variable, add Cylinders to the vector for select and then use the pairs() function on cars.subset.

Box plots

To draw a box plot like the one shown earlier, in Figure 3-6, you use a formula to show that Horsepower is the dependent variable and Cylinders is the independent variable:

```
> boxplot(Cars93$Horsepower ~ Cars93$Cylinders, xlab="Cylinders",
          ylab="Horsepower")
```

If you get tired of typing the $-signs, here's another way:

```
> boxplot(Horsepower ~ Cylinders, data = Cars93,
          xlab="Cylinders", ylab="Horsepower")
```

TIP

With the arguments laid out as in either of the two preceding code examples, plot() works exactly like boxplot().

Graduating to ggplot2

The Base R graphics toolset will get you started, but if you really want to shine at visualization, it's a good idea to learn ggplot2. Created by R-megastar Hadley Wickham, the "gg" in the package name stands for "grammar of graphics" and that's a good indicator of what's ahead. That's also the title of the book (by Leland Wilkinson) that is the source of the concepts for this package.

In general, a *grammar* is a set of rules for combining things. In the grammar we're most familiar with, the things happen to be words, phrases, and clauses: The grammar of our language tells you how to combine these components to produce valid sentences.

So a "grammar of graphics" is a set of rules for combining graphics components to produce graphs. Wilkinson proposed that all graphs have underlying common components — like data, a coordinate system (the x- and y-axes you know so well, for example), statistical transformations (like frequency counts), and objects within the graph (e.g., dots, bars, lines, or pie slices), to name a few.

Just as combining words and phrases produces grammatical sentences, combining graphics components produces graphs. And just as some sentences are grammatical but make no sense ("Colorless green ideas sleep furiously."), some ggplot2 creations are beautiful graphs that aren't always useful. It's up to the speaker/writer to make sense for his audience, and it's up to the graphic developer to create useful graphs for people who use them.

Histograms

In ggplot2, Wickham's implementation of Wilkinson's grammar is an easy-to-learn structure for R graphics code. To learn that structure, make sure you have ggplot2 in the library so that you can follow what comes next. (Find ggplot2 on the Packages tab and click its check box.)

A graph starts with ggplot(), which takes two arguments. The first argument is the source of the data. The second argument maps the data components of interest into components of the graph. The function that does the job is aes().

To begin a histogram for Price in Cars93, the function is

```
> ggplot(Cars93, aes(x=Price))
```

The aes() function associates Price with the x-axis. In ggplot-world, this is called an *aesthetic mapping*. In fact, each argument to aes() is called an *aesthetic*.

This line of code draws Figure 3-17, which is just a grid with a gray background and Price on the x-axis.

Well, what about the y-axis? Does anything in the data map into it? No. That's because this is a histogram and nothing explicitly in the data provides a y-value for each x. So you can't say "y=" in aes(). Instead, you let R do the work to calculate the heights of the bars in the histogram.

And what about that histogram? How do you put it into this blank grid? You have to add something indicating that you want to plot a histogram and let R take care of the rest. What you add is a geom function ("geom" is short for "geometric object").

These geom functions come in a variety of types. ggplot2 supplies one for almost every graphing need, and provides the flexibility to work with special cases. To draw a histogram, the geom function to use is called geom_histogram().

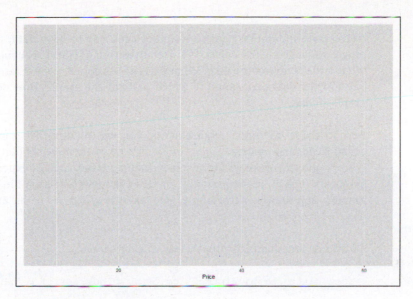

How do you add `geom_histogram()` to `ggplot()`? With a plus sign:

```
ggplot(Cars93, aes(x=Price)) +
  geom_histogram()
```

This produces Figure 3-18. The grammar rules tell ggplot2 that when the geometric object is a histogram, R does the necessary calculations on the data and produces the appropriate plot.

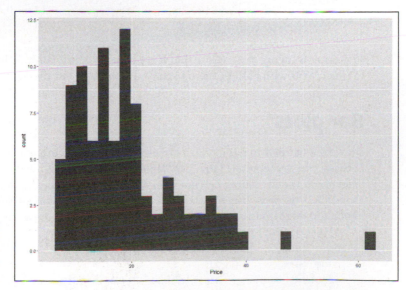

At the bare minimum, ggplot2 graphics code has to have data, aesthetic mappings, and a geometric object. It's like answering a logical sequence of questions: What's the source of the data? What parts of the data are you interested in? Which parts of the data correspond to which parts of the graph? How do you want the graph to look?

Beyond those minimum requirements, you can modify the graph. Each bar is called a *bin*, and by default, `ggplot()` uses 30 of them. After plotting the histogram, `ggplot()` displays an onscreen message that advises experimenting with `binwidth` (which, unsurprisingly, specifies the width of each bin) to change the graph's appearance. Accordingly, you use `binwidth = 5` as an argument in `geom_histogram()`.

Additional arguments modify the way the bars look:

```
geom_histogram(binwidth=5, color = "black", fill = "white")
```

With another function, `labs()`, you modify the labels for the axes and supply a title for the graph:

```
labs(x = "Price (x $1000)", y="Frequency",title="Prices of 93
        Models of 1993 Cars")
```

Altogether now:

```
ggplot(Cars93, aes(x=Price)) +
    geom_histogram(binwidth=5,color="black",fill="white") +
    labs(x = "Price (x $1000)", y="Frequency", title="Prices of
            93 Models of 1993 Cars")
```

The result is Figure 3-19. (Note that it's a little different from Figure 3-2. I'd have to tinker a bit with both of them to make them come out the same.)

Bar plots

Drawing a bar plot in ggplot2 is a little easier than drawing one in base R: It's not necessary to first create a table like Table 3-1 in order to draw the graph. As in the example in the preceding section, you don't specify an aesthetic mapping for `y`. This time, the `geom` function is `geom_bar()`, and the rules of the grammar tell ggplot2 to do the necessary work with the data and then draw the plot:

```
ggplot(Cars93, aes(x=Type))+
    geom_bar() +
    labs(y="Frequency", title="Car Type and Frequency in Cars93")
```

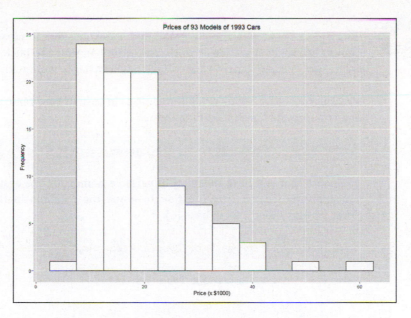

FIGURE 3-19:
The finished Price
histogram.

Figure 3-20 shows the resulting bar plot.

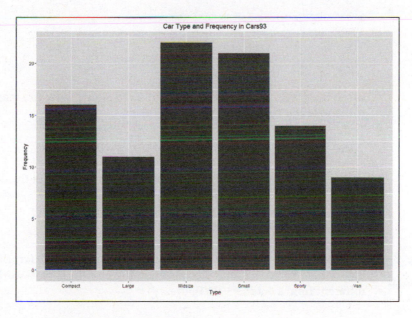

FIGURE 3-20:
Bar plot for Car
Type.

Dot charts

Earlier in this chapter, I show you the dot chart as an alternative to the pie graph.
In this section, I tell you how to use `ggplot()` to draw one.

TIP

Why didn't I lead with the pie graph and show you how to create one with the ggplot2 package? It's a lot of work, and little bang for the buck. If you want to create one, the base R pie() function is much easier to work with.

Making a dot chart begins much the same as in base R: You create a table for Type, and you turn the table into a data frame.

```
type.frame <- data.frame(table(Cars$93.Type))
```

To ensure that you have meaningful variable names for the aesthetic mapping, you apply the colnames() function to name the columns in this data frame. (That's a step I didn't do in base R.)

```
colnames(type.frame)<- c("Type","Frequency")
```

Now type.frame looks just like Table 3-1:

```
> type.frame
      Type Frequency
1  Compact        16
2    Large        11
3  Midsize        22
4    Small        21
5   Sporty        14
6      Van         9
```

On to the graph. To orient the dot chart as in Figure 3-11, you map Frequency to the x-axis and Type to the y-axis:

```
ggplot(type.frame, aes(x=Frequency,y= Type))
```

Again, usually the independent variable is on the x-axis and the dependent variable is on the y-axis, but that's not the case in this graph.

Next, you add a geom function.

WARNING

A geom function called geom_dotplot() is available, but surprisingly, it's not appropriate here. That one draws something else. In ggplot-world, a dot *plot* is different from a dot *chart*. Go figure.

The geom function for the dot chart is geom_point(). So this code

```
ggplot(type.frame, aes(x=Frequency,y=Type)) +
   geom_point()
```

results in Figure 3-21.

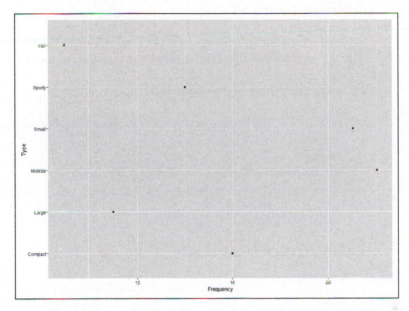

FIGURE 3-21:
The initial dot
chart for Type.

A couple of modifications are in order. First, with a graph like this, it's a nice touch to rearrange the categories on the y-axis with respect to how they order on what you're measuring on the x-axis. That necessitates a slight change in the aesthetic mapping to the y-axis:

```
ggplot(type.frame, aes(x=Frequency,y=reorder(Type,Frequency))
```

Larger dots would make the chart look a little nicer:

```
geom_point(size =4)
```

Additional functions modify the graph's overall appearance. One family of these functions is called *themes*. One member of this family, theme_bw(), removes the gray background. Adding theme() with appropriate arguments a) removes the vertical lines in the grid and b) blackens the horizontal lines and makes them dotted:

```
theme_bw() +
theme(panel.grid.major.x=element_blank(),
      panel.grid.major.y=element_line(color = "black",
          linetype = "dotted"))
```

Finally, labs() changes the y-axis label:

```
labs(y= "Type")
```

Without that change, the y-axis label would be "reorder(Type,Frequency)". Though picturesque, that label makes little sense to the average viewer.

Here's the code from beginning to end:

```
ggplot(type.frame, aes(x=Frequency,y=reorder(Type,Frequency))) +
  geom_point(size = 4) +
  theme_bw() +
  theme(panel.grid.major.x=element_blank(),
        panel.grid.major.y=element_line(color = "black",linetype
          = "dotted"))+
  labs(y="Type")
```

Figure 3-22 shows the dot chart.

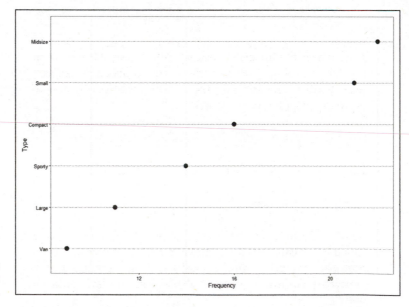

FIGURE 3-22: The modified dot chart for Type.

Bar plots re-revisited

As was the case with the first few graphs in base R, the graphs I've shown so far in this section have frequencies (or "counts") as the dependent variable. And, of course, as Table 3-2 shows, that's not always the case.

In the section on base R, I show you how to create a grouped bar plot. Here, I show you how to use `ggplot()` to create one from `space.rev`, the data set I created from the data in Table 3-2. The finished product will look like Figure 3-23.

The first order of business is to get the data ready. It's not in the format that `ggplot()` uses. This format

```
> space.rev
                                1990 1991 1992 1993 1994
Commercial Satellites Delivered 1000 1300 1300 1100 1400
Satellite Services               800 1200 1500 1850 2330
Satellite Ground Equipment       860 1300 1400 1600 1970
Commercial Launches              570  380  450  465  580
Remote Sensing Data              155  190  210  250  300
```

is called *wide* format. `ggplot()`, however, works with *long* format, which looks like this:

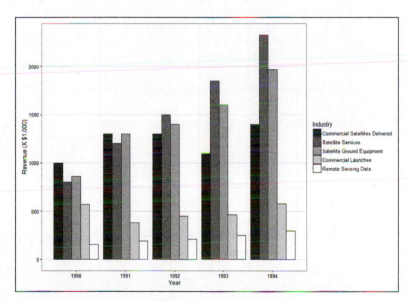

FIGURE 3-23:
Bar plot for the data in Table 3-2, created with `ggplot()`.

```
  Industry Year Revenue
1 Commercial Satellites Delivered 1990    1000
2               Satellite Services 1990     800
3       Satellite Ground Equipment 1990     860
4              Commercial Launches 1990     570
5              Remote Sensing Data 1990     155
6 Commercial Satellites Delivered 1991    1300
```

Those are just the first six rows for this data set. The total number of rows is 25 (because 5 rows and 5 columns are in the wide format).

Hadley Wickham (there's that name again!) created a package called reshape2 that provides everything for a seamless transformation. The function melt() turns wide format into long. Another function, cast(), does the reverse. These functions are a huge help because they eliminate the need to go schlepping around in spreadsheets to reshape a data set.

So, with reshape2 in the library (click its check box on the Packages tab), the code is

```
> space.melt <- melt(space.rev)
```

Yes, that's really all there is to it. Here, I'll prove it to you:

```
> head(space.melt)
                              Var1 Var2 value
1 Commercial Satellites Delivered 1990  1000
2                Satellite Services 1990   800
3       Satellite Ground Equipment 1990   860
4              Commercial Launches 1990   570
5               Remote Sensing Data 1990   155
6 Commercial Satellites Delivered 1991  1300
```

Next, you give meaningful names to the columns:

```
> colnames(space.melt) <- c("Industry","Year","Revenue")
> head(space.melt)
                           Industry Year Revenue
1 Commercial Satellites Delivered 1990    1000
2                Satellite Services 1990     800
3       Satellite Ground Equipment 1990     860
4              Commercial Launches 1990     570
5               Remote Sensing Data 1990     155
6 Commercial Satellites Delivered 1991    1300
```

And now you're ready to roll. You start with ggplot(). The aesthetic mappings are straightforward:

```
ggplot(space.melt, aes(x=Year,y=Revenue,fill=Industry))
```

You add the geom function for the bar, and you specify three arguments:

```
geom_bar(stat = "identity", position = "dodge", color ="black")
```

The first argument is absolutely necessary for a graph of this type. If left on its own, geom_bar defaults to the bar plot I showed you earlier — a graph based on frequencies. Because you defined an aesthetic mapping for y, and that type of graph is incompatible with an aesthetic for y, not setting this argument results in an error message.

Accordingly, you let ggplot() know that this is a graph based on explicit data values. So stat="identity" means "use the given numbers as the data."

The value for the next argument, position, is a cute name that means the bars "dodge" each other and line up side-by-side. (Omit this argument and see what happens.) It's analogous to "beside =T" in base R.

The third argument sets the color of the borders for each bar. The fill-color scheme for the bars is the province of the next function:

```
scale_fill_grey(start = 0,end = 1)
```

As its name suggests, this function fills the bars with shades of gray (excuse me, "grey"). The start value, 0, is black, and the end value, 1, is white. (Reminiscent of "grey0" = "black" and "grey100" = "white.') The effect is to fill the five bars with five shades from black to white.

You'd like to relabel the y-axis, so that's

```
labs(y="Revenue (X $1,000)")
```

and then remove the gray background

```
theme_bw()
```

and, finally, remove the vertical lines from the grid

```
theme(panel.grid.major.x = element_blank())
```

The whole chunk for producing Figure 3-23 is

```
ggplot(space.melt, aes(x=Year,y=Revenue,fill=Industry)) +
    geom_bar(stat = "identity", position = "dodge", color="black") +
    scale_fill_grey(start = 0,end = 1)+
    labs(y="Revenue (X $1,000)")+
    theme_bw()+
    theme(panel.grid.major.x = element_blank())
```

Scatter plots

As I describe earlier, a scatter plot is a great way to show the relationship between two variables, like horsepower and miles per gallon for city driving. And `ggplot()` is a great way to draw the scatter plot. If you've been following along, the grammar of this will be easy for you:

```
ggplot(Cars93,aes(x=Horsepower,y=MPG.city))+
  geom_point()
```

Figure 3-24 shows the scatter plot. I'll leave it to you to change the y-axis label to "Miles per Gallon (City)" and to add a descriptive title.

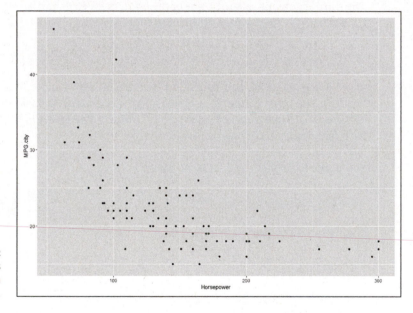

FIGURE 3-24:
MPG.city vs
Horsepower in
Cars93.

About that plot twist . . .

Take another look at Figure 3-15, the relationship between MPG.city and Horsepower. In that one, the points in the plot aren't dots. Instead, each data point is the number of cylinders, which is a label that appears as a text character.

How do you do make that happen in ggplot-world? First, you need an additional aesthetic mapping in `aes()`. That mapping is `label`, and you set it to `Cylinders`:

```
ggplot(Cars93, aes(x=Horsepower, y=MPG.city, label = Cylinders))
```

You add a geometric object for text and voilà:

```
ggplot(Cars93, aes(x = Horsepower,y = MPG.city,label =
    Cylinders)) +
    geom_text()
```

Figure 3-25 shows the graph this code produces. One difference from base R is "rotary" rather than "r" as a data point label.

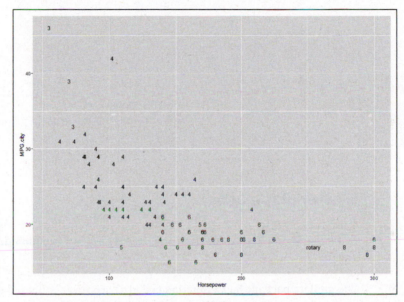

FIGURE 3-25:
The initial ggplot2 scatter plot for MPG.city vs Horsepower with Cylinders as the data point label.

Just for the heck of it, I used theme functions (see the earlier "Dot charts" section) to make the graph's appearance look more like the one shown in Figure 3-15. As in the dot chart example, theme_bw() eliminates the gray background. The theme() function (with a specific argument) eliminates the grid:

```
theme(panel.grid=element_blank())
```

element_blank() is a function that draws a blank element.

Putting it all together

```
ggplot(Cars93, aes(x=Horsepower, y=MPG.city, label=Cylinders)) +
    geom_text() +
    theme_bw() +
    theme(panel.grid=element_blank())
```

produces Figure 3-26. Once again, I leave it to you to use labs() to change the y-axis label and to add a descriptive title.

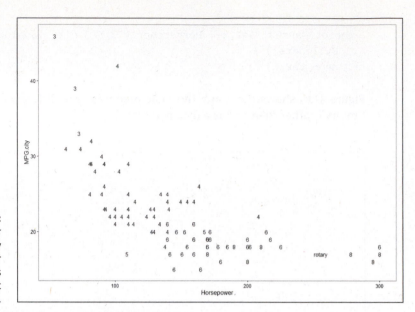

FIGURE 3-26:
Modified scatter
plot for MPG.city
vs Horsepower
with Cylinders as
the data point
label.

Scatter plot matrix

A matrix of scatter plots shows the pairwise relationships among more than two variables. Figure 3-16 shows how the base R `pairs()` function draws this kind of matrix.

The ggplot2 package had a function called `plotpairs()` that did something similar, but not anymore. GGally, a package built on ggplot2, provides `ggpairs()` to draw scatter plot matrices, and it does this in a flamboyant way.

TIP

The GGally package isn't on the Packages tab. You have to select Install and type **GGally** in the Install Packages dialog box. When it appears on the Packages tab, click the check box next to it.

Earlier, I created a subset of `Cars93` that includes MPG.city, Price, and Horsepower:

```
> cars.subset <- subset(Cars93, select = c(MPG.
   city,Price,Horsepower))
```

With the GGally package in your library, this code creates the scatter plot matrix in Figure 3-27:

```
> ggpairs(cars.subset)
```

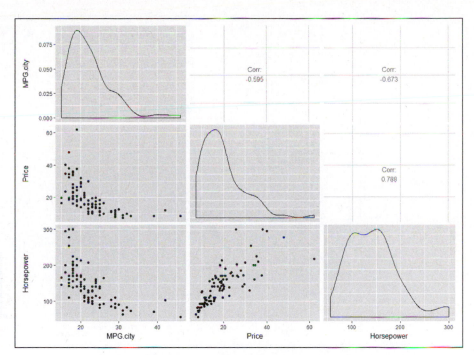

FIGURE 3-27:
Scatter plot matrix for MPG. city, Price, and Horsepower.

As Figure 3-27 shows, this one's a beauty. The cells along the main diagonal present density plots of the variables. (See the earlier subsection "Adding graph features," and also see Chapter 8.) One drawback is that the y-axis is visible for the variable MPG.city only in the first row and first column.

The three scatter plots are in the cells below the main diagonal. Rather than show the same scatter plots with the axes reversed in the cells above the main diagonal (like pairs() does), each above-the-diagonal cell shows a *correlation coefficient* that summarizes the relationship between the cell's row variable and its column variable. (Correlation coefficients? No, I'm not going to explain them now. See Chapter 15.)

For a real visual treat, add Cylinders to cars.subset, and then apply ggpairs():

```
> cars.subset <- subset(Cars93, select = c(MPG.city,Price,
        Horsepower,Cylinders))
> ggpairs(cars.subset)
```

Figure 3-28 shows the new scatter plot matrix, in all its finery.

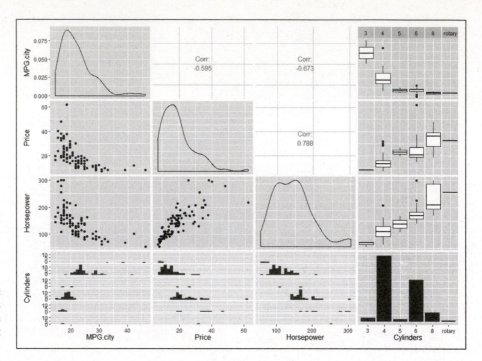

FIGURE 3-28:
Adding Cylinders
produces this
scatter plot
matrix.

Cylinders is not a variable that lends itself to scatter plots, density plots, or correlation coefficients. (Thought question: Why not?) Thus, the cell in the fourth column, fourth row, has a bar plot rather than a density plot. Bar plots relating Cylinders (on each y-axis) to the other three variables (on the x-axes) are in the remaining three cells in row 4. Box plots relating Cylinders (on each x-axis) to the other three variables (on the y-axes) are in the remaining three cells in column 4.

Which brings me to the next graph type. . . .

Box plots

Statisticians use box plots to quickly show how groups differ from one another. As in the base R example, I show you the box plot for Cylinders and Horsepower. This is a replication of the graph in row 3, column 4 of Figure 3-28.

At this point, you can probably figure out the ggplot() function:

```
ggplot(Cars93, aes(x=Cylinders, y= Horsepower))
```

What's the geom function? If you guessed geom_boxplot(), you're right!

So the code is

```
ggplot(Cars93, aes(x=Cylinders,y=Horsepower)) +
    geom_boxplot()
```

And that gives you Figure 3-29.

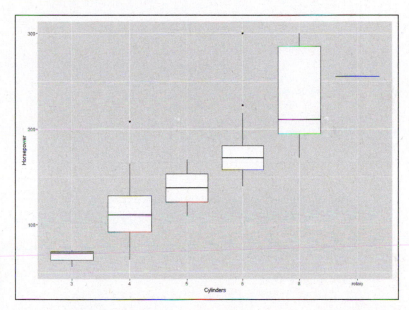

FIGURE 3-29:
Box plot for
Horsepower vs
Cylinders.

Want to show all the data points in addition to the boxes? Add the geom function for points

```
ggplot(Cars93, aes(x=Cylinders,y=Horsepower)) +
    geom_boxplot()+
    geom_point()
```

to produce the graph in Figure 3-30.

Remember that this is data for 93 cars. Do you see 93 data points? Neither do I. This, of course, is because many points overlap. Graphics gurus refer to this as *overplotting*.

One way to deal with overplotting is to randomly reposition the points so as to reveal them but not change what they represent. This is called *jittering*. And ggplot2 has a geom function for that: geom_jitter(). Adding this function to the code

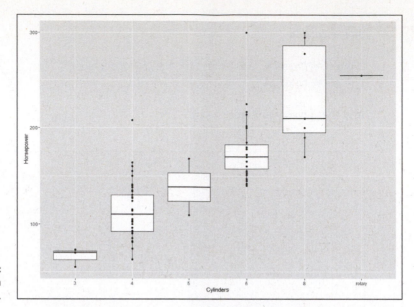

FIGURE 3-30:
Box plot with
data points.

```
gplot(Cars93, aes(x=Cylinders,y=Horsepower)) +
    geom_boxplot()+
    geom_point()+
    geom_jitter()
```

draws Figure 3-31.

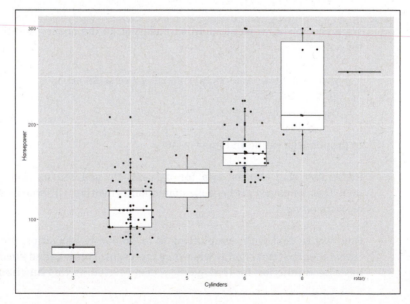

FIGURE 3-31:
Box plot with
jittered data
points.

Wrapping Up

As far as graphics goes, I've just scratched the surface. R has a rich set of graphics tools and packages — way more than I could show you in this chapter. In the chapters to come, every time I show you an analytic technique, I also show you how to visualize its results. I'll use what you've read in this chapter, along with new tools and packages as necessary.

Chapter **4**

Finding Your Center

f you've ever worked with a set of numbers and had to figure out how to summarize them with a single number, you've faced a situation that statisticians deal with all the time. Where would this ideal "single number" come from?

A good idea might be to select a number from somewhere in the middle of the set. That number could then represent the entire set of numbers. When you're looking around in the middle of the set, you're looking at *central tendency*. You can address central tendency in a variety of ways.

Means: The Lure of Averages

We've all used averages. Statisticians refer to the average as the *mean*. The mean is an easy way to summarize your spending, your school grades, your performance in a sport over time.

In the course of their work, scientists calculate means. When a researcher does a study, she applies some kind of treatment or procedure to a small sample of people or things. Then she measures the results and estimates the effects of the procedure on the population that produced the sample. Statisticians have shown that the sample mean is the estimate of the mean of the population.

I think you know how to calculate the mean, but I'll go through it anyway. Then I show you the statistical formula. My objective is that you understand statistical formulas in general, and then I'll show you how R calculates means.

A *mean* is just the sum of a set of numbers divided by how many numbers you added up. Suppose you measure the heights (in inches) of six 5-year-old children and find that their heights are

36, 42, 43, 37, 40, 45

The average height of these six children is

$$\frac{36 + 42 + 43 + 37 + 40 + 45}{6} = 40.5$$

The mean of this sample, then, is 40.5 inches.

A first attempt at a formula for the mean might be

$$\text{Mean} = \frac{\text{Sum of Numbers}}{\text{Amount of Numbers You Added Up}}$$

Formulas, though, usually involve abbreviations. A common abbreviation for "Number" is X. Statisticians usually abbreviate "Amount of Numbers You Added Up" as N. So the formula becomes

$$\text{Mean} = \frac{\text{Sum of } X}{N}$$

Statisticians also use an abbreviation for *Sum of* — the uppercase Greek letter for *S*. Pronounced "sigma," it looks like this: Σ. So the formula with the sigma is

$$\text{Mean} = \frac{\Sigma X}{N}$$

I'm not done yet. Statisticians abbreviate "mean," too. You might think that M would be the abbreviation, and some statisticians agree with you, but most prefer a symbol that's related to X. For this reason, the most popular abbreviation for the mean is $\bar{X}$, which is pronounced "X bar." And here's the formula:

$$\bar{X} = \frac{\Sigma X}{N}$$

I have to tie up one more loose end. In Chapter 1, I discuss samples and populations. Symbols in formulas have to reflect the distinction between the two. The convention is that English letters, like $\bar{X}$, stand for characteristics of samples, and Greek letters stand for characteristics of populations. For the population mean, the symbol is the Greek equivalent of *M*, which is µ. It's pronounced like "you" but with "m" in front of it. The formula for the population mean, then, is

$$\mu = \frac{\sum X}{N}$$

The Average in R: mean()

R provides an extremely straightforward way of calculating the mean of a set of numbers: mean(). I apply it to the example of the heights of six children.

First, I create a vector of the heights:

```
> heights <- c(36, 42, 43, 37, 40, 45)
```

Then I apply the function:

```
> mean(heights)
[1] 40.5
```

And there you have it.

What's your condition?

When you work with a data frame, sometimes you want to calculate the mean of just the cases (rows) that meet certain conditions, rather than the mean of all the cases. This is easy to do in R.

For the discussion that follows, I use the same Cars93 data frame that I use in Chapter 3. It's the one that has data for a sample of 93 cars from 1993. It's in the MASS package. So make sure you have the MASS package in your library. (Find MASS on the Packages tab and click its check box.)

Suppose I'm interested in the average horsepower of the cars made in the USA. First I select those cars and put their horsepowers into a vector:

```
Horsepower.USA <- Cars93$Horsepower[Cars93$Origin == "USA"]
```

(If the right-hand part of that line looks strange to you, reread Chapter 2.)

The average horsepower is then

```
> mean(Horsepower.USA)
[1] 147.5208
```

Hmm, I wonder what that average is for cars not made in the USA:

```
Horsepower.NonUSA <- Cars93$Horsepower[Cars93$Origin ==
        "non-USA"]
> mean(Horsepower.NonUSA)
[1] 139.8889
```

So the averages differ a bit. (Can we examine that difference more closely? Yes we can, which is just what I do in Chapter 11.)

Eliminate $-signs forth `with()`

In the preceding R-code, the $-signs denote variables in the `Cars93` data frame. R provides a way out of using the name of the data frame (and hence, the $-sign) each time you refer to one of its variables.

In Chapter 3, I show that graphics functions take, as their first argument, the data source. Then, in the argument list, it's not necessary to repeat the source along with the $-sign to denote a variable to plot.

The function `with()` does this for other R functions. The first argument is the data source, and the second argument is the function to apply to a variable in that data source.

To find the mean horsepower of USA cars in Cars93:

```
> with(Cars93, mean(Horsepower[Origin == "USA"]))
[1] 147.5208
```

This also skips the step of creating the `Horsepower.USA` vector.

How about multiple conditions, like the average horsepower of USA 4-cylinder cars?

```
> with(Cars93, mean(Horsepower[Origin == "USA" & Cylinders ==4]))
[1] 104.0909
```

R also provides the `attach()` function as a way of eliminating $-signs and keystrokes. Attach the data frame (`attach(Cars93)`, for example) and you don't have to refer to it again when you use its variables. Numerous R authorities recommend against this, however, as it can lead to errors.

Exploring the data

Now that we've examined the horsepower means of USA and non-USA cars, how about the overall distributions?

That calls for a little data exploration. I use the ggplot2 package (see Chapter 3) to create side-by-side histograms from the Cars93 data frame so that I can compare them. (Make sure you have ggplot2 in the library.) Figure 4-1 shows what I mean.

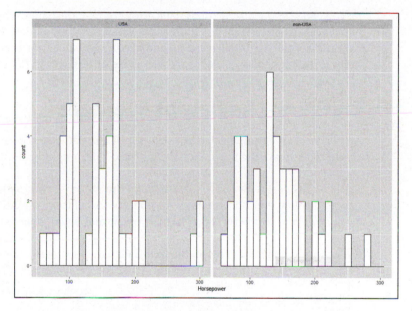

FIGURE 4-1:
Horsepower histograms for USA and Non-USA cars in Cars93.

To create the histograms in the figure, I begin the usual way:

```
ggplot(Cars93, aes(x=Horsepower))
```

and then add a geom function

```
geom_histogram(color="black", fill="white",binwidth = 10)
```

I tinkered around a little to arrive at that `binwidth` value.

The code so far creates an ordinary histogram with Horsepower on the x-axis. How can I create Figure 4-1? To do that, I add a ggplot capability called *faceting*. Simply put, faceting splits the data according to a nominal variable — like Origin, which is either "USA" or "non-USA." A couple of faceting functions are available. The one I use here is called facet_wrap(). To split the data according to Origin, it's

```
facet_wrap(~Origin)
```

Just a reminder: The tilde operator (~) means "depends on," so think of Origin as an independent variable. The full code for Figure 4-1 is

```
ggplot(Cars93, aes(x=Horsepower)) +
  geom_histogram(color="black", fill="white",binwidth = 10)+
  facet_wrap(~Origin)
```

As you can see, the distributions have different overall shapes. The USA cars seem to have a gap between the low 200s and the next-highest values, and the non-USA cars not so much. You also see higher maximum values for the USA cars. What other differences do you see? (I address those differences in Chapter 7.)

Outliers: The flaw of averages

An *outlier* is an extreme value in a data set. If the data set is a sample and you're trying to estimate the population mean, the outlier might bias the estimate.

Statisticians deal with outliers by *trimming* the mean — eliminating extreme values at the low end and the high end before calculating the sample mean. The amount of trim is a percentage, like the upper and lower 5 percent of the scores.

For example, the histogram on the left of Figure 4-1 shows some extreme values. To trim the upper and lower 5 percent, I add the trim argument to mean():

```
> mean(Horsepower.USA, trim =.05)
[1] 144.1818
```

The result is a bit lower than the untrimmed mean.

REMEMBER

What's the appropriate percentage for trim? That's up to you. It depends on what you're measuring, how extreme your scores can be, and how well you know the area you're studying. When you report a trimmed mean, let your audience know that you've done this and tell them the percentage you've trimmed.

In the upcoming section about the median, I show you another way to deal with extreme scores.

Other means to an end

In this section, I tell you about two additional averages that are different from the mean you're accustomed to working with.

REMEMBER

The everyday, garden-variety mean is called the *arithmetic* (pronounced "arith-MET-ic") *mean*.

How many different kinds of means are possible? Ancient Greek mathematicians came up with 11!

Geometric mean

Suppose you have a 5-year investment that yields these percentages: 10 percent, 15 percent, 10 percent, 20 percent, and 5 percent. (Yes, yes. I know. This is fiction.) What's the average annual rate of return?

Your first guess might be to average those percentages. That average is 12 percent. And it would be incorrect.

Why? It misses an important point. At the end of the first year, you *multiply* your investment by .10 — you don't add 1.10 to it. At the end of the second year, you multiply the first-year result by 1.15, and so on.

The arithmetic mean won't give you the average rate of return. Instead, you calculate that average this way:

$$\text{Average Rate of Return} = \sqrt[5]{1.10 \times 1.15 \times 1.10 \times 1.20 \times 1.05} = 1.118847$$

The average rate of return is a little less than 12 percent. This kind of average is called the *geometric mean*.

In this example, the geometric mean is the fifth root of the product of five numbers. Is it always the nth root of the product of n numbers? Yep.

Base R doesn't provide a function for calculating the geometric mean, but it's easy enough to calculate.

I begin by creating a vector of the numbers:

```
invest <- c(1.10,1.15,1.10,1.20,1.05)
```

I use the `prod()` function to calculate the product of the numbers in the vector, and the `length()` function to calculate how many numbers are in the vector. The calculation is then

```
> gm.invest <- prod(invest)^(1/(length(invest)))
> gm.invest
[1] 1.118847
```

Harmonic mean

Here's a situation you sometimes encounter in real life, but more often in algebra textbooks.

Suppose you're in no hurry to get to work in the morning and you drive from your home to your job at a rate of 30 miles per hour. At the end of the day, on the other hand, you'd like to get home quickly. So on the return trip (over exactly the same distance), you drive from your job to your home at 50 miles per hour. What is the average rate for your total time on the road?

It's not 40 miles per hour, because you're on the road a different amount of time for each leg of the trip. Without going into this too deeply, the formula for figuring this out is

$$\frac{1}{\text{Average}} = \frac{1}{2}\left[\frac{1}{30} + \frac{1}{50}\right] = \frac{1}{37.5}$$

The average is 37.5. This type of average is called a *harmonic mean*. This example consists of two numbers, but you can calculate it for any amount of numbers. Just put each number in the denominator of a fraction with 1 as the numerator. Mathematicians call this the *reciprocal* of a number. (So $\frac{1}{30}$ is the reciprocal of 30.) Add all the reciprocals together and take their average. The result is the reciprocal of the harmonic mean.

Base R doesn't have a function for the harmonic mean, but (again) it's easy to calculate. You begin by creating a vector of the two speeds:

```
speeds <- c(30,50)
```

Taking the reciprocal of the vector results in a vector of reciprocals:

```
> 1/speeds
[1] 0.03333333 0.02000000
```

So the harmonic mean is

```
> hm.speeds <- 1/mean(1/speeds)
> hm.speeds
[1] 37.5
```

Medians: Caught in the Middle

The mean is a useful way to summarize a group of numbers. One drawback ("the flaw of averages") is that it's sensitive to extreme values. If one number is out of whack, the mean is out of whack, too. When that happens, the mean might not be a good representative of the group.

Here, for example, are the reading speeds (in words per minute) for a group of children:

56, 78, 45, 49, 55, 62

The mean is

```
> reading.speeds <- c(56, 78, 45, 49, 55, 62)
> mean(reading.speeds)
[1] 57.5
```

Suppose the child who reads at 78 words per minute leaves the group and an exceptionally fast reader replaces him. Her reading speed is a phenomenal 180 words per minute:

```
> reading.speeds.new <-
          replace(reading.speeds,reading.speeds == 78,180)
> reading.speeds.new
[1]   56 180   45   49   55   62
```

Now the mean is

```
> mean(reading.speeds.new)
[1] 74.5
```

The new average is misleading. Except for the new child, no one else in the group reads nearly that fast. In a case like this, it's a good idea to use a different measure of central tendency — the median.

Median is a fancy name for a simple concept: It's the middle value in a group of numbers. Arrange the numbers in order, and the median is the value below which half the scores fall and above which half the scores fall:

```
> sort(reading.speeds)
[1] 45 49 55 56 62 78
> sort(reading.speeds.new)
[1]  45  49  55  56  62 180
```

In each case, the median is halfway between 55 and 56, or 55.5.

The Median in R: median()

So it's no big mystery how to use R to find the median:

```
> median(reading.speeds)
[1] 55.5
> median(reading.speeds.new)
[1] 55.5
```

With larger data sets, you might encounter replication of scores. In any case, the median is still the middle value. For example, here are the horsepowers for 4-cylinder cars in Cars93:

```
> with(Cars93, Horsepower.Four <- Horsepower[Cylinders == 4])
> sort(Horsepower.Four)
 [1]  63  74  81  81  82  82  85  90  90  92  92  92  92  92
[15]  93  96 100 100 100 102 103 105 110 110 110 110 110 110
[29] 110 114 115 124 127 128 130 130 130 134 135 138 140 140
[43] 140 141 150 155 160 164 208
```

You see quite a bit of duplication in these numbers — particularly around the middle. Count through the sorted values and you'll see that 24 scores are equal to or less than 110, and 24 scores are greater than or equal to 110, which makes the median

```
> median(Horsepower.Four)
[1] 110
```

Statistics à la Mode

One more measure of central tendency, the *mode*, is important. It's the score that occurs most frequently in a group of scores.

Sometimes the mode is the best measure of central tendency to use. Imagine a small company that consists of 30 consultants and two high-ranking officers. Each consultant has an annual salary of $40,000. Each officer has an annual salary of $250,000. The mean salary in this company is $53,125.

Does the mean give you a clear picture of the company's salary structure? If you were looking for a job with that company, would the mean influence your expectations? You're probably better off if you consider the mode, which in this case is $40,000 (unless you happen to be high-priced executive talent!).

Nothing is complicated about finding the mode. Look at the scores and find the one that occurs most frequently, and you've found the mode. Do two scores tie for that honor? In that case, your set of scores has two modes. (The technical name is *bimodal.*)

Can you have more than two modes? Absolutely.

If every score occurs equally often, you have no mode.

The Mode in R

Base R does not provide a function for finding the mode. It does have a function called mode(), but it's for something *much* different. Instead, you need a package called *modeest* in your library. (On the Packages tab, select Install, and then in the Install dialog box, type **modeest** in the Packages box and click Install. Then check its check box when it appears on the Packages tab.)

One function in the modeest package is called mfv() ("most frequent value"), and that's the one you need. Here's a vector with two modes (2 and 4):

```
> scores <- c(1,2,2,2,3,4,4,4,5,6)
> mfv(scores)
[1] 2 4
```

Chapter **5**

Deviating from the Average

H ere's a well-known statistician joke: Three statisticians go deer hunting with bows and arrow. They spot a deer and take aim. One shoots and his arrow flies off ten feet to the left. The second shoots and his arrow goes ten feet to the right. The third statistician happily yells out, "We got him!"

Moral of the story: Calculating the mean is a great way to summarize a set of numbers, but the mean might mislead you. How? By not giving you all the information you typically need. If you rely only on the mean, you might miss something important about the set of numbers.

To avoid missing important information, another type of statistic is necessary — a statistic that measures *variation*. Think of variation as a kind of average of how much each number in a group of numbers differs from the group mean. Several statistics are available for measuring variation. They all work the same way: The larger the value of the statistic, the more the numbers differ from their mean. The smaller the value, the less they differ.

Measuring Variation

Suppose you measure the heights of a group of children and you find that their heights (in inches) are

48, 48, 48, 48, and 48

Then you measure another group and find that their heights are

50, 47, 52, 46, and 45

If you calculate the mean of each group, you'll find they're the same — 48 inches. Just looking at the numbers tells you the two groups of heights are different: The heights in the first group are all the same, whereas the heights in the second vary quite a bit.

Averaging squared deviations: Variance and how to calculate it

One way to show the dissimilarity between the two groups is to examine the deviations in each one. Think of a "deviation" as the difference between a score and the mean of all the scores in a group.

Here's what I'm talking about. Table 5-1 shows the first group of heights and their deviations.

TABLE 5-1 **The First Group of Heights and Their Deviations**

Height	Height-Mean	Deviation
48	48-48	0
48	48-48	0
48	48-48	0
48	48-48	0
48	48-48	0

One way to proceed is to average the deviations. Clearly, the average of the numbers in the Deviation column is zero.

Table 5-2 shows the second group of heights and their deviations.

TABLE 5-2   **The Second Group of Heights and Their Deviations**

Height	Height-Mean	Deviation
50	50-48	2
47	47-48	–1
52	52-48	4
46	46-48	–2
45	45-48	–3

What about the average of the deviations in Table 5-2? That's . . . zero!

So now what?

Averaging the deviations doesn't help you see a difference between the two groups, because the average of deviations from the mean in any group of numbers is *always* zero. In fact, veteran statisticians will tell you that's a defining property of the mean.

The joker in the deck here is the negative numbers. How do statisticians deal with them?

The trick is to use something you might recall from algebra: A minus times a minus is a plus. Sound familiar?

So . . . does this mean that you multiply each deviation times itself and then average the results? Absolutely. Multiplying a deviation times itself is called *squaring a deviation.* The average of the squared deviations is so important that it has a special name: *variance.*

Table 5-3 shows the group of heights from Table 5-2, along with their deviations and squared deviations.

TABLE 5-3   **The Second Group of Heights and Their Squared Deviations**

Height	Height-Mean	Deviation	Squared Deviation
50	50-48	2	4
47	47-48	–1	1
52	52-48	4	16
46	46-48	–2	4
45	45-48	–3	9

The variance — the average of the squared deviations for this group — is $(4+1+16+4+9)/5 = 34/5 = 6.8$. This, of course, is quite different from the first group, whose variance is zero.

To develop the variance formula for you and show you how it works, I use symbols to show all this. X represents the Height heading in the first column of the table, and $\bar{X}$ represents the mean.

A deviation is the result of subtracting the mean from each number, so

$$\left(X - \bar{X}\right)$$

symbolizes a deviation. How about multiplying a deviation by itself? That's

$$\left(X - \bar{X}\right)^2$$

To calculate variance, you square each deviation, add them up, and find the average of the squared deviations. If N represents the amount of squared deviations you have (in this example, five), the formula for calculating the variance is

$$\frac{\sum\left(X - \bar{X}\right)^2}{N}$$

Σ is the uppercase Greek letter sigma, and it means "the sum of."

What's the symbol for variance? As I mention in Chapter 1, Greek letters represent population parameters, and English letters represent sample statistics. Imagine that our little group of five numbers is an entire population. Does the Greek alphabet have a letter that corresponds to V in the same way that μ (the symbol for the population mean) corresponds to M?

Nope. Instead, you use the *lowercase* sigma! It looks like this: σ. And on top of that, because you're talking about squared quantities, the symbol for population variance is σ^2.

Bottom line: The formula for calculating population variance is

$$\sigma^2 = \frac{\sum\left(X - \bar{X}\right)^2}{N}$$

REMEMBER

A large value for the variance tells you the numbers in a group vary greatly from their mean. A small value for the variance tells you the numbers are very similar to their mean.

Sample variance

The variance formula I just showed you is appropriate if the group of five measurements is a population. Does this mean that variance for a sample is different? It does, and here's why.

If your set of numbers is a sample drawn from a large population, your objective is most likely to use the variance of the sample to estimate the variance of the population.

The formula in the preceding section doesn't work as an estimate of the population variance. Although the mean calculated in the usual way is an accurate estimate of the population mean, that's not the case for the variance, for reasons far beyond the scope of this book.

REMEMBER

It's pretty easy to calculate an accurate estimate of the population variance. All you have to do is use $N-1$ in the denominator rather than N. (Again, for reasons way beyond this book's scope.)

And because you're working with a characteristic of a sample (rather than of a population), you use the English equivalent of the Greek letter — s rather than σ. This means that the formula for the sample variance (as an estimate of the population variance) is

$$s^2 = \frac{\sum(X - \bar{X})^2}{N-1}$$

The value of s^2, given the squared deviations in the set of five numbers, is

$$(4 + 1 + 16 + 4 + 9)/4 = 34/4 = 8.5$$

So if these numbers

50, 47, 52, 46, and 45

are an entire population, their variance is 6.8. If they're a sample drawn from a larger population, the best estimate of that population's variance is 8.5.

Variance in R

Calculating variance in R is simplicity itself. You use the var() function. But which variance does it give you? The one with N in the denominator or the one with $N-1$? Let's find out:

```
> heights <- c(50, 47, 52, 46, 45)
```

```
> var(heights)
[1] 8.5
```

It calculates the estimated variance (with $N-1$ in the denominator). To calculate that first variance I showed you (with N in the denominator), I have to multiply this number by $(N-1)/N$. Using `length()` to calculate N, that's

```
> var(heights)*(length(heights)-1)/length(heights)
[1] 6.8
```

If I were going to work with this kind of variance frequently, I'd define a function `var.p()`:

```
var.p = function(x){var(x)*(length(x)-1)/length(x)}
```

And here's how to use it:

```
> var.p(heights)
[1] 6.8
```

For reasons that will become clear later, I'd like you to think of the denominator of a variance estimate (like $N-1$) as *degrees of freedom*. Why? Stay tuned. (Chapter 12 reveals all!)

Back to the Roots: Standard Deviation

After you calculate the variance of a set of numbers, you have a value whose units are different from your original measurements. For example, if your original measurements are in inches, their variance is in *square* inches. This is because you square the deviations before you average them. So the variance in the five-score population in the preceding example is 6.8 square inches.

It might be hard to grasp what that means. Often, it's more intuitive if the variation statistic is in the same units as the original measurements. It's easy to turn variance into that kind of statistic. All you have to do is take the square root of the variance.

Like the variance, this square root is so important that it is has a special name: standard deviation.

Population standard deviation

The *standard deviation* of a population is the square root of the population variance. The symbol for the population standard deviation is σ (sigma). Its formula is

$$\sigma = \sqrt{\sigma^2} = \sqrt{\frac{\sum(X-\bar{X})^2}{N}}$$

For this 5-score population of measurements (in inches):

50, 47, 52, 46, and 45

the population variance is 6.8 square inches, and the population standard deviation is 2.61 inches (rounded off).

Sample standard deviation

The standard deviation of a sample — an estimate of the standard deviation of a population — is the square root of the sample variance. Its symbol is s and its formula is

$$s = \sqrt{s^2} = \sqrt{\frac{\sum(X-\bar{X})^2}{N-1}}$$

For this sample of measurements (in inches):

50, 47, 52, 46, and 45

the estimated population variance is 8.4 square inches, and the estimated population standard deviation is 2.92 inches (rounded off).

Standard Deviation in R

As is the case with variance, using R to compute the standard deviation is easy: You use the sd() function. And like its variance counterpart, sd() calculates s, not σ:

```
> sd(heights)
[1] 2.915476
```

For σ — treating the five numbers as a self-contained population, in other words — you have to multiply the sd() result by the square root of $(N-1)/N$:

```
> sd(heights)*(sqrt((length(heights)-1)/length(heights)))
[1] 2.607681
```

Again, if you're going to use this one frequently, defining a function is a good idea:

```
sd.p=function(x){sd(x)*sqrt((length(x)-1)/length(x))}
```

And here's how you use this function:

```
> sd.p(heights)
[1] 2.607681
```

Conditions, Conditions, Conditions . . .

In Chapter 4, I point out that with larger data frames, you sometimes want to calculate statistics on cases (rows) that meet certain conditions, rather than on all the cases.

As in Chapters 3 and 4, I use the Cars93 data frame for the discussion that follows. That data frame has data for a sample of 93 cars from 1993. You'll find it in the MASS package, so be sure you have the MASS package in your library. (Find MASS on the Packages tab and click its check box.)

I calculate the variance of the horsepowers of cars that originated in the USA. Using the with() function I show you in Chapter 4, that's

```
> with(Cars93, var(Horsepower[Origin == "USA"]))
[1] 2965.319
```

How many of those cars are in this group?

```
> with(Cars93, length(Horsepower[Origin == "USA"]))
[1] 48
```

How about the non-USA cars?

```
> with(Cars93, var(Horsepower[Origin == "non-USA"]))
[1] 2537.283
> with(Cars93, length(Horsepower[Origin == "non-USA"]))
[1] 45
```

Can you compare those variances? Sure — but not until Chapter 11.

I'll leave it as an exercise for you to compute the standard deviations for the USA cars and for the non-USA cars.

Chapter **6**

Meeting Standards and Standings

I n my left hand, I hold 100 Philippine pesos. In my right, I hold 1,000 Colombian pesos. Which is worth more? Both are called *pesos*, right? So shouldn't the 1,000 be greater than the 100? Not necessarily. *Peso* is just a coincidence of names. Each one comes out of a different country, and each country has its own economy.

To compare the two amounts of money, you have to convert each currency into a standard unit. The most intuitive standard for U.S. citizens is our own currency. How much is each amount worth in dollars and cents? As I write this, 100 Philippine pesos are worth over $2. One thousand Colombian pesos are worth 34 cents.

So when you compare numbers, context is important. To make valid comparisons across contexts, you often have to convert numbers into standard units. In this chapter, I show you how to use statistics to do just that. Standard units show you where a score stands in relation to other scores within a group. I also show you other ways to determine a score's standing within a group.

Catching Some Z's

A number in isolation doesn't provide much information. To fully understand what a number means, you have to take into account the process that produced it. To compare one number to another, they have to be on the same scale.

When you're converting currency, it's easy to figure out a standard. When you convert temperatures from Fahrenheit to Celsius, or lengths from feet to meters, a formula guides you.

When it's not so clear-cut, you can use the mean and standard deviation to standardize scores that come from different processes. The idea is to take a set of scores and use its mean as a zero point, and its standard deviation as a unit of measure. Then you make comparisons: You calculate the deviation of each score from the mean, and then you compare that deviation to the standard deviation. You're asking, "How big is a particular deviation relative to (something like) an average of all the deviations?"

To make a comparison, you divide the score's deviation by the standard deviation. This transforms the score into another kind of score. The transformed score is called a *standard score*, or a *z-score*.

The formula for this is

$$z = \frac{X - \bar{X}}{s}$$

if you're dealing with a sample, and

$$z = \frac{X - \mu}{\sigma}$$

if you're dealing with a population. In either case, x represents the score you're transforming into a z-score.

Characteristics of z-scores

A z-score can be positive, negative, or zero. A negative z-score represents a score that's less than the mean, and a positive z-score represents a score that's greater than the mean. When the score is equal to the mean, its z-score is zero.

When you calculate the z-score for every score in the set, the mean of the z-scores is 0, and the standard deviation of the z-scores is 1.

After you do this for several sets of scores, you can legitimately compare a score from one set to a score from another. If the two sets have different means and different standard deviations, comparing without standardizing is like comparing apples with kumquats.

In the examples that follow, I show how to use z-scores to make comparisons.

Bonds versus the Bambino

Here's an important question that often comes up in the context of serious metaphysical discussions: Who is the greatest home run hitter of all time: Barry Bonds or Babe Ruth? Although this is a difficult question to answer, one way to get your hands around it is to look at each player's best season and compare the two. Bonds hit 73 home runs in 2001, and Ruth hit 60 in 1927. On the surface, Bonds appears to be the more productive hitter.

The year 1927 was very different from 2001, however. Baseball (and everything else) went through huge, long-overdue changes in the intervening years, and player statistics reflect those changes. A home run was harder to hit in the 1920s than in the 2000s. Still, 73 versus 60? Hmmm. . . .

Standard scores can help decide whose best season was better. To standardize, I took the top 50 home run hitters of 1927 and the top 50 from 2001. I calculated the mean and standard deviation of each group and then turned Ruth's 60 and Bonds's 73 into z-scores.

The average from 1927 is 12.68 homers with a standard deviation of 10.49. The average from 2001 is 37.02 homers with a standard deviation of 9.64. Although the means differ greatly, the standard deviations are pretty close.

And the z-scores? Ruth's is

$$z = \frac{60 - 12.68}{10.49} = 4.51$$

Bonds's is

$$z = \frac{73 - 37.02}{9.64} = 3.73$$

The clear winner in the z-score best-season home run derby is Babe Ruth. Period.

Just to show you how times have changed, Lou Gehrig hit 47 home runs in 1927 (finishing second to Ruth) for a z-score of 3.27. In 2001, 47 home runs amounted to a z-score of 1.04.

Exam scores

Getting away from sports debates, one practical application of z-scores is the assignment of grades to exam scores. Based on percentage scoring, instructors traditionally evaluate a score of 90 points or higher (out of 100) as an A, 80–89 points as a B, 70–79 points as a C, 60–69 points as a D, and less than 60 points as an F. Then they average scores from several exams together to assign a course grade.

Is that fair? Just as a peso from the Philippines is worth more than a peso from Colombia, and a home run was harder to hit in 1927 than in 2001, is a "point" on one exam worth the same as a "point" on another? Like "pesos," isn't "points" just a coincidence?

Absolutely. A point on a difficult exam is, by definition, harder to come by than a point on an easy exam. Because points might not mean the same thing from one exam to another, the fairest thing to do is convert scores from each exam into z-scores before averaging them. That way, you're averaging numbers on a level playing field.

I do that in the courses I teach. I often find that a lower numerical score on one exam results in a higher z-score than a higher numerical score from another exam. For example, on an exam where the mean is 65 and the standard deviation is 12, a score of 71 results in a z-score of .5. On another exam, with a mean of 69 and a standard deviation of 14, a score of 75 is equivalent to a z-score of .429. (Yes, it's like Ruth's 60 home runs versus Bonds's 73.) Moral of the story: Numbers in isolation tell you very little. You have to understand the process that produces them.

Standard Scores in R

The R function for calculating standard scores is called scale(). Supply a vector of scores, and scale() returns a vector of z-scores along with, helpfully, the mean and the standard deviation.

To show scale() in action, I isolate a subset of the Cars93 data frame. (It's in the MASS package. On the Packages tab, check the box next to MASS if it's unchecked.)

Specifically, I create a vector of the horsepowers of 8-cylinder cars from the USA:

```
> Horsepower.USA.Eight <- Cars93$Horsepower[Origin ==
        "USA" & Cylinders == 8]
> Horsepower.USA.Eight
[1] 200 295 170 300 190 210
```

And now for the z-scores:

```
> scale(Horsepower.USA.Eight)
           [,1]
[1,] -0.4925263
[2,]  1.2089283
[3,] -1.0298278
[4,]  1.2984785
[5,] -0.6716268
[6,] -0.3134259
attr(,"scaled:center")
[1] 227.5
attr(,"scaled:scale")
[1] 55.83458
```

That last value is s, not σ. If you have to base your z-scores on σ, divide each element in the vector by the square root of $(N-1)/N$:

```
> N <- length(Horsepower.USA.Eight)
> scale(Horsepower.USA.Eight)/sqrt((N-1)/N)
           [,1]
[1,] -0.5395356
[2,]  1.3243146
[3,] -1.1281198
[4,]  1.4224120
[5,] -0.7357303
[6,] -0.3433408
attr(,"scaled:center")
[1] 227.5
attr(,"scaled:scale")
[1] 55.83458
```

Notice that scale() still returns s.

CACHING SOME Z'S

Because negative z-scores might have connotations that are, well, negative, educators sometimes change the z-score when they evaluate students. In effect, they're hiding the z-score, but the concept is the same — standardization with the standard deviation as the unit of measure.

One popular transformation is called the T-score. The T-score eliminates negative scores because a set of T-scores has a mean of 50 and a standard deviation of 10. The idea is to give an exam, grade all the tests, and calculate the mean and standard deviation. Next, turn each score into a z-score. Then follow this formula:

$$T = (z)(10) + 50$$

People who use the T-score often like to round to the nearest whole number.

Here's how to transform the vector from the example into a set of T-scores:

```
T.Hp.USA.Eight <- round((10*scale(Horsepower.USA.Eight)+50),
    digits = 0)
```

The `digits=0` argument in the `round()` function rounds off the result to the nearest whole number.

SAT scores are another transformation of the z-score. (Some refer to the SAT as a C-score.) Under the old scoring system, the SAT has a mean of 500 and a standard deviation of 100. After the exams are graded, and their mean and standard deviation calculated, each exam score becomes a z-score in the usual way. This formula converts the z-score into a SAT score:

$$SAT = (z)(100) + 50$$

Rounding to the nearest whole number is part of the procedure here, too.

The IQ score is still another transformed z. Its mean is 100, and its standard deviation is 15. What's the procedure for computing an IQ score? You guessed it. In a group of IQ scores, calculate the mean and standard deviation, and then calculate the z-score. Then it's

$$IQ = (z)(15) + 100$$

As with the other two, IQ scores are rounded to the nearest whole number.

Where Do You Stand?

Standard scores show you how a score stands in relation to other scores in the same group. To do this, they use the standard deviation as a unit of measure.

If you don't want to use the standard deviation, you can show a score's relative standing in a simpler way. You can determine the score's rank within the group: In ascending order, the lowest score has a rank of 1, the second lowest has a rank of 2, and so on. In descending order, the highest score is ranked 1, the second highest 2, and so on.

Ranking in R

Unsurprisingly, the rank() function ranks the scores in a vector. The default order is ascending:

```
> Horsepower.USA.Eight
[1] 200 295 170 300 190 210
> rank(Horsepower.USA.Eight)
[1] 3 5 1 6 2 4
```

For descending order, put a minus sign (−) in front of the vector name:

```
> rank(-Horsepower.USA.Eight)
[1] 4 2 6 1 5 3
```

Tied scores

R handles tied scores by including the optional ties.method argument in rank(). To show you how this works, I create a new vector that replaces the sixth value (210) in Horsepower.USA.Eight with 200:

```
> tied.Horsepower <- replace(Horsepower.USA.Eight,6,200)
> tied.Horsepower
[1] 200 295 170 300 190 200
```

One way of dealing with tied scores is to give each tied score the average of the ranks they would have attained. So the two scores of 200 would have been ranked 3 and 4, and their average 3.5 is what this method assigns to both of them:

```
> rank(tied.Horsepower, ties.method = "average")
[1] 3.5 5.0 1.0 6.0 2.0 3.5
```

Another method assigns the minimum of the ranks:

```
> rank(tied.Horsepower, ties.method = "min")
[1] 3 5 1 6 2 3
```

And still another assigns the maximum of the ranks:

```
> rank(tied.Horsepower, ties.method = "max")
[1] 4 5 1 6 2 4
```

A couple of other methods are available. Type **?rank** into the console window for the details (which appear on the Help tab).

Nth smallest, Nth largest

You can turn the ranking process inside out by supplying a rank (like second-lowest) and asking which score has that rank. This procedure begins with the sort() function, which arranges the scores in increasing order:

```
> sort(Horsepower.USA.Eight)
[1] 170 190 200 210 295 300
```

For the second-lowest score, supply the index value 2:

```
> sort(Horsepower.USA.Eight)[2]
[1] 190
```

How about from the other end? Start by assigning the length of the vector to N:

```
> N <- length(Horsepower.USA.Eight)
```

Then, to find the second-highest score, it's

```
> sort(Horsepower.USA.Eight)[N-1]
[1] 295
```

Percentiles

Closely related to rank is the *percentile*, which represents a score's standing in the group as the percent of scores below it. If you've taken standardized tests like the SAT, you've encountered percentiles. An SAT score in the 80th percentile is higher than 80 percent of the other SAT scores.

Sounds simple, doesn't it? Not so fast. "Percentile" can have a couple of definitions, and hence, a couple (or more) ways to calculate it. Some define percentile as "greater than" (as in the preceding paragraph), some define percentile as "greater than or equal to." "Greater than" equates to "exclusive." "Greater than or equal to" equates to "inclusive."

The function quantile() calculates percentiles. If left to its own devices, it calculates the 0th, 25th, 50th, 75th, and 100th percentiles. It calculates the percentiles in a manner that's consistent with "inclusive" and (if necessary) interpolates values for the percentiles.

I begin by sorting the Horsepower.USA.Eight vector so that you can see the scores in order and compare with the percentiles:

```
> sort(Horsepower.USA.Eight)
[1] 170 190 200 210 295 300
```

And now the percentiles:

```
> quantile(Horsepower.USA.Eight)
    0%    25%    50%    75%   100%
170.00 192.50 205.00 273.75 300.00
```

Notice that the 25th, 50th, and 75th percentiles are values that aren't in the vector.

To calculate percentiles consistent with "exclusive," add the type argument and set it equal to 6:

```
> quantile(Horsepower.USA.Eight, type = 6)
    0%    25%    50%    75%   100%
170.00 185.00 205.00 296.25 300.00
```

The default type (the first type I showed you) is 7, by the way. Seven other types (ways of calculating percentiles) are available. To take a look at them, type **?quantile** into the Console window (and then read the documentation on the Help tab.)

Moving forward, I use the default type for percentiles.

The 25th, 50th, 75th, and 100th percentiles are often used to summarize a group of scores. Because they divide a group of scores into fourths, they're called *quartiles*.

You're not stuck with quartiles, however. You can get `quantile()` to return any percentile. Suppose you want to find the 54th, 68th, and 91st percentiles. Include a vector of those numbers (expressed as proportions) and you're in business:

```
> quantile(Horsepower.USA.Eight, c(.54, .68, .91))
    54%    68%    91%
 207.00 244.00 297.75
```

Percent ranks

The `quantile()` function gives you the scores that correspond to given percentiles. You can also work in the reverse direction — find the percent ranks that correspond to given scores in a data set. For example, in `Horsepower.USA.Eight`, 170 is lowest in the list of six, so its rank is 1 and its percent rank is 1/6, or 16.67 percent.

Base R doesn't provide a function for this, but it's easy enough to create one:

```
percent.ranks <-
        function(x){round((rank(x)/length(x))*100, digits = 2)}
```

The `round()` function with `digits = 2` rounds the results to two decimal places.

Applying this function:

```
> percent.ranks(Horsepower.USA.Eight)
[1]  50.00  83.33  16.67 100.00  33.33  66.67
```

A NEAT TRICK

Sometimes, you might want to know only the percent rank of a single score in a set of scores — even if that score isn't in the data set. For example, what is the percent rank of 273 in `Horsepower.USA.Eight`?

To answer this question, you can harness `mean()`. Using this function along with logical operators yields interesting results. Here's what I mean:

```
xx <- c(15,20,25,30,35,40,45,50)
```

Here's a result you'd expect:

```
> mean(xx)
[1] 32.5
```

But here's one you might not:

```
> mean(xx > 15)
[1] 0.875
```

The result is the proportion of scores in xx that are greater than 15.

Here are a few more:

```
> mean(xx < 25)
[1] 0.25
> mean(xx <= 25)
[1] 0.375
> mean(xx <= 28)
[1] 0.375
```

That <= operator, of course, means "less than or equal to," so that last one gives the proportion of scores in xx that are less than or equal to 28.

Are you catching my drift? To find the percent rank of a score (or a potential score) in a vector like Horsepower.USA.Eight, it's

```
> mean(Horsepower.USA.Eight <= 273)*100
[1] 66.66667
```

Summarizing

In addition to the functions for calculating percentiles and ranks, R provides a couple of functions that quickly summarize data and do a lot of the work I discuss in this chapter.

One is called fivenum(). This function, unsurprisingly, yields five numbers. They're the five numbers that box plot creator John Tukey used to summarize a data set. Then he used those numbers in his box plots. (See Chapter 3.)

```
> fivenum(Horsepower.USA.Eight)
[1] 170 190 205 295 300
```

From left to right, that's the minimum, lower hinge, median, upper hinge, and maximum. Remember the quantile() function and the nine available ways (types) to calculate quantiles? This function's results are what type = 2 yields in quantile().

Another function, summary(), is more widely used:

```
> summary(Horsepower.USA.Eight)
   Min. 1st Qu.  Median    Mean 3rd Qu.    Max.
  170.0   192.5   205.0   227.5   273.8   300.0
```

It provides the mean along with the quantiles (as the default type in quantile() calculates them).

The summary() function is versatile. You can use it to summarize a wide variety of objects, and the results can look very different from object to object. I use it quite a bit in upcoming chapters.

IN THIS CHAPTER

» **Working with things great and small**

» **Understanding symmetry, peaks, and plateaus**

» **Experiencing special moments**

» **Finding frequencies**

» **Getting descriptive**

Chapter **7**

Summarizing It All

The measures of central tendency and variability that I discuss in earlier chapters aren't the only ways of summarizing a set of scores. These measures are a subset of descriptive statistics. Some descriptive statistics — like maximum, minimum, and range — are easy to understand. Some — like skewness and kurtosis — are not.

This chapter covers descriptive statistics and shows you how to calculate them in R.

How Many?

Perhaps the fundamental descriptive statistic is the number of scores in a set of data. In earlier chapters, I work with length(), the R function that calculates this number. As in earlier chapters, I work with the Cars93 data frame, which is in the MASS package. (If it isn't selected, click the check box next to MASS on the Packages tab.)

Cars93 holds data on 27 variables for 93 cars available in 1993. What happens when you apply length() to the data frame?

```
> length(Cars93)
[1] 27
```

So length() returns the number of variables in the data frame. The function ncol() does the same thing:

```
> ncol(Cars93)
[1] 27
```

I already know the number of cases (rows) in the data frame, but if I had to find that number, nrow() would get it done:

```
> nrow(Cars93)
[1] 93
```

If you want to know how many cases in the data frame meet a particular condition — like how many cars originated in the USA — you have to take into account the way R treats conditions: R attaches the label "TRUE" to cases that meet a condition, and "FALSE" to cases that don't. Also, R assigns the value 1 to "TRUE" and 0 to "FALSE."

To count the number of USA-originated cars, then, you state the condition and then add up all the 1s:

```
> sum(Cars93$Origin == "USA")
[1] 48
```

To count the number of non-USA cars in the data frame, you can change the condition to "non-USA", of course, or you can use != — the "not equal to" operator:

```
> sum(Cars93$Origin != "USA")
[1] 45
```

More complex conditions are possible. For the number of 4-cylinder USA cars:

```
> sum(Cars93$Origin == "USA" & Cars93$Cylinders == 4)
[1] 22
```

Or, if you prefer no $-signs:

```
> with(Cars93, sum(Origin == "USA" & Cylinders == 4))
[1] 22
```

To calculate the number of elements in a vector, length(), as you may have read earlier, is the function to use. Here is a vector of horsepowers for 4-cylinder USA cars:

```
> Horsepower.USA.Four <- Cars93$Horsepower[Origin ==
        "USA" & Cylinders == 4]
```

and here's the number of horsepower values in that vector:

```
> length(Horsepower.USA.Four)
[1] 22
```

The High and the Low

Two descriptive statistics that need no introduction are the maximum and minimum value in a set of scores:

```
> max(Horsepower.USA.Four)
[1] 155
> min(Horsepower.USA.Four)
[1] 63
```

If you happen to need both values at the same time:

```
> range(Horsepower.USA.Four)
[1]   63 155
```

Living in the Moments

In statistics, *moments* are quantities that are related to the shape of a set of numbers. By "shape of a set of numbers," I mean "what a histogram based on the numbers looks like" — how spread out it is, how symmetric it is, and more.

A *raw moment* of order k is the average of all numbers in the set, with each number raised to the kth power before you average it. So the *first* raw moment is the arithmetic mean. The *second* raw moment is the average of the squared scores. The *third* raw moment is the average of the cubed scores, and so on.

A *central moment* is based on the average of *deviations* of numbers from their mean. (Beginning to sound vaguely familiar?) If you square the deviations before you average them, you have the *second* central moment. If you cube the deviations before you average them, that's the *third* central moment. Raise each one to the fourth power before you average them, and you have the *fourth* central moment. I could go on and on, but you get the idea.

Two quick questions: 1. For any set of numbers, what's the first central moment? 2. By what other name do you know the second central moment?

Two quick answers: 1. Zero. 2. Population variance. Reread Chapter 5 if you don't believe me.

A teachable moment

Before I proceed, I think it's a good idea to translate into R everything I've said so far in this chapter. That way, when you get to the next R package to install (which calculates moments), you'll know what's going on behind the scenes.

Here's a function for calculating a central moment of a vector:

```
cen.mom <-function(x,y){mean((x - mean(x))^y)}
```

The first argument, x, is the vector. The second argument, y, is the order (second, third, fourth . . .).

Here's a vector to try it out on:

```
Horsepower.USA <- Cars93$Horsepower[Origin == "USA"]
```

And here are the second, third, and fourth central moments:

```
> cen.mom(Horsepower.USA,2)
[1] 2903.541
> cen.mom(Horsepower.USA,3)
[1] 177269.5
> cen.mom(Horsepower.USA,4)
[1] 37127741
```

Back to descriptives

What does all this about moments have to do with descriptive statistics? As I said . . . well . . . a moment ago, think of a histogram based on a set of numbers. The first raw moment (the mean) locates the *center* of the histogram. The second central moment indicates the *spread* of the histogram. The third central moment is involved in the *symmetry* of the histogram, which is called *skewness*. The fourth central moment figures into how fat or thin the tails (extreme ends) of the histogram are. This is called *kurtosis*. Getting into moments of higher order than that is way beyond the scope of this book.

But let's get into symmetry and "tailedness."

Skewness

Figure 7-1 shows three histograms. The first is symmetric; the other two are not. The symmetry and the asymmetry are reflected in the skewness statistic.

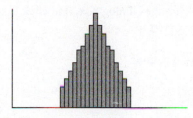

Symmetric: Skewness = 0

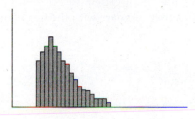

Skewed to the right: Skewness is positive

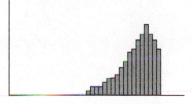

Skewed to the left: Skewness is negative

FIGURE 7-1:
Three histograms, showing three kinds of skewness.

For the symmetric histogram, the skewness is 0. For the second histogram — the one that tails off to the right — the value of the skewness statistic is *positive*. It's also said to be "skewed to the right." For the third histogram (which tails off to the left), the value of the skewness statistic is *negative*. It's also said to be "skewed to the left."

Now for a formula. I'll let M_k represent the kth central moment. To calculate skewness, it's

$$skewness = \frac{\sum \left(X - \bar{X} \right)^3}{(N-1)s^3}$$

In English, the *skewness* of a set of numbers is the third central moment divided by the second central moment raised to the three-halves power. With the R function I defined earlier, it's easier done than said:

```
> cen.mom(Horsepower.USA,3)/cen.mom(Horsepower.USA,2)^1.5
[1] 1.133031
```

With the `moments` package, it's easier still. On the Packages tab, click Install and type **moments** into the Install Packages dialog box, and click Install. Then on the Packages tab, click the check box next to `moments`.

Here's its `skewness()` function in action:

```
> skewness(Horsepower.USA)
[1] 1.133031
```

So the skew is positive. How does that compare with the horsepower for non-USA cars?

```
> Horsepower.NonUSA <- Cars93$Horsepower[Origin == "non-USA"]
> skewness(Horsepower.NonUSA)
[1] 0.642995
```

The skew is more positive for USA cars than for non-USA cars. What do the two histograms look like?

I produced them side-by-side in Figure 4-1, over in Chapter 4. For convenience, I show them here as Figure 7-2.

The code that produces them is

```
ggplot(Cars93, aes(x=Horsepower)) +
   geom_histogram(color="black", fill="white",binwidth = 10)+
   facet_wrap(~Origin)
```

Consistent with the skewness values, the histograms show that in the USA cars, the scores are more bunched up on the left than they are in the non-USA cars.

It's sometimes easier to see trends in a density plot rather than in a histogram. A density plot shows the proportions of scores between a given lower boundary and a given upper boundary (like the proportion of cars with horsepower between 100 and 140). I discuss density in more detail in Chapter 8.

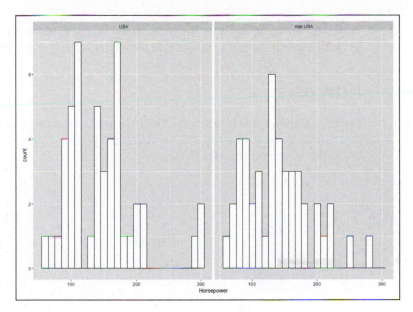

FIGURE 7-2:
Horsepower
histograms for
USA cars and
non-USA cars.

Changing one line of code produces the density plots:

```
ggplot(Cars93, aes(x=Horsepower)) +
    geom_density() +
    facet_wrap(~Origin)
```

Figure 7-3 shows the two density plots.

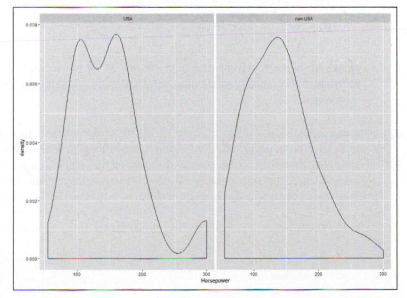

FIGURE 7-3:
Horsepower
density plots for
USA cars and
non-USA cars.

With the density plots, it seems to be easier (for me, anyway) to see the more leftward tilt (and hence, more positive skew) in the plot on the left.

Kurtosis

Figure 7-4 shows two histograms. The first has fatter tails than the second. The first is said to be *leptokurtic*. The second is *platykurtic*. The kurtosis for the first histogram is greater than for the second.

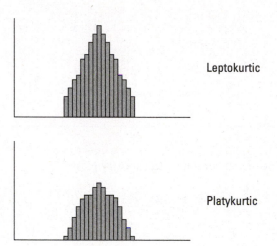

Leptokurtic

Platykurtic

FIGURE 7-4:
Two histograms, showing two kinds of kurtosis.

The formula for kurtosis is

$$kurtosis = \frac{\sum \left(X - \bar{X}\right)^2}{(N-1)s^4} - 3$$

where M_4 is the fourth central moment and M_2 is the second central moment. So kurtosis is the fourth central moment divided by the square of the second central moment.

TIP

Many statisticians subtract 3 from the result of the kurtosis formula. They refer to that value as *excess kurtosis*. By "excess," they mean kurtosis that's greater (or possibly less) than the kurtosis of something called the *standard normal distribution*, which I discuss in Chapter 8. Because of the subtraction, excess kurtosis can be negative. Why does 3 represent the kurtosis of the standard normal distribution? Don't ask.

Using the function I defined earlier, the kurtosis of horsepower for USA cars is

```
> cen.mom(Horsepower.USA,4)/cen.mom(Horsepower.USA,2)^2
[1] 4.403952
```

Of course, the `kurtosis()` function in the `moments` package makes this a snap:

```
> kurtosis(Horsepower.USA)
[1] 4.403952
```

The fatter tail in the left-side density plot in Figure 7-3 suggests that the USA cars have a higher kurtosis than the non-USA cars. Is this true?

```
> kurtosis(Horsepower.NonUSA)
[1] 3.097339
```

Yes, it is!

TIP

In addition to `skewness()` and `kurtosis()`, the `moments` package provides a function called `moment()` that does everything `cen.mom()` does and a bit more. I just thought it would be a good idea to show you a user-defined function that illustrates what goes into calculating a central moment. (Was I being "momentous" . . . or did I just "seize the moment"? Okay. I'll stop.)

Tuning in the Frequency

A good way to explore data is to find out the frequencies of occurrence for each category of a nominal variable, and for each interval of a numerical variable.

Nominal variables: table() et al

For nominal variables, like Type of Automobile in `Cars93`, the easiest way to get the frequencies is the `table()` function I use earlier:

```
> car.types <-table(Cars93$Type)
> car.types

Compact   Large Midsize   Small  Sporty     Van
     16      11      22      21      14       9
```

Another function, `prop.table()`, expresses these frequencies as proportions of the whole amount:

```
> prop.table(car.types)

   Compact     Large   Midsize     Small    Sporty
       Van
```

```
0.17204301 0.11827957 0.23655914 0.22580645 0.15053763
        0.09677419
```

REMEMBER

The values here appear out of whack because the page isn't as wide as the Console window. If I round off the proportions to two decimal places, the output looks a lot better on the page:

```
> round(prop.table(car.types),2)

Compact  Large Midsize  Small Sporty   Van
   0.17   0.12    0.24   0.23   0.15  0.10
```

Another function, `margin.table()`, adds up the frequencies:

```
> margin.table(car.types)
[1] 93
```

Numerical variables: hist()

Tabulating frequencies for intervals of numerical data is part and parcel of creating histograms. (See Chapter 3.) To create a table of frequencies, use the graphic function `hist()`, which produces a list of components when the `plot` argument is FALSE:

```
> prices <- hist(Cars93$Price, plot=F, breaks=5)
> prices
$breaks
[1]  0 10 20 30 40 50 60 70

$counts
[1] 12 50 19  9  2  0  1

$density
[1] 0.012903226 0.053763441 0.020430108 0.009677419 0.002150538
        0.000000000
[7] 0.001075269

$mids
[1]  5 15 25 35 45 55 65

$xname
[1] "Cars93$Price"

$equidist
[1] TRUE
```

(In Cars93, remember, each price is in thousands of dollars.)

Although I specified five breaks, hist() uses a number of breaks that makes everything look "prettier." From here, I can use mids (the interval-midpoints) and counts to make a matrix of the frequencies, and then a data frame:

```
> prices.matrix <- matrix(c(prices$mids,prices$counts), ncol = 2)
> prices.frame <- data.frame(prices.matrix)
> colnames(prices.frame) <- c("Price Midpoint (X
        $1,000)","Frequency")
> prices.frame
  Price Midpoint (X $1,000) Frequency
1                         5        12
2                        15        50
3                        25        19
4                        35         9
5                        45         2
6                        55         0
7                        65         1
```

Cumulative frequency

Another way of looking at frequencies is to examine *cumulative frequencies*: Each interval's cumulative frequency is the sum of its own frequency and all frequencies in the preceding intervals.

The cumsum() function does the arithmetic on the vector of frequencies:

```
> prices$counts
[1] 12 50 19  9  2  0  1
> cumsum(prices$counts)
[1] 12 62 81 90 92 92 93
```

To plot a cumulative frequency histogram, I substitute the cumulative frequencies vector for the original one:

```
> prices$counts <- cumsum(prices$counts)
```

and then apply plot():

```
> plot(prices, main = "Cumulative Histogram", xlab = "Price",
        ylab = "Cumulative Frequency")
```

The result is Figure 7-5.

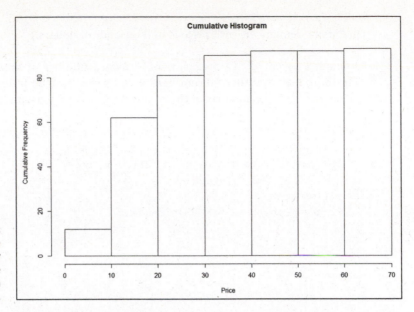

FIGURE 7-5:
Cumulative
frequency
histogram of the
price data in
Cars93.

Step by step: The empirical cumulative distribution function

The *empirical cumulative distribution function* (ecdf) is closely related to cumulative frequency. Rather than show the frequency in an interval, however, the ecdf shows the proportion of scores that are less than or equal to each score. If this sounds familiar, it's probably because you read about percentiles in Chapter 6.

In base R, it's easy to plot the ecdf:

```
> plot(ecdf(Cars93$Price), xlab = "Price", ylab = "Fn(Price)")
```

This produces Figure 7-6.

The uppercase *F* on the y-axis is a notational convention for a cumulative distribution. The Fn means, in effect, "cumulative function" as opposed to f or fn, which just means "function." (The y-axis label could also be Percentile(Price).)

Look closely at the plot. When consecutive points are far apart (like the two on the top right), you can see a horizontal line extending rightward out of a point. (A line extends out of every point, but the lines aren't visible when the points are bunched up.) Think of this line as a "step" and then the next dot is a step higher than the previous one. How much higher? That would be 1/N, where N is the number of scores in the sample. For Cars93, that would be 1/93, which rounds off to .011. (Now reconsider the title of this subsection. See what I did there?)

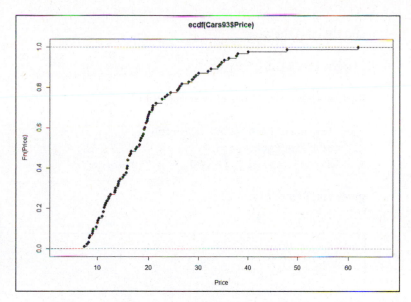

FIGURE 7-6:
Empirical
cumulative
distribution
function for the
price data in
Cars93.

Why is this called an "empirical" cumulative distribution function? Something that's *empirical* is based on observations, like sample data. Is it possible to have a non-empirical cumulative distribution function (cdf)? Yes — and that's the cdf of the population that the sample comes from. (See Chapter 1.) One important use of the ecdf is as a tool for estimating the population cdf.

So the plotted ecdf is an estimate of the cdf for the population, and the estimate is based on the sample data. To create an estimate, you assign a probability to each point and then add up the probabilities, point by point, from the minimum value to the maximum value. This produces the cumulative probability for each point. The probability assigned to a sample value is the estimate of the proportion of times that value occurs in the population. What is the estimate? That's the afore-mentioned $1/N$ for each point — .011, for this sample. For any given value, that might not be the exact proportion in the population. It's just the best estimate from the sample.

I prefer to use `ggplot()` to visualize the ecdf. Because I base the plot on a vector (`Cars93$Price`), the data source is `NULL`:

```
ggplot(NULL, aes(x=Cars93$Price))
```

In keeping with the step-by-step nature of this function, the plot consists of steps, and the geom function is `geom_step`. The statistic that locates each step on the plot is the ecdf, so that's

```
geom_step(stat="ecdf")
```

and I'll label the axes:

```
labs(x= "Price X $1,000",y = "Fn(Price)")
```

Putting those three lines of code together

```
ggplot(NULL, aes(x=Cars93$Price)) +
  geom_step(stat="ecdf") +
  labs(x= "Price X $1,000",y = "Fn(Price)")
```

gives you Figure 7-7.

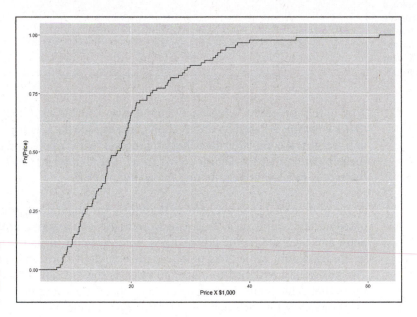

FIGURE 7-7:
The ecdf for the price data in Cars93, plotted with ggplot().

To put a little pizzazz in the graph, I add a dashed vertical line at each quartile. Before I add the geom function for a vertical line, I put the quartile information in a vector:

```
price.q <-quantile(Cars93$Price)
```

And now

```
geom_vline(aes(xintercept=price.q),linetype = "dashed")
```

adds the vertical lines. The aesthetic mapping sets the x-intercept of each line at a quartile value.

So these lines of code

```
ggplot(NULL, aes(x=Cars93$Price)) +
    geom_step(stat="ecdf") +
    labs(x= "Price X $1,000",y = "Fn(Price)") +
    geom_vline(aes(xintercept=price.q),linetype = "dashed")
```

result in Figure 7-8.

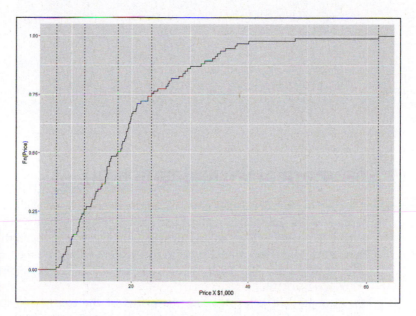

FIGURE 7-8:
The ecdf for price
data, with a
dashed vertical
line at each
quartile.

A nice finishing touch is to put the quartile-values on the x-axis. The function scale_x_continuous() gets that done. It uses one argument called breaks (which sets the location of values to put on the axis) and another called labels (which puts the values on those locations). Here's where that price.q vector comes in handy:

```
scale_x_continuous(breaks = price.q,labels = price.q)
```

And here's the R code that creates Figure 7-9:

```
ggplot(NULL, aes(x=Cars93$Price)) +
    geom_step(stat="ecdf") +
    labs(x= "Price X $1,000",y = "Fn(Price)") +
    geom_vline(aes(xintercept=price.q),linetype = "dashed")+
    scale_x_continuous(breaks = price.q,labels = price.q)
```

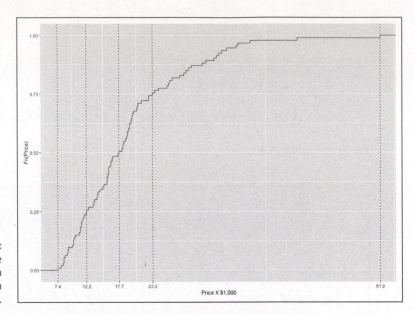

Numerical variables: stem()

Box plot creator John Tukey popularized the *stem-and-leaf plot* as a way to quickly visualize a distribution of numbers. It's not a "plot" in the usual sense of a graph in the Plot window. Instead, it's an arrangement of numbers in the Console window. With each score rounded off to the nearest whole number, each "leaf" is a score's rightmost digit. Each "stem" consists of all the other digits.

An example will help. Here are the prices of the cars in Cars93, arranged in ascending order and rounded off to the nearest whole number (remember that each price is in thousands of dollars):

```
> rounded <- (round(sort(Cars93$Price),0))
```

I use cat() to display the rounded values on this page. (Otherwise, it would look like a mess.) The value of its fill argument limits the number of characters (including spaces) on each line:

```
> cat(rounded, fill = 50)
7 8 8 8 8 9 9 9 9 10 10 10 10 10 11 11 11 11 11
11 12 12 12 12 12 13 13 14 14 14 14 14 15 15 16
16 16 16 16 16 16 16 16 16 17 18 18 18 18 18 18
19 19 19 19 19 20 20 20 20 20 20 20 21 21 21 22
23 23 23 24 24 26 26 26 27 28 29 29 30 30 32 32
34 34 35 35 36 38 38 40 48 62
```

The `stem()` function produces a stem-and-leaf plot of these values:

```
> stem(Cars93$Price)

  The decimal point is 1 digit(s) to the right of the |

  0 | 788889999
  1 | 00000111111222233344444556666666667788888999999
  2 | 00000001112333446667899
  3 | 00234455688
  4 | 08
  5 |
  6 | 2
```

In each row, the number to the left of the vertical line is the stem. The remaining numbers are the leaves for that row. The message about the decimal point means "multiply each stem by 10." Then add each leaf to that stem. So the bottom row tells you that one rounded score in the data is 62. The next row up reveals that no rounded score is between 50 and 59. The row above that one indicates that one score is 40 and another is 48. I'll leave it to you to figure out (and verify) the rest.

WARNING

As I reviewed the leaves, I noticed that the stem plot shows one score of 32 and another of 33. By contrast, the rounded scores show two 32s and no 33s. Apparently, `stem()` rounds differently than `round()` does.

Summarizing a Data Frame

If you're looking for descriptive statistics for the variables in a data frame, the `summary()` function will find them for you. I illustrate with a subset of the `Cars93` data frame:

```
> autos <- subset(Cars93, select = c(MPG.city,Type, Cylinders,
  Price, Horsepower))
> summary(autos)
   MPG.city          Type       Cylinders        Price
 Min.   :15.00   Compact:16   3     : 3    Min.   : 7.40
 1st Qu.:18.00   Large  :11   4     :49    1st Qu.:12.20
 Median :21.00   Midsize:22   5     : 2    Median :17.70
 Mean   :22.37   Small  :21   6     :31    Mean   :19.51
 3rd Qu.:25.00   Sporty :14   8     : 7    3rd Qu.:23.30
 Max.   :46.00   Van    : 9   rotary: 1    Max.   :61.90
   Horsepower
```

```
Min.    : 55.0
1st Qu.:103.0
Median :140.0
Mean    :143.8
3rd Qu.:170.0
Max.    :300.0
```

Notice the maxima, minima, and quartiles for the numerical variables and the frequency tables for Type and for Cylinders.

Two functions from the Hmisc package also summarize data frames. To use these functions, you need Hmisc in your library. (On the Packages tab, click Install and type **Hmisc** into the Packages box in the Install dialog box. Then click Install.)

One function, describe.data.frame(), provides output that's a bit more extensive than what you get from summary():

```
> describe.data.frame(autos)
autos

 5  Variables        93  Observations
----------------------------------------------------------------------

MPG.city
        n missing  unique     Info     Mean      .05      .10
       93       0      21     0.99    22.37     16.6     17.0
      .25      .50     .75      .90      .95
     18.0     21.0    25.0     29.0     31.4

lowest : 15 16 17 18 19, highest: 32 33 39 42 46
----------------------------------------------------------------------


Type
        n missing  unique
       93       0       6

          Compact Large Midsize Small Sporty Van
Frequency        16    11      22    21     14   9
%                17    12      24    23     15  10
----------------------------------------------------------------------
```

```
Cylinders
        n missing  unique
       93        0       6

            3   4 5  6 8 rotary
Frequency 3  49 2 31 7       1
%            3  53 2 33 8       1
_____


Price
        n missing  unique    Info    Mean    .05    .10
       93        0      81       1   19.51   8.52   9.84
      .25      .50     .75     .90     .95
    12.20    17.70   23.30   33.62   36.74


lowest :   7.4  8.0  8.3  8.4  8.6
highest: 37.7 38.0 40.1 47.9 61.9
_____


Horsepower
        n missing  unique    Info    Mean    .05    .10
       93        0      57       1   143.8   78.2   86.0
      .25      .50     .75     .90     .95
    103.0    140.0   170.0   206.8   237.0


lowest :   55  63  70  73  74, highest: 225 255 278 295 300
_____
```

A value labeled `Info` appears in the summaries of the numerical variables. That value is related to the number of tied scores — the greater the number of ties, the lower the value of `Info`. (The calculation of the value is fairly complicated.)

Another `Hmisc` function, `datadensity()`, gives graphic summaries, as in Figure 7-10:

```
> datadensity(autos)
```

If you plan to use the `datadensity()` function, arrange for the first data frame variable to be numerical. If the first variable is categorical (and thus appears at the top of the chart), longer bars in its plot are cut off at the top.

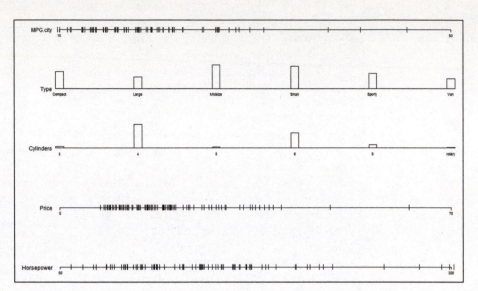

FIGURE 7-10:
Chart created by
`datadensity`
`(autos)`.

Chapter **8**

What's Normal?

One of the main jobs of a statistician is to estimate characteristics of a population. The job becomes easier if the statistician can make some assumptions about the populations he or she studies.

Here's an assumption that works over and over again: A specific attribute, ability, or trait is distributed throughout a population so that (1) most people have an average or near-average amount of the attribute, and (2) progressively fewer people have increasingly extreme amounts of the attribute. In this chapter, I discuss this assumption and its implications for statistics. I also discuss R functions related to this assumption.

Hitting the Curve

Attributes in the physical world, like length or weight, are all about objects you can see and touch. It's not that easy in the world of social scientists, statisticians, market researchers, and businesspeople. They have to be creative when they measure traits that they can't put their hands around — like "intelligence," "musical ability," or "willingness to buy a new product."

The assumption I mention in this chapter's introduction — that most people are around the average and progressively fewer people are toward the extremes — seems to work out well for those intangible traits. Because this happens often, it's become an assumption about how most traits are distributed.

It's possible to capture this assumption in a graphical way. Figure 8-1 shows the well-known *bell curve* that describes the distribution of a wide variety of attributes. The horizontal axis represents measurements of the ability under consideration. A vertical line drawn down the center of the curve would correspond to the average of the measurements.

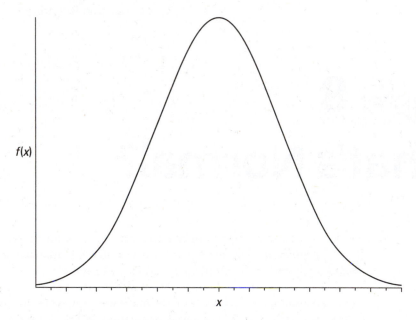

FIGURE 8-1:
The bell curve.

Assume that it's possible to measure a trait like intelligence and assume that this curve represents the distribution of intelligence in the population: The bell curve shows that most people have about average intelligence, only a few have little intelligence, and only a few are geniuses. That seems to fit nicely with what we know about people, doesn't it?

Digging deeper

On the horizontal axis of Figure 8-1 you see x, and on the vertical axis, $f(x)$. What do these symbols mean? The horizontal axis, as I mention, represents measurements, so think of each measurement as an x.

The explanation of $f(x)$ is a little more involved. A mathematical relationship between x and $f(x)$ creates the bell curve and enables you to visualize it. The relationship is rather complex, and I won't burden you with it right now. (I discuss it in a little while.) Just understand that $f(x)$ represents the height of the curve for a specified value of x. This means that you supply a value for x (and for a couple of other things), and then that complex relationship returns a value of $f(x)$.

Let me get into specifics. The formal name for "bell curve" is *normal distribution*. The term *f(x)* is called *probability density*, so a normal distribution is an example of a *probability density function*. Rather than give you a technical definition of probability density, I ask you to think of probability density as something that allows you to think about area under the curve as probability. Probability of . . . what? That's coming up in the next subsection.

Parameters of a normal distribution

You often hear people talk about "*the* normal distribution." That's a misnomer. It's really a *family* of distributions. The members of the family differ from one another in terms of two parameters — yes, *parameters* because I'm talking about populations. Those two parameters are the mean (μ) and the standard deviation (σ). The *mean* tells you where the center of the distribution is, and the *standard deviation* tells you how spread out the distribution is around the mean. The mean is in the middle of the distribution. Every member of the normal distribution family is symmetric — the left side of the distribution is a mirror image of the right. (Remember skewness, from Chapter 7? "Symmetric" means that the skewness of a normal distribution is zero.)

The characteristics of the normal distribution family are well known to statisticians. More important, you can apply those characteristics to your work.

How? This brings me back to probability. You can find some useful probabilities if you

>> Can lay out a line that represents the scale of the attribute you're measuring (the x-axis, in other words)

>> Can indicate on the line where the mean of the measurements is

>> Know the standard deviation

>> Can assume that the attribute is normally distributed throughout the population

I'll work with IQ scores to show you what I mean. Scores on the IQ test follow a normal distribution. The mean of the distribution of these scores is 100, and the standard deviation is 15. Figure 8-2 shows the probability density for this distribution.

TECHNICAL STUFF

You might have read elsewhere that the standard deviation for IQ is 16 rather than 15. That's the case for the Stanford–Binet version of the IQ test. For other versions, the standard deviation is 15.

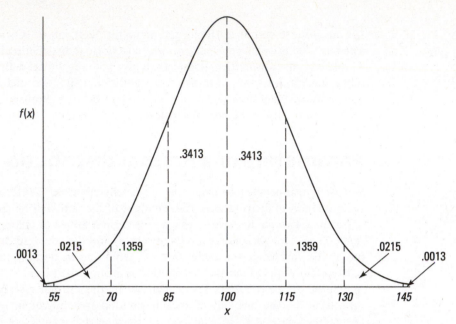

FIGURE 8-2:
The normal
distribution of IQ,
divided into
standard
deviations.

As Figure 8-2 shows, I've laid out a line for the IQ scale (the x-axis). Each point on the line represents an IQ score. With the mean (100) as the reference point, I've marked off every 15 points (the standard deviation). I've drawn a dashed line from the mean up to *f(100)* (the height of the distribution where x = 100) and drawn a dashed line from each standard deviation point.

The figure also shows the proportion of area bounded by the curve and the horizontal axis, and by successive pairs of standard deviations. It also shows the proportion beyond three standard deviations on either side (55 and 145). Note that the curve never touches the horizontal. It gets closer and closer, but it never touches. (Mathematicians say that the curve is *asymptotic* to the horizontal.)

So between the mean and one standard deviation — between 100 and 115 — are .3413 (or 34.13 percent) of the scores in the population. Another way to say this: The probability that an IQ score is between 100 and 115 is .3413. At the extremes, in the tails of the distribution, .0013 (.13 percent) of the scores are on each side (less than 55 or greater than 145).

REMEMBER

The proportions in Figure 8-2 hold for every member of the normal distribution family, not just for IQ scores. For example, in the "Caching Some z's" sidebar in Chapter 6, I mention SAT scores, which have a mean of 500 and a standard deviation of 100. They're normally distributed, too. That means 34.13 percent of SAT scores are between 500 and 600, 34.13 percent between 400 and 500, and . . . well, you can use Figure 8-2 as a guide for other proportions.

Working with Normal Distributions

The complex relationship I told you about between x and $f(x)$ is

$$f(x) = \frac{1}{\sigma\sqrt{2\pi}} e^{\left[\frac{(x-\mu)^2}{2\sigma^2}\right]}$$

If you supply values for μ (the mean), σ (the standard deviation), and x (a score), the equation gives you back a value for $f(x)$, the height of the normal distribution at x. π and e are important constants in mathematics: π is approximately 3.1416 (the ratio of a circle's circumference to its diameter); e is approximately 2.71828. It's related to something called natural logarithms (described in Chapter 16) and to numerous other mathematical concepts.

Distributions in R

The normal distribution family is one of many distribution families baked into R. Dealing with these families is intuitive. Follow these guidelines:

» Begin with the distribution family's name in R (norm for the normal family, for example).

» To the beginning of the family name, add d to work with the probability density function. For the probability density function for the normal family, then, it's dnorm( ) — which is equivalent to the equation I just showed you.

» For the cumulative density function (cdf), add p (pnorm( ), for example).

» For quantiles, add q (qnorm( ), which in mathematical terms is the *inverse* of the cdf).

» To generate random numbers from a distribution, add r. So rnorm( ) generates random numbers from a member of the normal distribution family.

Normal density function

When working with any normal distribution function, you have to let the function know which member of the normal distribution family you're interested in. You do that by specifying the mean and the standard deviation.

So, if you happen to need the height of the IQ distribution for IQ = 100, here's how to find it:

```
> dnorm(100,m=100,s=15)
[1] 0.02659615
```

REMEMBER

This does *not* mean that the probability of finding an IQ score of 100 is .027. Probability density is *not* the same as probability. With a probability density function, it only makes sense to talk about the probability of a score between two boundaries —
like the probability of a score between 100 and 115.

Plotting a normal curve

dnorm() is useful as a tool for plotting a normal distribution. I use it along with ggplot() to draw a graph for IQ that looks a lot like Figure 8-2.

Before I set up a ggplot() statement, I create three helpful vectors. The first

```
x.values <- seq(40,160,1)
```

is the vector I'll give to ggplot() as an aesthetic mapping for the x-axis. This statement creates a sequence of 121 numbers, beginning with 40 (4 standard deviations below the mean) to 160 (4 standard deviations above the mean).

The second

```
sd.values <- seq(40,160,15)
```

is a vector of the nine standard deviation-values from 40 to 160. This figures into the creation of the vertical dashed lines at each standard deviation in Figure 8-2.

The third vector

```
zeros9 <- rep(0,9)
```

will also be part of creating the vertical dashed lines. It's just a vector of nine zeros.

On to ggplot(). Because the data is a vector, the first argument is NULL. The aesthetic mapping for the x-axis is, as I mentioned earlier, the x.values vector. What about the mapping for the y-axis? Well, this is a plot of a normal density function for mean = 100 and sd =15, so you'd expect the y-axis mapping to be dnorm(x.values, m=100, s=15), wouldn't you? And you'd be right! Here's the ggplot() statement:

```
ggplot(NULL,aes(x=x.values,y=dnorm(x.values,m=100,s=15)))
```

Add a line geom function for the plot and labels for the axes, and here's what I have:

```
ggplot(NULL,aes(x=x.values,y=dnorm(x.values,m=100,s=15))) +
    geom_line() +
    labs(x="IQ",y="f(IQ)")
```

And that draws Figure 8-3.

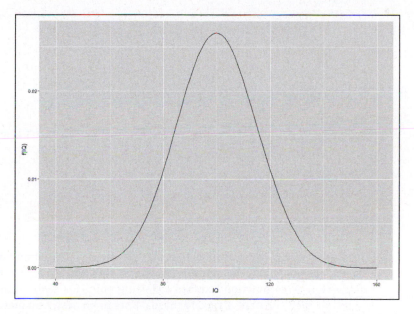

FIGURE 8-3:
Initial plot of the
normal density
function for IQ.

As you can see, ggplot() has its own ideas about the values to plot on the x-axis. Instead of sticking with the defaults, I want to place the sd.values on the x-axis. To change those values, I use scale_x_continuous() to rescale the x-axis. One of its arguments, breaks, sets the points on the x-axis for the values, and the other, labels, supplies the values. For each one, I supply sd.values:

```
scale_x_continuous(breaks=sd.values,labels = sd.values)
```

Now the code is

```
ggplot(NULL,aes(x=x.values,y=dnorm(x.values,m=100,s=15))) +
    geom_line() +
    labs(x="IQ",y="f(IQ)")+
    scale_x_continuous(breaks=sd.values,labels = sd.values)
```

and the result is Figure 8-4.

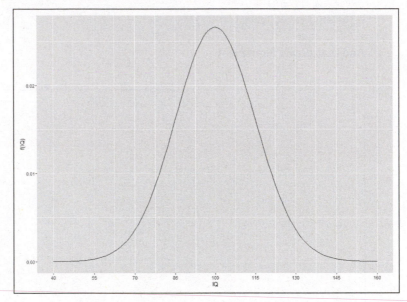

FIGURE 8-4:
The normal
density function
for IQ with
standard
deviations on the
x-axis.

In ggplot world, vertical lines that start at the x-axis and end at the curve are called *segments*. So the appropriate geom function to draw them is geom_segment(). This function requires a starting point for each segment and an end point for each segment. I specify those points in an aesthetic mapping within the geom. The x-coordinates for the starting points for the nine segments are in sd.values. The segments start at the x-axis, so the nine y-coordinates are all zeros — which happens to be the contents of the zeros9 vector. The segments end at the curve, so the x-coordinates for the end-points are once again, sd.values. The y-coordinates? Those would be dnorm(sd.values, m=100,s=15). Adding a statement about dashed lines, the rather busy geom_segment() statement is

```
geom_segment((aes(x=sd.values,y=zeros9,xend =
            sd.values,yend=dnorm(sd.values,m=100,s=15))),
        linetype = "dashed")
```

The code now becomes

```
ggplot(NULL,aes(x=x.values,y=dnorm(x.values,m=100,s=15))) +
    geom_line() +
    labs(x="IQ",y="f(IQ)")+
    scale_x_continuous(breaks=sd.values,labels = sd.values) +
    geom_segment((aes(x=sd.values,y=zeros9,xend =
            sd.values,yend=dnorm(sd.values,m=100,s=15))),
            linetype = "dashed")
```

which produces Figure 8-5.

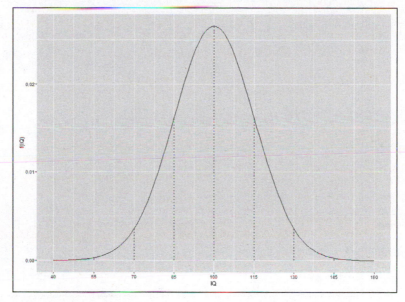

FIGURE 8-5:
The IQ plot with vertical dashed line segments at the standard deviations.

One more little touch and I'm done showing you how it's done. I'm not all that crazy about the space between the x-values and the x-axis. I'd like to remove that little slice of the graph and move the values up closer to where (at least I think) they should be.

To do that, I use scale_y_continuous(), whose expand argument controls the space between the x-values and the x-axis. It's a two-element vector with defaults that set the amount of space you see in Figure 8-5. Without going too deeply into it, setting that vector to c(0,0) removes the spacing.

These lines of code draw the aesthetically pleasing Figure 8-6:

```
ggplot(NULL,aes(x=x.values,y=dnorm(x.values,m=100,s=15))) +
   geom_line() +
   labs(x="IQ",y="f(IQ)")+
   scale_x_continuous(breaks=sd.values,labels = sd.values) +
   geom_segment((aes(x=sd.values,y=zeros9,xend =
         sd.values,yend=dnorm(sd.values,m=100,s=15))),
         linetype = "dashed")+
   scale_y_continuous(expand = c(0,0))
```

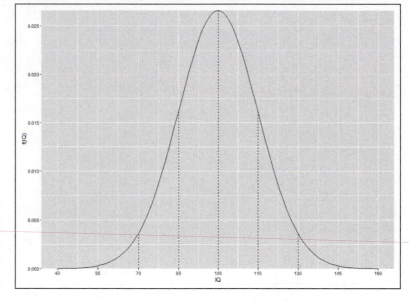

FIGURE 8-6:
The finished product: The IQ plot with no spacing between the x-values and the x-axis.

Cumulative density function

The cumulative density function pnorm(x,m,s) returns the probability of a score less than x in a normal distribution with mean m and standard deviation s.

As you'd expect from Figure 8-2 (and the subsequent plots I created):

```
> pnorm(100,m=100,s=15)
[1] 0.5
```

How about the probability of less than 85?

```
> pnorm(85,m=100,s=15)
[1] 0.1586553
```

If you want to find the probability of a score greater than 85, pnorm() can handle that, too. It has an argument called lower.tail whose default value, TRUE, returns the probability of "less than." For "greater than," set the value to FALSE:

```
> pnorm(85,m=100,s=15, lower.tail = FALSE)
[1] 0.8413447
```

It's often the case that you want the probability of a score between a lower bound and an upper bound — like the probability of an IQ score between 85 and 100. Multiple calls to pnorm() combined with a little arithmetic will get that done.

That's not necessary, however. A function called pnormGC() in a terrific package called tigerstats does that and more. The letters GC stand for graphical calculator, but they could also stand for Georgetown College (in Georgetown, Kentucky), the school from which this package originates. (On the Packages tab, click Install, and then in the Install Packages dialog box, type **tigerstats** and click Install. When you see tigerstats on the Packages tab, select its check box.)

Now watch closely:

```
>pnormGC(c(85,100),region="between",m=100,s=15,graph=TRUE)
[1] 0.3413447
```

In addition to the answer, the graph=TRUE argument produces Figure 8-7.

Plotting the cdf

Given that I've already done the heavy lifting when I showed you how to plot the density function, the R code for the cumulative density function is a snap:

```
ggplot(NULL,aes(x=x.values,y=pnorm(x.values,m=100,s=15))) +
  geom_line() +
  labs(x="IQ",y="Fn(IQ)")+
  scale_x_continuous(breaks=sd.values,labels = sd.values) +
  geom_segment((aes(x=sd.values,y=zeros9,xend =
          sd.values,yend=pnorm(sd.values,mean=100,sd=15))),
          linetype = "dashed")+
  scale_y_continuous(expand=c(0,0))
```

Yes, all you do is change dnorm to pnorm and edit the y-axis label. Code reuse — it's a beautiful thing. And so (I hope you agree) is Figure 8-8.

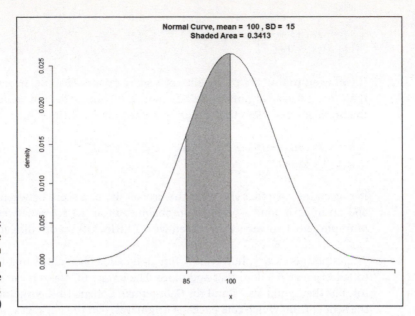

FIGURE 8-7: Visualizing the probability of an IQ score between 85 and 100 (in the `tigerstats` package)

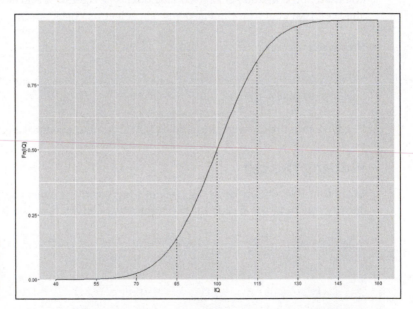

FIGURE 8-8: Cumulative density function of the IQ distribution.

The line segments shooting up from the x-axis clearly show that 100 is at the 50th percentile (.50 of the scores are below 100). Which brings me to quantiles of normal distributions, the topic of the next section.

Quantiles of normal distributions

The qnorm() function is the inverse of pnorm(). Give qnorm() an area, and it returns the score that cuts off that area (to the left) in the specified normal distribution:

```
> qnorm(0.1586553,m=100,s=15)
[1] 85
```

The area (to the left), of course, is a percentile (described in Chapter 6).

To find a score that cuts off an indicated area to the right:

```
> qnorm(0.1586553,m=100,s=15, lower.tail = FALSE)
[1] 115
```

Here's how qnormGC() (in the tigerstats package) handles it:

```
> qnormGC(.1586553, region = "below",m=100,s=15, graph=TRUE)
[1] 85
```

This function also creates Figure 8-9.

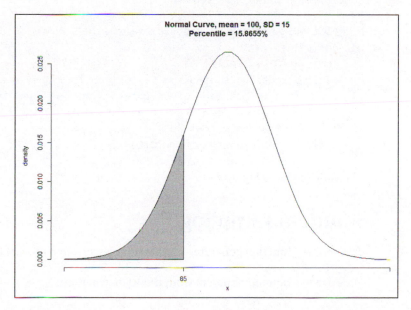

FIGURE 8-9:
Plot created by qnormGC().

You're typically not concerned with the 15.86553rd percentile. Usually, it's quartiles that attract your attention:

```
> qnorm(c(0,.25,.50,.75,1.00),m=100,s=15)
[1]       -Inf  89.88265 100.00000 110.11735         Inf
```

The 0th and 100th percentiles (— Infinity and Infinity) show that the cdf never completely touches the x-axis nor reaches an exact maximum. The middle quartiles are of greatest interest, and best if rounded:

```
> round(qnorm(c(.25,.50,.75),m=100,s=15))
[1]  90 100 110
```

Plotting the cdf with quartiles

To replace the standard deviation values in Figure 8-8 with the three quartile values, you begin by creating two new vectors:

```
> q.values <-round(qnorm(c(.25,.50,.75),m=100,s=15))
> zeros3 <- c(0,0,0)
```

Now all you have to do is put those vectors in the appropriate places in scale_x_continuous() and in geom_segment():

```
ggplot(NULL,aes(x=x.values,y=pnorm(x.values,m=100,s=15))) +
  geom_line() +
  labs(x="IQ",y="Fn(IQ)")+
  scale_x_continuous(breaks=q.values,labels = q.values) +
  geom_segment((aes(x=q.values,y=zeros3,xend =
          q.values,yend=pnorm(q.values,mean=100,sd=15))),
          linetype = "dashed")+
  scale_y_continuous(expand=c(0,0))
```

The code produces Figure 8-10.

Random sampling

The rnorm() function generates random numbers from a normal distribution.

Here are five random numbers from the IQ distribution:

```
> rnorm(5,m=100,s=15)
[1] 127.02944  75.18125  66.49264 113.98305 103.39766
```

Here's what happens when you run that again:

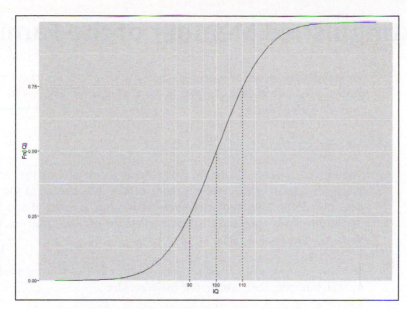

FIGURE 8-10:
The normal
cumulative
density function
with quartile
values.

```
> rnorm(5,m=100,s=15)
[1] 73.73596 91.79841 82.33299 81.59029 73.40033
```

Yes, the numbers are all different. (In fact, when you run rnorm(), I can almost guarantee your numbers will be different from mine.) Each time you run the function it generates a new set of random numbers. The randomization process starts with a number called a *seed*. If you want to reproduce randomization results, use the set.seed() function to set the seed to a particular number before randomizing:

```
> set.seed(7637060)
> rnorm(5,m=100,s=15)
[1]   71.99120   98.67231   92.68848 103.42207   99.61904
```

If you set the seed to that same number the next time you randomize, you get the same results:

```
> set.seed(7637060)
> rnorm(5,m=100,s=15)
[1]   71.99120   98.67231   92.68848 103.42207   99.61904
```

If you don't, you won't.

Randomization is the foundation of simulation, which comes up in Chapters 9 and 19. Bear in mind that R (or most any other software) doesn't generate "true" random numbers. R generates "pseudo-random" numbers which are sufficiently unpredictable for most tasks that require randomization — like the simulations I discuss later.

A Distinguished Member of the Family

To standardize a set of scores so that you can compare them to other sets of scores, you convert each one to a z-score. (I discuss z-scores in Chapter 6.) The formula for converting a score to a z-score (also known as a standard score) is

$$z = \frac{x - \mu}{\sigma}$$

The idea is to use the standard deviation as a unit of measure. For example, the Wechsler version of the IQ test (among others) has a mean of 100 and a standard deviation of 15. The Stanford–Binet version has a mean of 100 and a standard deviation of 16. How does a Wechsler score of, say, 110, stack up against a Stanford–Binet score of 110?

One way to answer this question is to put the two versions on a level playing field by standardizing both scores. For the Wechsler:

$$z = \frac{110 - 100}{15} = .667$$

For the Stanford–Binet:

$$z = \frac{110 - 100}{16} = .625$$

So 110 on the Wechsler is a slightly higher score than 110 on the Stanford–Binet.

Now, if you standardize all the scores in a normal distribution (such as either version of the IQ), you have a normal distribution of z-scores. Any set of z-scores (normally distributed or not) has a mean of 0 and a standard deviation of 1. If a normal distribution has those parameters, it's a *standard normal distribution* — a normal distribution of standard scores. Its equation is

$$f(z) = \frac{1}{\sqrt{2\pi}} e^{\left[\frac{-z^2}{2}\right]}$$

Figure 8-11 shows the standard normal distribution. It looks like Figure 8-2, except that I've substituted 0 for the mean and I've entered standard deviation units in the appropriate places.

WARNING

This is the member of the normal distribution family that most people are familiar with. It's the one they remember most from statistics courses, and it's the one that most people have in mind when they (mistakenly) say *the* normal distribution. It's also what people think of when they hear about "z-scores." This distribution leads many to the mistaken idea that converting to z-scores somehow transforms a set of scores into a normal distribution.

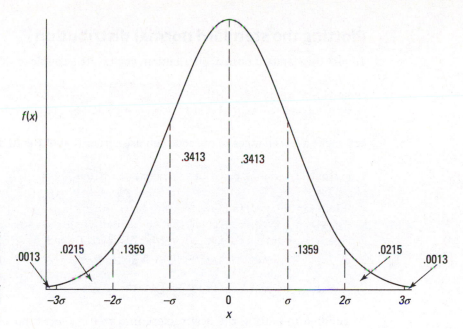

FIGURE 8-11: The standard normal distribution, divided up by standard deviations.

The standard normal distribution in R

Working with the standard normal distribution in R couldn't be easier. The only change you make to the four norm functions is to *not* specify a mean and a standard deviation — the defaults are 0 and 1.

Here are some examples:

```
> dnorm(0)
[1] 0.3989423
> pnorm(0)
[1] 0.5
> qnorm(c(.25,.50,.75))
[1] -0.6744898  0.0000000  0.6744898
> rnorm(5)
[1] -0.4280188 -0.9085506  0.6746574  1.0728058 -1.2646055
```

This also applies to the tigerstats functions:

```
> pnormGC(c(-1,0),region="between")
[1] 0.3413447
> qnormGC(.50, region = "below")
[1] 0
```

Plotting the standard normal distribution

To plot the standard normal distribution, you create a couple of new vectors

```
z.values <-seq(-4,4,.01)
z.sd.values <- seq(-4,4,1)
```

and make a few changes to the code you use earlier to plot the IQ distribution:

```
ggplot(NULL,aes(x=z.values,y=dnorm(z.values))) +
    geom_line() +
    labs(x="z",y="f(z)")+
    scale_x_continuous(breaks=z.sd.values,labels=z.sd.values) +
    geom_segment((aes(x=z.sd.values,y=zeros9,xend =
            z.sd.values,yend=dnorm(z.sd.values))),linetype =
            "dashed")+
    scale_y_continuous(expand=c(0,0))
```

In addition to putting the new vectors into scale_x_continuous() and geom_segment(), the notable change is to drop the mean and standard deviation arguments from dnorm(). The code creates Figure 8-12.

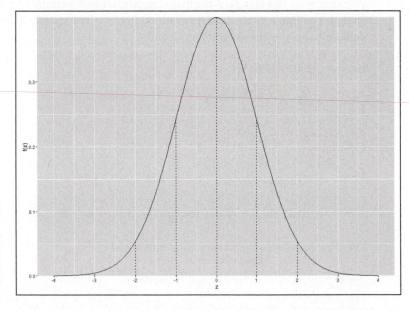

FIGURE 8-12:
The standard normal distribution, divided by standard deviations and plotted in ggplot().

I leave it to you as an exercise to plot the cumulative density function for the standard normal distribution.

3 Drawing Conclusions from Data

Chapter **9**

The Confidence Game: Estimation

"Population" and "sample" are pretty easy concepts to understand. A *population* is a huge collection of individuals, and a *sample* is a group of individuals you draw from a population. Measure the sample-members on some trait or attribute, calculate statistics that summarize the sample, and you're off and running.

In addition to those summary statistics, you can use the statistics to estimate the population parameters. This is a big deal: Just on the basis of a small percentage of individuals from the population, you can draw a picture of the entire population.

How definitive is that picture? In other words, how much confidence can you have in your estimates? To answer this question, you have to have a context for your estimates. How probable are they? How likely is the true value of a parameter to be within a particular lower bound and upper bound?

In this chapter, I introduce the context for estimates, show how that context plays into confidence in those estimates, and show you how to use R to calculate confidence levels.

Understanding Sampling Distributions

So you have a population, and you pull a sample out of this population. You measure the sample-members on some attribute and calculate the sample mean. Return the sample-members to the population. Draw another sample, assess the new sample-members, and then calculate *their* mean. Repeat this process again and again, always with same number of individuals as in the original sample. If you could do this an infinite amount of times (with the same sample size every time), you'd have an infinite amount of means. Those sample means form a distribution of their own. This distribution is called *the sampling distribution of the mean.*

For a sample mean, this is the "context" I mention at the beginning of this chapter. Like any other number, a statistic makes no sense by itself. You have to know where it comes from in order to understand it. Of course, a statistic *comes from* a calculation performed on sample data. In another sense, a statistic is part of a sampling distribution.

REMEMBER

In general, *a sampling distribution is the distribution of all possible values of a statistic for a given sample size.*

I've italicized the definition for a reason: It's extremely important. After many years of teaching statistics, I can tell you that this concept usually sets the boundary line between people who understand statistics and people who don't.

So . . . if you understand what a sampling distribution is, you'll understand what the field of statistics is all about. If you don't, you won't. It's almost that simple.

If you don't know what a sampling distribution is, statistics will be a cookbook type of subject for you: Whenever you have to apply statistics, you'll find yourself plugging numbers into formulas and hoping for the best. On the other hand, if you're comfortable with the idea of a sampling distribution, you'll grasp the big picture of inferential statistics.

To help clarify the idea of a sampling distribution, take a look at Figure 9-1. It summarizes the steps in creating a sampling distribution of the mean.

A sampling distribution — like any other group of scores — has a mean and a standard deviation. The symbol for the mean of the sampling distribution of the mean (yes, I know that's a mouthful) is $\mu_{\bar{x}} = \mu$.

REMEMBER

The standard deviation of a sampling distribution is a pretty hot item. It has a special name: *standard error.* For the sampling distribution of the mean, the standard deviation is called *the standard error of the mean.* Its symbol is $\sigma_{\bar{x}} = \sigma / \sqrt{N}$.

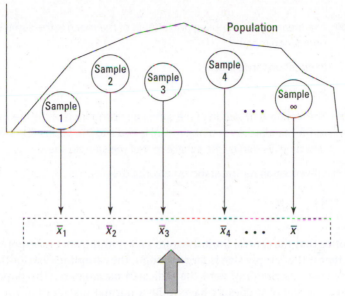

FIGURE 9-1:
Creating the
sampling
distribution
of the mean.

Sampling Distribution of the Mean

An EXTREMELY Important Idea: The Central Limit Theorem

The situation I asked you to imagine never happens in the real world. You never take an infinite amount of samples and calculate their means, and you never actually create a sampling distribution of the mean. Typically, you draw one sample and calculate its statistics.

So if you have only one sample, how can you ever know anything about a sampling distribution — a theoretical distribution that encompasses an infinite number of samples? Is this all just a wild-goose chase?

No, it's not. You can figure out a lot about a sampling distribution because of a great gift from mathematicians to the field of statistics: the central limit theorem.

REMEMBER

According to the *central limit theorem*:

>> The sampling distribution of the mean is approximately a normal distribution if the sample size is large enough.

Large enough means about 30 or more.

» The mean of the sampling distribution of the mean is the same as the population mean.

In equation form, that's

$$\mu_{\bar{x}} = \mu$$

» The standard deviation of the sampling distribution of the mean (also known as the standard error of the mean) is equal to the population standard deviation divided by the square root of the sample size.

The equation for the standard error of the mean is

$$\sigma_{\bar{x}} = \sigma / \sqrt{N}$$

Notice that the central limit theorem says nothing about the population. All it says is that if the sample size is large enough, the sampling distribution of the mean is a normal distribution, with the indicated parameters. The population that supplies the samples doesn't have to be a normal distribution for the central limit theorem to hold.

What if the population is a normal distribution? In that case, the sampling distribution of the mean is a normal distribution, regardless of the sample size.

Figure 9-2 shows a general picture of the sampling distribution of the mean, partitioned into standard error units.

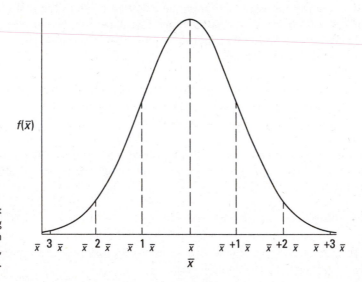

FIGURE 9-2:
The sampling distribution of the mean, partitioned.

$f(\bar{x})$

$\bar{x}\ 3\ \bar{x}$ $\bar{x}\ 2\ \bar{x}$ $\bar{x}\ 1\ \bar{x}$ $\bar{x}$ $\bar{x}\ +1\ \bar{x}$ $\bar{x}\ +2\ \bar{x}$ $\bar{x}\ +3\ \bar{x}$

$\bar{x}$

(Approximately) Simulating the central limit theorem

It almost doesn't sound right: How can a population that's not normally distributed produce a normally distributed sampling distribution?

To give you an idea of how the central limit theorem works, I walk you through a simulation. This simulation creates something like a sampling distribution of the mean for a very small sample, based on a population that's not normally distributed. As you'll see, even though the population is not a normal distribution, and even though the sample is small, the sampling distribution of the mean looks quite a bit like a normal distribution.

Imagine a huge population that consists of just three scores — 1, 2, and 3, and each one is equally likely to appear in a sample. That kind of population is definitely *not* a normal distribution.

Imagine also that you can randomly select a sample of three scores from this population. Table 9-1 shows all possible samples and their means.

TABLE 9-1 **ALL Possible Samples of Three Scores (and Their Means) from a Population Consisting of the Scores 1, 2, and 3**

Sample	Mean	Sample	Mean	Sample	Mean
1,1,1	1.00	2,1,1	1.33	3,1,1	1.67
1,1,2	1.33	2,1,2	1.67	3,1,2	2.00
1,1,3	1.67	2,1,3	2.00	3,1,3	2.33
1,2,1	1.33	2,2,1	1.67	3,2,1	2.00
1,2,2	1.67	2,2,2	2.00	3,2,2	2.33
1,2,3	2.00	2,2,3	2.33	3,2,3	2.67
1,3,1	1.67	2,3,1	2.00	3,3,1	2.33
1,3,2	2.00	2,3,2	2.33	3,3,2	2.67
1,3,3	2.33	2,3,3	2.67	3,3,3	3.00

If you look closely at the table, you can almost see what's about to happen in the simulation. The sample mean that appears most frequently is 2.00. The sample means that appear least frequently are 1.00 and 3.00. Hmmm. . . .

In the simulation, you randomly select a score from the population and then randomly select two more. That group of three scores is a sample. Then you calculate the mean of that sample. You repeat this process for a total of 600 samples, resulting in 600 sample means. Finally, you graph the distribution of the sample means.

What does the simulated sampling distribution of the mean look like? I walk you through it in R. You begin by creating a vector for the possible scores, and another for the probability of sampling each score:

```
values <- c(1,2,3)
probabilities <- c(1/3,1/3,1/3)
```

One more vector will hold the 600 sample means:

```
smpl.means <- NULL
```

To draw a sample, you use the `sample( )` function:

```
smpl <-sample(x=values,prob = probabilities,
    size=3,replace=TRUE)
```

The first two arguments, of course, provide the scores to sample and the probability of each score. The third is the sample size. The fourth indicates that after you select a score for the sample, you replace it. (You put it back in the population, in other words.) This procedure (unsurprisingly called "sampling with replacement") simulates a huge population from which you can select any score at any time.

Each time you draw a sample, you take its mean and append it (add it to the end of) the `smpl.means` vector:

```
smpl.means <- append(smpl.means, mean(smpl))
```

I don't want you to have to manually repeat this whole process 600 times. Fortunately, like all computer languages, R has a way of handling this: Its `for`-loop does all the work. To do the sampling, the calculation, and the appending 600 times, the `for`-loop looks like this:

```
for(i in 1:600){
    smpl <-sample(x = values,prob = probabilities,
               size = 3,replace=TRUE)
    smpl.means <- append(smpl.means, mean(smpl))
    }
```

As you can see, the curly brackets enclose what happens in each iteration of the loop, and i is a counter for how many times the loop occurs.

If you'd like to run this, here's all the code preceding the for-loop, including the seed so that you can replicate my results:

```
> values <- c(1,2,3)
> probabilities <- c(1/3,1/3,1/3)
> smpl.means <- NULL
> set.seed(7637060)
```

Then run the for-loop. If you want to run the loop over and over again, make sure you reset smpl.means to NULL each time. If you want to get different results each time, don't set the seed to the same number (or don't set it at all).

What does the sampling distribution look like? Use ggplot() to do the honors. The data values (the 600 sample means) are in a vector, so the first argument is NULL. The smpl.means vector maps to the x-axis. And you're creating a histogram, so the geom function is geom_histogram():

```
ggplot(NULL,aes(x=smpl.means)) +
    geom_histogram()
```

Figure 9-3 shows the histogram for the sampling distribution of the mean.

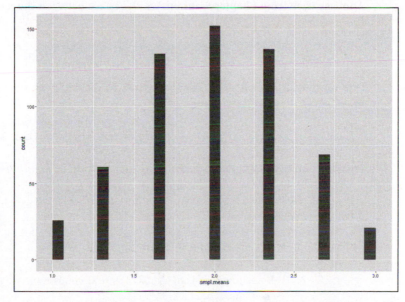

FIGURE 9-3:
Sampling distribution of the mean based on 600 samples of size 3 from a population consisting of the equally probable scores 1, 2, and 3.

Looks a lot like the beginnings of a normal distribution, right? I explore the distribution further in a moment, but first I'll show you how to make the graph a bit more informative. Suppose you want the labeled points on the x-axis to reflect the values of the mean in the `smpl.means` vector. You can't just specify the vector values for the x-axis, because the vector has 600 of them. Instead, you list the *unique* values:

```
> unique(smpl.means)
[1] 2.333333 1.666667 1.333333 2.000000 2.666667 3.000000
[7] 1.000000
```

They look better if you round them to two decimal places:

```
> round(unique(smpl.means),2)
[1] 2.33 1.67 1.33 2.00 2.67 3.00 1.00
```

Finally, you store these values in a vector called `m.values`, which you'll use to rescale the x-axis:

```
> m.values <-round(unique(smpl.means),2)
```

For the rescaling, use a trick that I show you in Chapter 8:

```
scale_x_continuous(breaks=m.values,label=m.values)
```

Another trick from Chapter 8 eliminates the space between the x-axis values and the x-axis:

```
scale_y_continuous(expand = c(0,0))
```

One more trick uses R's `expression` syntax to display $\bar{X}$ as the x-axis label and $frequency\left(\bar{X}\right)$ as the y-axis label:

```
labs(x=expression(bar(X)),y=expression(frequency(bar(X))))
```

Putting it all together gives the sampling distribution in Figure 9-4:

```
ggplot(NULL,aes(x=smpl.means)) +
    geom_histogram()+
    scale_x_continuous(breaks=m.values,label=m.values)+
    scale_y_continuous(expand = c(0,0)) +

            labs(x=expression(bar(X)),y=expression
            (frequency(bar(X))))
```

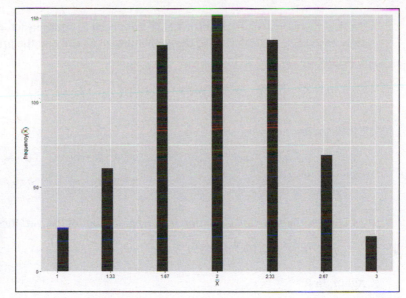

FIGURE 9-4:
The sampling distribution of the mean with the x-axis rescaled and cool axis labels.

Predictions of the central limit theorem

How do the characteristics of the sampling distribution match up with what the central limit theorem predicts?

To derive the predictions, you have to start with the population. Think of each population value (1, 2, or 3) as an X, and think of each probability as $pr(X)$. Mathematicians would refer to X as a *discrete random variable*.

The mean of a discrete random variable is called its *expected value*. The notation for the expected value of X is $E(X)$.

To find $E(X)$, you multiply each X by its probability and then add all those products together. For this example, that's

$$E(X) = \sum X(pr(X)) = 1\left(\frac{1}{3}\right) + 2\left(\frac{1}{3}\right) + 3\left(\frac{1}{3}\right) = 2$$

Or, if you prefer R:

```
> E.values<-sum(values*probabilities)
> E.values
[1] 2
```

To find the variance of X, subtract $E(X)$ from each X, square each deviation, multiply each squared deviation by the probability of X, and add the products. For this example:

$$\text{var}(X) = \sum (X - E(X))^2 pr(x) = (1-2)^2\left(\tfrac{1}{3}\right) + (2-2)^2\left(\tfrac{1}{3}\right) + (3-2)^2\left(\tfrac{1}{3}\right) = .67$$

In R:

```
> var.values <- sum((values-E.values)^2*probabilities)
> var.values
[1] 0.6666667
```

As always, the standard deviation is the square root of the variance:

$$\sigma = \sqrt{\text{var}(X)} = \sqrt{.67} = .82$$

Again, in R:

```
> sd.values<-sqrt(var.values)
> sd.values
[1] 0.8164966
```

So the population has a mean of 2 and a standard deviation of .82.

According to the central limit theorem, the mean of the sampling distribution should be

$$\mu_{\bar{x}} = \mu = 2$$

and the standard deviation should be

$$\sigma_{\bar{x}} = \sigma \big/ \sqrt{N} = .82 \big/ \sqrt{3} = .4714$$

How do these predicted values match up with the characteristics of the sampling distribution?

```
> mean(smpl.means)
[1] 2.002222
> sd(smpl.means)
[1] 0.4745368
```

Pretty close! Even with a non-normally distributed population and a small sample size, the central limit theorem gives an accurate picture of the sampling distribution of the mean.

Confidence: It Has Its Limits!

I tell you about sampling distributions because they help answer the question I pose at the beginning of this chapter: How much confidence can you have in the estimates you create?

The procedure is to calculate a statistic and then use that statistic to establish upper and lower bounds for the population parameter with, say, 95 percent confidence. (The interpretation of confidence limits is a bit more involved than that, as you'll see.) You can do this only if you know the sampling distribution of the statistic and the standard error of the statistic. In the next section, I show how to do this for the mean.

Finding confidence limits for a mean

The FarBlonJet Corporation manufactures navigation systems. (Corporate motto: "Taking a trip? Get FarBlonJet.") The company has developed a new battery to power its portable model. To help market this system, FarBlonJet wants to know how long, on average, each battery lasts before it burns out.

The FarBlonJet employees like to estimate that average with 95 percent confidence. They test a sample of 100 batteries and find that the sample mean is 60 hours, with a standard deviation of 20 hours. The central limit theorem, remember, says that with a large enough sample (30 or more), the sampling distribution of the mean approximates a normal distribution. The standard error of the mean (the standard deviation of the sampling distribution of the mean) is

$$\sigma_{\bar{x}} = \sigma / \sqrt{N}$$

The sample size, N, is 100. What about σ? That's unknown, so you have to estimate it. If you know σ, that would mean you know μ, and establishing confidence limits would be unnecessary.

The best estimate of σ is the standard deviation of the sample. In this case, that's 20. This leads to an estimate of the standard error of the mean.

$$s_{\bar{x}} = s / \sqrt{N} = 20 / \sqrt{100} = 20 / 10 = 2$$

The best estimate of the population mean is the sample mean: 60. Armed with this information — estimated mean, estimated standard error of the mean, normal distribution — you can envision the sampling distribution of the mean, which is shown in Figure 9-5. Consistent with Figure 9-2, each standard deviation is a standard error of the mean.

Now that you have the sampling distribution, you can establish the 95 percent confidence limits for the mean. Starting at the center of the distribution, how far out to the sides do you have to extend until you have 95 percent of the area under the curve? (For more on area under a normal distribution and what it means, see Chapter 8.)

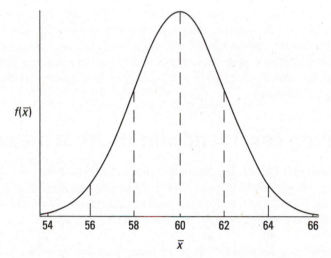

FIGURE 9-5:
The sampling distribution of the mean for the FarBlonJet battery.

One way to answer this question is to work with the standard normal distribution and find the z-score that cuts off 2.5 percent of the area in the upper tail. Then multiply that z-score by the standard error. Add the result to the sample mean to get the upper confidence limit; subtract the result from the mean to get the lower confidence limit.

Here's how to do all that in R. First, the setup:

```
> mean.battery <- 60
> sd.battery <- 20
> N <- 100
> error <- qnorm(.025,lower.tail=FALSE)*sd.battery/sqrt(N)
```

Then the limits:

```
> lower <- mean.battery - error
> upper <- mean.battery + error
> lower
[1] 56.08007
> upper
[1] 63.91993
```

Figure 9-6 shows these bounds on the sampling distribution.

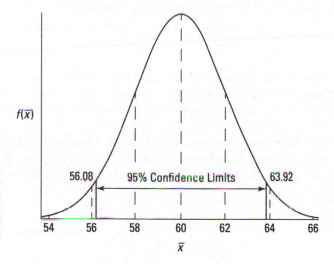

FIGURE 9-6:
The 95 percent
confidence limits
on the FarBlonJet
sampling
distribution.

56.08 95% Confidence Limits 63.92

$f(\bar{x})$

54   56   58   60   62   64   66

$\bar{x}$

What does this tell you, exactly? One interpretation is that if you repeat this sampling and estimation procedure many times, the confidence intervals you calculate (which would be different every time you do it) would include the population mean 95 percent of the time.

Fit to a t

The central limit theorem specifies (approximately) a normal distribution for large samples. In the real world, however, you deal with smaller samples, and the normal distribution isn't appropriate. What do you do?

First of all, you pay a price for using a smaller sample — you have a larger standard error. Suppose the FarBlonJet Corporation found a mean of 60 and a standard deviation of 20 in a sample of 25 batteries. The estimated standard error is

$$s_{\bar{x}} = s/\sqrt{N} = 20/\sqrt{25} = 20/5 = 4$$

which is twice as large as the standard error for $N=100$.

Second, you don't get to use the standard normal distribution to characterize the sampling distribution of the mean. For small samples, the sampling distribution of the mean is a member of a family of distributions called the *t-distribution*. The parameter that distinguishes members of this family from one another is called *degrees of freedom*.

REMEMBER

As I said in Chapter 5, think of "degrees of freedom" as the denominator of your variance estimate. For example, if your sample consists of 25 individuals, the sample variance that estimates population variance is

$$s^2 = \frac{\sum(x-\bar{x})^2}{N-1} = \frac{\sum(x-\bar{x})^2}{25-1} = \frac{\sum(x-\bar{x})^2}{24}$$

The number in the denominator is 24, and that's the value of the degrees of freedom parameter. In general, degrees of freedom (df) = $N-1$ (N is the sample size) when you use the t-distribution the way I show you in this section.

Figure 9-7 shows two members of the t-distribution family (df = 3 and df = 10), along with the normal distribution for comparison. As the figure shows, the greater the df, the more closely t approximates a normal distribution.

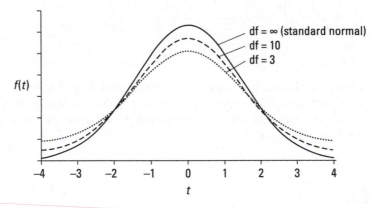

FIGURE 9-7:
Some members
of the
t-distribution
family.

To determine the lower and upper bounds for the 95 percent confidence level for a small sample, work with the member of the t-distribution family that has the appropriate df. Find the value that cuts off the upper 2.5 percent of the area in the upper tail of the distribution. Then multiply that value by the standard error.

Add the result to the mean to get the upper confidence limit; subtract the result from the mean to get the lower confidence limit.

R provides `dt()` (density function), `pt()` (cumulative density function), `qt()` (quantile), and `rt()` (random number generation) for working with the t-distribution. For the confidence intervals, I use `qt()`.

In the FarBlonJet batteries example:

```
> mean.battery <- 60
> sd.battery <- 20
```

```
> N <- 25
> error <- qt(.025,N-1,lower.tail=FALSE)*sd.battery/sqrt(N)
> lower <- mean.battery - error
> upper <- mean.battery + error
> lower
[1] 51.74441
> upper
[1] 68.25559
```

The lower and upper limits are 51.74 and 68.26. Notice that with the smaller sample, the range is wider than in the previous example.

If you have the raw data, you can use t.test() to generate confidence intervals:

```
> battery.data <- c(82,64,68,44,54,47,50,85,51,41,61,84,
        53,83,91,43,35,36,33,87,90,86,49,37,48)
```

Here's how to use t.test() to generate the lower and upper bounds for 90 percent confidence — the default value is .95:

```
> t.test(battery.data, conf.level=.90)

            One Sample t-test

data:  c(82, 64, 68, 44, 54, 47, 50, 85, 51, 41, 61, 84,
          53, 83, 91,  ...
t = 15, df = 24, p-value = 1.086e-13
alternative hypothesis: true mean is not equal to 0
90 percent confidence interval:
 53.22727 66.93273
sample estimates:
mean of x
    60.08
```

The t.test() function is really more appropriate for the next chapter. . . .

Chapter **10**

One-Sample Hypothesis Testing

Whatever your occupation, you often have to assess whether something new and different has happened. Sometimes you start with a population that you know a lot about (like its mean and standard deviation) and you draw a sample. Is that sample like the rest of the population, or does it represent something out of the ordinary?

To answer that question, you measure each individual in the sample and calculate the sample's statistics. Then you compare those statistics with the population's parameters. Are they the same? Are they different? Is the sample extraordinary in some way? Proper use of statistics helps you make the decision.

Sometimes, though, you don't know the parameters of the population that the sample came from. What happens then? In this chapter, I discuss statistical techniques and R functions for dealing with both cases.

Hypotheses, Tests, and Errors

A *hypothesis* is a guess about the way the world works. It's a tentative explanation of some process, whether that process occurs in nature or in a laboratory.

Before studying and measuring the individuals in a sample, a researcher formulates hypotheses that predict what the data should look like.

Generally, one hypothesis predicts that the data won't show anything new or out of the ordinary. This is called the *null hypothesis* (abbreviated H_0). According to the null hypothesis, if the data deviates from the norm in any way, that deviation is due strictly to chance. Another hypothesis, the *alternative hypothesis* (abbreviated H_1), explains things differently. According to the alternative hypothesis, the data show something important.

After gathering the data, it's up to the researcher to make a decision. The way the logic works, the decision centers around the null hypothesis. The researcher must decide to either reject the null hypothesis or to not reject the null hypothesis.

In *hypothesis testing*, you

>> Formulate null and alternative hypotheses

>> Gather data

>> Decide whether to reject or not reject the null hypothesis.

Nothing in the logic involves *accepting* either hypothesis. Nor does the logic involve making any decisions about the alternative hypothesis. It's all about rejecting or not rejecting H_0.

Regardless of the reject-don't-reject decision, an error is possible. One type of error occurs when you believe that the data shows something important and you reject H_0, but in reality the data are due just to chance. This is called a *Type I error*. At the outset of a study, you set the criteria for rejecting H_0. In so doing, you set the probability of a Type I error. This probability is called *alpha* (α).

The other type of error occurs when you don't reject H_0 and the data is really due to something out of the ordinary. For one reason or another, you happened to miss it. This is called a *Type II error*. Its probability is called *beta* (β). Table 10-1 summarizes the possible decisions and errors.

TABLE 10-1 **Decisions and Errors in Hypothesis Testing**

		"True State" of the World	
		H_0 is True	H_1 is True
	Reject H_0	Type I Error	Correct Decision
Decision			
	Do Not Reject H_0	Correct Decision	Type II Error

Note that you never know the true state of the world. (If you do, it's not necessary to do the study!) All you can ever do is measure the individuals in a sample, calculate the statistics, and make a decision about H_0. (I discuss hypotheses and hypothesis testing in Chapter 1.)

Hypothesis Tests and Sampling Distributions

In Chapter 9, I discuss sampling distributions. A sampling distribution, remember, is the set of all possible values of a statistic for a given sample size.

Also in Chapter 9, I discuss the central limit theorem. This theorem tells you that the sampling distribution of the mean approximates a normal distribution if the sample size is large (for practical purposes, at least 30). This works whether or not the population is normally distributed. If the population is a normal distribution, the sampling distribution is normal for any sample size. Here are two other points from the central limit theorem:

» The mean of the sampling distribution of the mean is equal to the population mean.

The equation for this is

$$\mu_{\bar{x}} = \mu$$

» The standard error of the mean (the standard deviation of the sampling distribution) is equal to the population standard deviation divided by the square root of the sample size.

This equation is

$$\sigma_{\bar{x}} = \sigma / \sqrt{N}$$

The sampling distribution of the mean figures prominently into the type of hypothesis testing I discuss in this chapter. Theoretically, when you test a null hypothesis versus an alternative hypothesis, each hypothesis corresponds to a separate sampling distribution.

Figure 10-1 shows what I mean. The figure shows two normal distributions. I placed them arbitrarily. Each normal distribution represents a sampling distribution of the mean. The one on the left represents the distribution of possible sample means if the null hypothesis is truly how the world works. The one on the right represents the distribution of possible sample means if the alternative hypothesis is truly how the world works.

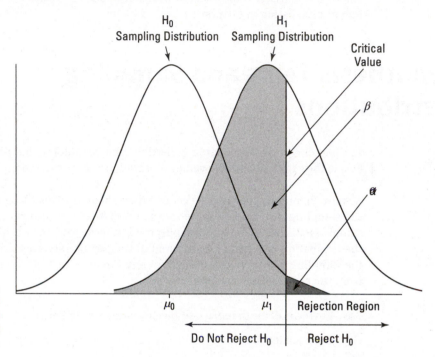

FIGURE 10-1:
H_0 and H_1 each correspond to a sampling distribution.

Of course, when you do a hypothesis test, you never know which distribution produces the results. You work with a sample mean — a point on the horizontal axis. The reject-or-don't reject decision boils down to deciding which distribution the sample mean is part of. You set up a *critical value* — a decision criterion. If the sample mean is on one side of the critical value, you reject H_0. If not, you don't.

In this vein, the figure also shows α and β. These, as I mention earlier in this chapter, are the probabilities of decision errors. The area that corresponds to α is in the H_0 distribution. I've shaded it in dark gray. It represents the probability that a sample mean comes from the H_0 distribution, but it's so extreme that you reject H_0.

REMEMBER

Where you set the critical value determines α. In most hypotheses testing, you set α at .05. This means that you're willing to tolerate a Type I error (rejecting H_0 when you shouldn't) 5 percent of the time. Graphically, the critical value cuts off 5 percent of the area of the sampling distribution. By the way, if you're talking about the 5 percent of the area that's in the right tail of the distribution (refer to Figure 10-1), you're talking about the *upper* 5 percent. If it's the 5 percent in the left tail you're interested in, that's the *lower* 5 percent.

The area that corresponds to β is in the H_1 distribution. I've shaded it in light gray. This area represents the probability that a sample mean comes from the H_1 distribution, but it's close enough to the center of the H_0 distribution that you don't reject H_0 (but you should have). You don't get to set β. The size of this area depends on the separation between the means of the two distributions, and that's up to the world we live in — not up to you.

These sampling distributions are appropriate when your work corresponds to the conditions of the central limit theorem: if you know that the population you're working with is a normal distribution or if you have a large sample.

Catching Some Z's Again

Here's an example of a hypothesis test that involves a sample from a normally distributed population. Because the population is normally distributed, any sample size results in a normally distributed sampling distribution. Because it's a normal distribution, you use z-scores in the hypothesis test:

$$z = \frac{\bar{x} - \mu}{\sigma / \sqrt{N}}$$

One more "because": Because you use the z-score in the hypothesis test, the z-score here is called the *test statistic.*

Suppose you think that people living in a particular zip code have higher-than-average IQs. You take a sample of nine people from that zip code, give them IQ tests, tabulate the results, and calculate the statistics. For the population of IQ scores, $\mu = 100$ and $\sigma = 15$.

The hypotheses are

$H_0: \mu_{ZIP\ code} \leq 100$

$H_1: \mu_{ZIP\ code} > 100$

Assume that $\alpha = .05$. That's the shaded area in the tail of the H_0 distribution in Figure 10-1.

Why the ≤ in H_0? You use that symbol because you'll reject H_0 only if the sample mean is larger than the hypothesized value. Anything else is evidence in favor of not rejecting H_0.

Suppose the sample mean is 108.67. Can you reject H_0?

The test involves turning 108.67 into a standard score in the sampling distribution of the mean:

$$z = \frac{\bar{x} - \mu}{\sigma / \sqrt{N}} = \frac{108.67 - 100}{\left(15 / \sqrt{9}\right)} = \frac{8.67}{\left(15 / 3\right)} = \frac{8.67}{5} = 1.73$$

Is the value of the test statistic large enough to enable you to reject H_0 with $\alpha = .05$? It is. The critical value — the value of z that cuts off 5 percent of the area in a standard normal distribution — is 1.645. (After years of working with the standard normal distribution, I happen to know this. Read Chapter 8, find out about R's qnorm( ) function, and you can have information like that at your fingertips, too.) The calculated value, 1.73, exceeds 1.645, so it's in the rejection region. The decision is to reject H_0.

This means that if H_0 is true, the probability of getting a test statistic value that's at least this large is less than .05. That's strong evidence in favor of rejecting H_0.

REMEMBER

In statistical parlance, any time you reject H_0, the result is said to be *statistically significant*.

This type of hypothesis testing is called *one-tailed* because the rejection region is in one tail of the sampling distribution.

A hypothesis test can be one-tailed in the other direction. Suppose you have reason to believe that people in that zip code have lower-than-average IQs. In that case, the hypotheses are

H_0: $\mu_{\text{ZIP code}} \geq 100$

H_1: $\mu_{\text{ZIP code}} < 100$

For this hypothesis test, the critical value of the test statistic is −1.645 if $\alpha = .05$.

A hypothesis test can be *two-tailed*, meaning that the rejection region is in both tails of the H_0 sampling distribution. That happens when the hypotheses look like this:

H_0: $\mu_{\text{ZIP code}} = 100$

H_1: $\mu_{\text{ZIP code}} \neq 100$

In this case, the alternative hypothesis just specifies that the mean is different from the null-hypothesis value, without saying whether it's greater or whether it's less. Figure 10-2 shows what the two-tailed rejection region looks like for $\alpha = .05$. The 5 percent is divided evenly between the left tail (also called the *lower tail*) and the right tail (the *upper tail*).

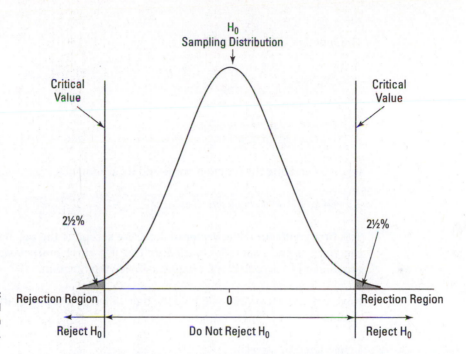

H₀
Sampling Distribution

Critical
Value

Critical
Value

2½%

2½%

FIGURE 10-2:
The two-tailed
rejection region
for α = .05.

Rejection Region

0

Rejection Region

Reject H₀

Do Not Reject H₀

Reject H₀

For a standard normal distribution, incidentally, the z-score that cuts off 2.5 percent in the right tail is 1.96. The z-score that cuts off 2.5 percent in the left tail is –1.96. (Again, I happen to know these values after years of working with the standard normal distribution.) The z-score in the preceding example, 1.73, does not exceed 1.96. The decision, in the two-tailed case, is to *not* reject H₀.

TIP

This brings up an important point. A one-tailed hypothesis test can reject H₀, while a two-tailed test on the same data might not. A two-tailed test indicates that you're looking for a difference between the sample mean and the null-hypothesis mean, but you don't know in which direction. A one-tailed test shows that you have a pretty good idea of how the difference should come out. For practical purposes, this means you should try to have enough knowledge to be able to specify a one-tailed test: That gives you a better chance of rejecting H₀ when you should.

Z Testing in R

An R function called z.test() would be great for doing the kind of testing I discuss in the previous section. One problem: That function does not exist in base R. Although you can find one in other packages, it's easy enough to create one and learn a bit about R programming in the process.

The function will work like this:

```
> IQ.data <- c(100,101,104,109,125,116,105,108,110)
> z.test(IQ.data,100,15)
z = 1.733
one-tailed probability = 0.042
two-tailed probability = 0.084
```

Begin by creating the function name and its arguments:

```
z.test = function(x,mu,popvar){
```

The first argument is the vector of data, the second is the population mean, and the third is the population variance. The left curly bracket signifies that the remainder of the code is what happens inside the function.

Next, create a vector that will hold the one-tailed probability of the z-score you'll calculate:

```
one.tail.p <- NULL
```

Then you calculate the z-score and round it to three decimal places:

```
z.score <- round((mean(x)-mu)/(popvar/sqrt(length(x))),3)
```

Without the rounding, R might calculate many decimal places, and the output would look messy.

Finally, you calculate the one-tailed probability (the proportion of area beyond the calculated z-score), and again round to three decimal places:

```
one.tail.p <- round(pnorm(abs(z.score),lower.tail = FALSE),3)
```

Why put abs() (absolute value) in the argument to pnorm? Remember that an alternative hypothesis can specify a value below the mean, and the data might result in a negative z-score.

The next order of business is to set up the output display. For this, you use the cat() function. I use this function in Chapter 7 to display a fairly sizable set of numbers in an organized way. The name *cat* is short for *concatenate and print*, which is exactly what I want you to do here: Concatenate (put together) strings (like one-tailed probability =) with expressions (like one.tail.p), and then show that whole thing onscreen. I also want you to start a new line for each concatenation, and \n is R's way of making that happen.

Here's the cat statement:

```
cat(" z =",z.score,"\n",
    "one-tailed probability =", one.tail.p,"\n",
    "two-tailed probability =", 2*one.tail.p )}
```

The space between the left quote and z lines up the first line with the next two onscreen. The right curly bracket closes off the function.

Here it is, all together:

```
z.test = function(x,mu,popvar){
  one.tail.p <- NULL
  z.score <- round((mean(x)-mu)/(popvar/sqrt(length(x))),3)
  one.tail.p <- round(pnorm(abs(z.score),lower.tail
        = FALSE),3)
  cat(" z =",z.score,"\n",
      "one-tailed probability =", one.tail.p,"\n",
      "two-tailed probability =", 2*one.tail.p )}
```

Running this function produces what you see at the beginning of this section.

t for One

In the preceding example, you work with IQ scores. The population of IQ scores is a normal distribution with a well-known mean and standard deviation. Thus, you can work with the central limit theorem and describe the sampling distribution of the mean as a normal distribution. You can then use z as the test statistic.

In the real world, however, you usually don't have the luxury of working with well-defined populations. You usually have small samples, and you're typically measuring something that isn't as well-known as IQ. The bottom line is that you often don't know the population parameters, nor do you know if the population is normally distributed.

When that's the case, you use the sample data to estimate the population standard deviation, and you treat the sampling distribution of the mean as a member of a family of distributions called the t-distribution. You use t as a test statistic. In Chapter 9, I introduce this distribution and mention that you distinguish members of this family by a parameter called *degrees of freedom* (df).

The formula for the test statistic is

$$t = \frac{\bar{x} - \mu}{s / \sqrt{N}}$$

Think of df as the denominator of the estimate of the population variance. For the hypothesis tests in this section, that's $N-1$, where N is the number of scores in the sample. The higher the df, the more closely the t-distribution resembles the normal distribution.

Here's an example. FarKlempt Robotics, Inc., markets microrobots. The company claims that its product averages four defects per unit. A consumer group believes this average is higher. The consumer group takes a sample of nine FarKlempt microrobots and finds an average of seven defects, with a standard deviation of 3.12. The hypothesis test is

$H_0: \mu \leq 4$

$H_1: \mu > 4$

$\alpha = .05$

The formula is

$$t = \frac{\bar{x} - \mu}{s / \sqrt{N}} = \frac{7 - 4}{\left(3.12 / \sqrt{9} \right)} = \frac{3}{\left(3.12 / 3 \right)} = 2.88$$

Can you reject H_0? The R function in the next section tells you.

t Testing in R

I preview the t.test() function in Chapter 2 and talk about it in a bit more detail in Chapter 9. Here, you use it to test hypotheses.

Start with the data for FarKlempt Robotics:

```
> FarKlempt.data <- c(3,6,9,9,4,10,6,4,12)
```

Then apply t.test(). For the example, it looks like this:

```
t.test(FarKlempt.data,mu=4, alternative="greater")
```

The second argument specifies that you're testing against a hypothesized mean of 4, and the third argument indicates that the alternative hypothesis is that the true mean is greater than 4.

Here it is in action:

```
> t.test(FarKlempt.data,mu=4, alternative="greater")

            One Sample t-test

data:  c(3, 6, 9, 9, 4, 10, 6, 4, 12)
t = 2.8823, df = 8, p-value = 0.01022
alternative hypothesis: true mean is greater than 4
95 percent confidence interval:
 5.064521       Inf
sample estimates:
mean of x
        7
```

The output provides the t-value and the low p-value shows that you can reject the null hypothesis with α = .05.

This t.test() function is versatile. I work with it again in Chapter 11 when I test hypotheses about two samples.

Working with t-Distributions

Just as you can use d, p, q, and r prefixes for the normal distribution family, you can use dt() (density function), pt() (cumulative density function), qt() (quantiles), and rt() (random number generation) for the t-distribution family.

Here are dt() and rt() at work for a t-distribution with 12 df:

```
> t.values <- seq(-4,4,1)
> round(dt(t.values,12),2)
[1] 0.00 0.01 0.06 0.23 0.39 0.23 0.06 0.01 0.00
> round(pt(t.values,12),2)
[1] 0.00 0.01 0.03 0.17 0.50 0.83 0.97 0.99 1.00
```

I show you how to use dt() more in the next section. (Way more. Trust me.)

For quantile information about the t-distribution with 12 df:

```
> quartiles <- c(0,.25,.50,.75,1)
> qt(quartiles,12)
[1]       -Inf -0.6954829  0.0000000  0.6954829           Inf
```

The -Inf and Inf tell you that the curve never touches the x-axis at either tail.

To generate eight (rounded) random numbers from the t-distribution with 12 df:

```
> round(rt(8,12),2)
[1]  0.73  0.13 -1.32  1.33 -1.27  0.91 -0.48 -0.83
```

All these functions give you the option of working with t-distributions not centered around zero. You do this by entering a value for ncp (the *noncentrality* parameter). In most applications of the t-distribution, noncentrality doesn't come up. For completeness, I explain this concept in greater detail in Appendix 3 online.

Visualizing t-Distributions

Visualizing a distribution often helps you understand it. The process can be a bit involved in R, but it's worth the effort. Figure 9-7 shows three members of the t-distribution family on the same graph. The first has df=3, the second has df=10, and the third is the standard normal distribution (df=infinity).

In this section, I show you how to create that graph in base R graphics and in ggplot2.

With either method, the first step is to set up a vector of the values that the density functions will work with:

```
t.values <- seq(-4,4,.1)
```

One more thing and I'll get you started. After the graphs are complete, you'll put the infinity symbol, ∞ on the legends to denote the df for the standard normal distribution. To do that, you have to install a package called grDevices: On the Packages tab, click Install, and then in the Install Packages dialog box, type **grDevices** and click Install. When grDevices appears on the Packages tab, select its check box.

With grDevices installed, this adds the infinity symbol to a legend:

```
expression(infinity)
```

But I digress. . . .

Plotting t in base R graphics

Begin with the `plot()` function, and plot the t-distribution with 3 df:

```
plot(x = t.values,y = dt(t.values,3),  type = "l", lty =
        "dotted", ylim = c(0,.4), xlab = "t", ylab = "f(t)")
```

The first two arguments are pretty self-explanatory. The next two establish the type of plot — type = "l" means *line plot* (that's a lowercase "L" not the number 1), and lty = "dotted" indicates the type of line. The ylim argument sets the lower and upper limits of the y-axis — ylim = c(0,.4). A little tinkering shows that if you don't do this, subsequent curves get chopped off at the top. The final two arguments label the axes. Figure 10-3 shows the graph so far:

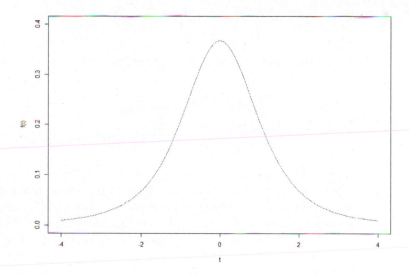

FIGURE 10-3:
t-distribution with
3 df, base R.

The next two lines add the t-distribution for df=10, and for the standard normal (df = infinity):

```
lines(t.values,dt(t.values,10),lty = "dashed")
lines(t.values,dnorm(t.values))
```

The line for the standard normal is solid (the default value for lty). Figure 10-4 shows the progress. All that's missing is the legend that explains which curve is which.

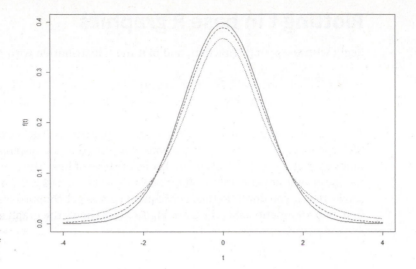

FIGURE 10-4:
Three distributions in search of a legend.

One advantage of base R is that positioning and populating the legend is not difficult:

```
legend("topright", title = "df",legend =
        c(expression(infinity),"10","3"), lty =
        c("solid","dashed","dotted"), bty = "n")
```

The first argument positions the legend in the upper-right corner. The second gives the legend its title. The third argument is a vector that specifies what's in the legend. As you can see, the first element is that infinity expression I showed you earlier, corresponding to the df for the standard normal. The second and third elements are the df for the remaining two t-distributions. You order them this way because that's the order in which the curves appear at their centers. The lty argument is the vector that specifies the order of the linetypes (they correspond with the df). The final argument bty="n" removes the border from the legend.

And this produces Figure 10-5.

Plotting t in ggplot2

The grammar-of-graphics approach takes considerably more effort than base R. But follow along and you'll learn a lot about ggplot2.

You start by putting the relevant numbers into a data frame:

```
t.frame = data.frame(t.values,
                     df3 = dt(t.values,3),
                     df10 = dt(t.values,10),
                     std_normal = dnorm(t.values))
```

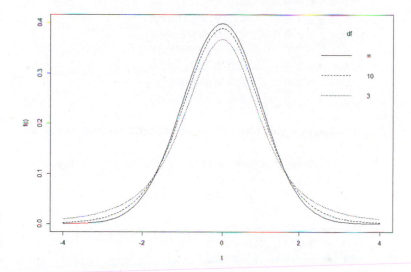

FIGURE 10-5:
The final graph,
including the
legend.

The first six rows of the data frame look like this:

```
> head(t.frame)
  t.values         df3         df10      std_normal
1    -4.0 0.009163361 0.002031034 0.0001338302
2    -3.9 0.009975671 0.002406689 0.0001986555
3    -3.8 0.010875996 0.002854394 0.0002919469
4    -3.7 0.011875430f 0.003388151 0.0004247803
5    -3.6 0.012986623 0.004024623 0.0006119019
6    -3.5 0.014224019 0.004783607 0.0008726827
```

That's a pretty good-looking data frame, but it's in wide format. As I point out in Chapter 3, ggplot() prefers long format — which is the three columns of density-numbers stacked into a single column. To get to that format — it's called *reshaping the data* — make sure you have the reshape2 package installed. Select its check box on the Packages tab and you're ready to go.

Reshaping from wide format to long format is called *melting* the data, so the function is

```
t.frame.melt <- melt(t.frame,id="t.values")
```

The `id` argument specifies that `t.values` is the variable whose numbers *don't* get stacked with the rest. Think of it as the variable that stores the data. The first six rows of `t.frame.melt` are:

```
> head(t.frame.melt)
  t.values variable       value
1     -4.0      df3 0.009163361
2     -3.9      df3 0.009975671
3     -3.8      df3 0.010875996
4     -3.7      df3 0.011875430
5     -3.6      df3 0.012986623
6     -3.5      df3 0.014224019
```

It's always a good idea to have meaningful column names, so . . .

```
> colnames(t.frame.melt)= c("t","df","density")
> head(t.frame.melt)
     t  df     density
1 -4.0 df3 0.009163361
2 -3.9 df3 0.009975671
3 -3.8 df3 0.010875996
4 -3.7 df3 0.011875430
5 -3.6 df3 0.012986623
6 -3.5 df3 0.014224019
```

Now for one more thing before I have you start on the graph. This is a vector that will be useful when you lay out the x-axis:

```
x.axis.values <- seq(-4,4,2)
```

Begin with `ggplot()`:

```
ggplot(t.frame.melt, aes(x=t,y=f(t),group =df))
```

The first argument is the data frame. The aesthetic mappings tell you that `t` is on the x-axis, `density` is on the y-axis, and the data falls into groups specified by the `df` variable.

This is a line plot, so the appropriate `geom` function to add is `geom_line`:

```
geom_line(aes(linetype=df))
```

Geom functions can work with aesthetic mappings. The aesthetic mapping here maps `df` to the type of line.

Rescale the x-axis so that it goes from −4 to 4, by twos. Here's where to use that x.axis.values vector:

```
scale_x_continuous(breaks=x.axis.values,labels=x.axis.values)
```

The first argument sets the breakpoints for the x-axis, and the second provides the labels for those points. Putting these three statements together

```
ggplot(t.frame.melt, aes(x=t,y=density,group =df)) +
    geom_line(aes(linetype=df)) +
    scale_x_continuous(breaks = x.axis.values,labels =
          x.axis.values)
```

results in Figure 10-6. One of the benefits of ggplot2 is that the code automatically produces a legend.

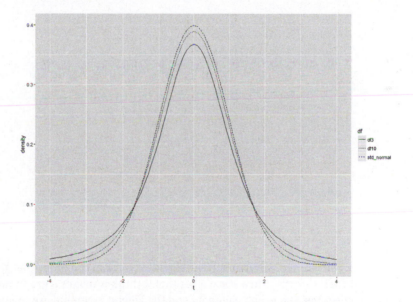

FIGURE 10-6:
Three
t-distribution
curves, plotted
in ggplot2.

You still have some work to do. First of all, the default linetype assignments are not what you want, so you have to redo them:

```
scale_linetype_manual(values =
          c("dotted","dashed","solid"),
    labels = c("3","10", expression(infinity)))
```

The four statements

```
ggplot(t.frame.melt, aes(x=t,y=density,group =df)) +
    geom_line(aes(linetype=df)) +
    scale_x_continuous(breaks = x.axis.values,labels =
            x.axis.values)+
    scale_linetype_manual(values =
            c("dotted","dashed","solid"),
            labels = c("3","10", expression(infinity)))
```

produce Figure 10-7.

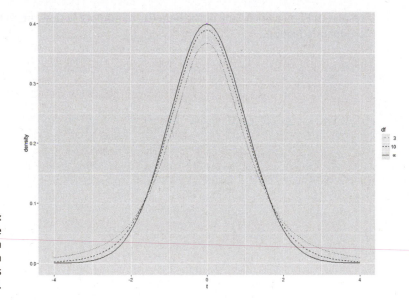

FIGURE 10-7:
Three
t-distribution
curves, with
the linetypes
reassigned.

As you can see, the items in the legend are not in the order that the curves appear at their centers. I'm a stickler for that. I think it makes a graph more comprehensible when the graph elements and the legend elements are in sync. ggplot2 provides `guide` functions that enable you to control the legend's details. To reverse the order of the linetypes in the legend, here's what you do:

```
guides(linetype=guide_legend(reverse = TRUE))
```

Putting all the code together, finally, yields Figure 10-8.

```
ggplot(t.frame.melt, aes(x=t,y=density,group =df)) +
    geom_line(aes(linetype=df)) +
```

```
scale_x_continuous(breaks = x.axis.values,labels =
        x.axis.values)+
scale_linetype_manual(values =
        c("dotted","dashed","solid"),
        labels = c("3","10", expression(infinity)))+
guides(linetype=guide_legend(reverse = TRUE))
```

I leave it to you as an exercise to relabel the y-axis f(t).

Base R graphics versus ggplot2: It's like driving a car with a standard transmission versus driving with an automatic transmission — but I'm not always sure which is which!

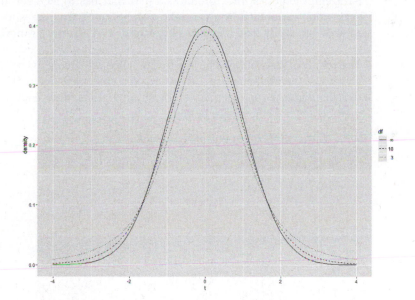

FIGURE 10-8:
The final product,
with the legend
rearranged.

One more thing about ggplot2

I could have had you plot all this without creating and reshaping a data frame. An alternative approach is to set NULL as the data source, map t.values to the x-axis, and then add three geom_line statements. Each of those statements would map a vector of densities (created on the fly) to the y-axis, and each one would have its own linetype.

The problem with that approach? When you do it that way, the grammar does not automatically create a legend. Without a data frame, it has nothing to create a legend from. It's something like using ggplot() to create a base R graph.

Is it ever a good idea to use this approach? Yes, it is — when you don't want to include a legend but you want to annotate the graph in some other way. I provide an example in the later section "Visualizing Chi-Square Distributions."

Testing a Variance

So far, I discuss one-sample hypothesis testing for means. You can also test hypotheses about variances.

This topic sometimes comes up in the context of manufacturing. Suppose FarKlempt Robotics, Inc., produces a part that has to be a certain length with a very small variability. You can take a sample of parts, measure them, find the sample variability, and perform a hypothesis test against the desired variability.

The family of distributions for the test is called *chi-square*. Its symbol is χ^2. I won't go into all the mathematics. I'll just tell you that, once again, df is the parameter that distinguishes one member of the family from another. Figure 10-9 shows two members of the chi-square family.

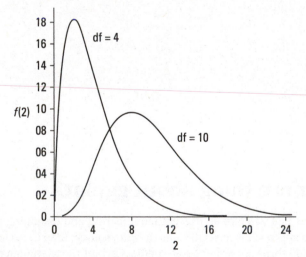

FIGURE 10-9:
Two members of the chi-square family.

As the figure shows, chi-square is not like the previous distribution families I showed you. Members of this family can be skewed, and none of them can take a value less than zero.

The formula for the test statistic is

$$\chi^2 = \frac{(N-1)s^2}{\sigma^2}$$

N is the number of scores in the sample, s^2 is the sample variance, and σ^2 is the population variance specified in H_0.

With this test, you have to assume that what you're measuring has a normal distribution.

Suppose the process for the FarKlempt part has to have, at most, a standard deviation of 1.5 inches for its length. (Notice that I use *standard deviation.* This allows me to speak in terms of inches. If I use *variance,* the units would be square inches.) After measuring a sample of 10 parts, you find a standard deviation of 1.80 inches.

The hypotheses are

H_0: $\sigma^2 \leq 2.25$ (remember to square the "at-most" standard deviation of 1.5 inches)

H_1: $\sigma^2 > 2.25$

$\alpha = .05$

Working with the formula,

$$\chi^2 = \frac{(N-1)s^2}{\sigma^2} = \frac{(10-1)(1.80)^2}{(1.5)^2} = \frac{(9)(3.25)}{2.25} = 12.96$$

can you reject H_0? Read on.

Testing in R

At this point, you might think that the function `chisq.test()` would answer the question. Although base R provides this function, it's not appropriate here. As you can see in Chapters 18 and 20, statisticians use this function to test other kinds of hypotheses.

Instead, turn to a function called `varTest`, which is in the `EnvStats` package. On the Packages tab, click Install. Then type **EnvStats** into the Install Packages dialog box and click Install. When EnvStats appears on the Packages tab, select its check box.

Before you use the test, you create a vector to hold the ten measurements described in the example in the preceding section:

```
FarKlempt.data2 <- c(12.43, 11.71, 14.41, 11.05, 9.53,
        11.66, 9.33,11.71,14.35,13.81)
```

And now, the test:

```
varTest(FarKlempt.data2,alternative="greater",conf.level
        = 0.95,sigma.squared = 2.25)
```

The first argument is the data vector. The second specifies the alternative hypothesis that the true variance is greater than the hypothesized variance, the third gives the confidence level $(1-\alpha)$, and the fourth is the hypothesized variance.

Running that line of code produces these results:

```
Results of Hypothesis Test
--------------------------

Null Hypothesis:          variance = 2.25

Alternative Hypothesis:   True variance is greater than 2.25

Test Name:                Chi-Squared Test on Variance

Estimated Parameter(s):   variance = 3.245299

Data:                     FarKlempt.data2

Test Statistic:           Chi-Squared = 12.9812

Test Statistic Parameter: df = 9

P-value:                  0.163459

95% Confidence Interval:  LCL = 1.726327
                          UCL =       Inf
```

Among other statistics, the output shows the chi-square (12.9812) and the p-value (0.163459). (The chi-square value in the previous section is a bit lower because of rounding.) The p-value is greater than .05. Therefore, you cannot reject the null hypothesis.

How high would chi-square (with df=9) have to be in order to reject? Hmmm. . . .

Working with Chi-Square Distributions

As is the case for the distribution families I've discussed in this chapter, R provides functions for working with the chi-square distribution family: dchisq() (for the density function), pchisq() (for the cumulative density function), qchisq() (for quantiles), and rchisq() (for random-number generation).

To answer the question I pose at the end of the previous section, I use qchisq():

```
> qchisq(.05,df=9,lower.tail = FALSE)
[1] 16.91898
```

The observed value missed that critical value by quite a bit.

Here are examples of the other chisq functions with df=9. For this set of values,

```
> chisq.values <- seq(0,16,2)
```

here are the densities

```
> round(dchisq(chisq.values,9),3)
[1] 0.000 0.016 0.066 0.100 0.101 0.081 0.056 0.036 0.021
```

and here are the cumulative densities

```
> round(pchisq(chisq.values,9),3)
[1] 0.000 0.009 0.089 0.260 0.466 0.650 0.787 0.878 0.933
```

Here are six random numbers selected from this chi-square distribution:

```
> round(rchisq(n=6,df=9),3)
[1] 13.231  5.674  7.396  6.170 11.806  7.068
```

Visualizing Chi-Square Distributions

Figure 10-9 nicely shows a couple of members of the chi-square family, with each member annotated with its degrees of freedom. In this section, I show you how to use base R graphics and ggplot2 to re-create that picture. You'll learn some more about graphics, and you'll know how to visualize any member of this family.

Plotting chi-square in base R graphics

To get started, you create a vector of values from which dchisq() calculates densities:

```
chi.values <- seq(0,25,.1)
```

Start the graphing with a plot statement:

```
plot(x=chi.values,
     y=dchisq(chi.values,df=4),
     type = "l",
     xlab=expression(chi^2),
     ylab="")
```

The first two arguments indicate what you're plotting — the chi-square distribution with four degrees of freedom versus the chi.values vector. The third argument specifies a line (that's a lowercase "L", not the number 1). The third argument labels the x-axis with the Greek letter chi (χ) raised to the second power. The fourth argument gives the y-axis a blank label.

Why did I have you do that? When I first created the graph, I found that ylab locates the y-axis label too far to the left, and the label was cut off slightly. To fix that, I blank out ylab and then use mtext():

```
mtext(side = 2, text = expression(f(chi^2)), line = 2.5)
```

The side argument specifies the side of the graph to insert the label: bottom = 1, left = 2, top = 3, and right = 4. The text argument sets $f\left(\chi^2\right)$ as the label for the axis. The line argument specifies the distance from the label to the y-axis: The distance increases with the value.

Next, you add the curve for chi-square with ten degrees of freedom:

```
lines(x=chi.values,y=dchisq(chi.values,df= 10))
```

Rather than add a legend, follow Figure 10-9 and add an annotation for each curve. Here's how:

```
text(x=6,y=.15, label="df=4")
text(x=16, y=.07, label = "df=10")
```

The first two arguments locate the annotation, and the third one provides the content.

Putting it all together:

```
plot(x=chi.values,
     y=dchisq(chi.values,df=4),
     type = "l",
     xlab=expression(chi^2),
     ylab="")
mtext(side = 2, expression(f(chi^2)), line = 2.5)
lines(x=chi.values,y=dchisq(chi.values,df= 10))
text(x=6,y=.15, label="df=4")
text(x=16, y=.07, label = "df=10")
```

creates Figure 10-10.

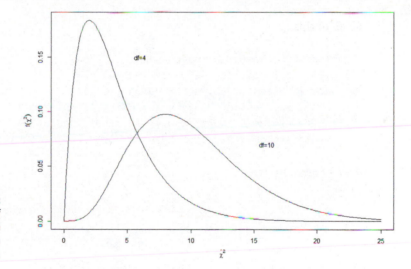

FIGURE 10-10:
Two members of the chi-square family, plotted in base R graphics.

Plotting chi-square in ggplot2

In this plot, I again have you use annotations rather than a legend, so you set NULL as the data source and work with a vector for each line. The first aesthetic maps chi.values to the x-axis:

```
ggplot(NULL, aes(x=chi.values))
```

Then you add a geom_line for each chi-square curve, with the mapping to the y-axis as indicated:

```
geom_line(aes(y=dchisq(chi.values,4)))
geom_line(aes(y=dchisq(chi.values,10)))
```

As I point out earlier in this chapter, this is like using ggplot2 to create a base R graph, but in this case it works (because it doesn't create an unwanted legend).

Next, you label the axes:

```
labs(x=expression(chi^2),y=expression(f(chi^2)))
```

And finally, the aptly named `annotate()` function adds the annotations:

```
annotate(geom = "text",x=6,y=.15,label="df=4")
annotate(geom = "text",x=16,y=.07,label="df=10")
```

The first argument specifies that the annotation is a text object. The next two locate the annotation in the graph, and the fourth provides the label.

So all of this

```
ggplot(NULL, aes(x=chi.values))+
    geom_line(aes(y=dchisq(chi.values,4))) +
    geom_line(aes(y=dchisq(chi.values,10))) +
    labs(x=expression(chi^2),y=expression(f(chi^2)))+
    annotate(geom = "text",x=6,y=.15,label = "df=4")+
    annotate(geom = "text",x=16,y=.07,label = "df=10")
```

draws Figure 10-11.

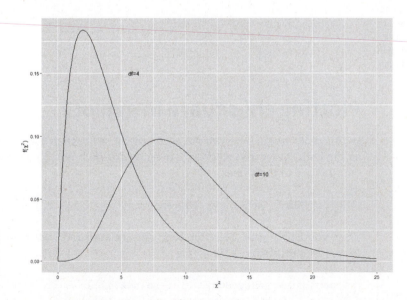

FIGURE 10-11:
Two members of the chi-square family, plotted in ggplot2.

Chapter **11**

Two-Sample Hypothesis Testing

n a variety of fields, the need often arises to compare one sample with another. Sometimes the samples are independent, and sometimes they're matched in some way. Each sample comes from a separate population. The objective is to decide whether these populations are different from one another.

Usually, this involves tests of hypotheses about population means. You can also test hypotheses about population variances. In this chapter, I show you how to carry out these tests, and how to use R to get the job done.

Hypotheses Built for Two

As in the one-sample case (see Chapter 10), hypothesis testing with two samples starts with a null hypothesis (H_0) and an alternative hypothesis (H_1). The null hypothesis specifies that any differences you see between the two samples are due strictly to chance. The alternative hypothesis says, in effect, that any differences you see are real and not due to chance.

It's possible to have a *one-tailed test,* in which the alternative hypothesis specifies the direction of the difference between the two means, or a *two-tailed test* in which the alternative hypothesis does not specify the direction of the difference.

For a one-tailed test, the hypotheses look like this:

$$H_0: \mu_1 - \mu_2 = 0$$

$$H_1: \mu_1 - \mu_2 > 0$$

or like this:

$$H_0: \mu_1 - \mu_2 = 0$$

$$H_1: \mu_1 - \mu_2 < 0$$

For a two-tailed test, the hypotheses are:

$$H_0: \mu_1 - \mu_2 = 0$$

$$H_1: \mu_1 - \mu_2 \neq 0$$

The zero in these hypotheses is the typical case. It's possible, however, to test for any value — just substitute that value for zero.

To carry out the test, you first set α, the probability of a Type I error that you're willing to live with. (See Chapter 10.) Then you calculate the mean and standard deviation of each sample, subtract one mean from the other, and use a formula to convert the result into a test statistic. Compare the test statistic to a sampling distribution of test statistics. If it's in the rejection region that α specifies (again, see Chapter 10), reject H_0. If it's not, don't reject H_0.

Sampling Distributions Revisited

In Chapter 9, I introduce the idea of a sampling distribution — a distribution of all possible values of a statistic for a particular sample size. In that chapter, I describe the sampling distribution of the mean. In Chapter 10, I show its connection with one-sample hypothesis testing.

For two-sample hypothesis testing, another sampling distribution is necessary. This one is the sampling distribution of the difference between means.

REMEMBER

The *sampling distribution of the difference between means* is the distribution of all possible values of differences between pairs of sample means with the sample sizes held constant from pair to pair. (Yes, that's a mouthful.) *Held constant from pair to pair* means that the first sample in the pair always has the same size, and the second sample in the pair always has the same size. The two sample sizes are not necessarily equal.

Within each pair, each sample comes from a different population. All samples are independent of one another so that picking individuals for one sample has no effect on picking individuals for another.

Figure 11-1 shows the steps in creating this sampling distribution. This is something you never do in practice. It's all theoretical. As the figure shows, the idea is to take a sample out of one population and a sample out of another, calculate their means, and subtract one mean from the other. Return the samples to the populations, and repeat over and over and over. The result of the process is a set of differences between means. This set of differences is the sampling distribution.

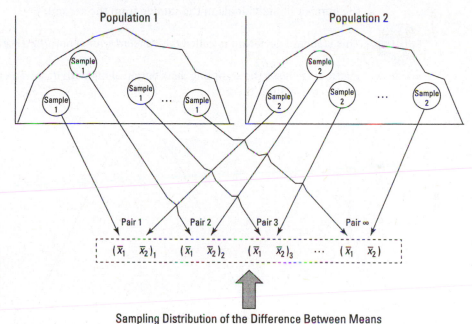

FIGURE 11-1:
Creating the sampling distribution of the difference between means.

Sampling Distribution of the Difference Between Means

Applying the central limit theorem

Like any other set of numbers, this sampling distribution has a mean and a standard deviation. As is the case with the sampling distribution of the mean (see Chapters 9 and 10), the central limit theorem applies here.

According to the central limit theorem, if the samples are large, the sampling distribution of the difference between means is approximately a normal distribution. If the populations are normally distributed, the sampling distribution is a normal distribution even if the samples are small.

The central limit theorem also has something to say about the mean and standard deviation of this sampling distribution. Suppose that the parameters for the first population are μ_1 and σ_1, and the parameters for the second population are μ_2 and σ_2. The mean of the sampling distribution is

$$\mu_{\bar{x}_1 - \bar{x}_2} = \mu_1 - \mu_2$$

The standard deviation of the sampling distribution is

$$\sigma_{\bar{x}_1 - \bar{x}_2} = \sqrt{\frac{\sigma_1^2}{N_1} + \frac{\sigma_2^2}{N_2}}$$

N_1 is the number of individuals in the sample from the first population, and N_2 is the number of individuals in the sample from the second.

REMEMBER

This standard deviation is called *the standard error of the difference between means*.

Figure 11-2 shows the sampling distribution along with its parameters, as specified by the central limit theorem.

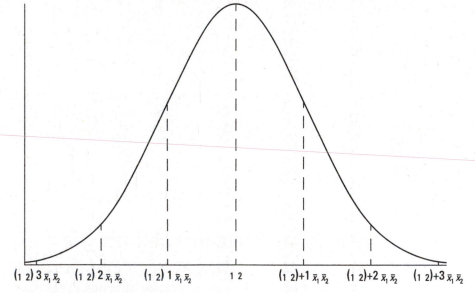

FIGURE 11-2:
The sampling
distribution of the
difference
between means,
according to the
central limit
theorem.

Z's once more

Because the central limit theorem says that the sampling distribution is approximately normal for large samples (or for small samples from normally distributed populations), you use the z-score as your test statistic. Another way to say "use the z-score as your test statistic" is "perform a z-test." Here's the formula:

$$z = \frac{(\bar{x}_1 - \bar{x}_2) - (\mu_1 - \mu_2)}{\sigma_{\bar{x}_1 - \bar{x}_2}}$$

The term $(\mu_1 - \mu_2)$ represents the difference between the means in H_0.

This formula converts the difference between sample means into a standard score. Compare the standard score against a standard normal distribution — a normal distribution with $\mu = 0$ and $\sigma = 1$. If the score is in the rejection region defined by α, reject H_0. If it's not, don't reject H_0.

You use this formula when you know the value of σ_1^2 and σ_2^2.

Here's an example. Imagine a new training technique designed to increase IQ. Take a sample of nine people and train them under the new technique. Take another sample of nine people and give them no special training. Suppose that the sample mean for the new technique sample is 110.222, and for the no-training sample it's 101. The hypothesis test is

$$H_0: \mu_1 - \mu_2 \leq 0$$

$$H_1: \mu_1 - \mu_2 > 0$$

I'll set α at .05.

The IQ is known to have a standard deviation of 15, and I assume that standard deviation would be the same in the population of people trained on the new technique. Of course, that population doesn't exist. The assumption is that if it did, it should have the same value for the standard deviation as the regular population of IQ scores. Does the mean of that (theoretical) population have the same value as the regular population? H_0 says it does. H_1 says it's larger.

The test statistic is

$$z = \frac{(\bar{x}_1 - \bar{x}_2) - (\mu_1 - \mu_2)}{\sigma_{\bar{x}_1 - \bar{x}_2}} = \frac{(\bar{x}_1 - \bar{x}_2) - (\mu_1 - \mu_2)}{\sqrt{\dfrac{\sigma_1^2}{N_1} + \dfrac{\sigma_2^2}{N_2}}} = \frac{(107 - 101.2)}{\sqrt{\dfrac{16^2}{25} + \dfrac{16^2}{25}}} = \frac{5.8}{4.53} = 1.28$$

With $\alpha = .05$, the critical value of z — the value that cuts off the upper 5 percent of the area under the standard normal distribution — is 1.645. (You can use the qnorm() function from Chapter 8 to verify this.) The calculated value of the test statistic is less than the critical value, so the decision is to not reject H_0. Figure 11-3 summarizes this.

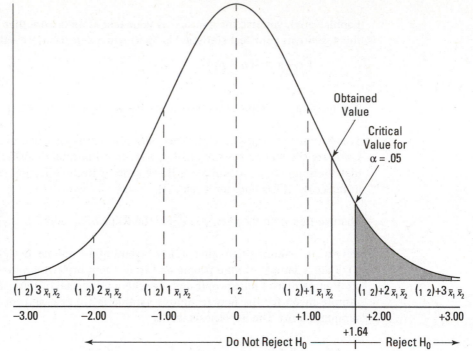

| Obtained Value |
| Critical Value for $\alpha = .05$ |

| $(\bar{x}_1 - \bar{x}_2) - 3\sigma_{\bar{x}_1 - \bar{x}_2}$ | $(\bar{x}_1 - \bar{x}_2) - 2\sigma_{\bar{x}_1 - \bar{x}_2}$ | $(\bar{x}_1 - \bar{x}_2) - 1\sigma_{\bar{x}_1 - \bar{x}_2}$ | $\bar{x}_1 - \bar{x}_2$ | $(\bar{x}_1 - \bar{x}_2) + 1\sigma_{\bar{x}_1 - \bar{x}_2}$ | $(\bar{x}_1 - \bar{x}_2) + 2\sigma_{\bar{x}_1 - \bar{x}_2}$ | $(\bar{x}_1 - \bar{x}_2) + 3\sigma_{\bar{x}_1 - \bar{x}_2}$ |

| −3.00 | −2.00 | −1.00 | 0 | +1.00 | +2.00 | +3.00 |

+1.64

← Do Not Reject H$_0$ ———— | ———— Reject H$_0$ →

FIGURE 11-3:
The sampling distribution of the difference between means, along with the critical value for $\alpha = .05$ and the obtained value of the test statistic in the IQ example.

Z-testing for two samples in R

As is the case for one-sample testing (explained in Chapter 10), base R provides no function for a two-sample z-test. If this function existed, you'd probably want it to work like this for the example:

```
> sample1 <-c(100,118,97,92,118,125,136,95,111)
> sample2 <-c(91,109,83,88,115,108,127,102,86)
> z.test2(sample1,sample2,15,15)
mean1 = 110.2222    mean2 = 101
standard error = 7.071068
z = 1.304
one-tailed probability = 0.096
two-tailed probability = 0.192
```

Because this function isn't available, I'll show you how to create one.

Begin with the function name and the arguments:

```
z.test2 = function(x,y,popsd1,popsd2){
```

The first two arguments are data vectors, and the second two are the population standard deviations. The left curly bracket indicates that subsequent statements are what occurs inside the function.

Next, you initialize a vector that will hold the one-tailed probability:

```
one.tail.p <- NULL
```

Then you calculate the standard error of the difference between means

```
std.error <- sqrt((popsd1^2/length(x) + popsd2^2/length(y)))
```

and then the (rounded) z-score

```
z.score <- round((mean(x)-mean(y))/std.error,3)
```

Finally, you calculate the rounded one-tailed probability:

```
one.tail.p <- round(pnorm(abs(z.score),lower.tail = FALSE),3)
```

The abs() function (absolute value) ensures the appropriate calculation for a negative z-score.

Last but not least, a cat() (concatenate-and-print) statement displays the output:

```
cat(" mean1 =", mean(x)," ", "mean2 =", mean(y), "\n",
    "standard error =", std.error, "\n",
    "z =", z.score,"\n",
    "one-tailed probability =", one.tail.p,"\n",
    "two-tailed probability =", 2*one.tail.p )}
```

I use a cat() function like this for the one-sample case in Chapter 10. The right curly bracket closes off the function.

Here's the newly defined function:

```
z.test2 = function(x,y,popsd1,popsd2){
  one.tail.p <- NULL
  std.error <- sqrt((popsd1^2/length(x) + popsd2^2/length(y)))
  z.score <- round((mean(x)-mean(y))/std.error,3)
  one.tail.p <- round(pnorm(abs(z.score),lower.tail = FALSE),3)
  cat(" mean1 =", mean(x)," ", "mean2 =", mean(y), "\n",
      "standard error =", std.error, "\n",
```

```
   "z =", z.score,"\n",
   "one-tailed probability =", one.tail.p,"\n",
   "two-tailed probability =", 2*one.tail.p )}
```

t for Two

The example in the preceding section involves a situation you rarely encounter — known population variances. If you know a population's variance, you're likely to know the population mean. If you know the mean, you probably don't have to perform hypothesis tests about it.

Not knowing the variances takes the central limit theorem out of play. This means that you can't use the normal distribution as an approximation of the sampling distribution of the difference between means. Instead, you use the t-distribution, a family of distributions I introduce in Chapter 9 and apply to one-sample hypothesis testing in Chapter 10. The members of this family of distributions differ from one another in terms of a parameter called *degrees of freedom* (df). Think of df as the denominator of the variance estimate you use when you calculate a value of *t* as a test statistic. Another way to say "calculate a value of *t* as a test statistic" is "Perform a t-test."

Unknown population variances lead to two possibilities for hypothesis testing. One possibility is that although the variances are unknown, you have reason to assume they're equal. The other possibility is that you cannot assume they're equal. In the sections that follow, I discuss these possibilities.

Like Peas in a Pod: Equal Variances

When you don't know a population variance, you use the sample variance to estimate it. If you have two samples, you average (sort of) the two sample variances to arrive at the estimate.

REMEMBER

Putting sample variances together to estimate a population variance is called *pooling*. With two sample variances, here's how you do it:

$$s_p{}^2 = \frac{(N_1-1)s_1^2 + (N_2-1)s_2^2}{(N_1-1)+(N_2-1)}$$

In this formula, $s_p{}^2$ stands for the pooled estimate. Notice that the denominator of this estimate is $(N_1-1) + (N_2-1)$. Is this the df? Absolutely!

The formula for calculating t is

$$t = \frac{(\bar{x}_1 - \bar{x}_2) - (\mu_1 - \mu_2)}{s_p \sqrt{\frac{1}{N_1} + \frac{1}{N_2}}}$$

On to an example. FarKlempt Robotics is trying to choose between two machines to produce a component for its new microrobot. Speed is of the essence, so the company has each machine produce ten copies of the component, and time each production run. The hypotheses are

$H_0: \mu_1 - \mu_2 = 0$

$H_1: \mu_1 - \mu_2 \neq 0$

They set α at .05. This is a two-tailed test because they don't know in advance which machine might be faster.

Table 11-1 presents the data for the production times in minutes.

TABLE 11-1   **Sample Statistics from the FarKlempt Machine Study**

	Machine 1	Machine 2
Mean Production Time	23.00	20.00
Standard Deviation	2.71	2.79
Sample Size	10	10

The pooled estimate of σ^2 is

$$s_p^2 = \frac{(N_1 - 1)s_1^2 + (N_2 - 1)s_2^2}{(N_1 - 1) + (N_2 - 1)} = \frac{(10-1)(2.71)^2 + (10-1)(2.79)^2}{(10-1) + (10-1)}$$

$$= \frac{(9)(2.71)^2 + (9)(2.79)^2}{(9) + (9)} = \frac{66 + 70}{18} = 7.56$$

The estimate of σ is 2.75, the square root of 7.56.

The test statistic is

$$t = \frac{(\bar{x}_1 - \bar{x}_2) - (\mu_1 - \mu_2)}{s_p \sqrt{\frac{1}{N_1} + \frac{1}{N_2}}} = \frac{(23 - 20)}{2.75 \sqrt{\frac{1}{10} + \frac{1}{10}}} = \frac{3}{1.23} = 2.44$$

For this test statistic, df = 18, the denominator of the variance estimate. In a t-distribution with 18 df, the critical value is 2.10 for the right-side (upper) tail and −2.10 for the left-side (lower) tail. If you don't believe me, apply `qt()`. (See Chapter 10.) The calculated value of the test statistic is greater than 2.10, so the decision is to reject H_0. The data provide evidence that Machine 2 is significantly faster than Machine 1. (You can use the word *significant* whenever you reject H_0.)

t-Testing in R

Here are a couple of vectors for the sample data in the example in the preceding section:

```
machine1 <-c(24.58, 22.09, 23.70, 18.89, 22.02, 28.71, 24.44,
        20.91, 23.83, 20.83)
```

```
machine2 <- c(21.61, 19.06, 20.72, 15.77, 19, 25.88, 21.48,
        17.85, 20.86, 17.77)
```

R provides two ways for performing the t-test. Both involve `t.test()`, which I use in Chapters 9 and 10.

Working with two vectors

Here's how to test the hypotheses with two vectors and the equal variances assumption:

```
t.test(machine1,machine2,var.equal = TRUE, alternative="two.
        sided", mu=0)
```

The `alternative=two-sided` argument reflects the type of alternative hypothesis specified in the example, and the last argument indicates the hypothesized difference between means.

Running that function produces this output:

```
Two Sample t-test
data:   c(24.58, 22.09, 23.7, 18.89, 22.02, 28.71, 24.44, 20.91,
        23.83,   ... and c(21.61, 19.06, 20.72, 15.77, 19,
        25.88, 21.48, 17.85, 20.86,   ...
t = 2.4396, df = 18, p-value = 0.02528
alternative hypothesis: true difference in means is not
        equal to 0
```

```
95 percent confidence interval:
 0.4164695 5.5835305
sample estimates:
mean of x mean of y
        23        20
```

The t-value and the low p-value indicate that you can reject the null hypothesis. Machine 2 is significantly faster than Machine 1.

Working with a data frame and a formula

The other way of carrying out this test is to create a data frame and then use a formula that looks like this:

```
prod.time ~ machine
```

The formula expresses the idea that production time depends on the machine you use. Although it's not necessary to do the test this way, it's a good idea to get accustomed to formulas. I use them quite a bit in later chapters.

The first thing to do is create a data frame in long format. First you create a vector for the 20 production times — machine1's times first and then machine2's:

```
prod.time <- c(machine1,machine2)
```

Next, you create a vector of the two machine names:

```
machine <-c("machine1","machine2")
```

Then you turn that vector into a vector of ten repetitions of "machine1" followed by ten repetitions of "machine2". It's a little tricky, but here's how:

```
machine <- rep(machine, times = c(10,10))
```

And the data frame is

```
FarKlempt.frame <-data.frame(machine,prod.time)
```

Its first six rows are

```
> head(FarKlempt.frame)
   machine prod.time
1 machine1     24.58
2 machine1     22.09
3 machine1     23.70
```

```
4 machine1        18.89
5 machine1        22.02
6 machine1        28.71
```

The `t.test()` function is then

```
with (FarKlempt.frame,t.test(prod.time~machine,
                              var.equal = TRUE,
                              alternative="two.sided",
                              mu=0))
```

This produces the same output as the two-vector version.

Visualizing the results

In studies like in the preceding section, two ways of presenting the results are boxplots and bar graphs.

Boxplots

Boxplots depict the data in each sample along with the sample median (as explained in Chapter 3). They're easy to create in base R and in ggplot2. For base R graphics, the code looks quite a bit like the formula method for `t.test()`:

```
with (FarKlempt.frame,boxplot(prod.time~machine, xlab =
          "Machine", ylab="Production Time (minutes)"))
```

The plot looks like Figure 11-4.

Figure 11-5 shows the boxplot rendered in ggplot2. The code that produces that boxplot is

```
ggplot(FarKlempt.frame, aes(x=machine, y=prod.time))+
    stat_boxplot(geom="errorbar", width =.5) +
    geom_boxplot()
```

The only new function is `stat_boxplot()`, which adds the perpendicular line to the end of each whisker. The default width of those lines is the width of the box. I added `width =.5` to cut that width in half.

TECHNICAL STUFF

In ggplot2, `stat` is a way of summarizing the data so that a `geom` function can use it. The `stat` function used here calculates the components for the boxplot. You use it to override the default appearance of the boxplot — which is without the perpendicular line at the end of each whisker. In earlier examples (and in the next one), you use `stat= "identity"` to instruct `geom_bar()` to use table data rather than counts.

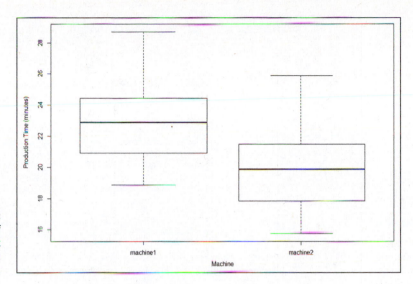

FIGURE 11-4:
Boxplot of
FarKlempt
Machines data
in base R.

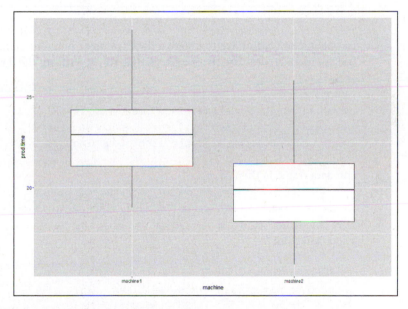

FIGURE 11-5:
Boxplot of
FarKlempt
Machines data in
ggplot2.

Bar graphs

Traditionally, researchers report and plot sample means and standard errors. It's easy to do that in ggplot2. Figure 11-6 shows what I mean.

The t-shaped bars that extend above and below the top of each bar are the *error bars* that denote the standard error of the mean.

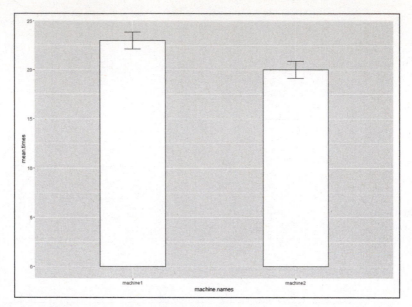

FIGURE 11-6:
FarKlempt
Machine means
and standard
errors.

To use ggplot2, you have to create a data frame of machine names, mean times, and standard errors. The three vectors that will constitute the data frame are

```
machine.names <-c("machine1","machine2")
mean.times <- c(mean(machine1),mean(machine2))
se.times <- c(sd(machine1)/sqrt(length(machine1)),
         sd(machine2)/sqrt(length(machine2)))
```

The data frame is then

```
FKmeans.frame <-data.frame(machine.names,mean.times,se.times)
```

It looks like this:

```
> FKmeans.frame
  machine.names mean.times  se.times
1      machine1         23 0.8570661
2      machine2         20 0.8818339
```

The code to create Figure 11-6 is

```
ggplot(FKmeans.frame, aes(x=machine.names, y=mean.
         times))+
```

```
geom_bar(stat="identity", width=.4,color="black",
        fill="white")+
geom_errorbar(aes(ymin=mean.times-se.times, ymax=mean.
        times+se.times),width=.1)
```

The first function sets the stage with the aesthetic mappings, and the second plots the bars. The `stat = identity` argument instructs `geom_bar` to use the tabled statistics rather than to count instances of `machine1` and `machine2`. The other arguments set the appearance of the bars.

The third function is the `geom` that plots the error bars. The aesthetic mappings set the minimum point and maximum point for each error bar. The `width` argument sets the width for the perpendicular line at the end of each error bar.

TIP

In most scientific publications, you see graphs like this with only the positive error bar — the one extending above the mean. To graph it that way in this example, set `ymin=mean.times` rather than `ymin=mean.times-se.times`.

Like p's and q's: Unequal variances

The case of unequal variances presents a challenge. As it happens, when variances are not equal, the t-distribution with $(N_1-1) + (N_2-1)$ degrees of freedom is not as close an approximation to the sampling distribution as statisticians would like.

Statisticians meet this challenge by reducing the degrees of freedom. To accomplish the reduction, they use a fairly involved formula that depends on the sample standard deviations and the sample sizes.

Because the variances aren't equal, a pooled estimate is not appropriate. So you calculate the t-test in a different way:

$$t = \frac{(\bar{x}_1 - \bar{x}_2) - (\mu_1 - \mu_2)}{\sqrt{\dfrac{s_1^2}{N_1} + \dfrac{s_2^2}{N_2}}}$$

You evaluate the test statistic against a member of the t-distribution family that has the reduced degrees of freedom.

Here's what `t.test()` produces for the FarKlempt example if I assume the variances are not equal:

```
with (FarKlempt.frame,t.test(prod.time~machine,
                        var.equal = FALSE,
                        alternative="two.sided",
                        mu=0))
```

```
Welch Two Sample t-test
data:  prod.time by machine
t = 2.4396, df = 17.985, p-value = 0.02529
alternative hypothesis: true difference in means is not
          equal to 0
95 percent confidence interval:
 0.4163193 5.5836807
sample estimates:
mean in group machine1 mean in group machine2
                    23                     20
```

You can see the slight reduction in degrees of freedom. The variances are so close that little else changes.

A Matched Set: Hypothesis Testing for Paired Samples

In the hypothesis tests I describe so far, the samples are independent of one another. Choosing an individual for one sample has no bearing on the choice of an individual for the other.

Sometimes, the samples are matched. The most obvious case is when the same individual provides a score under each of two conditions — as in a before-after study. Suppose ten people participate in a weight-loss program. They weigh in before they start the program and again after one month on the program. The important data is the set of before-after differences. Table 11-2 shows the data:

The idea is to think of these differences as a sample of scores and treat them as you would in a one-sample t-test. (See Chapter 10.)

You carry out a test on these hypotheses:

$$H_0: \mu_d \leq 0$$
$$H_1: \mu_d > 0$$

The *d* in the subscripts stands for "difference." Set $\alpha = .05$.

TABLE 11-2   ## Data for the Weight-Loss Example

Person	Weight Before Program	Weight After One Month	Difference
1	198	194	4
2	201	203	-2
3	210	200	10
4	185	183	2
5	204	200	4
6	156	153	3
7	167	166	1
8	197	197	0
9	220	215	5
10	186	184	2
Mean			2.9
Standard Deviation			3.25

The formula for this kind of t-test is

$$t = \frac{\bar{d} - \mu_d}{s_{\bar{d}}}$$

In this formula, $\bar{d}$ is the mean of the differences. To find $s_{\bar{d}}$, you calculate the standard deviation of the differences and divide by the square root of the number of pairs:

$$s_{\bar{d}} = \frac{s}{\sqrt{N}}$$

The df is N 1 (where N is the number of pairs).

From Table 11-2,

$$t = \frac{\bar{d} - \mu_d}{s_{\bar{d}}} = \frac{2.9}{\left(3.25 \big/ \sqrt{10} \right)} = 2.82$$

With df = 9 (Number of pairs − 1), the critical value for α = .05 is 1.83. (Use qt( ) to verify.) The calculated value exceeds this value, so the decision is to reject H_o.

Paired Sample t-testing in R

For paired sample t-tests, it's the same formula as for independent samples t-tests. As you'll see, you add an argument. Here's the data from Table 11-2:

```
before <-c(198,201,210,185,204,156,167,197,220,186)
after <- c(194,203,200,183,200,153,166,197,215,184)
```

And the t-test:

```
t.test(before,after,alternative = "greater",paired=TRUE)
```

That last argument, of course, specifies a paired-samples test. The default value for that one is FALSE.

Running that test yields

```
          Paired t-test

data:  before and after
t = 2.8241, df = 9, p-value = 0.009956
alternative hypothesis: true difference in means is greater
          than 0
95 percent confidence interval:
 1.017647      Inf
sample estimates:
mean of the differences
          2.9
```

Because of the very low p-value, you reject the null hypothesis.

Testing Two Variances

The two-sample hypothesis testing I describe in this chapter pertains to means. It's also possible to test hypotheses about variances.

In this section, I extend the one-variance manufacturing example I use in Chapter 10. FarKlempt Robotics, Inc., produces a part that has to be a certain length with a very small variability. The company is considering two machines to produce this part, and it wants to choose the one that results in the least variability. FarKlempt Robotics takes a sample of parts from each machine, measures them, finds the variance for each sample, and performs a hypothesis test to see whether one machine's variance is significantly greater than the other's.

The hypotheses are:

$$H_0: \sigma_1^2 = \sigma_2^2$$

$$H_1: \sigma_1^2 \neq \sigma_2^2$$

As always, an α is a must–have item. As usual, I set it to .05.

When you test two variances, you don't subtract one from the other. Instead, you divide one by the other to calculate the test statistic. Sir Ronald Fisher is a famous statistician who worked out the mathematics and the family of distributions for working with variances in this way. The test statistic is named in his honor. It's called an *F-ratio* and the test is the *F-test*. The family of distributions for the test is called the *F-distribution*.

Without going into all the mathematics, I'll just tell you that, once again, df is the parameter that distinguishes one member of the family from another. What's different about this family is that two variance estimates are involved, so each member of the family is associated with two values of df, rather than one as in the t-test. Another difference between the *F*-distribution and the others you've seen is that the *F* cannot have a negative value. Figure 11-7 shows two members of the *F*-distribution family.

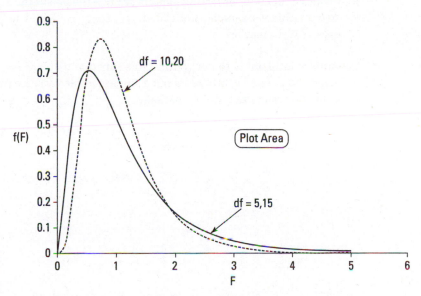

FIGURE 11-7:
Two members of the *F*-distribution family.

The test statistic is

$$F = \frac{\text{larger } s^2}{\text{smaller } s^2}$$

Suppose FarKlempt Robotics produces 10 parts with Machine 1 and finds a sample variance of .81 square inches. It produces 15 parts with Machine 2 and finds a sample variance of .64 square inches. Can the company reject H_0?

Calculating the test statistic,

$$F = \frac{.81}{.64} = 1.27$$

The df's are 9 and 14: The variance estimate in the numerator of the F-ratio is based on 10 cases, and the variance estimate in the denominator is based on 15 cases.

When the df's are 9 and 14 and it's a two-tailed test at $\alpha = .05$, the critical value of F is 3.21. (In a moment, I show you an R function that calculates this.) The calculated value is less than the critical value, so the decision is to not reject H_0.

REMEMBER

It makes a difference which df is in the numerator and which df is in the denominator. The F-distribution for df = 9 and df = 14 is different from the F-distribution for df = 14 and df = 9. For example, the critical value in the latter case is 3.80, not 3.21.

F-testing in R

R provides a function for testing hypotheses like the one in the FarKlempt Robotics two-machines example. It's called var.test(). Should it have been called F.test()? Well, maybe.

The important point is to not confuse this function with varTest(), which I use in Chapter 10 to test hypotheses about a single sample variance (with chi-square). That function is in the EnvStats package.

To apply var.test(), you first create the vectors that hold the data for the parts that machine 1 and machine 2 produce:

```
> var.test(m1.parts,m2.parts,ratio=1,alternative="two.sided")


Results of Hypothesis Test


--------------------------

Null Hypothesis:              ratio of variances = 1

Alternative Hypothesis:       True ratio of variances is not equal to 1

Test Name:                    F test to compare two variances
```

```
Estimated Parameter(s):          ratio of variances = 1.26482


Data:                            m1.parts and m2.parts


Test Statistic:                  F = 1.26482


Test Statistic Parameters:       num df   = 9
                                 denom df = 14
P-value:                         0.6690808


95% Confidence Interval:         LCL = 0.3941108
                                 UCL = 4.8037262
```

The low F-ratio and high p-value indicate that you cannot reject the null hypothesis. (The slight discrepancy between this F-ratio and the one calculated in the example is due to rounding.)

F in conjunction with t

One use of the F-distribution is in conjunction with the t-test for independent samples. Before you do the t-test, you use F to help decide whether to assume equal variances or unequal variances in the samples.

In the equal variances t-test example I show you earlier, the standard deviations are 2.71 and 2.79. The variances are 7.34 and 7.78. The F-ratio of these variances is

$$F = \frac{7.78}{7.34} = 1.06$$

Each sample is based on ten observations, so df = 9 for each sample variance. An F-ratio of 1.06 cuts off the upper 47 percent of the F-distribution whose df are 9 and 9, so it's safe to use the equal variances version of the t-test for these data.

How does all this play out in the context of hypothesis testing? On rare occasions, H_0 is a desirable outcome and you'd rather not reject it. In that case, you stack the deck against *not* rejecting by setting α at a high level so that small differences cause you to reject H_0.

This is one of those rare occasions. It's more desirable to use the equal variances t-test, which typically provides more degrees of freedom than the unequal variances t-test. Setting a high value of α (.20 is a good one) for the F-test enables you to be confident when you assume equal variances.

Working with *F*-Distributions

Just like the other distribution-families I cover earlier (normal, t, chi-square), R provides functions for dealing with *F*-distributions: qf() gives quantile information, df() provides the density function, pf() provides the cumulative density function, and rf() generates random numbers.

TIP

Note that throughout this section, I spell out "degrees of freedom" rather than use the abbreviation "df" as I do elsewhere. That's to avoid confusion with the density function df().

That critical value I refer to earlier for a two-tailed F-test with 9 and 14 degrees of freedom is

```
> qf(.025,9,14,lower.tail = FALSE)
[1] 3.2093
```

It's a two-tailed test at α = .05, so .025 is in each tail.

To watch df() and pf() in action, you create a vector for them to operate on:

```
F.scores <-seq(0,5,1)
```

With 9 and 14 degrees of freedom, the (rounded) densities for these values are

```
> round(df(F.scores,9,14),3)
[1] 0.000 0.645 0.164 0.039 0.011 0.004
```

The (rounded) cumulative densities are

```
> round(pf(F.scores,9,14),3)
[1] 0.000 0.518 0.882 0.968 0.990 0.996
```

To generate five random numbers from this member of the *F*-family:

```
> rf(5,9,14)
[1] 0.6409125 0.4015354 1.1601984 0.6552502 0.8652722
```

Visualizing *F*-Distributions

As I've said, visualizing distributions helps you learn them. *F*-distributions are no exception, and with density functions and ggplot2, it's easy to plot them. My objective in this section is to show you how to use ggplot2 to create a graph that looks like Figure 11-7, which depicts an *F*-distribution with 5 and 15 degrees of freedom and another with 10 and 20 degrees of freedom. To make the graph look like the figure, I have to add annotations with arrows pointing to the appropriate curves.

Begin with a vector of values for `df()` to do its work on:

```
F.values <-seq(0,5,.05)
```

Then create a vector of densities for an *F*-distribution with 5 and 15 degrees of freedom:

```
F5.15 <- df(F.values,5,15)
```

and another for an *F*-distribution with 10 and 20 degrees of freedom:

```
F10.20 <- df(F.values,10,20)
```

Now for a data frame for ggplot2:

```
F.frame <- data.frame(F.values,F5.15,F10.20)
```

This is what the first six rows of `F.frame` look like:

```
> head(F.frame)
  F.values       F5.15       F10.20
1     0.00 0.00000000 0.000000000
2     0.05 0.08868702 0.001349914
3     0.10 0.21319965 0.015046816
4     0.15 0.33376038 0.053520748
5     0.20 0.43898395 0.119815721
6     0.25 0.52538762 0.208812406
```

This is in wide format. As I point out earlier, `ggplot()` prefers long format, in which the data values are stacked on top of one another in one column. This is called *melting* the data and is part and parcel of the reshape2 package. (On the Packages tab, find the check box next to reshape2. If it's unchecked, click on it.)

To appropriately reshape the data,

```
F.frame.melt <- melt(F.frame,id="F.values")
```

The id argument tells `melt()` what *not* to include in the stack. (`F.values` is the "identifier," in other words.) Next, assign meaningful column names:

```
colnames(F.frame.melt)=c("F","deg.fr","density")
```

The first six rows of the melted data frame are

```
> head(F.frame.melt)
     F deg.fr    density
1 0.00  F5.15 0.00000000
2 0.05  F5.15 0.08868702
3 0.10  F5.15 0.21319965
4 0.15  F5.15 0.33376038
5 0.20  F5.15 0.43898395
6 0.25  F5.15 0.52538762
```

To begin the visualizing, the first statement, as always, is `ggplot()`:

```
ggplot(F.frame.melt,aes(x=F,y=density,group=deg.fr))
```

The first argument is the data frame. The first two aesthetic mappings associate *F* with the x-axis, and density with the y-axis. The third mapping forms groups based on the `deg.fr` variable.

Next, you add a `geom_line`:

```
geom_line(stat="identity",aes(linetype=deg.fr))
```

The `stat` argument tells the `geom` function to use the tabled data. The aesthetic mapping associates the linetype ("solid" and "dotted" are the default values) with `deg.fr`.

If you prefer "solid" and "dashed," as in Figure 11-7, you have to change things manually:

```
scale_linetype_manual(values = c("solid","dashed"),
        labels = c("5,15","10,20"))
```

The values and labels will appear in the legend that the grammar automatically creates.

Here's the code so far:

```
ggplot(F.frame.melt,aes(x=F,y=density,group=deg.fr)) +
   geom_line(stat="identity",aes(linetype=deg.fr))+
   scale_linetype_manual(values = c("solid","dashed"),
        labels = c("5,15","10,20"))
```

Figure 11-8 shows the progress.

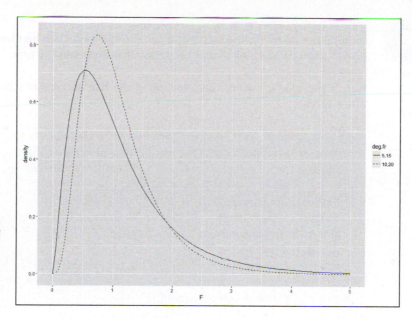

FIGURE 11-8:
Two members of the *F*-distribution family in ggplot2 — intermediate graph.

But the objective is to create a graph without a legend, just like Figure 11-7. You use `guides()` to manipulate the legend, and the legend is based on `linetype`. So here's how to remove the legend:

```
guides(linetype=FALSE)
```

Finally, add a couple of annotations that show the degrees of freedom for each curve. The annotation for the curve with 10 and 20 degrees of freedom is

```
annotate(geom="text",x=1.98,y=.78,label="df=10,20")
```

The first argument specifies a `text` geom, the next two position the `text` geom within the graph (centered on the indicated coordinates), and the fourth sets what the annotation says.

Now for the arrow that points from the annotation to the curve. It consists of a line segment and an arrowhead. The line-segment part of the arrow is a `segment` geom. The arrowhead part of the arrow is the product of a function called `arrow()`, which is in the `grid` package. On the Packages tab, find the check box next to `grid`, and click it.

Another `annotate()` function sets the arrow:

```
annotate(geom="segment",x=2.0,xend=1.15,y=0.75,yend = .6,
        arrow=arrow())
```

The four arguments after the `geom` function locate the start-point and the end-point for the segment. The final argument plots the arrowhead.

Finding the values for the start point and the end-point can involve some trial and error. It's not a bad idea to plot the arrow first and then the text.

Here's the code for everything, including the two `annotate()` functions for the other curve:

```
ggplot(F.frame.melt,aes(x=F,y=density,group=deg.fr)) +
   geom_line(stat="identity",aes(linetype=deg.fr))+
   scale_linetype_manual(values = c("solid","dashed"),
         labels = c("5,15","10,20")) +
   guides(linetype=FALSE) +
   annotate(geom="text",x=1.98,y=.78,label="df=10,20")+
   annotate(geom="segment",y=0.75,yend=.6,
   arrow=arrow())+
   annotate(geom="text",x=3.3,y=.28,label="df=5,15")+
   annotate(geom="segment",x = 3.35, xend=2.45,y =0.25,
         yend=.1,arrow=arrow())
```

And Figure 11-9 is the result.

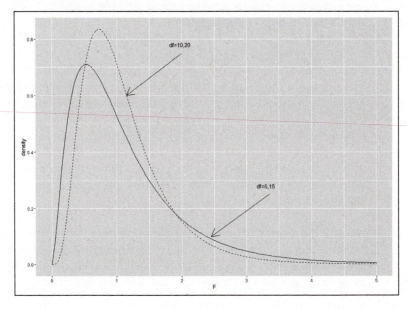

FIGURE 11-9:
Two members of
the *F*-distribution
family in
ggplot2 — final
product.

Experiment with other values for degrees of freedom and see what the curves look like.

Chapter **12**

Testing More than Two Samples

Statistics would be limited if you could only make inferences about one or two samples. In this chapter, I discuss the procedures for testing hypotheses about three or more samples. I show what to do when samples are independent of one another, and what to do when they're not. In both cases, I discuss what to do after you test the hypotheses. I also discuss R functions that do the work for you.

Testing More Than Two

Imagine this situation. Your company asks you to evaluate three different methods for training its employees to do a particular job. You randomly assign 30 employees to one of the three methods. Your plan is to train them, test them, tabulate the results, and make some conclusions. Before you can finish the study, three people leave the company — one from the Method 1 group and two from the Method 3 group.

Table 12-1 shows the data.

TABLE 12-1 **Data from Three Training Methods**

	Method 1	Method 2	Method 3
	95	83	68
	91	89	75
	89	85	79
	90	89	74
	99	81	75
	88	89	81
	96	90	73
	98	82	77
	95	84	
		80	
Mean	93.44	85.20	75.25
Variance	16.28	14.18	15.64
Standard Deviation	4.03	3.77	3.96

Do the three methods provide different results, or are they so similar that you can't distinguish among them? To decide, you have to carry out a hypothesis test

$H_0: \mu_1 = \mu_2 = \mu_3$

H_1: Not H_0

with $\alpha = .05$.

A thorny problem

Finding differences among three groups sounds pretty easy, particularly if you've read Chapter 11. Take the mean of the scores from Method 1, the mean of the scores from Method 2, and do a t-test to see whether they're different. Follow the same procedure for Method 1 versus Method 3, and for Method 2 versus Method 3. If at least one of those t-tests shows a significant difference, reject H_0. Nothing to it, right? Wrong. If your α is .05 for each t-test, you're setting yourself up for a Type I error with a probability higher than you planned on. The probability that at least one of the three t-tests results in a significant difference is way above .05. In fact, it's .14, which is way beyond acceptable. (The mathematics behind calculating that number is a little involved, so I won't elaborate.)

With more than three samples, the situation gets even worse. Four groups require six t-tests, and the probability that at least one of them is significant is .26. Table 12-2 shows what happens with increasing numbers of samples.

TABLE 12-2

The Incredible Increasing Alpha

Number of Samples t	Number of Tests	Pr (At Least One Significant t)
3	3	.14
4	6	.26
5	10	.40
6	15	.54
7	21	.66
8	28	.76
9	36	.84
10	45	.90

Carrying out multiple t-tests is clearly not the answer. What do you do?

A solution

It's necessary to take a different approach. The idea is to think in terms of variances rather than means.

I'd like you to think of variance in a slightly different way. The formula for estimating population variance, remember, is

$$s^2 = \frac{\sum (x - \bar{x})^2}{N - 1}$$

Because the variance is almost a mean of squared deviations from the mean, statisticians also refer to it as *mean-square*. In a way, that's an unfortunate nickname: It leaves out "deviation from the mean," but there you have it.

The numerator of the variance — excuse me, mean-square — is the sum of squared deviations from the mean. This leads to another nickname, *sum of squares*. The denominator, as I say in Chapter 10, is *degrees of freedom* (df). So, the slightly different way to think of variance is

$$\text{Mean Square} = \frac{\text{Sum of Squares}}{\text{df}}$$

You can abbreviate this as

$$MS = \frac{SS}{df}$$

Now, on to solving the thorny problem. One important step is to find the mean-squares hiding in the data. Another is to understand that you use these mean-squares to estimate the variances of the populations that produced these samples. In this case, assume that those variances are equal, so you're really estimating one variance. The final step is to understand that you use these estimates to test the hypotheses I show you at the beginning of the chapter.

Three different mean-squares are inside the data in Table 12-1. Start with the whole set of 27 scores, forgetting for the moment that they're divided into three groups. Suppose that you want to use those 27 scores to calculate an estimate of the population variance. (A dicey idea, but humor me.) The mean of those 27 scores is 85. I'll call that mean the *grand mean* because it's the average of everything.

So the mean-square would be

$$\frac{(95-85)^2 + (91-85)^2 + \ldots + (73-85)^2 + (77-85)^2}{(27-1)} = 68.08$$

The denominator has 26 (27 − 1) degrees of freedom. I refer to that variance as the total variance, or in the new way of thinking about this, the MS_{Total}. It's often abbreviated as MS_T.

Here's another variance to consider. In Chapter 11, I describe the t-test for two samples with equal variances. For that test, you put together the two sample variances to create a *pooled* estimate of the population variance. The data in Table 12-1 provides three sample variances for a pooled estimate: 16.28, 14.18, and 15.64. Assuming that these numbers represent equal population variances, the pooled estimate is

$$s_p^2 = \frac{(N_1-1)s_1^2 + (N_2-1)s_2^2 + (N_3-1)s_3^2}{(N_1-1) + (N_2-1) + (N_3-1)}$$

$$= \frac{(9-1)(16.28) + (10-1)(14.18) + (8-1)(15.64)}{(9-1) + (10-1) + (8-1)} = 15.31$$

Because this pooled estimate comes from the variance within the groups, it's called MS_{Within}, or MS_W.

One more mean-square to go — the variance of the sample means around the grand mean. In this example, that means the variance in these numbers 93.44, 85.20, and 75.25 — sort of. I say "sort of" because these are means, not scores. When you deal with means, you have to take into account the number of scores that produced each mean. To do that, you multiply each squared deviation by the number of scores in that sample.

So this variance is

$$\frac{(9)(93.44-85)^2+(10)(85.20-85)^2+(8)(75.25-85)^2}{3-1}=701.34$$

The df for this variance is 2 (the number of samples − 1).

Statisticians, not known for their crispness of usage, refer to this as the variance *between* sample means. (*Among* is the correct word when you're talking about more than two items.) This variance is known as $MS_{Between}$, or MS_B.

So you now have three estimates of population variance: MS_T, MS_W, and MS_B. What do you do with them?

Remember that the original objective is to test a hypothesis about three means. According to H_0, any differences you see among the three sample means are due strictly to chance. The implication is that the variance among those means is the same as the variance of any three numbers selected at random from the population.

If you could somehow compare the variance among the means (that's MS_B, remember) with the population variance, you could see if that holds up. If only you had an estimate of the population variance that's independent of the differences among the groups, you'd be in business.

Ah . . . but you do have that estimate. You have MS_W, an estimate based on pooling the variances within the samples. Assuming that those variances represent equal population variances, this is a solid estimate. In this example, it's based on 24 degrees of freedom.

The reasoning now becomes: If MS_B is about the same as MS_W, you have evidence consistent with H_0. If MS_B is significantly larger than MS_W, you have evidence that's inconsistent with H_0. In effect, you transform these hypotheses

$H_0: \mu_1 = \mu_2 = \mu_3$

$H_1:$ Not H_0

into these

$H_0: \sigma_B^2 \le \sigma_W^2$

$H_1: \sigma_B^2 > \sigma_W^2$

Rather than perform multiple t-tests among sample means, you perform a test of the difference between two variances.

What is that test? In Chapter 11, I show you the test for hypotheses about two variances. It's called the F-test. To perform this test, you divide one variance by the other. You evaluate the result against a family of distributions called the F-distribution. Because two variances are involved, two values for degrees of freedom define each member of the family.

For this example, F has df = 2 (for the MS_B) and df = 24 (for the MS_W). Figure 12-1 shows what this member of the F family looks like. For our purposes, it's the distribution of possible f-values if H_0 is true. (See the section in Chapter 11 about visualizing F-distributions.)

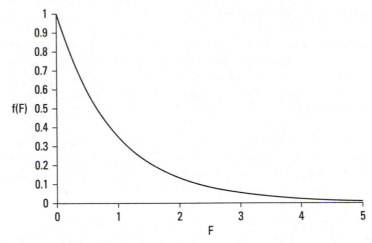

The test statistic for the example is

$$F = \frac{701.34}{15.31} = 45.82$$

What proportion of area does this value cut off in the upper tail of the F-distribution? From Figure 12-1, you can see that this proportion is microscopic, as the values on the horizontal axis only go up to 5. (And the proportion of area beyond 5 is tiny.) It's way less than .05.

This means that it's highly unlikely that differences among the means are due to chance. It means that you reject H_0.

REMEMBER

This whole procedure for testing more than two samples is called the *analysis of variance*, often abbreviated as ANOVA. In the context of an ANOVA, the denominator of an F-ratio has the generic name *error term*. The independent variable is sometimes called a *factor*. So this is a single-factor or (1-factor) ANOVA.

In this example, the factor is Training Method. Each instance of the independent variable is called a *level.* The independent variable in this example has three levels.

More complex studies have more than one factor, and each factor can have many levels.

Meaningful relationships

Take another look at the mean-squares in this example, each with its sum of squares and degrees of freedom. Before, when I calculated each mean-square for you, I didn't explicitly show you each sum of squares, but here I include them:

$$MS_B = \frac{SS_B}{df_B} = \frac{1402.68}{2} = 701.34$$

$$MS_W = \frac{SS_W}{df_W} = \frac{367.32}{24} = 15.31$$

$$MS_T = \frac{SS_T}{df_T} = \frac{1770}{26} = 68.08$$

Start with the degrees of freedom: $df_B = 2$, $df_W = 24$, and $df_T = 26$. Is it a coincidence that they add up? Hardly. It's always the case that

$$df_B + df_W = df_T$$

How about those sums of squares?

$$1402.68 + 367.32 = 1770$$

Again, this is no coincidence. In the analysis of variance, this always happens:

$$SS_B + SS_W = SS_T$$

In fact, statisticians who work with the analysis of variance speak of partitioning (read "breaking down into non-overlapping pieces") the SS_T into one portion for the SS_B and another for the SS_W, and partitioning the df_T into one amount for the df_B and another for the df_W.

ANOVA in R

In this section, I walk you through the previous section's example and show you how straightforward an analysis of variance is in R. In fact, I start at the finish line so that you can see where I'm heading.

The R function for ANOVA is `aov()`. Here's how it looks generically:

```
aov(Dependent_variable ~ Independent_variable, data)
```

In the example, the scores are the dependent variable and the method is the independent variable. So you need a 2-column data frame with *Method* in the first column and Score in the second. (This is equivalent to the "long-form" data format, which I discuss in Chapters 10 and 11.)

Start with a vector for each column in Table 12-1:

```
method1.scores <- c(95,91,89,90,99,88,96,98,95)
method2.scores <- c(83,89,85,89,81,89,90,82,84,80)
method3.scores <- c(68,75,79,74,75,81,73,77)
```

Then create a single vector that consists of all these scores:

```
Score <- c(method1.scores, method2.scores, method3.scores)
```

Next, create a vector consisting of the names of the methods, matched up against the scores. In other words, this vector has to consist of "method1" repeated nine times, followed by "method2" repeated ten times, followed by "method3" repeated eight times:

```
Method <- rep(c("method1", "method2", "method3"),
          times=c(length(method1.scores),
          length(method2.scores), length(method3.scores)))
```

The data frame is then

```
Training.frame <- data.frame(Method,Score)
```

And the ANOVA is

```
analysis <-aov(Score ~ Method,data = Training.frame)
```

For a table of the analysis, use `summary()`.

```
> summary(analysis)
            Df Sum Sq Mean Sq F value   Pr(>F)
Method       2 1402.7   701.3   45.82 6.38e-09 ***
Residuals   24  367.3    15.3
---
Signif. codes: 0 '***' 0.001 '**' 0.01 '*' 0.05 '.' 0.1 ' ' 1
```

The first column consists of Method and Residuals, which map onto Between and Within from the preceding section. A *residual,* in this context, is a score's deviation from its group mean. (I have more to say about residuals in Chapter 14.) The next columns provide degrees of freedom, SS, MS, F, and p.

The high value of F and the tiny value of p (listed here as `Pr(>F)`) tell you to reject the null hypothesis. The significance codes tell you that F is so high that you can reject the null hypothesis even if α is .0001.

Visualizing the results

One way of plotting the findings is to show them as a boxplot. Here's how to plot one in ggplot2.

The first statement maps variables to the axes:

```
ggplot(Training.frame, aes(x=Method, y=Score))
```

The next sets up the crossbars for the whiskers:

```
stat_boxplot(geom="errorbar", width =.5)
```

And the last plots the appropriate geom function:

```
geom_boxplot()
```

So these lines of R code

```
ggplot(Training.frame, aes(x=Method, y=Score))+
    stat_boxplot(geom="errorbar", width =.5) +
    geom_boxplot()
```

produce Figure 12-2.

After the ANOVA

The analysis ANOVA enables you to decide whether or not to reject H_0. After you decide to reject, then what? All you can say is that somewhere within the set of means, something is different from something else. The analysis doesn't specify what those "somethings" are.

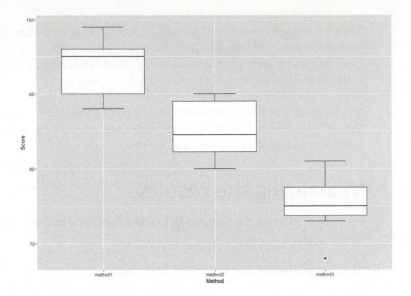

FIGURE 12-2:
Boxplot of the
sample results.

Planned comparisons

In order to get more specific, you have to do some further tests. Not only that, you have to plan those tests in advance of carrying out the ANOVA.

These post-ANOVA tests are called *planned comparisons*. Some statisticians refer to them as *a priori tests* or *contrasts*. I illustrate by following through with the example. Suppose that before you gathered the data, you had reason to believe that Method 2 would result in higher scores than Method 3 and that Method 1 would result in higher scores than Method 2 and Method 3 averaged together. In that case, you plan in advance to compare the means of those samples in the event your ANOVA-based decision is to reject H_0.

As I mention earlier, the overall analysis partitions the SS_T into the SS_B and the SS_W, and the df_T into the df_B and the df_W. Planned comparisons further partition the SS_B and the df_B. Each contrast (remember, that's another name for "planned comparison") has its own SS along with 1 df. I refer to Method 2 versus Method 3 as *Contrast1* and Method 1 versus the average of Method 2 and 3 as *Contrast2*. For this example,

$$SS_{Contrast1} + SS_{Contrast2} = SS_B$$

and

$$df_{Contrast1} + df_{Contrast2} = df_B$$

Because each SS has 1 df, it's equal to its corresponding MS. Dividing the SS for the contrast by MS_W yields an F-ratio for the contrast. The F has df=1 and df_W. If that

F cuts off less than .05 in the upper tail of its F-distribution, reject the null hypothesis for that contrast (and you can refer to the contrast as "statistically significant").

It's possible to set up a contrast between two means as an expression that involves all three of the sample means. For example, to compare Method 2 versus Method 3, I can write the difference between them as

$$(0)\bar{x}_1 + (+1)\bar{x}_2 + (-1)\bar{x}_3$$

The 0, +1, and −1 are *comparison coefficients*. I refer to them, in a general way, as c_1, c_2, and c_3. To compare Method 1 versus the average of Method 2 and Method 3, it's

$$(+2)\bar{x}_1 + (-1)\bar{x}_2 + (-1)\bar{x}_3$$

The important point is that the coefficients add up to 0. How do you use the comparison coefficients and the means to calculate a SS for a contrast? For this example, here's $SS_{Contrast1}$:

$$SS_{Contrast1} = \frac{\left((0)(93.44) + (+1)(85.20) + (-1)(75.25)\right)^2}{\frac{(0)^2}{9} + \frac{(+1)^2}{10} + \frac{(-1)^2}{8}} = 358.5$$

And here's $SS_{Contrast2}$:

$$SS_{Contrast2} = \frac{\left((+2)(93.44) + (-1)(85.20) + (-1)(75.25)\right)^2}{\frac{(2)^2}{9} + \frac{(-1)^2}{10} + \frac{(-1)^2}{8}} = 1044.2$$

In general, the formula is

$$SS_{Contrast} = \frac{\sum c_j \bar{x}_j}{\sum \left(\frac{c_j^2}{n_j}\right)}$$

in which the j subscript stands for "level of the independent variable" (for Method 1, $j=1$, for example).

For Contrast 1

$$F_{1,24} = \frac{SS_{Contrast1}}{MS_{Within}} = \frac{358.5}{15.3} = 23.42$$

and for Contrast 2

$$F_{1,24} = \frac{SS_{Contrast2}}{MS_{Within}} = \frac{1044.2}{15.3} = 68.22$$

Are these contrasts significant? Yes they are — meaning that Method 2 yields significantly higher learning than Method 3, and that Method 1 results in significantly higher learning than the average of Methods 2 and 3. You can use pf() to verify (or wait until the upcoming subsection "Contrasts in R.")

Another word about contrasts

Earlier, I say that the important thing about a contrast is that its coefficients add up to 0. Another important thing is the relationship between the coefficients in a set of contrasts. In the two contrasts I show you, the sum of the products of corresponding coefficients is 0:

$$((0)(+2)) + ((+1)(-1)) + ((-1)(-1)) = 0$$

When this happens, the contrasts are *orthogonal*. This means they have no overlapping information. It doesn't mean that other contrasts aren't possible. It's just that other contrasts would be part of a different set (or sets) of orthogonal contrasts.

The two other sets of orthogonal contrasts for this example are: (1) Method 1 versus Method 2, and Method 3 versus the average of Method 1 and Method 2; (2) Method 1 versus Method 3, and Method 2 versus the average of Method 1 and Method 3.

Contrasts in R

The objective here is to create a table of the ANOVA that shows the contrasts partitioning the SS_B and will show the associated F-ratios and p-values. It will look like this:

```
                   Df Sum Sq Mean Sq F value   Pr(>F)
Method              2 1402.7   701.3   45.82 6.38e-09 ***
  Method: 2 vs 3    1  358.5   358.5   23.42 6.24e-05 ***
  Method: 1 vs 2 & 3 1 1044.2  1044.2   68.22 1.78e-08 ***
Residuals          24  367.3    15.3
---
Signif. codes: 0 '***' 0.001 '**' 0.01 '*' 0.05 '.' 0.1 ' ' 1
```

To set up for the contrasts, you first create a matrix of the coefficients in the set of orthogonal contrasts:

```
contrasts(Training.frame$Method) <- matrix(c(0,1,-1,2,-1,-1),3,2)
```

On the left, the term inside the parentheses specifies what to contrast — the levels of the independent variable Method in the Training.frame. On the right, the matrix() function creates a matrix with the coefficients in the columns:

```
> contrasts(Training.frame$Method)
        [,1] [,2]
method1    0    2
method2    1   -1
method3   -1   -1
```

Next, you run the analysis of variance, but this time with a contrasts argument:

```
Anova.w.Contrasts <-aov(Score ~ Method,data=Training.frame,
        contrasts = contrasts(Training.frame$Method))
```

How do you create the table at the beginning of this subsection? With a summary()
statement that adds a little twist:

```
summary(Anova.w.Contrasts,split=list(Method=list("2 vs 3"= 1,
    "1 vs 2 & 3" = 2)))
```

The little twist (a little "split," actually) is in the second argument. The goal is to partition Method into two pieces — one that corresponds to the first contrast and one that corresponds to the second. You do that with split, which divides a list into the indicated number of components and reassembles the list with a name assigned to each component. In this case, the list is Method split into a list with two components. The name of each component corresponds to what's in the contrast.

Running that summary statement produces the table at the top of this subsection.

Unplanned comparisons

Things would get boring if your post-ANOVA testing is limited to comparisons you have to plan in advance. Sometimes you want to snoop around your data and see whether anything interesting reveals itself. Sometimes, something jumps out at you that you didn't anticipate.

When this happens, you can make comparisons you didn't plan on. These comparisons are called *a posteriori tests*, *post hoc tests*, or *simply unplanned comparisons*. Statisticians have come up with a wide variety of these tests, many of them with exotic names and many of them dependent on special sampling distributions.

The idea behind these tests is that you pay a price for not having planned them in advance. That price has to do with stacking the deck against rejecting H_0 for the particular comparison.

One of the best-known members of the post-hoc world is Tukey's HSD (Honest Significant Difference) test. This test performs all possible pairwise comparisons among the sample means.

Wait. What? In the earlier section "A thorny problem," I discuss why multiple pairwise t-tests don't work — if each test has $\alpha = .05$, the overall probability of a Type I error increases with the number of means.

So what's the story? The story is that Tukey's test adjusts for the number of sample means and compares the differences not to the t-distribution but to the *Studentized Range* distribution. The overall effect is to make it more difficult to reject the null hypothesis about any pairwise comparison than it would be if you compare the difference against the t-distribution. (I haven't heard multiple t-tests referred to as "Dishonestly Significant Differences," but maybe someday. . . .)

This test is easy to do in R:

```
> TukeyHSD(analysis)
  Tukey multiple comparisons of means
    95% family-wise confidence level

Fit: aov(formula = Score ~ Method, data = Training.frame)

$Method
                     diff        lwr        upr     p adj
method2-method1  -8.244444 -12.73337  -3.755523 0.0003383
method3-method1 -18.194444 -22.94172 -13.447166 0.0000000
method3-method2  -9.950000 -14.58423  -5.315769 0.0000481
```

The table shows each pairwise comparison along with the difference, lower and upper 95 percent confidence limits, and adjusted probability. Each probability is way lower than .05, so the conclusion is that each difference is statistically significant.

Another Kind of Hypothesis, Another Kind of Test

The preceding ANOVA works with independent samples. As Chapter 11 explains, sometimes you work with matched samples. For example, sometimes a person provides data in a number of different conditions. In this section, I introduce the ANOVA you use when you have more than two matched samples.

This type of ANOVA is called *repeated measures*. You'll see it called other names, too, like *randomized blocks* or *within subjects*.

Working with repeated measures ANOVA

To show how this works, I extend the example from Chapter 11. In that example, ten men participate in a weight-loss program. Table 12-3 shows their data over a three-month period.

TABLE 12-3 ## Data for the Weight-Loss Example

Person	Before	One Month	Two Months	Three Months	Mean
Al	198	194	191	188	192.75
Bill	201	203	200	196	200.00
Charlie	210	200	192	188	197.50
Dan	185	183	180	178	181.50
Ed	204	200	195	191	197.50
Fred	156	153	150	145	151.00
Gary	167	166	167	166	166.50
Harry	197	197	195	192	195.25
Irv	220	215	209	205	212.25
Jon	186	184	179	175	181.00
Mean	192.4	189.5	185.8	182.4	187.525

Is the program effective? This question calls for a hypothesis test:

H_0: $\mu_{Before} = \mu_1 = \mu_2 = \mu_3$

H_1: Not H_0

Once again, you set $\alpha = .05$

As in the previous ANOVA, start with the variances in the data. The MS_T is the variance in all 40 scores from the grand mean, which is 187.525:

$$MS_T = \frac{(198-187.525)^2 + (201-187.525)^2 + \ldots + (175-187.525)^2}{(40-1)} = 318.20$$

The people participating in the weight-loss program also supply variance. Each one's overall mean (his average over the four measurements) varies from the grand mean. Because these data are in the rows, I call this MS_{Rows}:

$$MS_{Rows} = \frac{(192.75 - 187.525)^2 + (200 - 187.525)^2 + \ldots + (181 - 187.525)^2}{(10 - 1)} = 1292.41$$

The means of the columns also vary from the grand mean:

$$MS_{Columns} = \frac{(192.4 - 187.525)^2 + (189.5 - 187.525)^2 + (185.8 - 187.525)^2 + (182.4 - 187.525)^2}{(4 - 1)}$$
$$= 189.69$$

One more source of variance is in the data. Think of it as the variance left over after you pull out the variance in the rows and the variance in the columns from the total variance. Actually, it's more correct to say that it's the sum of squares that's left over when you subtract the SS_{Rows} and the $SS_{Columns}$ from the SS_T.

This variance is called MS_{Error}. As I say earlier, in the ANOVA the denominator of an F is called an *error term*. So the word *error* here gives you a hint that this MS is a denominator for an F.

To calculate MS_{Error}, you use the relationships among the sums of squares and among the df.

$$MS_{Error} = \frac{SS_{Error}}{df_{Error}} = \frac{SS_T - SS_{Rows} - SS_{Columns}}{df_T - df_{Rows} - df_{Columns}} = \frac{209.175}{27} = 7.75$$

Here's another way to calculate the df_{Error}:

$$df_{Error} = (\text{number of rows - 1})(\text{number of columns - 1})$$

To perform the hypothesis test, you calculate the F:

$$F = \frac{MS_{Columns}}{MS_{Error}} = \frac{189.69}{7.75} = 24.49$$

With 3 and 27 degrees of freedom, the critical F for $\alpha = .05$ is 2.96. (Use qf( ) to verify.) The calculated F is larger than the critical F, so the decision is to reject H_0.

What about an F involving MS_{Rows}? That one doesn't figure into H_0 for this example. If you find a significant F, all it shows is that people are different from one another with respect to weight and that doesn't tell you much.

Repeated measures ANOVA in R

To set the stage for the repeated measures analysis, put the columns of Table 12-3 into vectors:

```
Person <-c("Al", "Bill", "Charlie", "Dan", "Ed", "Fred",
          "Gary","Harry","Irv","Jon")
Before <- c(198,201,210,185,204,156,167,197,220,186)
OneMonth <- c(194,203,200,183,200,153,166,197,215,184)
TwoMonths <- c(191,200,192,180,195,150,167,195,209,179)
ThreeMonths <- c(188,196,188,178,191,145,166,192,205,175)
```

Then create a data frame:

```
Weight.frame <- data.frame(Person, Before, OneMonth,
            TwoMonths, ThreeMonths)
```

The data frame looks like this:

```
> Weight.frame
    Person Before OneMonth TwoMonths ThreeMonths
1       Al    198      194       191         188
2     Bill    201      203       200         196
3  Charlie    210      200       192         188
4      Dan    185      183       180         178
5       Ed    204      200       195         191
6     Fred    156      153       150         145
7     Gary    167      166       167         166
8    Harry    197      197       195         192
9      Irv    220      215       209         205
10     Jon    186      184       179         175
```

It's in wide format, and you have to reshape it. With the reshape2 package installed (on the Packages tab, select the check box next to reshape2), melt the data into long format:

```
Weight.frame.melt <- melt(Weight.frame,id="Person")
```

Next, assign column names to the melted data frame:

```
colnames(Weight.frame.melt) = c("Person","Time","Weight")
```

And now, the first six rows of the new data frame are

```
> head(Weight.frame.melt)
    Person   Time Weight
1       Al Before    198
2     Bill Before    201
3  Charlie Before    210
4      Dan Before    185
5       Ed Before    204
6     Fred Before    156
```

In addition to `Person`, you now have `Time` as an independent variable.

I'm going to use R as a teaching tool: To give you an idea of how this analysis works, I'll start by pretending that it's an independent samples analysis, like the first one in this chapter. Then I'll run it as a repeated measures analysis so that you can see the differences and perhaps better understand what a repeated measures analysis does.

As independent samples:

```
> ind.anova <- aov(Weight ~ Time, data=Weight.frame.melt)
> summary(ind.anova)
            Df Sum Sq Mean Sq F value Pr(>F)
Time         3    569   189.7   0.577  0.634
Residuals   36  11841   328.9
```

This analysis shows no significant differences among the levels of the `Time`. The key is to tease out the effects of having each row represent the data from one person. That will break down the SS for `Residuals` into two components — one SS for `Person` (which has nine degrees of freedom) and another SS that has the remaining 27 degrees of freedom. Divide that second SS by its degrees of freedom, and you have the MS_{Error} I mention earlier (although R doesn't refer to it that way).

Here's how to get that done:

```
rm.anova <- aov(Weight ~ Time + Error(Person/Time),
          data = Weight.frame.melt)
```

The new term indicates that `Weight` depends not only on `Time` but also on `Person`, and that each `Person` experiences all levels of `Time`. The effect of `Time` — decreasing body weight over the four levels of `Time` — is evident within each `Person`. (It's easier to see that in the wide format than in the long.)

REMEMBER

In some fields, the word *subject* means *person:* That's why a repeated measures analysis is also called a *within-subjects* analysis, as I point out earlier.

And now for the table

```
> summary(rm.anova)

Error: Person
          Df Sum Sq Mean Sq F value Pr(>F)
Residuals  9  11632    1292

Error: Person:Time
          Df Sum Sq Mean Sq F value  Pr(>F)
Time       3  569.1  189.69   24.48 7.3e-08 ***
Residuals 27  209.2    7.75

Signif. codes:  0 '***' 0.001 '**' 0.01 '*' 0.05 '.' 0.1 ' ' 1
```

Now the analysis shows the significant effect of `Time`.

Visualizing the results

One way to visualize the results is to plot the mean weight loss on the y-axis and the month (0, 1, 2, 3) on the x-axis. Notice I use 0–3 to represent the levels of `Time` (Before, OneMonth, TwoMonths, ThreeMonths).

Figure 12-3 shows the plot, along with the standard error of the mean (reflected in the error bars).

The foundation for the plot is a data frame that holds time (for convenience, as a numerical variable), mean weight, and standard error:

```
time <- c(0,1,2,3)

mean.weight <- c(mean(Before),mean(OneTime),
        mean(TwoTimes),mean(ThreeTimes))
```

```
se.weight <- c(sd(Before), sd(OneTime), sd(TwoTimes),
        sd(ThreeTimes))/sqrt(length(Person))
```

```
wt.means.frame <- data.frame(time,mean.weight,se.weight)
```

```
> wt.means.frame
  time mean.weight se.weight
```

1	0	192.4	6.144917
2	1	189.5	5.856146
3	2	185.8	5.466667
4	3	182.4	5.443038

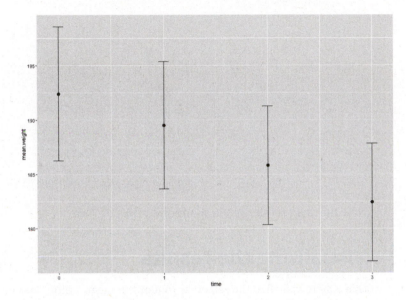

FIGURE 12-3:
The means and
standard errors
for the weight-
loss example.

Plotting in ggplot2:

```
ggplot(wt.means.frame,aes(x=time,y=mean.weight)) +
    geom_point(size=3)+
    geom_errorbar(aes(ymin=mean.weight-se.weight,
            ymax=mean.weight+se.weight),width=.1)
```

The first statement maps the independent variable into the x-axis, and the dependent variable into the y-axis. The second statement specifies a point as the geometric object and sets its size. The third statement gives the boundaries and size for the error-bars.

Getting Trendy

In situations like the one in the weight-loss example, you have an independent variable that's quantitative — its levels are numbers (0 months, 1 month, 2 months, 3 months). Not only that, but in this case, the intervals are equal.

With that kind of an independent variable, it's often a good idea to look for trends in the data rather than just plan comparisons among means. As Figure 12-3 shows, the means in the weight-loss example seem to fall along a line.

Trend analysis is the statistical procedure that examines that pattern. The objective is to see whether the pattern contributes to the significant differences among the means.

A trend can be linear, as it apparently is in this example, or nonlinear (in which the means fall on a curve). The two nonlinear types of curves for four means are called *quadratic* and *cubic*. If the means show a quadratic trend, they align in a pattern that shows one change of direction. Figure 12-4 shows what I mean.

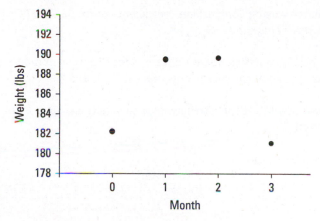

FIGURE 12-4:
A quadratic trend with four means.

If the means show a cubic trend, they align in a pattern that shows two changes of direction. Figure 12-5 shows what a cubic trend looks like.

The three components are orthogonal, so

$$SS_{Linear} + SS_{Quadratic} + SS_{Cubic} = SS_{Time}$$

and

$$df_{Linear} + df_{Quadratic} + df_{Cubic} = df_{Time}$$

To analyze a trend, you use comparison coefficients — those numbers you use in contrasts. You use them in a slightly different way than you did before. The formula for computing a SS for a trend component is

$$SS_{Component} = \frac{N\left(\sum c\bar{x}\right)^2}{\sum c^2}$$

In this formula, N is the number of people and c represents the coefficients.

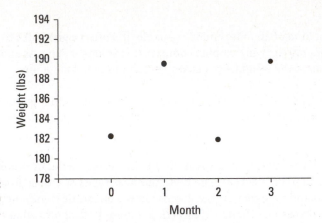

FIGURE 12-5:
A cubic trend with
four means.

So you start by using comparison coefficients to find a sum of squares for linear trend. I abbreviate that as SS_{Linear}.

The comparison coefficients are different for different numbers of samples. For four samples, the linear coefficients are −3, −1, 1, and 3.

TIP

The easiest way to get the coefficients is to look them up in a stat textbook or on the Internet!

For this example, the SS_{Linear} is

$$SS_{Linear} = \frac{N(\sum c\bar{x})^2}{\sum c^2} = \frac{10\left[(-3)(192.4)+(-1)(189.5)+(1)(185.8)+(3)(182.4)\right]^2}{(-3)^2+(-1)^2+(3)^2+(1)^2} = 567.845$$

After you calculate SS_{Linear}, you divide it by df_{Linear} to produce MS_{Linear}. This is extremely easy because df_{Linear} = 1. Divide MS_{Linear} by MS_{Error} and you have an F. If that F is higher than the critical value of F with df = 1 and df_{Error} at your α, then weight is decreasing in a linear way over the period of the weight-loss program. The F-ratio here is

$$F = \frac{MS_{Linear}}{MS_{Error}} = \frac{567.85}{7.75} = 73.30$$

The critical value for F with 1 and 27 degrees of freedom and α = .05 is 4.21. Because the calculated value is larger than the critical value, statisticians would say the data shows a *significant linear component.* This, of course, verifies what you see in Figure 12-3.

The linear component of SS_{Time} is so large that the other two components are very small. I'll walk you through the computations anyway.

The coefficients for the quadratic component are 1,–1,–1,1. So the $SS_{Quadratic}$ is

$$SS_{Quadratic} = \frac{N\left(\sum c\bar{x}\right)^2}{\sum c^2} = \frac{10\left[(1)(192.4)+(-1)(189.5)+(-1)(185.8)+(1)(182.4)\right]^2}{(1)^2+(-1)^2+(-1)^2+(1)^2} = 0.6$$

The coefficients for the cubic component are –1,3,–3,1, and the SS_{Cubic} is

$$SS_{Cubic} = \frac{N\left(\sum c\bar{x}\right)^2}{\sum c^2} = \frac{10\left[(-1)(192.4)+(3)(189.5)+(-3)(185.8)+(1)(182.4)\right]^2}{(-1)^2+(3)^2+(-3)^2+(1)^2} = 0.6$$

Rather than complete the final calculations to get the microscopic F–ratios, I'll let R do the work for you in the next subsection.

A LITTLE MORE ON TREND

Linear, quadratic, and cubic are as far as you can go with four means. With five means, you can look for those three plus a *quartic component* (three direction changes), and with six you can try to scope out all the preceding plus a *quintic component* (four direction changes). What do the coefficients look like?

For five means, they're:

Linear: –2, –1, 0, 1, 2

Quadratic: 2, –1, –2, –1, 2

Cubic: -1, 2, 0, –2, 1

Quartic: 1, –4, 6, –4, 1

And for six means. They're:

Linear: –5, –3, –1, 1, 3, 5

Quadratic: 5, –1, –4, –4, –1, 5

Cubic: –5, 7, 4, –4, –7, 5

Quartic: 1, –3, 2, 2, –3, 1

Quintic: –1, 5, –10, 10, –5, 1

I could go on with more means, coefficients, and exotic component names (hextic? septic?), but enough already. This should hold you for a while.

Trend Analysis in R

I treat this analysis pretty much the same way as contrasts for the independent samples example. I begin by creating a matrix of the coefficients for the three trend components:

```
contrasts(Weight.frame.melt$Time) <- matrix(c(-3,-1,1,3,1,-1,
       -1,1,-1,3,-3,1), 4, 3)
```

Then I run the ANOVA, adding the contrasts argument:

```
rm.anova <- aov(Weight ~ Time + Error(factor(Person)/Time),
        data=Weight.frame.melt,
        contrasts = contrasts(Weight.frame.melt$Time))
```

Finally, I apply summary() (including the split of Time into three components) to print the table of the analysis:

```
summary(rm.anova,split=list(Time=list("Linear" =1,
        "Quadratic"=2,"Cubic" =3)))
```

Running this statement produces this table:

```
Error: factor(Person)
          Df Sum Sq Mean Sq F value Pr(>F)
Residuals  9  11632    1292

Error: factor(Person):Time
                Df Sum Sq Mean Sq F value   Pr(>F)
Time             3  569.1   189.7  24.485 7.30e-08 ***
  Time: Linear   1  567.8   567.8  73.297 3.56e-09 ***
  Time: Quadratic 1    0.6     0.6   0.081    0.779
  Time: Cubic    1    0.6     0.6   0.078    0.782
Residuals       27  209.2     7.7
---
Signif. codes: 0 '***' 0.001 '**' 0.01 '*' 0.05 '.' 0.1 ' ' 1
```

Once again, you can see the overwhelming linearity of the trend — just as we would expect from Figure 12-3.

IN THIS CHAPTER

» Working with two variables

» Working with replications

» Understanding interactions

» Mixing variable types

» Working with multiple dependent variables

Chapter **13**

More Complicated Testing

I n Chapter 11, I show you how to test hypotheses with two samples. In Chapter 12, I show you how to test hypotheses when you have more than two samples. The common thread in both chapters is one independent variable (also called a *factor*).

Many times, you have to test the effects of more than one factor. In this chapter, I show how to analyze two factors within the same set of data. Several types of situations are possible, and I describe R functions that deal with each one.

Cracking the Combinations

Imagine that a company has two methods of presenting its training information: One is via a person who presents the information orally, and the other is via a text document. Imagine also that the information is presented in either a humorous way or a technical way. I refer to the first factor as Presentation Method and to the second as Presentation Style.

Combining the two levels of Presentation Method with the two levels of Presentation Style gives four combinations. The company randomly assigns 4 people to each combination, for a total of 16 people. After providing the training, they test the 16 people on their comprehension of the material.

Figure 13-1 shows the combinations, the four comprehension scores within each combination, and summary statistics for the combinations, rows, and columns.

Presentation Style

	Humorous		Technical	
Spoken	Spoken and Humorous	57 56 60 64	Spoken and Technical	22 21 29 25
	Mean = 59.25 Variance = 12.92		Mean = 24.25 Variance = 12.92		Mean = 41.75
Text	Text and Humorous	33 25 28 31	Text and Technical	66 65 71 72
	Mean = 29.25 Variance = 12.25		Mean = 68.50 Variance = 12.33		Mean = 48.88
	Mean = 44.25		Mean = 46.38		Grand Mean = 44.31

Presentation Method (row label on left of table)

FIGURE 13-1: Combining the levels of Presentation Method with the levels of Presentation Style.

REMEMBER

With each of two levels of one factor combined with each of two levels of the other factor, this kind of study is called a 2 X 2 *factorial* design.

Here are the hypotheses:

H_0: $\mu_{Spoken} = \mu_{Text}$

H_1: Not H_0

and

H_0: $\mu_{Humorous} = \mu_{Technical}$

H_1: Not H_0

Because the two presentation methods (Spoken and Text) are in the rows, I refer to Presentation Type as the *row factor*. The two presentation styles (Humorous and Technical) are in the columns, so Presentation Style is the *column factor*.

Interactions

When you have rows and columns of data and you're testing hypotheses about the row factor and the column factor, you have an additional consideration. Namely, you have to be concerned about the row–column combinations. Do the combinations result in peculiar effects?

For the example I present, it's possible that combining Spoken and Text with Humorous and Technical yields an unexpected result. In fact, you can see that in the data in Figure 13-1: For Spoken presentation, the Humorous style produces a higher average than the Technical style. For Text presentation, the Humorous style produces a lower average than the Technical style.

REMEMBER

A situation like that is called an *interaction*. In formal terms, an interaction occurs when the levels of one factor affect the levels of the other factor differently. The label for the interaction is row factor × column factor, so for this example, that's Method × Type.

The hypotheses for this are

H_0: Presentation Method does not interact with Presentation Style

H_1: Not H_0

The analysis

The statistical analysis is, once again, an analysis of variance (ANOVA). As is the case with the ANOVAs I show you earlier, it depends on the variances in the data. It's called a *two-factor* ANOVA, or a *two-way* ANOVA.

The first variance is the total variance, labeled MS_T. That's the variance of all 16 scores around their mean (the grand mean), which is 44.81:

$$MS_T = \frac{(57-45.31)^2 + (56-45.31)^2 + \ldots + (72-45.31)^2}{16-1} = \frac{5885.43}{15} = 392.36$$

The denominator tells you that df = 15 for MS_T.

The next variance comes from the row factor. That's MS_{Method}, and it's the variance of the row means around the grand mean:

$$MS_{Method} = \frac{(8)(41.75-45.31)^2 + (8)(48.88-45.31)^2}{2-1} = \frac{203.06}{1} = 203.06$$

The 8 in the equation multiplies each squared deviation because you have to take into account the number of scores that produced each row mean. The df for MS_{Method} is the number of rows − 1, which is 1.

Similarly, the variance for the column factor is

$$MS_{Style} = \frac{(8)(43.25 - 45.31)^2 + (8)(46.38 - 45.31)^2}{2 - 1} = \frac{18.06}{1} = 18.06$$

The df for MS_{Style} is 1 (the number of columns − 1).

Another variance is the pooled estimate based on the variances within the four row–column combinations. It's called the MS_{Within}, or MS_W. (For details on MS_W and pooled estimates, see Chapter 12.). For this example,

$$MS_W = \frac{(4-1)(12.92) + (4-1)(12.92) + (4-1)(12.25) + (4-1)(12.33)}{(4-1) + (4-1) + (4-1) + (4-1)}$$

$$= \frac{151.25}{12} = 12.60$$

This one is the error term (the denominator) for each F you calculate. Its denominator tells you that df = 12 for this MS.

The last variance comes from the interaction between the row factor and the column factor. In this example, it's labeled $MS_{Method \times Type}$. You can calculate this in a couple of ways. The easiest way is to take advantage of this general relationship:

$$SS_{Row \times Column} = SS_T - SS_{Row\ Factor} - SS_{Column\ Factor} - SS_W$$

And this one:

$$df_{Row \times Column} = df_T - df_{Row\ Factor} - df_{Column\ Factor} - df_W$$

Another way to calculate this is

$$df_{Row \times Column} = (\text{number of rows - 1})(\text{number of columns - 1})$$

The MS is

$$MS_{Row \times Column} = \frac{SS_{Row \times Column}}{df_{Row \times Column}}$$

For this example,

$$MS_{Method \times Style} = \frac{SS_{Method \times Style}}{df_{Method \times Style}} = \frac{5885.43 - 203.06 - 18.06 - 151.25}{15 - 12 - 1 - 1}$$

$$= \frac{5513.06}{1} = 5513.06$$

To test the hypotheses, you calculate three Fs:

$$F = \frac{MS_{Style}}{MS_W} = \frac{18.06}{12.60} = 1.43$$

$$F = \frac{MS_{Method}}{MS_W} = \frac{203.06}{12.60} = 16.12$$

$$F = \frac{MS_{Method \times Style}}{MS_W} = \frac{5513.06}{12.60} = 437.54$$

For df = 1 and 12, the critical F at α = .05 is 4.75. (You can use $qf()$ to verify). The decision is to reject H_0 for the Presentation Method and the Method X Style inter-action, and to not reject H_0 for the Presentation Style.

REMEMBER

It's possible, of course, to have more than two levels of each factor. It's also possible to have more than two factors. In that case, things (like interactions) become way more complex.

Two-Way ANOVA in R

As in any analysis, the first step is to get the data in shape, and in R that means getting the data into long format.

Start with vectors for the scores in each of the columns in Figure 13-1:

```
humorous <- c(57,56,60,64,33,25,28,31)
technical <- c(22,21,29,25,66,65,71,72)
```

Then combine them to produce a vector of all scores:

```
Score = c(humorous,technical)
```

Next, create vectors for Method and for Style:

```
Method =rep(c("spoken","text"),each=4,2)
Style =rep(c("humorous","technical"),each=8)
```

And then put everything into a data frame:

```
pres.frame <-data.frame(Method,Style,Score)
```

which looks like this:

```
> pres.frame
   Method      Style Score
1  spoken   humorous    57
2  spoken   humorous    56
3  spoken   humorous    60
4  spoken   humorous    64
5    text   humorous    33
6    text   humorous    25
7    text   humorous    28
8    text   humorous    31
9  spoken  technical    22
10 spoken  technical    21
11 spoken  technical    29
12 spoken  technical    25
13   text  technical    66
14   text  technical    65
15   text  technical    71
16   text  technical    72
```

And here's the two-way analysis of variance:

```
> two.way <- aov(Score ~ Style*Method,
                 data = pres.frame)
```

The `Style*Method` expression indicates that all levels of `Style` (humorous and technical) combine with all levels of `Method` (spoken and text).

Here's the ANOVA table:

```
> summary(two.way)
             Df Sum Sq Mean Sq F value   Pr(>F)
Style         1     18      18   1.433  0.25438
Method        1    203     203  16.111  0.00172 **
Style:Method  1   5513    5513 437.400 8.27e-11 ***
Residuals    12    151      13
---
Signif. codes: 0 '***' 0.001 '**' 0.01 '*' 0.05 '.' 0.1 ' ' 1
```

Again, the f-values and p-values indicate rejection of the null hypothesis for `Method` and for the `Style X Method` interaction, but not for `Style`.

With just two levels of each factor, no post-analysis tests are necessary to explore a significant result.

Visualizing the two-way results

The best way to show the results of a study like this one is with a grouped bar plot that shows the means and the standard errors. The foundation for the plot is a data frame that holds these statistics for each combination of levels of the independent variables:

```
> mse.frame
  Method      Style  Mean        SE
1 spoken   humorous 59.25 1.796988
2   text   humorous 29.25 1.750000
3 spoken technical 24.25 1.796988
4   text technical 68.50 1.755942
```

To create this data frame, start by creating four vectors:

```
Score.spk.hum <- with(pres.frame, Score[Method=="spoken" &
        Style=="humorous"])
Score.txt.hum <- with(pres.frame, Score[Method=="text" &
        Style=="humorous"])
Score.spk.tec <- with(pres.frame, Score[Method=="spoken" &
        Style=="technical"])
Score.txt.tec <- with(pres.frame, Score[Method=="text" &
        Style=="technical"])
```

Then concatentate the vector means into another vector:

```
mean.Scores <- c(mean(Score.spk.hum), mean(Score.txt.hum),
        mean(Score.spk.tec), mean(Score.txt.tec))
```

and concatenate the standard errors into still another vector:

```
se.Scores <- c(sd(Score.spk.hum), sd(Score.txt.hum), sd(Score.
        spk.tec), sd(Score.txt.tec))/2
```

In dividing by 2, I cheated a bit on that last one. Each combination consists of four scores, and the square root of 4 is 2.

Create a vector for the levels of Method and another for the levels of Style:

```
mse.Method =rep(c("spoken","text"),2)
mse.Style =rep(c("humorous","technical"),each=2)
```

Then create the data frame:

```
mse.frame <- data.frame(mse.Method,mse.Style,mean.Scores,se.Scores)
```

Finally, make the column-names a little nicer-looking:

```
colnames(mse.frame)=c("Method","Style","Mean","SE")
```

On to the visualization. In ggplot2, begin with a `ggplot()` statement that maps the components of the data to the components of the graph:

```
ggplot(mse.frame,aes(x=Method,y=Mean,fill=Style))
```

Now use a `geom_bar` that takes the given mean as its statistic:

```
geom_bar(stat = "identity", position = "dodge",
      color = "black", width = .5)
```

The `position` argument sets up this plot as a grouped bar plot, the `color` argument specifies "black" as the border color, and `width` sets up a size for nice-looking bars. You might experiment a bit to see whether another width is more to your liking.

If you don't change the colors of the bars, they appear as light red and light blue, which are pleasant enough but would be indistinguishable on a black-and-white page. Here's how to change the colors:

```
scale_fill_grey(start = 0,end = .8)
```

In the grey scale, 0 corresponds to black and 1 to white. Finally, the `geom_errorbar` adds the bars for the standard errors:

```
geom_errorbar(aes(ymin=Mean,ymax=Mean+SE), width=.2,
            position=position_dodge(width=.5))
```

Using `Mean` as the value of `ymin` ensures that you plot only the upper error bar, which is what you typically see in published bar plots. The `position` argument uses the `position_dodge()` function to center the error bars.

So, these lines of code

```
ggplot(mse.frame,aes(x=Method,y=Mean,fill=Style)) +
  geom_bar(stat = "identity", position = "dodge",
          color = "black", width = .5)+
```

```
scale_fill_grey(start = 0,end = .8)+
geom_errorbar(aes(ymin=Mean,ymax=Mean+SE), width=.2,
        position=position_dodge(width=.5))
```

produce Figure 13-2.

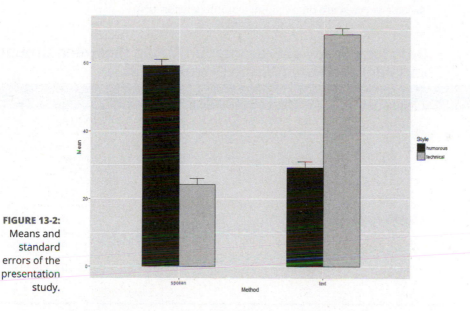

FIGURE 13-2:
Means and
standard
errors of the
presentation
study.

This graph clearly shows the `Method X Style` interaction. For the spoken presentation, humorous is more effective than technical, and it's the reverse for the text presentation.

Two Kinds of Variables . . . at Once

What happens when you have a Between Groups variable and a Within Groups variable . . . at the same time? How can that happen?

Very easily. Here's an example. Suppose you want to study the effects of presentation media on the reading speeds of fourth-graders. You randomly assign the fourth-graders (I'll call them *subjects*) to read either books or e-readers. So "Medium" is the Between Groups variable.

Let's say you're also interested in the effects of font. So you assign each subject to read each of these fonts: Haettenschweiler, Arial, and Calibri. (I've never seen a document in Haettenschweiler, but it's my favorite font because "Haettenschweiler" is fun to say. Try it. Am I right?) Because each subject reads all the fonts, "Font" is the Within Groups variable. For completeness, you have to randomly order the fonts for each subject.

Table 13-1 shows data that might result from a study like this. The dependent variable is the score on a reading comprehension test.

TABLE 13-1 **Data for a Study of Presentation Media (Between Groups variable) and Font (Within Groups variable)**

Medium	Subject	Haettenschweiler	Arial	Calibri
Book	Alice	48	40	38
	Brad	55	43	45
	Chris	46	45	44
	Donna	61	53	53
e-reader	Eddie	43	45	47
	Fran	50	52	54
	Gil	56	57	57
	Harriet	53	53	55

REMEMBER

Because this kind of analysis mixes a Between Groups variable with a Within Groups variable, it's called a *Mixed ANOVA*.

To show you how the analysis works, I present the kind of table that results from a Mixed ANOVA. It's a bit more complete than the output of an ANOVA in R, but bear with me. Table 13-2 shows it to you in a generic way. It's categorized into a set of sources that make up Between Groups variability and a set of sources that make up Within Groups (also known as Repeated Measures) variability.

In the Between category, A is the name of the Between Groups variable. (In the example, that's Medium.) Read "S/A" as "Subjects within A." This just says that the people in one level of A are different from the people in the other levels of A.

In the Within category, B is the name of the Within Groups variable. (In the example, that's Font.) A X B is the interaction of the two variables. B X S/A is something like the B variable interacting with subjects within A. As you can see, anything associated with B falls into the Within Groups category.

TABLE 13-2

The ANOVA Table for the Mixed ANOVA

Source	SS	df	MS	F
Between	$SS_{Between}$	$df_{Between}$		
A	SS_A	df_A	SS_A/df_A	$MS_A/MS_{S/A}$
S/A	$SS_{S/A}$	$df_{S/A}$	$SS_{S/A}/df_{S/A}$	
Within	SS_{Within}	df_{Within}		
B	SS_B	df_B	SS_B/df_B	$MS_B/MS_{B \times S/A}$
A X B	$SS_{A \times B}$	$df_{A \times B}$	$SS_{A \times B}/df_{A \times B}$	$MS_{A \times B}/MS_{B \times S/A}$
B X S/A	$SS_{B \times S/A}$	$df_{B \times S/A}$	$SS_{B \times S/A}/df_{B \times S/A}$	
Total	SS_{Total}	df_{Total}		

The first thing to note is the three F-ratios. The first one tests for differences among the levels of A, the second for differences among the levels of B, and the third for the interaction of the two. Notice also that the denominator for the first F-ratio is different from the denominator for the other two. This happens more and more as ANOVAs increase in complexity.

Next, it's important to be aware of some relationships. At the top level:

$$SS_{Between} + SS_{Within} = SS_{Total}$$

$$df_{Between} + df_{Within} = df_{Total}$$

The Between component breaks down further:

$$SS_A + SS_{S/A} = SS_{Between}$$

$$df_A + df_{S/A} = df_{Between}$$

The Within component breaks down, too:

$$SS_B + SS_{A \times B} + SS_{B \times S/A} = SS_{Within}$$

$$df_B + df_{A \times B} + df_{B \times S/A} = df_{Within}$$

REMEMBER

It's possible to have more than one Between Groups factor and more than one repeated measure in a study.

On to the analysis. . . .

Mixed ANOVA in R

First, I show you how to use the data from Table 13-1 to build a data frame in long format. When finished, it looks like this:

```
> mixed.frame
      Medium              Font Subject Score
1       Book Haettenschweiler   Alice    48
2       Book Haettenschweiler    Brad    55
3       Book Haettenschweiler   Chris    46
4       Book Haettenschweiler   Donna    61
5       Book            Arial   Alice    40
6       Book            Arial    Brad    43
7       Book            Arial   Chris    45
8       Book            Arial   Donna    53
9       Book          Calibri   Alice    38
10      Book          Calibri    Brad    45
11      Book          Calibri   Chris    44
12      Book          Calibri   Donna    53
13  E-reader Haettenschweiler   Eddie    43
14  E-reader Haettenschweiler    Fran    50
15  E-reader Haettenschweiler     Gil    56
16  E-reader Haettenschweiler  Harriet   53
17  E-reader            Arial   Eddie    45
18  E-reader            Arial    Fran    52
19  E-reader            Arial     Gil    57
20  E-reader            Arial  Harriet   53
21  E-reader          Calibri   Eddie    47
22  E-reader          Calibri    Fran    54
23  E-reader          Calibri     Gil    57
24  E-reader          Calibri  Harriet   55
```

I begin with a vector for the Book scores and a vector for the e-reader scores:

```
BkScores <- c(48,55,46,61,40,43,45,53,38,45,44,53)
ErScores <- c(43,50,56,53,45,52,57,53,47,54,57,55)
```

Then I combine them into a vector:

```
Score <-c(BkScores,ErScores)
```

I complete a similar process for the subjects: one vector for the Book subjects and another for the e-reader subjects. Note that I have to repeat each list three times:

```
BkSubjects <- rep(c("Alice","Brad","Chris","Donna"),3)
ErSubjects <- rep(c("Eddie","Fran","Gil","Harriet"),3)
```

Then I combine the two:

```
Subject <- c(BkSubjects,ErSubjects)
```

Next up is a vector for Book versus e-reader, and note that I repeat that list 12 times:

```
Medium <- rep(c("Book","E-reader"),each=12)
```

The vector for Font is a bit tricky. I have to repeat each font name four times and then repeat *that* again:

```
Font <- rep(c("Haettenschweiler","Arial","Calibri"),
            each=4,2)
```

I can now create the data frame:

```
mixed.frame <-data.frame(Medium,Font,Subject,Score)
```

The analysis is

```
mixed.anova <- aov(Score ~ Medium*Font + Error(Subject/Font),
            data=mixed.frame)
```

The arguments show that Score depends on Medium and Font and that Font is repeated throughout each Subject.

To see the table:

```
> summary(mixed.anova)

Error: Subject
          Df Sum Sq Mean Sq F value Pr(>F)
Medium     1  108.4  108.37   1.227   0.31
Residuals  6  529.9   88.32
```

```
Error: Subject:Font
             Df Sum Sq Mean Sq F value   Pr(>F)
Font          2  40.08   20.04   5.681 0.018366 *
Medium:Font   2 120.25   60.13  17.043 0.000312 ***
Residuals    12  42.33    3.53
---
Signif. codes: 0 '***' 0.001 '**' 0.01 '*' 0.05 '.' 0.1 ' ' 1
```

You can reject the null hypothesis about Font and about the interaction of Medium and Font, but not about Medium.

Visualizing the Mixed ANOVA results

You use ggplot() to create a bar plot of the means and standard errors. Begin by creating this data frame, which contains the necessary information:

```
> mse.frame
    Medium          Font  Mean       SE
1     Book Haettenschweiler 52.50 3.427827
2     Book          Arial 45.25 2.780138
3     Book         Calibri 45.00 3.082207
4 E-reader Haettenschweiler 50.50 2.783882
5 E-reader          Arial 51.75 2.495830
6 E-reader         Calibri 53.25 2.174665
```

To create this data frame, follow the same steps as in the earlier "Visualizing the two-way results" section, with appropriate changes. The ggplot code is also the same as in that earlier section, with changes to variable names:

```
ggplot(mse.frame,aes(x=Medium,y=Mean,fill=Font)) +
  geom_bar(stat = "identity", position =
           "dodge",color="black",width = .5) +
  scale_fill_grey(start = 0,end = .8) +
  geom_errorbar(aes(ymin=Mean,ymax=Mean+SE),
           width=.2,position=position_dodge(width=.5))
```

The result is Figure 13-3. The figure shows the Between Groups variable on the x-axis and levels of the repeated measure in the bars — but that's just my preference. You might prefer vice versa. In this layout, the different ordering of the heights of the bars from Book to e-reader reflects the interaction.

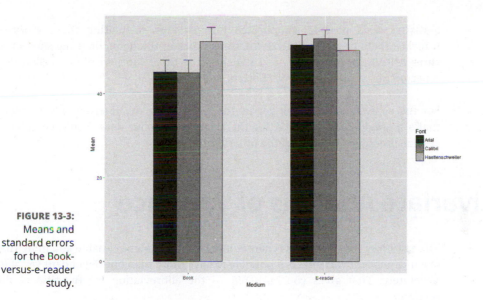

FIGURE 13-3:
Means and standard errors for the Book-versus-e-reader study.

After the Analysis

As I point out in Chapter 12, a significant result in an ANOVA tells you that an effect is lurking somewhere in the data. Post-analysis tests tell you where. Two types of tests are possible: planned or unplanned. Chapter 12 provides the details.

In this example, the Between Groups variable has only two levels. For this reason, if the result is statistically significant, no further test would be necessary. The Within Groups variable, Font, is significant. Ordinarily, the test would proceed as described in Chapter 12. In this case, however, the interaction between Media and Font necessitates a different path.

With the interaction, post-analysis tests can proceed in either (or both) of two ways. You can examine the effects of each level of the A variable (the Between Groups variable) on the levels of the B variable (the repeated measure), or you can examine the effects of each level of the B variable on the levels of the A variable. Statisticians refer to these as *simple main effects*.

For this example, the first way examines the means for the three fonts in a book and the means for the three fonts in the e-reader. The second way examines the means for the book versus the mean for the e-reader with Haettenschweiler font, with Arial, and with Calibri.

Statistics texts provide complicated formulas for calculating these analyses. R makes them easy. To analyze the three fonts in the book, do a repeated measures ANOVA for Subjects 1–4. To analyze the three fonts in the e-reader, do a repeated measures ANOVA for Subjects 5–8.

For the analysis of the book versus the e-reader in the Haettenschweiler font, that's a single-factor ANOVA for the Haettenschweiler data. You'd complete a similar procedure for each of the other fonts.

Multivariate Analysis of Variance

The examples thus far in this chapter involve a dependent variable and more than one independent variable. Is it possible to have more than one dependent variable? Absolutely! That gives you MANOVA — the abbreviation for the title of this section.

When might you encounter this type of situation? Suppose you're thinking of adopting one of three textbooks for a basic science course. You have 12 students, and you randomly assign four of them to read Book 1, another four to read Book 2, and the remaining four to read Book 3. You're interested in how each book promotes knowledge in physics, chemistry, and biology, so after the students read the books, they take a test of fundamental knowledge in each of those three sciences.

The independent variable is Book, and the dependent variable is multivariate — it's a vector that consists of Physics score, Chemistry score, and Biology score. Table 13-3 shows the data.

TABLE 13-3   **Data for the Science Textbook MANOVA Study**

Student	Book	Physics	Chemistry	Biology
Art	Book 1	50	66	71
Brenda	Book 1	53	45	56
Cal	Book 1	52	48	65
Dan	Book 1	54	51	68
Eva	Book 2	75	55	88
Frank	Book 2	72	58	85

Student	Book	Physics	Chemistry	Biology
Greg	Book 2	64	59	79
Hank	Book 2	76	59	82
Iris	Book 3	68	67	55
Jim	Book 3	61	56	59
Kendra	Book 3	62	66	63
Lee	Book 3	64	78	61

The dependent variable for the first student in the Book 1 sample is a vector consisting of 50, 66, and 71.

What are the hypotheses in a case like this? The null hypothesis has to take all components of the vector into account, so here are the null and the alternative:

$$H_0 : \begin{pmatrix} \mu_{Book1,Phys} \\ \mu_{Book1,Chem} \\ \mu_{Book1,Bio} \end{pmatrix} = \begin{pmatrix} \mu_{Book2,Phys} \\ \mu_{Book2,Chem} \\ \mu_{Book2,Bio} \end{pmatrix} = \begin{pmatrix} \mu_{Book3,Phys} \\ \mu_{Book3,Chem} \\ \mu_{Book3,Bio} \end{pmatrix}$$

$$H_1 : Not\ H_0$$

I don't go into the same depth on MANOVA in this chapter as I did on ANOVA. I don't discuss SS, MS, and df. That would require knowledge of math (matrix algebra) and other material that's beyond the scope of this chapter. Instead, I dive right in and show you how to get the analysis done.

MANOVA in R

The data frame for the MANOVA looks just like Table 13-3:

```
> Textbooks.frame
   Student   Book Physics Chemistry Biology
1      Art  Book1      50        66      71
2   Brenda  Book1      53        45      56
3      Cal  Book1      52        48      65
4      Dan  Book1      54        51      68
5      Eva  Book2      75        55      88
6    Frank  Book2      72        58      85
7     Greg  Book2      64        59      79
8     Hank  Book2      76        59      82
9     Iris  Book3      68        67      55
```

```
10      Jim  Book3       61          56       59
11   Kendra  Book3       62          66       63
12     Lee   Book3       64          78       61
```

In ANOVA, the dependent variable for the analysis is a single column. In MANOVA, the dependent variable for the analysis is a matrix. In this case, it's a matrix with 12 rows (one for each student) and three columns (Physics, Chemistry, and Biology).

To create the matrix, use the cbind() function to *bind* the appropriate columns together. You can do this inside the manova() function that performs the analysis:

```
m.analysis <- manova(cbind(Physics,Chemistry,Biology) ~ Book,
         data = Textbooks.frame)
```

The formula inside the parentheses shows the 12 X 3 matrix (the result of cbind()) depending on Book, with Textbooks.frame as the source of the data.

As always, apply summary() to see the table:

```
> summary(m.analysis)
          Df Pillai approx F num Df den Df    Pr(>F)
Book       2 1.7293   17.036      6     16 3.922e-06 ***
Residuals  9
---
Signif. codes: 0 '***' 0.001 '**' 0.01 '*' 0.05 '.' 0.1 ' ' 1
```

The only new item is Pillai, a test statistic that results from a MANOVA. It's a little complicated, so I'll leave it alone. Suffice to say that R turns Pillai into an F-ratio (with 6 and 16 df) and that's what you use as the test statistic. The high F and exceptionally low p-value indicate rejection of the null hypothesis.

Pillai is the default test. In the summary statement, you can specify other MANOVA test statistics. They're called "Wilks", "Hotelling-Lawley", and "Roy". For example:

```
> summary(m.analysis, test = "Roy")
          Df    Roy approx F num Df den Df    Pr(>F)
Book       2 10.926   29.137      3      8 0.0001175 ***
Residuals  9
---
Signif. codes: 0 '***' 0.001 '**' 0.01 '*' 0.05 '.' 0.1 ' ' 1
```

The different tests result in different values for F and df, but the overall decision is the same.

REMEMBER

This example is a MANOVA extension of an ANOVA with just one factor. It's possible to have multiple dependent variables with more complex designs (like the ones I discuss earlier in this chapter).

Visualizing the MANOVA results

The objective of the study is to show how the distribution of Physics, Chemistry, and Biology scores differs from book to book. A separate set of boxplots for each book visualizes the differences. Figure 13-4 shows what I'm talking about.

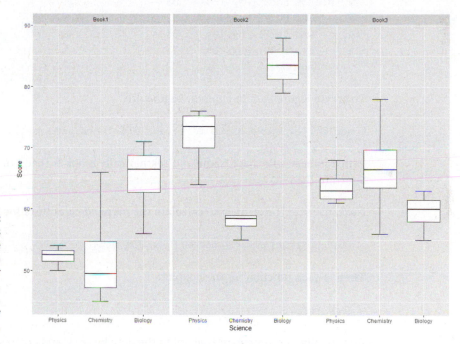

FIGURE 13-4: Three boxplots show the distribution of scores for Physics, Chemistry, and Biology for each book.

The ggplot2 *faceting* capability splits the data by Book and creates the three side-by-side graphs. Each graph is called a *facet*. (See the "Exploring the data" section in Chapter 4.)

To set this all up, you have to reshape the Textbooks.frame into long format. With the reshape2 package installed (on the Packages tab, select the check box next to reshape2), apply the melt() function:

```
Textbooks.frame.melt = melt(Textbooks.frame)
```

After assigning column names:

```
colnames(Textbooks.frame.melt) = c("Student", "Book", "Science",
        "Score")
```

the first six rows of the melted frame are

```
> head(Textbooks.frame.melt)
  Student  Book Science Score
1     Art Book1 Physics    50
2  Brenda Book1 Physics    53
3     Cal Book1 Physics    52
4     Dan Book1 Physics    54
5     Eva Book2 Physics    75
6   Frank Book2 Physics    72
```

To create Figure 13-4 in ggplot2, begin with

```
ggplot(Textbooks.frame.melt,(aes(x=Science,y=Score)))
```

which indicates the data frame and aesthetically maps Science to the x-axis and Score to the y-axis.

Next, use stat_boxplot() to calculate the perpendicular lines for the whiskers:

```
stat_boxplot(geom="errorbar", width =.5)
```

Then, a geom function for the boxplot:

```
geom_boxplot()
```

And, finally, the statement that splits the data by Book and creates a row of three graphs (excuse me — *facets*):

```
facet_grid(. ~ Book)
```

The dot followed by the tilde (~) followed by Book arranges the facets side-by-side. To put the three graphs in a column, it's

```
facet_grid(Book ~ .)
```

Putting it all together, the code for creating Figure 13-4 is

```
ggplot(Textbooks.frame.melt,(aes(x=Science,y=Score)))+
    stat_boxplot(geom="errorbar", width =.5) +
    geom_boxplot() +
    facet_grid(. ~ Book)
```

After the analysis

When a MANOVA results in rejection of the null hypothesis, one way to proceed is to perform an ANOVA on each component of the dependent variable. The results tell you which components contribute to the significant MANOVA.

The summary.aov() function does this for you. Remember that m.analysis holds the results of the MANOVA in this section's example:

```
> summary.aov(m.analysis)
 Response Physics :
            Df Sum Sq Mean Sq F value    Pr(>F)
Book         2 768.67  384.33  27.398 0.0001488 ***
Residuals    9 126.25   14.03
---
Signif. codes: 0 '***' 0.001 '**' 0.01 '*' 0.05 '.' 0.1 ' ' 1

 Response Chemistry :
            Df Sum Sq Mean Sq F value  Pr(>F)
Book         2  415.5 207.750  3.6341 0.06967 .
Residuals    9  514.5  57.167
---
Signif. codes: 0 '***' 0.001 '**' 0.01 '*' 0.05 '.' 0.1 ' ' 1

 Response Biology :
            Df Sum Sq Mean Sq F value    Pr(>F)
Book         2 1264.7  632.33  27.626 0.0001441 ***
Residuals    9  206.0   22.89
---
Signif. codes: 0 '***' 0.001 '**' 0.01 '*' 0.05 '.' 0.1 ' ' 1
```

These analyses show that Physics and Biology contribute to the overall effect, and Chemistry just misses significance.

TIP

Notice the word Response in these tables. This is R-terminology for "dependent variable."

TECHNICAL STUFF

This separate-ANOVAs procedure doesn't consider the relationships among pairs of components. The relationship is called *correlation*, which I discuss in Chapter 15.

Chapter **14**

Regression: Linear, Multiple, and the General Linear Model

One of the main things you do when you work with statistics is make predictions. The idea is to use data from one or more variables to predict the value of another variable. To do this, you have to understand how to summarize relationships among variables, and to test hypotheses about those relationships.

In this chapter, I introduce *regression*, a statistical way to do just that. Regression also enables you to use the details of relationships to make predictions. First, I show you how to analyze the relationship between one variable and another. Then I show you how to analyze the relationship between a variable and two others. Finally, I let you in on the connection between regression and ANOVA.

The Plot of Scatter

FarMisht Consulting, Inc., is a consulting firm with a wide range of specialties. It receives numerous applications from people interested in becoming FarMisht consultants. Accordingly, FarMisht Human Resources has to be able to predict which applicants will succeed and which ones will not. They've developed a Performance measure that they use to assess their current employees. The scale is 0–100, where 100 indicates top performance.

What's the best prediction for a new applicant? Without knowing anything about an applicant, and knowing only their own employees' Performance scores, the answer is clear: It's the average Performance score among their employees. Regardless of who the applicant is, that's all the Human Resources team can say if its members' knowledge is limited.

With more knowledge about the employees and about the applicants, a more accurate prediction becomes possible. For example, if FarMisht develops an aptitude test and assesses its employees, Human Resources can match up every employee's Performance score with their Aptitude score and see whether the two pieces of data are somehow related. If they are, an applicant can take the FarMisht aptitude test, and Human Resources can use that score (and the relationship between Aptitude and Performance) to help make a prediction.

Figure 14-1 shows the Aptitude-Performance matchup in a graphical way. Because the points are scattered, it's called a *scatter plot.* By convention, the vertical axis (the *y-axis*) represents what you're trying to predict. That's also called the *dependent variable,* or the *y-variable.* In this case, that's Performance. Also by convention, the horizontal axis (the *x-axis*) represents what you're using to make your prediction. That's also called the *independent variable,* or *x-variable.* Here, that's Aptitude.

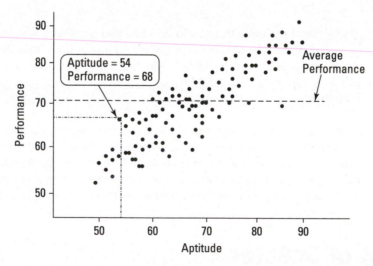

FIGURE 14-1: Aptitude and Performance at FarMisht Consulting.

Each point in the graph represents an individual's Performance and Aptitude. In a scatter plot for a real-life corporation, you'd see many more points than I show here. The general tendency of the set of points seems to be that high Aptitude scores are associated with high Performance scores and that low Aptitude scores are associated with low Performance scores.

I've singled out one of the points. It shows a FarMisht employee with an Aptitude score of 54 and a Performance score of 58. I also show the average Performance score, to give you a sense that knowing the Aptitude–Performance relationship provides an advantage over knowing only the mean.

How do you make that advantage work for you? You start by summarizing the relationship between Aptitude and Performance. The summary is a line through the points. How and where do you draw the line?

I get to that in a minute. First, I have to tell you about lines in general.

Graphing Lines

In the world of mathematics, a line is a way to picture a relationship between an independent variable (*x*) and a dependent variable (*y*). In this relationship,

$$y = 4 + 2x$$

If you supply a value for *x*, you can figure out the corresponding value for *y*. The equation says to multiply the *x*-value by 2 and then add 3.

If $x = 1$, for example, $y = 6$. If $x = 2$, $y = 8$. Table 14-1 shows a number of *x*-*y* pairs in this relationship, including the pair in which $x = 0$.

TABLE 14-1 **x-y Pairs in** $y = 4 + 2x$

x	y
0	4
1	6
2	8
3	10
4	12
5	14
6	16

Figure 14-2 shows these pairs as points on a set of *x-y* axes, along with a line through the points. Each time I list an *x-y* pair in parentheses, the *x-value* is first.

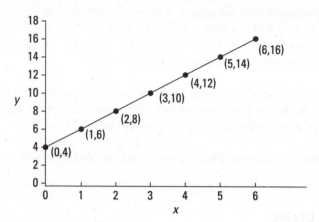

FIGURE 14-2:
The graph for
$y = 4 + 2x$.

As the figure shows, the points fall neatly onto the line. The line *graphs* the equation $y = 4 + 2x$. In fact, whenever you have an equation like this, where *x* isn't squared or cubed or raised to any power higher than 1, you have what mathematicians call a *linear* equation. (If *x* is raised to a higher power than 1, you connect the points with a curve, not a line.)

REMEMBER

A couple of things to keep in mind about a line: You can describe a line in terms of how slanted it is, and where it runs into the *y*-axis.

The how-slanted-it-is part is the slope. The *slope* tells you how much *y* changes when *x* changes by one unit. In the line shown in Figure 14-2, when *x* changes by one (from 4 to 5, for example), *y* changes by two (from 12 to 14).

The where-it-runs-into-the-*y*-axis part is called the *y-intercept* (or sometimes just the *intercept*). That's the value of *y* when *x* = 0. In Figure 14-2, the *y*-intercept is 4.

You can see these numbers in the equation. The slope is the number that multiplies *x*, and the intercept is the number you add to *x*. In general,

$$y = a + bx$$

where *a* represents the intercept and *b* represents the slope.

The slope can be a positive number, a negative number, or 0. In Figure 14-2, the slope is positive. If the slope is negative, the line is slanted in a direction opposite to what you see in Figure 14-2. A negative slope means that *y decreases* as *x* increases. If the slope is 0, the line is parallel to the horizontal axis. If the slope is 0, y doesn't change as x changes.

The same applies to the intercept — it can be a positive number, a negative number, or 0. If the intercept is positive, the line cuts off the y-axis *above* the x-axis. If the intercept is negative, the line cuts off the y-axis *below* the x-axis. If the intercept is 0, it intersects with the y-axis and the x-axis, at the point called the *origin*.

And now, back to what I was originally talking about.

Regression: What a Line!

I mention earlier that a line is the best way to summarize the relationship in the scatter plot in Figure 14-1. It's possible to draw an infinite amount of straight lines through the scatter plot. Which one best summarizes the relationship?

Intuitively, the "best fitting" line ought to be the one that passes through the maximum number of points and isn't too far away from the points it doesn't pass through. For statisticians, that line has a special property: If you draw that line through the scatter plot, then draw distances (in the vertical direction) between the points and the line, and then square those distances and add them up, the sum of the squared distances is a minimum.

Statisticians call this line the *regression line*, and they indicate it as

$$y' = a + bx$$

Each y' is a point on the line. It represents the best prediction of y for a given value of x.

To figure out exactly where this line is, you calculate its slope and its intercept. For a regression line, the slope and intercept are called *regression coefficients.*

The formulas for the regression coefficients are pretty straightforward. For the slope, the formula is

$$b = \frac{\sum (x - \bar{x})(y - \bar{y})}{\sum (x - \bar{x})^2}$$

The intercept formula is

$$a = \bar{y} - b\bar{x}$$

I illustrate with an example. To keep the numbers manageable and comprehensible, I use a small sample instead of the hundreds (or perhaps thousands) of employees you'd find in a scatter plot for a corporation. Table 14-2 shows a sample of data from 16 FarMisht consultants.

TABLE 14-2   **Aptitude Scores and Performance Scores for 16 FarMisht Consultants**

Consultant	Aptitude	Performance
1	45	56
2	81	74
3	65	56
4	87	81
5	68	75
6	91	84
7	77	68
8	61	52
9	55	57
10	66	82
11	82	73
12	93	90
13	76	67
14	83	79
15	61	70
16	74	66
Mean	72.81	70.63
Variance	181.63	126.65
Standard Deviation	13.48	11.25

For this set of data, the slope of the regression line is

$$b = \frac{(45-72.81)(56-70.63)+(81-72.81)(74-70.63)+...+(74-72.81)(66-70.63)}{(45-72.81)^2+(81-72.81)^2+...+(74-72.81)^2}$$

$$= 0.654$$

The intercept is

$$a = \bar{y} - b\bar{x} = 70.63 - 0.654(72.81) = 23.03$$

So the equation of the best-fitting line through these 16 points is

$$y' = 23.03 + 0.654x$$

Or, in terms of Performance and Aptitude, it's

$$Predicted\ Performance = 23.03 + 0.654(Aptitude)$$

REMEMBER

The slope and the intercept of a regression line are generically called *regression coefficients*.

Using regression for forecasting

Based on this sample and this regression line, you can take an applicant's Aptitude score — say, 85 — and predict the applicant's Performance:

$$Predicted\ Performance = 23.03 + 0.654(85) = 78.59$$

Without this regression line, the only prediction is the mean Performance, 70.63.

Variation around the regression line

In Chapter 5, I describe how the mean doesn't tell the whole story about a set of data. You have to show how the scores vary around the mean. For that reason, I introduce the variance and standard deviation.

You have a similar situation here. To get the full picture of the relationship in a scatter plot, you have to show how the scores vary around the regression line. Here, I introduce the *residual variance* and *standard error of estimate*, which are analogous to the variance and the standard deviation.

The residual variance is sort of an average of the squared deviations of the observed *y*-values around the predicted *y*-values. Each deviation of a data point from a predicted point $(y - y')$ is called a *residual*; hence, the name. The formula is

$$s_{yx}^2 = \frac{\sum(y - y')^2}{N - 2}$$

I say "sort of" because the denominator is $N-2$ rather than N. Telling you the reason for the -2 is beyond the scope of this discussion. As I mention earlier, the denominator of a variance estimate is *degrees of freedom* (df), and that concept comes in handy in a little while.

The standard error of estimate is

$$s_{yx} = \sqrt{s_{yx}^2} = \sqrt{\frac{\sum(y - y')^2}{N - 2}}$$

To show you how the residual error and the standard error of estimate play out for the data in the example, here's Table 14-3. This table extends Table 14-2 by showing the predicted Performance score for each given Aptitude score:

TABLE 14-3

Aptitude Scores, Performance Scores, and Predicted Performance Scores for 16 FarMisht Consultants

Consultant	Aptitude	Performance	Predicted Performance
1	45	56	52.44
2	81	74	75.98
3	65	56	65.52
4	87	81	79.90
5	68	75	67.48
6	91	84	82.51
7	77	68	73.36
8	61	52	62.90
9	55	57	58.98
10	66	82	66.17
11	82	73	76.63
12	93	90	83.82
13	76	67	72.71
14	83	79	77.28
15	61	70	62.90
16	74	66	71.40
Mean	72.81	70.63	
Variance	181.63	126.65	
Standard Deviation	13.48	11.25	

As the table shows, sometimes the predicted Performance score is pretty close, and sometimes it's not.

For these data, the residual variance is

$$s_{yx}^2 = \frac{\sum(y-y')^2}{N-2} = \frac{(56-52.44)^2 + (74-75.98)^2 + \ldots + (66-71.40)^2}{16-2} = \frac{735.65}{14}$$
$$= 52.54$$

The standard error of estimate is

$$s_{yx} = \sqrt{s_{yx}^2} = \sqrt{52.54} = 7.25$$

If the residual variance and the standard error of estimate are small, the regression line is a good fit to the data in the scatter plot. If the residual variance and the standard error of estimate are large, the regression line is a poor fit.

What's "small"? What's "large"? What's a "good" fit?

Keep reading.

Testing hypotheses about regression

The regression equation you are working with:

$$y' = a + bx$$

summarizes a relationship in a scatter plot of a sample. The regression coefficients *a* and *b* are sample statistics. You can use these statistics to test hypotheses about population parameters, and that's what you do in this section.

The regression line through the population that produces the sample (like the entire set of FarMisht consultants) is the graph of an equation that consists of parameters rather than statistics. By convention, remember, Greek letters stand for parameters, so the regression equation for the population is

$$y' = \alpha + \beta x + \varepsilon$$

The first two Greek letters on the right are α (alpha) and β (beta), the equivalents of *a* and *b*. What about that last one? It looks something like the Greek equivalent of *e*. What's it doing there?

That last term is the Greek letter *epsilon*. It represents "error" in the population. In a way, *error* is an unfortunate term. It's a catchall for "things you don't know or things you have no control over." Error is reflected in the residuals — the deviations from the predictions. The more you understand about what you're measuring, the more you decrease the error.

You can't measure the error in the relationship between Aptitude and Performance, but it's lurking there. Someone might score low on the Aptitude, for example, and then go on to have a wonderful consulting career with a higher-than-predicted Performance. On a scatter plot, this person's Aptitude–Performance point looks like an error in prediction. As you find out more about that person, you might discover that she was sick on the day of the Aptitude, and that explains the "error."

You can test hypotheses about α, β, and ε, and that's what you do in the upcoming subsections.

Testing the fit

You begin with a test of how well the regression line fits the scatter plot. This is a test of ε, the error in the relationship.

The objective is to decide whether or not the line really does represent a relationship between the variables. It's possible that what looks like a relationship is just due to chance and the equation of the regression line doesn't mean anything (because the amount of error is overwhelming) — or it's possible that the variables are strongly related.

These possibilities are testable, and you set up hypotheses to test them:

H$_0$: No real relationship

H$_1$: Not H$_0$

Although those hypotheses make nice light reading, they don't set up a statistical test. To set up the test, you have to consider the variances. To consider the variances, you start with the deviations. Figure 14-3 focuses on one point in a scatter plot and its deviation from the regression line (the residual) and from the mean of the y-variable. It also shows the deviation between the regression line and the mean.

As the figure shows, the distance between the point and the regression line and the distance between the regression line and the mean add up to the distance between the point and the mean:

$$(y-y')+(y'-\bar{y})=(y-\bar{y})$$

This sets the stage for some other important relationships.

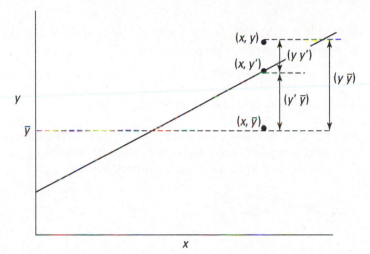

FIGURE 14-3:
The deviations in
a scatter plot.

Start by squaring each deviation. That gives you $(y-y')^2$, $(y'-\bar{y})^2$, and $(y-\bar{y})^2$. If you add up each of the squared deviations, you have

$$\sum(y-y')^2$$

You just saw this one. That's the numerator for the residual variance. It represents the variability around the regression line — the "error" I mention earlier. In the terminology of Chapter 12, the numerator of a variance is called a sum of squares, or SS. So this is $SS_{Residual}$.

$$\sum(y'-\bar{y})^2$$

This one is new. The deviation $(y'-\bar{y})$ represents the gain in prediction due to using the regression line rather than the mean. The sum reflects this gain and is called $SS_{Regression}$.

$$\sum(y-\bar{y})^2$$

I show you this one in Chapter 5 — although I use x rather than y. That's the numerator of the variance of y. In Chapter 12 terms, it's the numerator of *total variance*. This one is SS_{Total}.

This relationship holds among these three sums:

$$SS_{Residual} + SS_{Regression} = SS_{Total}$$

Each one is associated with a value for degrees of freedom — the denominator of a variance estimate. As I point out in the preceding section, the denominator for

$SS_{Residual}$ is $N-2$. The df for SS_{Total} is $N-1$. (See Chapters 5 and 12.) As with the SS, the degrees of freedom add up:

$$df_{Residual} + df_{Regression} = df_{Total}$$

This leaves one degree of freedom for Regression.

Where is this all headed, and what does it have to do with hypothesis testing? Well, since you asked, you get variance estimates by dividing SS by df. Each variance estimate is called a *mean-square*, abbreviated MS (again, see Chapter 12):

$$MS_{Regression} = \frac{SS_{Regression}}{df_{Regression}}$$

$$MS_{Residual} = \frac{SS_{Residual}}{df_{Residual}}$$

$$MS_{Total} = \frac{SS_{Total}}{df_{Total}}$$

Now for the hypothesis part. If H_0 is true and what looks like a relationship between x and y is really no big deal, the piece that represents the gain in prediction because of the regression line ($MS_{Regression}$) should be no greater than the variability around the regression line ($MS_{Residual}$). If H_0 is not true, and the gain in prediction is substantial, then $MS_{Regression}$ should be a lot bigger than $MS_{Residual}$.

So the hypotheses now set up as

$$H_0: \sigma^2_{Regression} \leq \sigma^2_{Residual}$$

$$H_1: \sigma^2_{Regression} > \sigma^2_{Residual}$$

These are hypotheses you can test. How? To test a hypothesis about two variances, you use an F test. (See Chapter 11.) The test statistic here is

$$F = \frac{MS_{Regression}}{MS_{Residual}}$$

To show you how it all works, I apply the formulas to the FarMisht example. The $MS_{Residual}$ is the same as syx2 from the preceding section, and that value is 18.61. The $MS_{Regression}$ is

$$MS_{Regression} = \frac{(59.64 - 70.63)^2 + (71.40 - 70.63)^2 + ... + (66.17 - 70.63)^2}{1} = 1164.1$$

This sets up the F:

$$F = \frac{MS_{Regression}}{MS_{Residual}} = \frac{1164.1}{52.55} = 22.15$$

With 1 and 14 df and α = .05, the critical value of F is 4.60. (Use $qf()$ to verify.) The calculated F is greater than the critical F, so the decision is to reject H_0. That means the regression line provides a good fit to the data in the sample.

Testing the slope

Another question that arises in linear regression is whether the slope of the regression line is significantly different from zero. If it's not, the mean is just as good a predictor as the regression line.

The hypotheses for this test are

H_0: $\beta \leq 0$

H_1: $\beta > 0$

The statistical test is t, which I discuss in Chapters 9, 10, and 11 in connection with means. The t-test for the slope is

$$t = \frac{b - \beta}{s_b}$$

with df = $N-2$. The denominator estimates the standard error of the slope. This term sounds more complicated than it is. The formula is

$$s_b = \frac{s_{yx}}{s_x \sqrt{(N-1)}}$$

where s_x is the standard deviation of the x-variable. For the data in the example,

$$s_b = \frac{s_{yx}}{s_x \sqrt{(N-1)}} = \frac{7.25}{(13.48)\sqrt{(16-1)}} = .139$$

$$t = \frac{b - \beta}{s_b} = \frac{.654 - 0}{.139} = 4.71$$

This is larger than the critical value of t for 14 df and α = .05 (2.14), so the decision is to reject H_0.

Testing the intercept

Finally, here's the hypothesis test for the intercept. The hypotheses are

H_0: $\alpha = 0$

H_1: $\alpha \neq 0$

The test, once again, is a t-test. The formula is

$$t = \frac{a - \alpha}{s_a}$$

The denominator is the estimate of the standard error of the intercept. Without going into detail, the formula for s_a is

$$s_a = s_{yx} \sqrt{\left[\frac{1}{N} + \frac{\bar{x}^2}{(N-1)s_x^2}\right]}$$

where s_x is the standard deviation of the x-variable, s_x^2 is the variance of the x-variable, and $\bar{x}^2$ is the squared mean of the x-variable. Applying this formula to the data in the example,

$$s_a = s_{yx} \sqrt{\left[\frac{1}{N} + \frac{\bar{x}^2}{(N-1)s_x^2}\right]} = 10.27$$

The t-test is

$$t = \frac{a - \alpha}{s_a} = \frac{23.03}{10.27} = 2.24$$

With 15 degrees of freedom, and the probability of a Type I error at .05, the critical t is 2.13 for a two-tailed test. It's a two-tailed test because H_1 is that the intercept doesn't equal zero — it doesn't specify whether the intercept is greater than zero or less than zero. Because the calculated value is greater than the critical value, the decision is to reject H_0.

Linear Regression in R

Time to see how R handles linear regression. To start the analysis for this example, create a vector for the Aptitude scores and another for the Performance scores:

```
Aptitude <- c(45, 81, 65, 87, 68, 91, 77, 61, 55, 66, 82, 93,
        76, 83, 61, 74)
Performance <- c(56, 74, 56, 81, 75, 84, 68, 52, 57, 82, 73, 90,
        67, 79, 70, 66)
```

Then use the two vectors to create a data frame

```
FarMisht.frame <- data.frame(Aptitude,Performance)
```

The `lm()` (linear model) function performs the analysis:

```
FM.reg <-lm(Performance ~ Aptitude, data=FarMisht.frame)
```

As always, the tilde (~) operator signifies "depends on," so this is a perfect example of a dependent variable and an independent variable.

Applying `summary()` to `FM.reg` produces the regression information:

```
> summary(FM.reg)

Call:
lm(formula = Performance ~ Aptitude, data = FarMisht.frame)

Residuals:
    Min       1Q   Median       3Q      Max
-10.9036  -5.3720  -0.4379   4.2111  15.8281

Coefficients:
            Estimate Std. Error t value Pr(>|t|)
(Intercept)  23.0299    10.2732   2.242 0.041697 *
Aptitude      0.6537     0.1389   4.707 0.000337 ***
---
Signif. codes: 0 '***' 0.001 '**' 0.01 '*' 0.05 '.' 0.1 ' ' 1

Residual standard error: 7.249 on 14 degrees of freedom
Multiple R-squared:  0.6128,    Adjusted R-squared:  0.5851
F-statistic: 22.15 on 1 and 14 DF,  p-value: 0.0003368
```

The first couple of lines provide summary information about the residuals. The coefficients table shows the intercept and slope of the regression line. If you divide each number in the `Estimate` column by the adjoining number in the `Std. Error` column, you get the number in the `t value` column. These t-values, of course, are the significance tests I mention earlier for the intercept and the slope. The extremely low p-values indicate rejection of the null hypothesis (that a coefficient = 0) for each coefficient.

The bottom part of the output shows the info on how well the line fits the scatter plot. It presents the standard error of the residual, followed by `Multiple R-squared` and `Adjusted R-squared`. These last two range from 0 to 1.00 (the higher the value, the better the fit). I discuss them in Chapter 15, but for now I'll leave them alone. The `F-statistic` corresponds to the F-ratio I show you earlier.

Its high value and low associated *p*-value indicate that the line is a great fit to the scatter plot.

REMEMBER

I refer to the result of the linear regression analysis as "the linear model."

Features of the linear model

The linear model produced by lm( ) is an object that provides information, if you ask for it in the right way. As I already showed you, applying summary( ) gives all the information you need about the analysis.

You can also zero in on the coefficients:

```
> coefficients(FM.reg)
(Intercept)     Aptitude
  23.029869     0.653667
```

and on their confidence intervals:

```
> confint(FM.reg)
                   2.5 %       97.5 %
(Intercept) 0.9961369  45.0636002
Aptitude    0.3558034   0.9515307
```

Applying fitted(FM.reg) produces the fitted values, and residuals(FM.reg) gives the residuals.

Making predictions

The value of linear regression is that it gives you the ability to predict, and R provides a function that does just that: predict( ) applies a set of x-values to the linear model and returns the predicted values. Imagine two applicants with Aptitude scores of 85 and 62:

```
predict(FM.reg,data.frame(Aptitude=c(85,62)))
```

The first argument is the linear model, and the second makes a data frame out of the vector of values for the independent variable. Running this function produces these predicted values:

```
        1         2
78.59157  63.55723
```

Visualizing the scatter plot and regression line

With the ggplot2 package, you can visualize a scatter plot and its regression line in three statements. The first statement, as always, indicates the data source and maps the components of the data to components of the plot:

```
ggplot(FarMisht.frame,aes(x=Aptitude,y=Performance))
```

The second statement plots points in the graph

```
geom_point()
```

and the third specifies a geom function that adds the regression line (as indicated by the method = lm argument):

```
geom_smooth(method=lm)
```

Putting all three together

```
ggplot(FarMisht.frame,aes(x=Aptitude,y=Performance)) +
    geom_point()+
    geom_smooth(method=lm)
```

produces Figure 14-4.

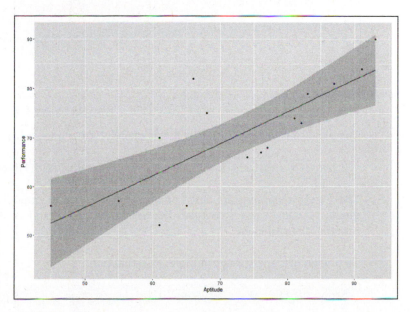

FIGURE 14-4: Scatter plot and regression line for the 16 FarMisht consultants.

The shaded area represents the 95 percent confidence interval around the regression line.

Plotting the residuals

After a regression analysis, it's a good idea to plot the residuals against the predicted values. If the residuals form a random pattern around a horizontal line at zero, that's evidence in favor of a linear relationship between the independent variable and the dependent variable.

Figure 14-5 shows the residual plot for the example. The pattern of residuals around the line is consistent with a linear model.

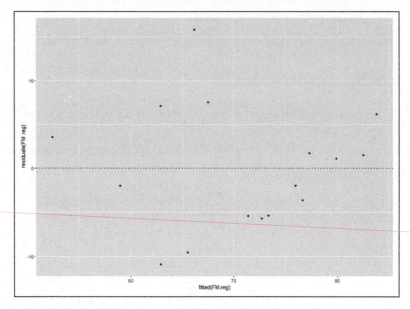

FIGURE 14-5:
Residuals plot for the FarMisht example.

The plot is based on FM.reg, the linear model. Here's the ggplot() statement:

```
ggplot(FM.reg, aes(x=fitted(FM.reg), y=residuals(FM.reg)))
```

The x and y mappings are based on information from the analysis. As you might guess, fitted(FM.reg) retrieves the predicted values, and residuals(FM.reg) retrieves the residuals.

To plot points, add the appropriate geom function:

```
geom_point()
```

and then a geom function for the dashed horizontal line whose y-intercept is 0:

```
geom_hline(yintercept = 0, linetype = "dashed" )
```

So the code for Figure 14-5 is

```
ggplot(FM.reg, aes(x=fitted(FM.reg), y=residuals(FM.reg)))+
    geom_point() +
    geom_hline(yintercept = 0, linetype = "dashed" )
```

Juggling Many Relationships at Once: Multiple Regression

Linear regression is a great tool for making predictions. When you know the slope and the intercept of the line that relates two variables, you can take a new x-value and predict a new y-value. In the example you've been working through in this chapter, you take an Aptitude score and predict a Performance score for a FarMisht applicant.

What if you knew more than just the Aptitude score for each applicant? For example, imagine that the FarMisht management team decides that a particular personality type is ideal for their consultants. So they develop the FarMisht Personality Inventory, a 20-point scale in which a higher score indicates greater compatibility with the FarMisht corporate culture and, presumably, predicts better performance. The idea is to use that data along with Aptitude scores to predict performance.

Table 14-4 shows the Aptitude, Performance, and Personality scores for the 16 current consultants. Of course, in a real-life corporation, you might have many more employees in the sample.

TABLE 14-4

Aptitude, Performance, and Personality Scores for 16 FarMisht Consultants

Consultant	Aptitude	Performance	Personality
1	45	56	9
2	81	74	15
3	65	56	11

(continued)

TABLE 14-4 *(continued)*

Consultant	Aptitude	Performance	Personality
4	87	81	15
5	68	75	14
6	91	84	19
7	77	68	12
8	61	52	10
9	55	57	9
10	66	82	14
11	82	73	15
12	93	90	14
13	76	67	16
14	83	79	18
15	61	70	15
16	74	66	12
Mean	72.81	70.63	13.63
Variance	181.63	126.65	8.65
Standard Deviation	13.48	11.25	2.94

When you work with more than one independent variable, you're in the realm of *multiple regression.* As in linear regression, you find regression coefficients. In the case of two independent variables, you're looking for the best-fitting *plane* through a three-dimensional scatter plot. Once again, "best-fitting" means that the sum of the squared distances from the data points to the plane is a minimum.

Here's the equation of the regression plane:

$$\text{standard residual} = \frac{\text{residual - average residual}}{s_{yx}}$$

For this example, that translates to

$$y' = a + b_1 x_1 + b_2 x_2$$

You can test hypotheses about the overall fit, and about all three of the regression coefficients.

I don't walk you through all the formulas for finding the coefficients, because that gets *really* complicated. Instead, I go right to the R analysis.

Here are a few things to bear in mind before I proceed:

>> You can have any number of *x*-variables. (I use two in this example.)

>> Expect the coefficient for Aptitude to change from linear regression to multiple regression. Expect the intercept to change, too.

>> Expect the standard error of estimate to decrease from linear regression to multiple regression. Because multiple regression uses more information than linear regression, it reduces the error.

Multiple regression in R

I begin by adding a vector for the personality scores in Column 4 of Table 14-4:

```
Personality <- c(9, 15, 11, 15, 14, 19, 12, 10, 9, 14, 15, 14,
        16, 18, 15, 12)
```

And then I add that vector to the data frame:

```
FarMisht.frame["Personality"] = Personality
```

Applying lm() produces the analysis:

```
FM.multreg <- lm(Performance ~ Aptitude + Personality,
        data = FarMisht.frame)
```

And applying summary() gives the information:

```
> summary(FM.multreg)

Call:
lm(formula = Performance ~ Aptitude + Personality, data
        = FarMisht.frame)

Residuals:
    Min      1Q Median     3Q    Max
-8.689 -2.834 -1.840  2.886 13.432
```

```
Coefficients:
            Estimate Std. Error t value Pr(>|t|)
(Intercept)  20.2825     9.6595   2.100   0.0558 .
Aptitude      0.3905     0.1949   2.003   0.0664 .
Personality   1.6079     0.8932   1.800   0.0951 .
---
Signif. codes:  0 '***' 0.001 '**' 0.01 '*' 0.05 '.' 0.1 ' ' 1

Residual standard error: 6.73 on 13 degrees of freedom
Multiple R-squared:   0.69,    Adjusted R-squared:  0.6423
F-statistic: 14.47 on 2 and 13 DF,  p-value: 0.0004938
```

So the generic equation for the regression plane is

$$Predicted\ GPA = a + b_1(SAT) + b_2(High\ School\ Average)$$

Or, in terms of this example

$$y' = a + .0025x_1 + .043x_2$$

Again, the high F-value and low p-value indicate that the regression plane is an excellent fit for the scatter plot.

Making predictions

Once again, `predict()` enables predictions of Performance. This time, I use it with the multiple regression model: `FM.multreg`. Imagine two applicants: One has Aptitude and Personality scores of 85 and 14, and the other has Aptitude and Personality scores of 62 and 17. This requires two vectors — one for the Aptitude scores and one for the Personality scores:

```
> predict(FM.multreg, data.frame(Aptitude = c(85,62),
          Personality=c(14,17)))
       1        2
75.98742 71.82924
```

Visualizing the 3D scatter plot and regression plane

The `ggplot2` package, for all its wonderful features, does not provide a way to draw 3-dimensional graphics — like a scatter plot for a dependent variable and two independent variables. Never fear, however: R has a number of other ways to do this. In this section, I show you two of them.

The scatterplot3d package

If you want to make a nifty three-dimensional scatter plot like the one shown in Figure 14-6 — a figure that looks good on a printed page, the scatterplot3d() function is for you.

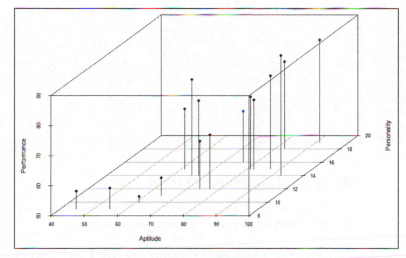

FIGURE 14-6:
Scatter plot for the FarMisht multiple regression example, rendered in scatter plot3d().

First, install the scatterplot3d package. On the Packages tab, find scatterplot3d and select its check box.

Next, write a statement that creates the plot:

```
with (FarMisht.frame,
  (splot <- scatterplot3d(Performance ~ Aptitude +
         Personality, type = "h", pch = 19)))
```

If you use with you don't have to repeat the name of the data frame three times. The first argument to scatterplot3d() is the formula for setting up the linear model. The second argument adds the vertical lines from the x-y plane to the data points. Those vertical lines aren't absolutely necessary, but I think they help the viewer understand where the points are in the plot. The third argument specifies what the plot characters look like.

The function produces an object that you can use to embellish the plot. For example, here's how to add the regression plane and produce Figure 14-7:

```
splot$plane3d(FM.multreg,lty="dashed")
```

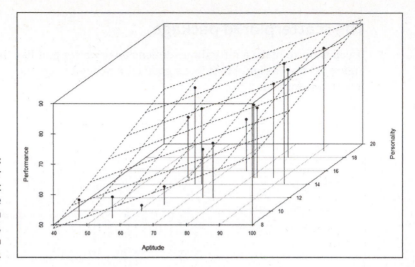

FIGURE 14-7:
Scatter plot for
the FarMisht
multiple
regression
example,
complete with
regression plane.

car and rgl: A package deal

If you have to present a 3D scatter plot to an audience and you want to dazzle them with an interactive plot, the next method is for you.

The plot-creating function is called scatter3d(), and it lives in the car package. On the Packages tab, click Install. In the Install Packages dialog box, type **car** and click Install. When car appears on the Packages tab, select its check box.

This function works with the rgl package, which uses tools from the Open Graphics Library (OpenGL), a toolset for creating 2D and 3D graphics. You'll find OpenGL tools at work in virtual reality, computer-aided design, flight simulation, and a number of other applications.

On the Packages tab, find rgl and select its check box.

With those two packages installed, run this function:

```
scatter3d(Performance ~ Aptitude + Personality,
          data=FarMisht.frame)
```

This opens an RGL window with the 3D scatter plot shown in Figure 14-8. As you can see, the scatter plot shows the regression plane and the residuals.

You can move the mouse inside this plot, press the left mouse button, and rotate the plot to present different angles. You can also use the scroll wheel to zoom in or out of the plot. Try it!

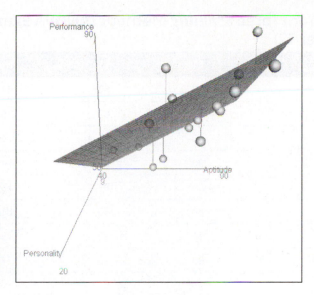

FIGURE 14-8:
Scatter plot for the FarMisht multiple regression example, rendered in scatter3d().

ANOVA: Another Look

Here's a statement you might find radical: Analysis of variance and linear regression *are really the same thing.*

They're both part of what's called the General Linear Model (GLM). In linear regression, the objective is to predict a value of a dependent variable given a value of an independent variable. In ANOVA, the objective is to decide whether several sample means differ enough from one another to enable you to reject the null hypothesis about levels of the independent variable.

How are they similar? It's easier to see the connection if you rethink ANOVA: Given the data, imagine that the objective is to predict the dependent variable given the level of the independent variable. What would be the best prediction? For any level of the independent variable, that would be the mean of the sample for that level — also known as the "group mean." This means that deviations from the group mean (the best predicted value) are residuals, and this is why, in an R ANOVA, the MS_{Error} is called $MS_{Residuals}$.

It goes deeper than that. To show you how, I revisit the ANOVA example from Chapter 12. For convenience, here's Table 12-1 reproduced as Table 14-5.

TABLE 14-5

Data from Three Training Methods (ANOVA Example from Chapter 12)

	Method 1	Method 2	Method 3
	95	83	68
	91	89	75
	89	85	79
	90	89	74
	99	81	75
	88	89	81
	96	90	73
	98	82	77
	95	84	
		80	
Mean	93.44	85.20	75.25
Variance	16.28	14.18	15.64
Standard Deviation	4.03	3.77	3.96

You have to test

$$H_0: \mu_1 = \mu_2 = \mu_3$$

$$H_1: \text{Not } H_0$$

To use the aov() function to produce an analysis of variance, set up the data in long format. Here are the first six rows:

```
> head(Training.frame)
  Method Score
1 method1    95
2 method1    91
3 method1    89
4 method1    90
5 method1    99
6 method1    88
```

The result of the analysis is

```
> analysis <-aov(Score~Method,data = Training.frame)
> summary(analysis)
            Df Sum Sq Mean Sq F value  Pr(>F)
Method       2 1402.7   701.3   45.82 6.38e-09 ***
Residuals   24  367.3    15.3
---
Signif. codes: 0 '***' 0.001 '**' 0.01 '*' 0.05 '.' 0.1 ' ' 1
```

What if you tried a linear regression analysis on the data?

```
> reg.analysis <-lm(Score~Method,data = Training.frame)
> summary(reg.analysis)

Call:
lm(formula = Score ~ Method, data = Training.frame)

Residuals:
   Min     1Q Median     3Q    Max
-7.250 -2.822 -0.250  3.775  5.750

Coefficients:
               Estimate Std. Error t value Pr(>|t|)
(Intercept)      93.444      1.304  71.657  < 2e-16 ***
Methodmethod2    -8.244      1.798  -4.587 0.000119 ***
Methodmethod3   -18.194      1.901  -9.571 1.15e-09 ***
---
Signif. codes: 0 '***' 0.001 '**' 0.01 '*' 0.05 '.' 0.1 ' ' 1

Residual standard error: 3.912 on 24 degrees of freedom
Multiple R-squared:  0.7925,    Adjusted R-squared:  0.7752
F-statistic: 45.82 on 2 and 24 DF,  p-value: 6.381e-09
```

You see a good bit more information than in the ANOVA table, but the bottom line shows the same F-ratio and associated information as the analysis of variance. Also, the coefficients provide the group means: The intercept (93.444) is the mean of Method 1, the intercept plus the second coefficient (−8.244) is the mean of Method 2 (85.20), and the intercept plus the third coefficient (−18.194) is the mean of Method 3 (75.25). Check the Means in Table 14-1, if you don't believe me.

A bit more on the coefficients: The Intercept represents Method 1, which is a baseline against which to compare each of the others. The t-value for Method 2 (along with its associated probability, which is much less than .05) shows that Method 2 differs significantly from Method 1. It's the same story for Method 3, which also differs significantly from Method 1.

Here's a question that should be forming in your mind: How can you perform a linear regression when the independent variable (Method) is categorical rather than numerical?

Glad you asked.

REMEMBER

To form a regression analysis with categorical data, R (and other statistical software packages) recode the levels of a variable like Method into combinations of numeric *dummy variables*. The only values a dummy variable can take are 0 or 1: 0 indicates the *absence* of a categorical value; 1 indicates the *presence* of a categorical value.

I'll do this manually. For the three levels of Method (Method 1, Method 2, and Method 3), I need two dummy variables. I'll call them D1 and D2. Here's how I (arbitrarily) assign the values:

» For Method 1, D1 = 0 and D2 = 0

» For Method 2, D1 = 1, and D2 = 0

» For Method 3, D1 = 0, and D2 = 1

To illustrate further, here's a data frame called Training.frame.w.Dummies. Ordinarily, I wouldn't show you all 27 rows of a data frame, but here I think it's instructive:

```
> Training.frame.w.Dummies
     Method D1 D2 Score
1   method1  0  0    95
2   method1  0  0    91
3   method1  0  0    89
4   method1  0  0    90
5   method1  0  0    99
6   method1  0  0    88
7   method1  0  0    96
8   method1  0  0    98
9   method1  0  0    95
10  method2  1  0    83
11  method2  1  0    89
12  method2  1  0    85
13  method2  1  0    89
14  method2  1  0    81
15  method2  1  0    89
16  method2  1  0    90
17  method2  1  0    82
18  method2  1  0    84
```

```
19  method2  1  0    80
20  method3  0  1    68
21  method3  0  1    75
22  method3  0  1    79
23  method3  0  1    74
24  method3  0  1    75
25  method3  0  1    81
26  method3  0  1    73
27  method3  0  1    77
```

These lines of code

```
model.w.Dummies <- lm(Score ~ D1 + D2,
                      data= Training.frame.w.Dummies)
summary(model.w.Dummies)
```

produce the same result as the analysis of variance and the linear regression I showed you earlier. The only difference is that the coefficients are expressed in terms of the dummy variables:

```
Coefficients:
              Estimate Std. Error t value Pr(>|t|)
(Intercept)     93.444      1.304  71.657  < 2e-16 ***
D1              -8.244      1.798  -4.587 0.000119 ***
D2             -18.194      1.901  -9.571 1.15e-09 ***
```

So, dummy variables enable a linear regression model with categorical independent variables. In fact, linear regression with categorical independent variables *is* the analysis of variance.

Analysis of Covariance: The Final Component of the GLM

In this chapter, I've shown you how linear regression works with a numeric independent (predictor) variable, and with a categorical independent (predictor) variable. Is it possible to have a study with both a numeric predictor variable and a categorical predictor variable?

Absolutely! The analytical tool for this type of study is called the Analysis of Covariance (ANCOVA). It's the third and final component of the General Linear Model. (Linear regression and ANOVA are the first two.) The easiest way to describe it is with an example.

Make sure you have the MASS package installed. On the Packages tab, find its check box and select it, if it isn't already. In the MASS package is a data frame called anorexia. (I use it in Chapter 2.) This data frame contains data for 72 young women randomly selected for one of three types of treatment for anorexia: Cont (a control condition with no therapy), CBT (cognitive behavioral therapy), or FT (family treatment).

Here are the first six rows:

```
> head(anorexia)
  Treat Prewt Postwt
1  Cont  80.7   80.2
2  Cont  89.4   80.1
3  Cont  91.8   86.4
4  Cont  74.0   86.3
5  Cont  78.1   76.1
6  Cont  88.3   78.1
```

Prewt is the weight before treatment, and Postwt is the weight after treatment. What you need, of course, is a variable that indicates the amount of weight gained during treatment. I'll call it WtGain, and here's how to add it to the data frame:

```
anorexia["WtGain"]=anorexia["Postwt"]-anorexia["Prewt"]
```

Now:

```
> head(anorexia)
  Treat Prewt Postwt WtGain
1  Cont  80.7   80.2   -0.5
2  Cont  89.4   80.1   -9.3
3  Cont  91.8   86.4   -5.4
4  Cont  74.0   86.3   12.3
5  Cont  78.1   76.1   -2.0
6  Cont  88.3   78.1  -10.2
```

Figure 14-9 plots the data points for this data frame.

Here's the code for this plot, in case you're curious:

```
ggplot(anorexia,aes(x=Treat,y=WtGain))+
  geom_point()
```

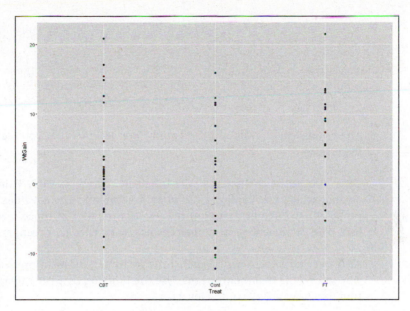

FIGURE 14-9:
Weight Gain
versus Treat in
the anorexia
data frame.

An analysis of variance or a linear regression analysis would be appropriate to test these:

H_0: $\mu_{Cont} = \mu_{CBT} = \mu_{FT}$

H_1: Not H_0

Here's the linear regression model:

```
> anorexia.linreg <-lm(WtGain ~ Treat, data=anorexia)
> summary(anorexia.linreg)

Call:
lm(formula = WtGain ~ Treat, data = anorexia)

Residuals:
    Min      1Q  Median      3Q     Max
-12.565  -4.543  -1.007   3.846  17.893

Coefficients:
            Estimate Std. Error t value Pr(>|t|)
(Intercept)    3.007      1.398   2.151   0.0350 *
TreatCont     -3.457      2.033  -1.700   0.0936 .
TreatFT        4.258      2.300   1.852   0.0684 .
---
```

```
Signif. codes: 0 '***' 0.001 '**' 0.01 '*' 0.05 '.' 0.1 ' ' 1

Residual standard error: 7.528 on 69 degrees of freedom
Multiple R-squared:  0.1358,   Adjusted R-squared:  0.1108
F-statistic: 5.422 on 2 and 69 DF,   p-value: 0.006499
```

The *F*-ratio and *p*-value in the bottom line tell you that you can reject the null hypothesis.

Let's look at the coefficients. The intercept represents CBT. This is the baseline against which you compare the other treatments. The *t*-values and associated probabilities (greater than .05) tell you that neither of those levels differs from CBT. The significant *F*-ratio must result from some other comparisons.

Also, check the coefficients against the treatment means. Here's a quick and easy way to find the treatment means: Use the function tapply( ) to apply mean( ) and find the mean WtGain in the levels of Treat:

```
> with (anorexia, tapply(WtGain,Treat,mean))
      CBT       Cont        FT
 3.006897 -0.450000  7.264706
```

The intercept, remember, is the mean for CBT. Add the intercept to the next coefficient to calculate the mean for Cont, and add the intercept to the final coefficient to calculate the mean for FT.

If you prefer to see the *F*-ratio and associated statistics in an ANOVA table, you can apply the anova( ) function to the model:

```
> anova(anorexia.linreg)
Analysis of Variance Table

Response: WtGain
          Df Sum Sq Mean Sq F value   Pr(>F)
Treat      2  614.6 307.322  5.4223 0.006499 **
Residuals 69 3910.7  56.677
---
Signif. codes: 0 '***' 0.001 '**' 0.01 '*' 0.05 '.' 0.1 ' ' 1
```

You can dig a little deeper. Suppose weight gain depends not only on type of treatment but also on a person's initial weight (which is called a *covariate*). Taking PreWt into consideration might yield a more accurate picture. Treat is a categorical variable, and Prewt is a numerical variable. Figure 14-10 shows a plot based on the two variables.

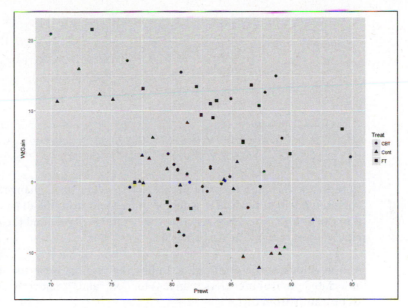

FIGURE 14-10:
Weight Gain
versus Treat
and Prewt in
the anorexia
data frame.

The code for this plot is

```
ggplot(anorexia, aes(x=Prewt,y=WtGain, shape = Treat)) +
   geom_point(size=2.5)
```

The first statement maps `Prewt` to the x-axis, `WtGain` to the y-axis, and `Treat` to shape. Thus, the shape of a data point reflects its treatment group. The second statement specifies that points appear in the plot. Its `size` argument enlarges the data points and makes them easier to see.

For the analysis of covariance, I use the `lm()` function to create a model based on both `Treat` and `Prewt`:

```
> anorexia.T.and.P <- lm(WtGain ~ Treat + Prewt, data=anorexia)
> summary(anorexia.T.and.P)

Call:
lm(formula = WtGain ~ Treat + Prewt, data = anorexia)

Residuals:
     Min      1Q   Median      3Q     Max
-14.1083  -4.2773  -0.5484  5.4838  15.2922

Coefficients:
            Estimate Std. Error t value Pr(>|t|)
(Intercept)  49.7711    13.3910    3.717 0.000410 ***
```

```
TreatCont     -4.0971    1.8935  -2.164 0.033999 *
TreatFT        4.5631    2.1333   2.139 0.036035 *
Prewt         -0.5655    0.1612  -3.509 0.000803 ***
---
Signif. codes: 0 '***' 0.001 '**' 0.01 '*' 0.05 '.' 0.1 ' ' 1

Residual standard error: 6.978 on 68 degrees of freedom
Multiple R-squared:  0.2683,    Adjusted R-squared:  0.236
F-statistic: 8.311 on 3 and 68 DF,  p-value: 8.725e-05
```

Note in the last line that the degrees of freedom have changed from the first analysis: Adding Prewt takes a degree of freedom from the df Residual and adds it to the df for Treat. Note also that the F-ratio is higher and the p-value considerably lower than in the first analysis.

And now look at the coefficients. Unlike the original analysis, the t-values and associated probabilities (less than .05) for Cont and FT show that each one differs significantly from CBT.

So it seems that adding Prewt to the analysis has helped uncover treatment differences. Bottom line: The ANCOVA shows that when evaluating the effect of an anorexia treatment, it's important to also know an individual's pretreatment weight.

But "it seems" is not really enough for statisticians. Can you really be sure that the ANCOVA adds value? To find out, you have to compare the linear regression model with the ANCOVA model. To make the comparison, use the anova() function, which does double-duty: In addition to creating an ANOVA table for a model (which is the way you saw it used earlier), you can use it to compare models. Here's how:

```
> anova(anorexia.linreg,anorexia.T.and.P)
Analysis of Variance Table

Model 1: WtGain ~ Treat
Model 2: WtGain ~ Treat + Prewt
  Res.Df    RSS Df Sum of Sq      F    Pr(>F)
1     69 3910.7
2     68 3311.3  1    599.48 12.311 0.0008034 ***
---
Signif. codes: 0 '***' 0.001 '**' 0.01 '*' 0.05 '.' 0.1 ' ' 1
```

What do the numbers in the table mean? The RSS indicates the residual sums of squares from each model. They're next to their degrees of freedom in the Res.DF column. In the Df column, 1 is the difference between the two Res.Dfs. In the Sum of Sq column, 599.48 is the difference between the two RSS. The F-ratio is the result of dividing two mean squares: The mean square for the numerator is 599.48 divided by its df (1), and the mean square for the denominator is 3311.3 divided by its df (68). The high F-ratio and low Pr(>F) (probability of a Type 1 error) tell you that adding `Prewt` significantly lowered the residual sum of squares. In English, that means it was a good idea to add `Prewt` to the mix.

TECHNICAL STUFF

Statisticians would say that this analysis statistically controls for the effects of the covariate (`Prewt`).

But wait — there's more

In an analysis of covariance, it's important to ask whether the relationship between the dependent variable and the numerical predictor variable is the same across the levels of the categorical variable. In this example, that's the same as asking if the slope of the regression line between `WtGain` and `Prewt` is the same for the scores in `Cont` as it is for the scores in `CBT` and for the scores in `FT`. If the slopes are the same, that's called *homogeneity of regression*. If not, you have an interaction of `Prewt` and `Treat`, and you have to be careful about how you state your conclusions.

Adding the regression lines to the plot in Figure 14-10 is helpful. To do this, I add this line to the code that produced Figure 14-10:

```
geom_smooth(method = lm,se = FALSE, aes(linetype=Treat))
```

This instructs ggplot to add a separate line that "smoothes" the data within each treatment group. The `method` argument specifies `lm` (linear modelling) so that each line is a regression line. The next argument, `se=FALSE`, prevents the plotting of the confidence interval around each line. Finally, the aesthetic mapping indicates that the line for each level of `Treat` will look different. So the full code is

```
ggplot(anorexia, aes(x=Prewt,y=WtGain, shape = Treat)) +
   geom_point(size=2.5) +
   geom_smooth(method = lm,se = FALSE, aes(linetype=Treat))
```

and the result is Figure 14-11.

As you can see, the three negatively sloped regression lines are not parallel. The line for `CBT` parallels the line for `FT`, but the line for `Cont` (the control condition) has a much greater negative slope. Assuming that patients in the control group received no treatment, this sounds fairly intuitive: Because they received no treatment, many of these anorexic patients (the heavier ones) continued to lose weight (rather than gain weight), resulting in the highly negative slope for that line.

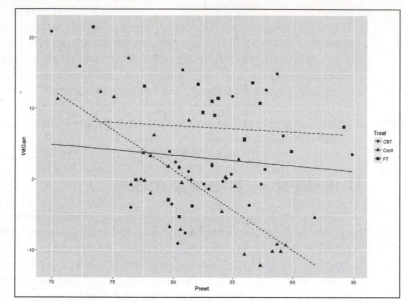

FIGURE 14-11:
Weight Gain versus Treat and Prewt in the anorexia data frame, with a regression line for the scores in each level of Treat.

Apparently, we have a `Treat X Prewt` interaction. Does analysis bear this out?

To include the interaction in the model, I have to add `Treat*Prewt` to the formula:

```
anorexia.w.interaction <- lm(WtGain ~ Treat + Prewt +
        Treat*Prewt, data=anorexia)
```

Does adding the interaction make a difference?

```
> anova(anorexia.T.and.P,anorexia.w.interaction)
Analysis of Variance Table

Model 1: WtGain ~ Treat + Prewt
Model 2: WtGain ~ Treat + Prewt + Treat * Prewt
  Res.Df    RSS Df Sum of Sq      F    Pr(>F)
1     68 3311.3
2     66 2844.8  2    466.48 5.4112 0.006666 **
---
Signif. codes: 0 '***' 0.001 '**' 0.01 '*' 0.05 '.' 0.1 ' ' 1
```

It sure does! In your conclusions about this study, you have to include the caveat that the relationship between pre-weight and weight-gain is different for the control than it is for the cognitive-behavioral treatment and for the family treatment.

Chapter **15**

Correlation: The Rise and Fall of Relationships

In Chapter 14, I introduce the concepts of regression, a tool for summarizing and testing relationships between (and among) variables. In this chapter, I introduce you to the ups and downs of correlation, another tool for looking at relationships. I use the example of employee aptitude and performance from Chapter 14 and show how to think about the data in a slightly different way. The new concepts connect to what I show you in Chapter 14, and you'll see how those connections work. I also show you how to test hypotheses about relationships and how to use R functions for correlation.

Scatter plots Again

A *scatter plot* is a graphical way of showing a relationship between two variables. In Chapter 14, I show you a scatter plot of the data for employees at FarMisht Consulting, Inc. I reproduce that scatter plot here as Figure 15-1. Each point represents one employee's score on a measure of Aptitude (on the x-axis) and on a measure of Performance (on the y-axis).

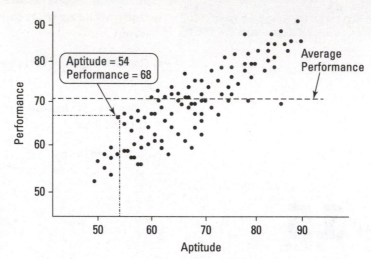

FIGURE 15-1:
Aptitude and
Performance at
FarMisht
Consulting.

Understanding Correlation

In Chapter 14, I refer to Aptitude as the *independent variable* and to Performance as the *dependent variable.* The objective in Chapter 14 is to use Aptitude to predict Performance.

REMEMBER

Although I use scores on one variable to *predict* scores on the other, I do *not* mean that the score on one variable *causes* a score on the other. "Relationship" doesn't necessarily mean "causality."

Correlation is a statistical way of looking at a relationship. When two things are correlated, it means that they vary together. *Positive* correlation means that high scores on one are associated with high scores on the other, and that low scores on one are associated with low scores on the other. The scatter plot in Figure 15-1 is an example of positive correlation.

Negative correlation, on the other hand, means that high scores on the first thing are associated with *low* scores on the second. Negative correlation also means that low scores on the first are associated with high scores on the second. An example is the correlation between body weight and the time spent on a weight-loss program. If the program is effective, the higher the amount of time spent on the program, the lower the body weight. Also, the lower the amount of time spent on the program, the higher the body weight.

Table 15-1, a repeat of Table 14-2, shows the data for 16 FarMisht consultants.

TABLE 15-1

Aptitude Scores and Performance Scores for 16 FarMisht Consultants

Consultant	Aptitude	Performance
1	45	56
2	81	74
3	65	56
4	87	81
5	68	75
6	91	84
7	77	68
8	61	52
9	55	57
10	66	82
11	82	73
12	93	90
13	76	67
14	83	79
15	61	70
16	74	66
Mean	72.81	70.63
Variance	181.63	126.65
Standard Deviation	13.48	11.25

In keeping with the way I use Aptitude and Performance in Chapter 14, Aptitude is the x-variable and Performance is the y-variable.

The formula for calculating the correlation between the two is

$$r = \frac{\left[\frac{1}{N-1}\right]\sum(x-\bar{x})(y-\bar{y})}{s_x s_y}$$

The term on the left, r, is called the *correlation coefficient*. It's also called *Pearson's product-moment correlation coefficient*, after its creator, Karl Pearson.

The two terms in the denominator on the right are the standard deviation of the x-variable and the standard deviation of the y-variable. The term in the numerator is called the *covariance*. Another way to write this formula is

$$r = \frac{\text{cov}(x,y)}{s_x s_y}$$

The covariance represents x and y varying together. Dividing the covariance by the product of the two standard deviations imposes some limits. The lower limit of the correlation coefficient is −1.00, and the upper limit is +1.00.

A correlation coefficient of −1.00 represents perfect negative correlation (low x-scores associated with high y-scores, and high x-scores associated with low y-scores). A correlation of +1.00 represents perfect positive correlation (low x-scores associated with low y-scores and high x-scores associated with high y-scores). A correlation of 0.00 means that the two variables are not related.

Applying the formula to the data in Table 15-1,

$$r = \frac{\left[\frac{1}{N-1}\right]\sum(x-\bar{x})(y-\bar{y})}{s_x s_y}$$

$$= \frac{\left[\frac{1}{16-1}\right]\left[(45-72.81)(56-70.63)+...+(74-72.81)(66-70.83)\right]}{(13.48)(11.25)} = .783$$

What, exactly, does this number mean? I'm about to tell you.

Correlation and Regression

Figure 15-2 shows the scatter plot of just the 16 employees in Table 15-1 with the line that "best fits" the points. It's possible to draw an infinite number of lines through these points. Which one is best?

To be the best, a line has to meet a specific standard: If you draw the distances in the vertical direction between the points and the line, and you square those distances, and then you add those squared distances, the best-fitting line is the one that makes the sum of those squared distances as small as possible. This line is called the *regression line*.

The regression line's purpose in life is to enable you to make predictions. As I mention in Chapter 14, without a regression line, the best predicted value of the y-variable is the mean of the y's. A regression line takes the x-variable into account and delivers a more precise prediction. Each point on the regression line represents a predicted value for *y*. In the symbology of regression, each predicted value is a *y'*.

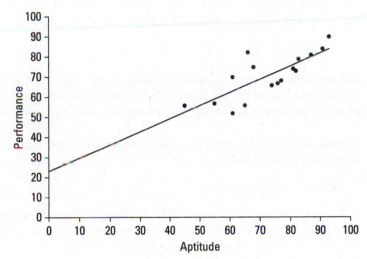

FIGURE 15-2:
Scatter plot of 16
FarMisht
consultants,
including the
regression line.

Why do I tell you all this? Because correlation is closely related to regression. Figure 15-3 focuses on one point in the scatter plot, and on its distance to the regression line and to the mean. (This is a repeat of Figure 14-3.)

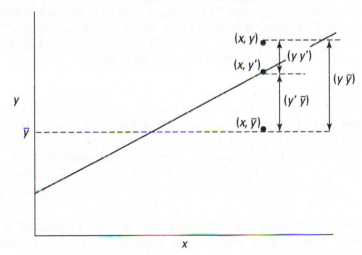

FIGURE 15-3:
One point in the
scatter plot and
its associated
distances

Notice the three distances laid out in the figure. The distance labeled (*y*–*y'*) is the difference between the point and the regression line's prediction for where the point should be. (In Chapter 14, I call that a *residual*.) The distance labeled (*y*–$\bar{y}$)

is the difference between the point and the mean of the y's. The distance labeled $(y'-\bar{y})$ is the gain in prediction capability that you get from using the regression line to predict the point instead of using the mean to predict the point.

Figure 15-3 shows that the three distances are related like this:

$$(y-y')+(y'-\bar{y})=(y-\bar{y})$$

As I point out in Chapter 14, you can square all the residuals and add them, square all the deviations of the predicted points from the mean and add them, and square all the deviations of the actual points from the mean and add them, too.

It turns out that these sums of squares are related in the same way as the deviations I just showed you:

$$SS_{Residual} + SS_{Regression} = SS_{Total}$$

If $SS_{Regression}$ is large in comparison to $SS_{Residual}$, the relationship between the x-variable and the y-variable is a strong one. It means that, throughout the scatter plot, the variability around the regression line is small.

On the other hand, if $SS_{Regression}$ is small in comparison to $SS_{Residual}$, the relationship between the x-variable and the y-variable is weak. In this case, the variability around the regression line is large throughout the scatter plot.

One way to test $SS_{Regression}$ against $SS_{Residual}$ is to divide each by its degrees of freedom (1 for $SS_{Regression}$ and $N-2$ for $SS_{Residual}$) to form variance estimates (also known as mean-squares, or MS), and then divide one by the other to calculate an F. If $MS_{Regression}$ is significantly larger than $MS_{Residual}$, you have evidence that the x-y relationship is strong. (See Chapter 14 for details.)

Here's the clincher, as far as correlation is concerned: Another way to assess the size of $SS_{Regression}$ is to compare it with SS_{Total}. Divide the first by the second. If the ratio is large, this tells you the x-y relationship is strong. This ratio has a name. It's called the *coefficient of determination*. Its symbol is r^2. Take the square root of this coefficient, and you have . . . the correlation coefficient!

$$r = \sqrt{r^2} = \pm\sqrt{\frac{SS_{Regression}}{SS_{Total}}}$$

The plus-or-minus sign ($\pm$) means that r is either the positive or negative square root, depending on whether the slope of the regression line is positive or negative.

So, if you calculate a correlation coefficient and you quickly want to know what its value signifies, just square it. The answer — the coefficient of determination — lets you know the proportion of the SS_{Total} that's tied up in the relationship between the x-variable and the y-variable. If it's a large proportion, the correlation coefficient signifies a strong relationship. If it's a small proportion, the correlation coefficient signifies a weak relationship.

In the Aptitude–Performance example, the correlation coefficient is .783. The coefficient of determination is

$$r^2 = (.783)^2 = .613$$

In this sample of 16 consultants, the $SS_{Regression}$ is 61.3 percent of the SS_{Total}. Sounds like a large proportion, but what's large? What's small? Those questions scream out for hypothesis tests.

Testing Hypotheses About Correlation

In this section, I show you how to answer important questions about correlation. Like any other kind of hypothesis testing, the idea is to use sample statistics to make inferences about population parameters. Here, the sample statistic is r, the correlation coefficient. By convention, the population parameter is ρ (rho), the Greek equivalent of r. (Yes, it does look like the letter p, but it really is the Greek equivalent of r.)

Two kinds of questions are important in connection with correlation: (1) Is a correlation coefficient greater than 0? (2) Are two correlation coefficients different from one another?

Is a correlation coefficient greater than zero?

Returning once again to the Aptitude–Performance example, you can use the sample r to test hypotheses about the population ρ — the correlation coefficient for all consultants at FarMisht Consulting.

Assuming that you know in advance (before you gather any sample data) that any correlation between Aptitude and Performance should be positive, the hypotheses are

$H_0: \rho \leq 0$

$H_1: \rho > 0$

Set $\alpha = .05$.

The appropriate statistical test is a t-test. The formula is

$$t = \frac{r - \rho}{s_r}$$

This test has $N-2$ df.

For the example, the values in the numerator are set: r is .783 and ρ (in H_0) is 0. What about the denominator? I won't burden you with the details. I'll just tell you that's

$$\sqrt{\frac{1 - r^2}{N - 2}}$$

With a little algebra, the formula for the t-test simplifies to

$$t = \frac{r\sqrt{N - 2}}{\sqrt{1 - r^2}}$$

For the example,

$$t = \frac{r\sqrt{N - 2}}{\sqrt{1 - r^2}} = \frac{.783\sqrt{16 - 2}}{\sqrt{1 - .783^2}} = 4.707$$

With df $= 14$ and $\alpha = .05$ (one-tailed), the critical value of t is 1.76. Because the calculated value is greater than the critical value, the decision is to reject H_0.

Do two correlation coefficients differ?

FarKlempt Robotics has a consulting branch that assesses aptitude and performance with the same measurement tools that FarMisht Consulting uses. In a sample of 20 consultants at FarKlempt Robotics, the correlation between Aptitude and Performance is .695. Is this different from the correlation (.783) at FarMisht Consulting? If you have no way of assuming that one correlation should be higher than the other, the hypotheses are

$$H_0: \rho_{FarMisht} = \rho_{FarKlempt}$$

$$H_1: \rho_{FarMisht} \neq \rho_{FarKlempt}$$

Again, $\alpha = .05$.

For highly technical reasons, you can't set up a t-test for this one. In fact, you can't even work with .783 and .695, the two correlation coefficients.

Instead, what you do is *transform* each correlation coefficient into something else and then work with the two "something elses" in a formula that gives you — believe it or not — a z-test.

TECHNICAL STUFF

The transformation is called *Fisher's r to z transformation*. Fisher is the statistician who is remembered as the F in F-test. He transforms the *r* into a *z* by doing this:

$$z_r = \frac{1}{2}\Big[\log_e(1+r) - \log_e(1-r)\Big]$$

If you know what $\log_e$ means, fine. If not, don't worry about it. (I explain it in Chapter 16.) R takes care of all of this for you, as you see in a moment.

Anyway, for this example

$$z_{.783} = \frac{1}{2}\Big[\log_e(1+.783) - \log_e(1-.783)\Big] = 1.0530$$

$$z_{.695} = \frac{1}{2}\Big[\log_e(1+.695) - \log_e(1-.695)\Big] = 0.8576$$

After you transform *r* to *z*, the formula is

$$Z = \frac{z_1 - z_2}{\sigma_{z_1 - z_2}}$$

The denominator turns out to be easier than you might think. It's

$$\sigma_{z_1-z_2} = \sqrt{\frac{1}{N_1 - 3} + \frac{1}{N_2 - 3}}$$

For this example,

$$\sigma_{z_1-z_2} = \sqrt{\frac{1}{N_1 - 3} + \frac{1}{N_2 - 3}} = \sqrt{\frac{1}{16-3} + \frac{1}{20-3}} = .368$$

The whole formula is

$$Z = \frac{z_1 - z_2}{\sigma_{z_1 - z_2}} = \frac{1.0530 - 0.8576}{.368} = .531$$

The next step is to compare the calculated value to a standard normal distribution. For a two-tailed test with $\alpha = .05$, the critical values in a standard normal distribution are 1.96 in the upper tail and −1.96 in the lower tail. The calculated value falls between those two, so the decision is to not reject H_0.

Correlation in R

In this section, I work with the FarMisht example. The data frame, `FarMisht.frame`, holds the data points shown over in Table 14-4. Here's how I created it:

```
Aptitude <- c(45, 81, 65, 87, 68, 91, 77, 61, 55, 66, 82, 93,
        76, 83, 61, 74)
Performance <- c(56, 74, 56, 81, 75, 84, 68, 52, 57, 82, 73, 90,
        67, 79, 70, 66)
Personality <- c(9, 15, 11, 15, 14, 19, 12, 10, 9, 14, 15, 14,
        16, 18, 15, 12)
FarMisht.frame <- data.frame(Aptitude, Performance, Personality)
```

Calculating a correlation coefficient

To find the correlation coefficient for the relationship between Aptitude and Performance, I use the function `cor()`:

```
> with(FarMisht.frame, cor(Aptitude,Performance))
[1] 0.7827927
```

TECHNICAL STUFF

The Pearson product-moment correlation coefficient that `cor()` calculates in this example is the default for its `method` argument:

```
cor(Farmisht.frame, method = "pearson")
```

Two other possible values for `method` are "spearman" and "kendall", which I cover in Appendix B.

Testing a correlation coefficient

To find a correlation coefficient, and test it at the same time, R provides `cor.test()`. Here is a one-tailed test (specified by `alternative = "greater"`):

```
> with(FarMisht.frame, cor.test(Aptitude,Performance,
        alternative = "greater"))

        Pearson's product-moment correlation

data:  Aptitude and Performance
t = 4.7068, df = 14, p-value = 0.0001684
alternative hypothesis: true correlation is greater than 0
```

```
95 percent confidence interval:
 0.5344414 1.0000000
sample estimates:
      cor
0.7827927
```

TECHNICAL STUFF

As is the case with cor(), you can specify "spearman" or "kendall" as the method for cor.test().

Testing the difference between two correlation coefficients

In the earlier section "Do two correlation coefficients differ?" I compare the Aptitude-Performance correlation coefficient (.695) for 20 consultants at FarKlempt Robotics with the correlation (.783) for 16 consultants at FarMisht Consulting.

The comparison begins with Fisher's r to z transformation for each coefficient. The test statistic (Z) is the difference of the transformed values divided by the standard error of the difference.

A function called r.test() does all the work if you provide the coefficients and the sample sizes. This function lives in the psych package, so on the Packages tab, click Insert. Then in the Insert Packages dialog box, type **psych**. When psych appears on the Packages tab, select its check box.

Here's the function, and its arguments:

```
r.test(r12=.783, n=16, r34=.695, n2=20)
```

This one is pretty particular about how you state the arguments. The first argument is the first correlation coefficient. The second is its sample size. The third argument is the second correlation coefficient, and the fourth is its sample size. The 12 label for the first coefficient and the 34 label for the second indicate that the two coefficients are independent.

If you run that function, this is the result:

```
Correlation tests
Call:r.test(n = 16, r12 = 0.783, r34 = 0.695, n2 = 20)
Test of difference between two independent correlations
 z value 0.53    with probability  0.6
```

Calculating a correlation matrix

In addition to finding a single correlation coefficient, cor( ) can find all the pair-wise correlation coefficients for a data frame, resulting in a correlation matrix:

```
> cor(FarMisht.frame)
             Aptitude Performance Personality
Aptitude    1.0000000   0.7827927   0.7499305
Performance 0.7827927   1.0000000   0.7709271
Personality 0.7499305   0.7709271   1.0000000
```

Visualizing correlation matrices

In Chapter 3, I describe a couple of ways to visualize a matrix like the one in the preceding section. Here's how to do it with base R graphics:

```
pairs(FarMisht.frame)
```

This function produces Figure 15-4.

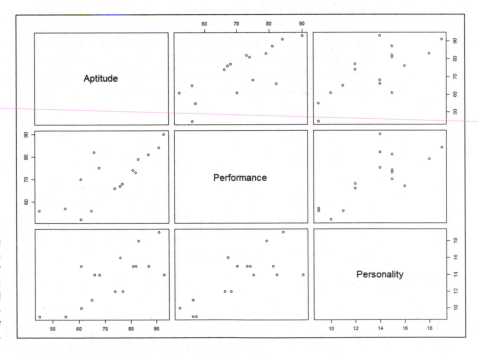

FIGURE 15-4:
The correlation matrix for Aptitude, Performance, and Personality, rendered in base R graphics.

The main diagonal, of course, holds the names of the variables. Each off-diagonal cell is a scatter plot of the pair of variables named in the row and the column. For example, the cell to the immediate right of Aptitude is the scatter plot of Aptitude (y-axis) and Performance (x-axis). The cell just below Aptitude is the reverse — it's the scatter plot of Performance (y-axis) and Aptitude (x-axis).

As I also mention in Chapter 3, a package called GGally (built on ggplot2) provides ggpairs(), which produces a bit more. Find GGally on the Packages tab and select its check box. Then

```
ggpairs(FarMisht.frame)
```

draws Figure 15-5.

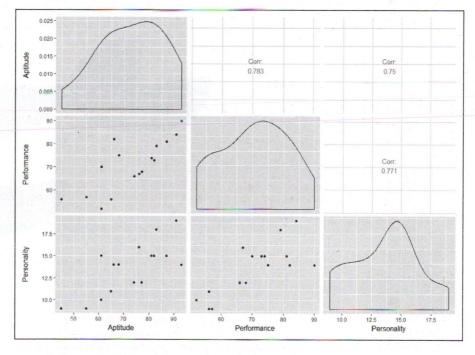

FIGURE 15-5: The correlation matrix for Aptitude, Performance, and Personality, rendered in GGally (a ggplot2-based package).

The main diagonal provides a density function for each variable, the upper off-diagonal cells present the correlation coefficients, and the remaining cells show pairwise scatter plots.

More elaborate displays are possible with the corrgram package. On the Packages tab, click Install, and in the Install dialog box, type **corrgram** and click Install. (Be patient. This package installs a *lot* of items.) Then, on the Packages tab, find corrgram and select its check box.

The `corrgram()` function works with a data frame and enables you to choose options for what goes into the main diagonal (`diag.panel`) of the resulting matrix, what goes into the cells in the upper half of the matrix (`upper.panel`), and what goes into the cells in the lower half of the matrix (`lower.panel`). For the main diagonal, I chose to show the minimum and maximum values for each variable. For the upper half, I specified a pie chart to show the value of a correlation coefficient: The filled-in proportion represents the value. For the lower half, I'd like a scatter plot in each cell:

```
corrgram(FarMisht.frame, diag.panel=panel.minmax,
                upper.panel = panel.pie,
                      lower.panel = panel.pts)
```

The result is Figure 15-6.

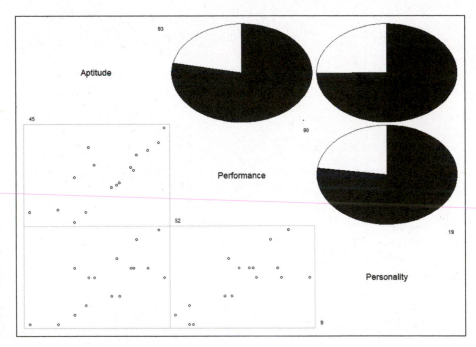

FIGURE 15-6: The correlation matrix for Aptitude, Performance, and Personality, rendered in the corrgram package.

Multiple Correlation

The correlation coefficients in the correlation matrix described in the preceding section combine to produce a *multiple correlation coefficient.* This is a number that summarizes the relationship between the dependent variable — Performance, in this example — and the two independent variables (Aptitude and Personality).

To show you how these correlation coefficients combine, I abbreviate Performance as P, Aptitude as A, and Personality as F (FarMisht Personality Inventory). So r_{PA} is the correlation coefficient for Performance and Aptitude (.7827927), r_{PF} is the correlation coefficient for Performance and Personality (.7709271), and r_{AF} is the correlation coefficient for Aptitude and Personality (.7499305).

Here's the formula that puts them all together:

$$R_{P.AF} = \sqrt{\frac{r_{PA}^2 + r_{PF}^2 - 2r_{PA}r_{PF}r_{AF}}{1 - r_{AF}^2}}$$

The uppercase R on the left indicates that this is a multiple correlation coefficient, as opposed to the lowercase r, which indicates a correlation between two variables. The subscript $P.AF$ means that the multiple correlation is between Performance and the combination of Aptitude and Personality.

For this example,

$$R_{P.AF} = \sqrt{\frac{(.7827927)^2 + (.7709271)^2 - 2(.7827927)(.7709271)(.7499305)}{1 - (.7499305)^2}} = .8306841$$

If you square this number, you get the *multiple coefficient of determination*. In Chapter 14, you met Multiple R-Squared, and that's what this is. For this example, that result is

$$R_{P.AF}^2 = (.830641)^2 = .6900361$$

Multiple correlation in R

The easiest way to calculate a multiple correlation coefficient is to use `lm()` and proceed as in multiple regression:

```
> FarMisht.multreg <- lm(Performance ~ Aptitude + Personality,
        data = FarMisht.frame)
> summary(FarMisht.multreg)

Call:
lm(formula = Performance ~ Aptitude + Personality, data =
        FarMisht.frame)
```

```
Residuals:
   Min      1Q Median     3Q     Max
 -8.689  -2.834 -1.840  2.886 13.432

Coefficients:
             Estimate Std. Error t value Pr(>|t|)
(Intercept)  20.2825     9.6595   2.100   0.0558 .
Aptitude      0.3905     0.1949   2.003   0.0664 .
Personality   1.6079     0.8932   1.800   0.0951 .
---
Signif. codes:  0 '***' 0.001 '**' 0.01 '*' 0.05 '.' 0.1 ' ' 1

Residual standard error: 6.73 on 13 degrees of freedom
Multiple R-squared:   0.69,   Adjusted R-squared:  0.6423
F-statistic: 14.47 on 2 and 13 DF,  p-value: 0.0004938
```

In the next-to-last line, `Multiple R-squared` is right there, waiting for you.

If you have to work with that quantity for some reason, that's

```
> summary(FarMisht.multreg)$r.squared
[1] 0.6900361
```

And to calculate R:

```
> Mult.R.sq <- summary(FarMisht.multreg)$r.squared
> Mult.R <- sqrt(Mult.R.sq)
> Mult.R
[1] 0.8306841
```

Adjusting R-squared

In the output of `lm()`, you see *Adjusted R-squared.* Why is it necessary to "adjust" R-squared?

In multiple regression, adding independent variables (like `Personality`) sometimes makes the regression equation less accurate. The multiple coefficient of determination, R-squared, doesn't reflect this. Its denominator is SS_{Total} (for the dependent variable), and that never changes. The numerator can only increase or stay the same. So any decline in accuracy doesn't result in a lower R-squared.

Taking degrees of freedom into account fixes the flaw. Every time you add an independent variable, you change the degrees of freedom, and that makes all the difference. Just so you know, here's the adjustment:

$$\text{Adjusted } R^2 = 1 - \left(1 - R^2\right)\left[\frac{(N-1)}{(N-k-1)}\right]$$

The k in the denominator is the number of independent variables.

If you ever have to work with this quantity (and I'm not sure why you would), here's how to retrieve it:

```
> summary(FarMisht.multreg)$adj.r.squared
[1] 0.6423494
```

Partial Correlation

Performance and Aptitude are associated with Personality (in the example). Each one's association with Personality might somehow hide the true correlation between them.

What would their correlation be if you could remove that association? Another way to ask this: What would be the Performance–Aptitude correlation if you could hold Personality constant?

One way to hold Personality constant is to find the Performance–Aptitude correlation for a sample of consultants who have one Personality score — 17, for example. In a sample like this, the correlation of each variable with Personality is 0. This usually isn't feasible in the real world, however.

Another way is to find the *partial correlation* between Performance and Aptitude. This is a statistical way of removing each variable's association with Personality in your sample. You use the correlation coefficients in the correlation matrix to do this:

$$r_{PA.F} = \frac{r_{PA} - r_{PF}r_{AF}}{\sqrt{1 - r_{PF}^2}\sqrt{1 - r_{AF}^2}}$$

Once again, P stands for Performance, A for Aptitude, and F for Personality. The subscript *PA.F* means that the correlation is between Performance and Aptitude with Personality "partialled out."

For this example,

$$r_{PA.F} = \frac{.7827927 - (.7709271)(.7499305)}{\sqrt{1 - (.7709271)^2}\sqrt{1 - (.7499305)^2}} = .4857198$$

Partial Correlation in R

A package called ppcor holds the functions for calculating partial correlation and for calculating semipartial correlation, which I cover in the next section.

On the Packages tab, click Install. In the Install Packages dialog box, type **ppcor** and then click Install. Next, find ppcor in the Packages dialog box and select its check box.

The function pcor.test() calculates the correlation between Performance and Aptitude with Personality partialled out:

```
> with (FarMisht.frame, pcor.test(x=Performance, y=Aptitude,
        z=Personality))
   estimate    p.value statistic  n gp  Method
1 0.4857199 0.06642269    2.0035 16  1 pearson
```

In addition to the correlation coefficient (shown below `estimate`), it calculates a t-test of the correlation with $N-3$ df (shown below `statistic`) and an associated p-value.

If you prefer to calculate all the possible partial correlations (and associated p-values and t-statistics) in the data frame, use `pcor()`:

```
> pcor(FarMisht.frame)
$estimate
             Aptitude  Performance  Personality
Aptitude    1.0000000    0.4857199    0.3695112
Performance 0.4857199    1.0000000    0.4467067
Personality 0.3695112    0.4467067    1.0000000

$p.value
             Aptitude   Performance  Personality
Aptitude    0.00000000   0.06642269   0.17525219
Performance 0.06642269   0.00000000   0.09506226
Personality 0.17525219   0.09506226   0.00000000

$statistic
             Aptitude  Performance  Personality
Aptitude    0.000000     2.003500     1.433764
Performance 2.003500     0.000000     1.800222
Personality 1.433764     1.800222     0.000000
```

Each cell under `$estimate` is the partial correlation of the cell's row variable with the cell's column variable, with the third variable partialled out. If you have more than three variables, each cell is the row-column partial correlation with everything else partialled out.

Semipartial Correlation

It's possible to remove the correlation with Personality from just Aptitude without removing it from Performance. This is called *semipartial correlation*. The formula for this one also uses the correlation coefficients from the correlation matrix:

$$r_{P(A.F)} = \frac{r_{PA} - r_{PF}r_{AF}}{\sqrt{1 - r_{AF}^2}}$$

The subscript $P(A.F)$ means that the correlation is between Performance and Aptitude with Personality partialled out of Aptitude only.

Applying this formula to the example,

$$r_{P(A.F)} = \frac{.7827927 - (.7709271)(.7499305)}{\sqrt{1 - (.7499305)^2}} = .3093663$$

Some statistics textbooks refer to semipartial correlation as *part correlation*.

Semipartial Correlation in R

As I mention earlier in this chapter, the ppcor package has the functions for calculating semipartial correlation. To find the semipartial correlation between Performance and Aptitude with Personality partialled out of Aptitude only, use spcor.test():

```
> with (FarMisht.frame, spcor.test(x=Performance, y=Aptitude,
          z=Personality))
    estimate   p.value statistic  n gp  Method
1 0.3093664 0.2618492  1.172979 16  1 pearson
```

As you can see, the output is similar to the output for pcor.test(). Again, estimate is the correlation coefficient and statistic is a *t*-test of the correlation coefficient with $N-3$ df.

To find the semipartial corrleations for the whole data frame, use spcor():

```
> spcor(FarMisht.frame)
$estimate
               Aptitude Performance Personality
Aptitude      1.0000000   0.3213118   0.2299403
Performance   0.3093664   1.0000000   0.2779778
Personality   0.2353503   0.2955039   1.0000000


$p.value
               Aptitude Performance Personality
Aptitude      0.0000000   0.2429000   0.4096955
Performance   0.2618492   0.0000000   0.3157849
Personality   0.3984533   0.2849315   0.0000000


$statistic
               Aptitude Performance Personality
Aptitude      0.0000000   1.223378   0.8518883
```

```
Performance 1.1729794    0.000000    1.0433855
Personality 0.8730923    1.115260    0.0000000
```

Notice that, unlike the matrices in the output for `pcor()`, in these matrices the numbers above the diagonal are not the same as the numbers below the diagonal.

The easiest way to explain is with an example. In the $estimate matrix, the value in the first column, second row (0.3093364) is the correlation between Performance (the row variable) and Aptitude (the column variable) with Personality partialled out of Aptitude. The value in the second column, first row (0.3213118) is the correlation between Aptitude (which is now the row variable) and Performance (which is now the column variable) with Personality partialled out of Performance.

What happens when you have more than three variables? In that case, each cell value is the row-column correlation with everything else partialled out of the column variable.

Chapter **16**

Curvilinear Regression: When Relationships Get Complicated

I n Chapters 14 and 15, I describe linear regression and correlation — two concepts that depend on the straight line as the best-fitting summary of a scatterplot.

But a line is isn't always the best fit. Processes in a variety of areas, from biology to business, conform more to curves than to lines.

For example, think about when you learned a skill — like tying your shoelaces. When you first tried it, it took quite a while didn't it? And then whenever you tried it again, it took progressively less time for you to finish, right? Until finally, you can tie your shoelaces very quickly but you can't really get any faster — you're now doing it is as efficiently as you can.

If you plotted shoelace-tying-time (in seconds) on the y-axis and trials (occasions when you tried to tie your shoes) on the x-axis, the graph might look something like Figure 16-1. A straight line is clearly not the best summary of a plot like this.

How do you find the best-fitting curve? (Another way to say this: "How do you formulate a model for these data?") I'll be happy to show you, but first I have to tell you about logarithms, and about an important number called *e*.

Why? Because those concepts form the foundation of three kinds of nonlinear regression.

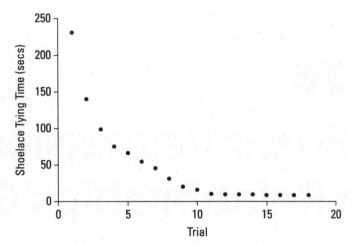

FIGURE 16-1: Hypothetical plot of learning a skill — like tying your shoelaces.

What Is a Logarithm?

Plainly and simply, a logarithm is an *exponent* — a power to which you raise a number. In the equation

$$10^2 = 100$$

2 is an exponent. Does that mean that 2 is also a logarithm? Well . . . yes. In terms of logarithms,

$$\log_{10} 100 = 2$$

That's really just another way of saying $10^2 = 100$. Mathematicians read it as "the logarithm of 100 to the base 10 equals 2." It means that if you want to raise 10 to some power to get 100, that power is 2.

How about 1,000? As you know

$$10^3 = 1000$$

so

$$\log_{10} 1000 = 3$$

How about 763? Uh. . . . Hmm. . . . That's like trying to solve

$$10^x = 763$$

What could that answer possibly be? 10^2 means 10×10 and that gives you 100. 10^3 means $10 \times 10 \times 10$ and that's 1,000. But 763?

Here's where you have to think outside the dialog box. You have to imagine exponents that aren't whole numbers. I know, I know: How can you multiply a number by itself a fraction at a time? If you could, somehow, the number in that 763 equation would have to be between 2 (which gets you to 100) and 3 (which gets you to 1,000).

In the 16th century, mathematician John Napier showed how to do it, and logarithms were born. Why did Napier bother with this? One reason is that it was a great help to astronomers. Astronomers have to deal with numbers that are, well, astronomical. Logarithms ease computational strain in a couple of ways. One way is to substitute small numbers for large ones: The logarithm of 1,000,000 is 6, and the logarithm of 100,000,000 is 8. Also, working with logarithms opens up a helpful set of computational shortcuts. Before calculators and computers appeared on the scene, this was a very big deal.

Incidentally,

$$10^{2.882525} = 763$$

which means that

$$\log_{10} 763 = 2.882525$$

You can use R's log10( ) function to check that out:

```
> log10(763)
[1] 2.882525
```

If you reverse the process, you'll see that

```
> 10^2.882525
[1] 763.0008
```

So, 2.882525 is a *tiny* bit off, but you get the idea.

A bit earlier, I mentioned "computational shortcuts" that result from logarithms. Here's one: If you want to multiply two numbers, add their logarithms, and then find the number whose logarithm is the sum. That last part is called "finding the antilogarithm." Here's a quick example: To multiply 100 by 1,000:

$$\log_{10}(100) + \log_{10}(1000) =$$
$$2 + 3 = 5$$
$$\text{antilog}_{10}(5) = 10^5 = 100,000$$

Here's another computational shortcut: Multiplying the logarithm of a number x by a number b corresponds to raising x to the b power.

Ten, the number that's raised to the exponent, is called the *base*. Because it's also the base of our number system and everyone is familiar with it, logarithms of base 10 are called *common logarithms*. And, as you just saw, a common logarithm in R is log10.

Does that mean you can have other bases? Absolutely. *Any* number (except 0 or 1 or a negative number) can be a base. For example,

$$7.8^2 = 60.84$$

So

$$\log_{7.8} 60.84 = 2$$

And you can use R's log( ) function to check *that* out:

```
> log(60.84,7.8)
[1] 2
```

In terms of bases, one number is special . . .

What Is e?

Which brings me to *e*, a constant that's all about growth.

Imagine the princely sum of $1 deposited in a bank account. Suppose that the interest rate is 2 percent a year. (Yes, this is just an example!) If it's simple interest, the bank adds $.02 every year, and in 50 years you have $2.

If it's compound interest, at the end of 50 years you have $(1+.02)^{50}$ — which is just a bit more than $2.68, assuming that the bank compounds the interest once a year.

Of course, if the bank compounds interest twice a year, each payment is $.01, and after 50 years the bank has compounded it 100 times. That gives you $(1+.01)^{100}$, or just over \$2.70. What about compounding it four times a year? After 50 years — 200 compoundings — you have $(1+.005)^{200}$, which results in the don't-spend-it-all-in-one-place amount of \$2.71 and a tiny bit more.

Focusing on "just a bit more" and "a tiny bit more," and taking it to extremes, after 100,000 compoundings, you have \$2.718268. After 100 million, you have \$2.718282.

If you could get the bank to compound many more times in those 50 years, your sum of money approaches a *limit* — an amount it gets ever so close to, but never quite reaches. That limit is *e*.

The way I set up the example, the rule for calculating the amount is

$$\left(1+\left(\frac{1}{n}\right)\right)^{n}$$

where *n* represents the number of payments. Two cents is 1/50th of a dollar and I specified 50 years — 50 payments. Then I specified two payments a year (and each year's payments have to add up to 2 percent) so that in 50 years you have 100 payments of 1/100th of a dollar, and so on.

To see this concept in action,

```
x <- c(seq(1,10,1),50,100,200,500,1000,10000,100000000)
> y <- (1+(1/x))^x
> data.frame(x,y)
        x         y
1   1e+00  2.000000
2   2e+00  2.250000
3   3e+00  2.370370
4   4e+00  2.441406
5   5e+00  2.488320
6   6e+00  2.521626
7   7e+00  2.546500
8   8e+00  2.565785
9   9e+00  2.581175
10  1e+01  2.593742
11  5e+01  2.691588
12  1e+02  2.704814
13  2e+02  2.711517
14  5e+02  2.715569
15  1e+03  2.716924
16  1e+04  2.718146
17  1e+08  2.718282
```

So *e* is associated with growth. Its value is 2.718282 . . . The three dots mean that you never quite get to the exact value (like π, the constant that enables you to find the area of a circle).

The number *e* pops up in all kinds of places. It's in the formula for the normal distribution (along with π; see Chapter 8), and it's in distributions I discuss in Chapter 18 and in Appendix A). Many natural phenomena are related to *e*.

It's so important that scientists, mathematicians, and business analysts use it as a base for logarithms. Logarithms to the base *e* are called *natural* logarithms. In many textbooks, a natural logarithm is abbreviated as *ln*. In R, it's log.

Table 16-1 presents some comparisons (rounded to three decimal places) between common logarithms and natural logarithms.

TABLE 16-1 **Some Common Logarithms (Log10) and Natural Logarithms (Log)**

Number	Log10	Log
e	0.434	1.000
10	1.000	2.303
50	1.699	3.912
100	2.000	4.605
453	2.656	6.116
1000	3.000	6.908

One more thing: In many formulas and equations, it's often necessary to raise *e* to a power. Sometimes the power is a fairly complicated mathematical expression. Because superscripts are usually printed in a small font, it can be a strain to have to constantly read them. To ease the eyestrain, mathematicians have invented a special notation: *exp*. Whenever you see *exp* followed by something in parentheses, it means to raise *e* to the power of whatever's in the parentheses. For example,

$$\exp(1.6) = e^{1.6} = 4.953032$$

R's exp() function does that calculation for you:

```
> exp(1.6)
[1] 4.953032
```

Applying the exp( ) function with natural logarithms is like finding the antilog with common logarithms.

Speaking of raising *e*, when executives at Google, Inc., filed its IPO, they said they wanted to raise $2,718,281,828, which is *e* times a billion dollars rounded to the nearest dollar.

And now . . . back to curvilinear regression.

Power Regression

Biologists have studied the interrelationships between the sizes and weights of parts of the body. One fascinating relationship is the relation between body weight and brain weight. One way to study this is to assess the relationship across different species. Intuitively, it seems like heavier animals should have heavier brains — but what's the exact nature of the relationship?

In the MASS package, you'll find a data frame called Animals that contains the body weights (in kilograms) and brain weights (in grams) of 28 species. (To follow along, on the Package tab click Install. Then, in the Install Packages dialog box, type **MASS**. When MASS appears on the Packages tab, select its check box.)

The first six rows of Animals are:

```
> head(Animals)
                  body brain
Mountain beaver    1.35   8.1
Cow              465.00 423.0
Grey wolf         36.33 119.5
Goat              27.66 115.0
Guinea pig         1.04   5.5
Dipliodocus    11700.00  50.0
```

Have you ever seen a dipliodocus? No? Outside of a natural history museum, no one else has, either. In addition to this dinosaur in row 6, Animals has triceratops in row 16 and brachiosaurus in row 26. Here, I'll show you:

```
> Animals[c(6,16,26),]
                body brain
Dipliodocus    11700  50.0
Triceratops     9400  70.0
Brachiosaurus  87000 154.5
```

To confine your work to living species, create

```
> Animals.living <- Animals[-c(6,16,26),]
```

which causes those three dinosaurs to vanish from the data frame as surely as they have vanished from the face of the earth.

Let's take a look at the data points. This code snippet

```
ggplot(Animals.living, aes(x=body, y=brain))+
    geom_point()
```

produces Figure 16-2. Note that the idea is to use body weight to predict brain weight.

Doesn't look much like a linear relationship, does it? In fact, it's not. Relationships in this field often take the form

$$y' = ax^b$$

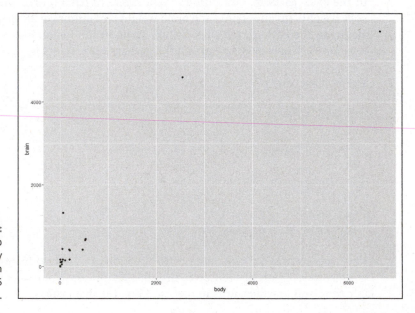

FIGURE 16-2:
The relationship between body weight and brain weight for 25 animal species.

Because the independent (predictor) variable x (body weight, in this case) is raised to a power, this type of model is called *power regression*.

R doesn't have a specific function for creating a power regression model. Its lm( ) function creates linear models, as described in Chapter 14. But you can use lm( ) in this situation if you can somehow transform the data so that the relationship between the transformed body weight and the transformed brain weight is linear.

And this is why I told you about logarithms.

You can "linearize" the scatterplot by working with the logarithm of the body weight and the logarithm of the brain weight. Here's some code to do just that. For good measure, I'll throw in the animal name for each data point:

```
ggplot(Animals.living, aes(x=log(body), y=log(brain)))+
    geom_point()+
    geom_text(aes(label=rownames(Animals.living)))
```

Figure 16-3 shows the result.

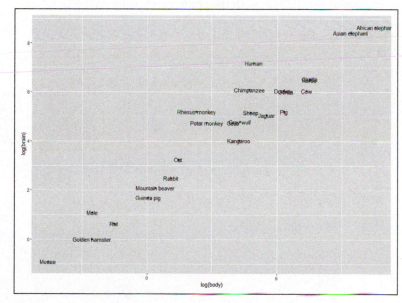

FIGURE 16-3: The relationship between the log of body weight and the log of brain weight for 25 animal species.

I'm surprised by the closeness of donkey and gorilla, but maybe my concept of gorilla comes from *King Kong*. Another surprise is the closeness of horse and giraffe.

Anyway, you can fit a regression line through this scatterplot. Here's the code for the plot with the line and without the animal names:

```
ggplot(Animals.living, aes(x=log(body), y=log(brain)))+
    geom_point()+
    geom_smooth(method = "lm",se=FALSE)
```

The first argument in the last statement (method = "lm") fits the regression line to the data points. The second argument (se=FALSE) prevents ggplot from plotting the 95 percent confidence interval around the regression line. These lines of code produce Figure 16-4.

This procedure — working with the log of each variable and then fitting a regression line — is exactly what to do in a case like this. Here's the analysis:

```
powerfit <- lm(log(brain) ~ log(body), data = Animals.living)
```

As always, lm() indicates a linear model, and the dependent variable is on the left side of the tilde (~) with the predictor variable on the right side. After running the analysis,

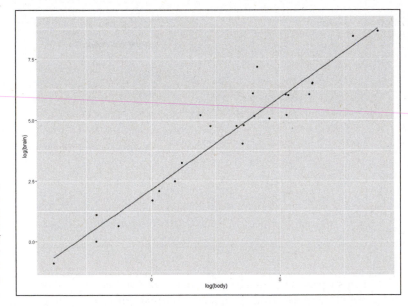

FIGURE 16-4:
The relationship between the log of body weight and the log of brain weight for 25 animal species, with a regression line.

```
> summary(powerfit)

Call:
lm(formula = log(brain) ~ log(body), data = Animals.living)

Residuals:
    Min      1Q  Median      3Q     Max
-0.9125 -0.4752 -0.1557  0.1940  1.9303

Coefficients:
             Estimate Std. Error t value Pr(>|t|)
(Intercept)  2.15041    0.20060   10.72 2.03e-10 ***
log(body)    0.75226    0.04572   16.45 3.24e-14 ***
---
Signif. codes:  0 '***' 0.001 '**' 0.01 '*' 0.05 '.' 0.1 ' ' 1

Residual standard error: 0.7258 on 23 degrees of freedom
Multiple R-squared:  0.9217,   Adjusted R-squared:  0.9183
F-statistic: 270.7 on 1 and 23 DF,  p-value: 3.243e-14
```

The high value of F (270.7) and the extremely low p-value let you know that the model is a good fit.

The coefficients tell you that in logarithmic form, the regression equation is

$$\log(y') = \log(a + bx)$$
$$\log(\text{brainweight}') = \log(2.15041 + (.75226 \times \text{bodyweight}))$$

For the power regression equation, you have to take the antilog of both sides. As I mention earlier, when you're working with natural logarithms, that's the same as applying the exp() function:

$$\exp(\log(y')) = \exp(\log(a + bx))$$
$$y' = \exp(a)x^b$$
$$\text{brainweight}' = \exp(2.15041) \times \text{bodyweight}^{.75226}$$
$$\text{brainweight}' = 8.588397 \times \text{bodyweight}^{.75226}$$

All this is in keeping with what I say earlier in this chapter:

» Adding the logarithms of numbers corresponds to multiplying the numbers.

» Multiplying the logarithm of x by b corresponds to raising x to the b power.

Here's how to use R to find the *exp* of the intercept:

```
> a <- exp(powerfit$coefficients[1])
> a
(Intercept)
   8.588397
```

You can plot the power regression equation as a curve in the original scatterplot:

```
ggplot(Animals.living, aes(x=body, y=brain))+
  geom_point()+
  geom_line(aes(y=exp(powerfit$fitted.values)))
```

That last statement is the business end, of course: `powerfit$fitted.values` contains the predicted brain weights in logarithmic form, and applying `exp()` to those values converts those predictions to the original units of measure. You map them to y to position the curve. Figure 16-5 shows the plot.

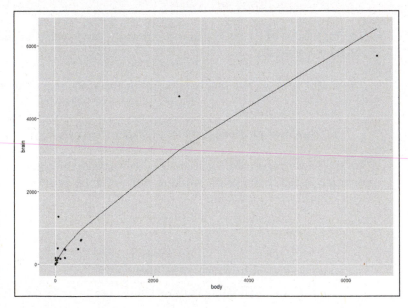

FIGURE 16-5:
Original plot of brain weights and body weights of 25 species, with the power regression curve.

Exponential Regression

As I mention earlier, *e* figures into processes in a variety of areas. Some of those processes, like compound interest, involve growth. Others involve decay.

Here's an example. If you've ever poured a glass of beer and let it stand, you might have noticed that the head gets smaller and smaller (it "decays," in other words) as time passes. You haven't done that? Okay. Go ahead and pour a tall, cool one and watch it for six minutes. I'll wait.

. . . And we're back. Was I right? Notice that I didn't ask you to measure the height of the head as it decayed. Physicist Arnd Leike did that for us for three brands of beer.

He measured head-height every 15 seconds from 0 to 120 seconds after pouring the beer, then every 30 seconds from 150 seconds to 240 seconds, and, finally, at 300 seconds and 360 seconds. (In the true spirit of science, he then drank the beer.) Here are those intervals as a vector:

```
seconds.after.pour <- c(seq(0,120,15), seq(150,240,30),
    c(300,360))
```

and here are the measured head-heights (in centimeters) for one of those brands:

```
head.cm <- c(17, 16.1, 14.9, 14, 13.2, 12.5, 11.9, 11.2,
        10.7, 9.7, 8.9, 8.3, 7.5, 6.3, 5.2)
```

I combine these vectors into a data frame:

```
beer.head <- data.frame(seconds.after.pour,head.cm)
```

Let's see what the plot looks like. This code snippet

```
ggplot(beer.head, aes(x=seconds.after.pour,y=head.cm))+
    geom_point()
```

produces Figure 16-6.

This one is crying out (in its beer?) for a curvilinear model, isn't it?

One way to linearize the plot (so that you can use lm() to create a model) is to work with the log of the y-variable:

```
ggplot(beer.head, aes(x=
            seconds.after.pour,y=log(head.cm)))+
    geom_point()+
    geom_smooth(method="lm",se=FALSE)
```

The last statement adds the regression line (method = "lm") and doesn't draw the confidence interval around the line (se = FALSE). You can see all this in Figure 16-7.

CHAPTER 16 **Curvilinear Regression: When Relationships Get Complicated**   347

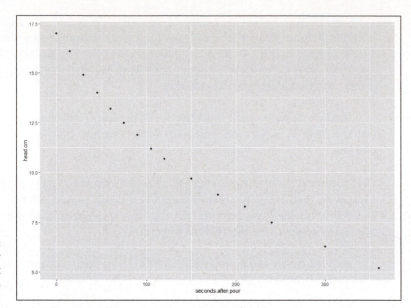

FIGURE 16-6:
How beer
head-height
(head.cm) decays
over time.

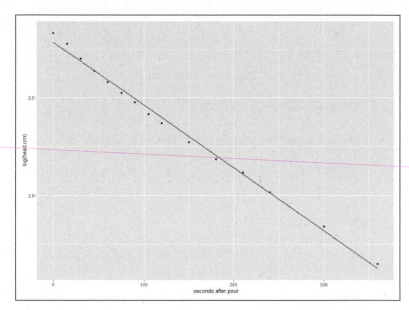

FIGURE 16-7:
How log(head.cm)
decays over time,
including the
regression line.

As in the preceding section, creating this plot points the way for carrying out the analysis. The general equation for the resulting model is

$$y' = ae^{bx}$$

Because the predictor variable appears in an exponent (to which e is raised), this is called *exponential* regression.

And here's how to do the analysis:

```
expfit <- lm(log(head.cm) ~ seconds.after.pour,
            data = beer.head)
```

Once again, `lm()` indicates a linear model, and the dependent variable is on the left side of the tilde (~), with the predictor variable on the right side. After running the analysis,

```
> summary(expfit)

Call:
lm(formula = log(head.cm) ~ seconds.after.pour, data = beer.
        head)

Residuals:
      Min        1Q     Median        3Q       Max
-0.031082 -0.019012 -0.001316   0.017338   0.047806

Coefficients:
                     Estimate Std. Error t value Pr(>|t|)
(Intercept)         2.785e+00  1.110e-02  250.99  < 2e-16 ***
seconds.after.pour -3.223e-03  6.616e-05  -48.72  4.2e-16 ***
---
Signif. codes: 0 '***' 0.001 '**' 0.01 '*' 0.05 '.' 0.1 ' ' 1

Residual standard error: 0.02652 on 13 degrees of freedom
Multiple R-squared:  0.9946,   Adjusted R-squared:  0.9941
F-statistic:  2373 on 1 and 13 DF,  p-value: 4.197e-16
```

The *F* and *p*-value show that this model is a phenomenally great fit. The `R-squared` is among the highest you'll ever see. In fact, Arnd did all this to show his students how an exponential process works. [If you want to see his data for the other two brands, check out Leike, A. (2002), "Demonstration of the exponential decay law using beer froth," *European Journal of Physics*, 23(1), 21–26.]

According to the coefficients, the regression equation in logarithmic form is

$$\log(y') = a + bx$$
$$\log(\text{head.cm}') = 2.785 + \left((-.003223) \times \text{seconds.after.pour} \right)$$

For the exponential regression equation, you have to take the exponential of both sides — in other words, you apply the $\exp()$ function:

$$\exp\big(\log(y')\big) = \exp\big(a + bx\big)$$

$$y' = \exp(a)e^{bx}$$

$$\text{head.cm}' = \exp(2.785) \times e^{-.003223\text{seconds.after.pour}}$$

$$\text{head.cm}' = 16.20642 \times e^{-.003223\text{seconds.after.pour}}$$

Analogous to what you did in the preceding section, you can plot the exponential regression equation as a curve in the original scatterplot:

```
ggplot(beer.head, aes(x= seconds.after.pour,y=head.cm))+
    geom_point()+
    geom_line(aes(y=exp(expfit$fitted.values)))
```

In the last statement, `expfit$fitted.values` contains the predicted beer head-heights in logarithmic form, and applying `exp()` to those values converts those predictions to the original units of measure. Mapping them to y positions the curve. Figure 16-8 shows the plot.

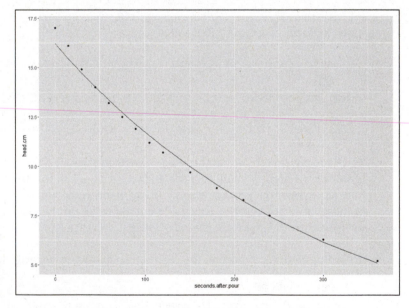

FIGURE 16-8: The decay of head.cm over time, with the exponential regression curve.

Logarithmic Regression

In the two preceding sections, I explain how power regression analysis works with the log of the x-variable and the log of the y-variable, and how exponential regression analysis works with the log of just the y-variable. As you might imagine, one more analytic possibility is available to you — working with just the log of the x-variable. The equation of the model looks like this:

$$y' = a + b\log(x)$$

Because the logarithm is applied to the predictor variable, this is called *logarithmic regression*.

Here's an example that uses the Cars93 data frame in the MASS package. (Make sure you have the MASS package installed. On the Packages tab, find the MASS check box and if it's not selected, click it.)

This data frame, featured prominently in Chapter 3, holds data on a number of variables for 93 cars in the model year 1993. Here, I focus on the relationship between Horsepower (the x-variable) and MPG.highway (the y-variable).

This is the code to create the scatterplot in Figure 16-9:

```
ggplot(Cars93, aes(x=Horsepower,y=MPG.highway))+
    geom_point()
```

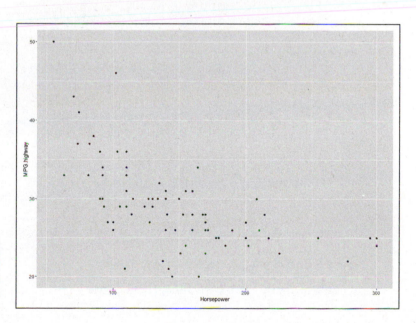

FIGURE 16-9:
MPG.highway and
Horsepower in
the Cars93 data
frame.

For this example, linearize the plot by taking the log of Horsepower. In the plot, include the regression line, and here's how to draw it:

```
ggplot(Cars93, aes(x=log(Horsepower),y=MPG.highway))+
  geom_point()+
  geom_smooth(method="lm",se=FALSE)
```

Figure 16-10 shows the result.

With `log(Horsepower)` as the x-variable, the analysis is

```
logfit <- lm(MPG.highway ~ log(Horsepower), data=Cars93)
```

After carrying out that analysis, `summary()` provides the details:

```
> summary(logfit)

Call:
lm(formula = MPG.highway ~ log(Horsepower), data = Cars93)

Residuals:
     Min       1Q   Median       3Q      Max
-10.3109  -2.2066  -0.0707   2.0031  14.0002

Coefficients:
                Estimate Std. Error t value Pr(>|t|)
(Intercept)       80.003      5.520  14.493  < 2e-16 ***
log(Horsepower)  -10.379      1.122  -9.248 9.55e-15 ***
---
Signif. codes: 0 '***' 0.001 '**' 0.01 '*' 0.05 '.' 0.1 ' ' 1

Residual standard error: 3.849 on 91 degrees of freedom
Multiple R-squared:  0.4845,  Adjusted R-squared:  0.4788
F-statistic: 85.53 on 1 and 91 DF,  p-value: 9.548e-15
```

The high value of F and the very low value of p indicate an excellent fit.

From the coefficients, the regression equation is

$$\text{MPG.highway'} = 80.03 - 10.379\log(\text{Horsepower})$$

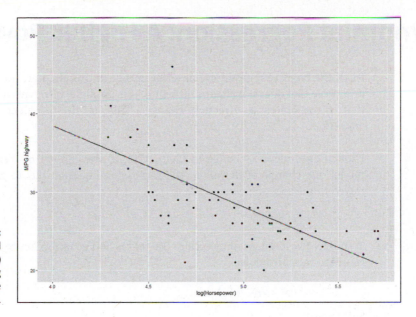

As in the preceding sections, I plot the regression curve in the original plot:

```
ggplot(Cars93, aes(x=Horsepower,y=MPG.highway))+
  geom_point()+
  geom_line(aes(y=logfit$fitted.values))
```

Figure 16-11 shows the plot with the regression curve.

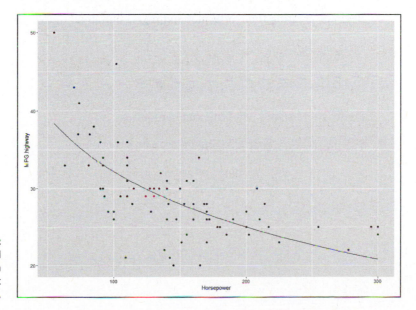

Polynomial Regression: A Higher Power

In all the types of regression I describe earlier in this chapter, the model is a line or a curve that does not change direction. It is possible, however, to create a model that incorporates a direction-change. This is the province of *polynomial regression*.

I touch on direction-change in Chapter 12, in the context of trend analysis. To model one change of direction, the regression equation has to have an *x*-term raised to the second power:

$$y' = a + b_1 x + b_2 x^2$$

To model two changes of direction, the regression equation has to have an *x*-term raised to the third power:

$$y' = a + b_1 x + b_2 x^2 + b_3 x^3$$

and so forth.

I illustrate polynomial regression with another data frame from the MASS package. (On the Packages tab, find MASS. If its check box isn't selected, click it.)

This data frame is called Boston. It holds data on housing values in the Boston suburbs. Among its 14 variables are rm (the number of rooms in a dwelling) and medv (the median value of the dwelling). I focus on those two variables in this example, with rm as the predictor variable.

Begin by creating the scatterplot and regression line:

```
ggplot(Boston, aes(x=rm,y=medv))+
   geom_point()+
   geom_smooth(method=lm, se=FALSE)
```

Figure 16-12 shows what this code produces.

The linear regression model is

```
linfit <- lm(medv ~ rm, data=Boston)
```

```
> summary(linfit)

Call:
lm(formula = medv ~ rm, data = Boston)
```

```
Residuals:
     Min       1Q   Median       3Q      Max
 -23.346   -2.547    0.090    2.986   39.433


Coefficients:
              Estimate Std. Error t value Pr(>|t|)
(Intercept)    -34.671      2.650  -13.08   <2e-16 ***
rm               9.102      0.419   21.72   <2e-16 ***
---
Signif. codes:  0 '***' 0.001 '**' 0.01 '*' 0.05 '.' 0.1 ' ' 1

Residual standard error: 6.616 on 504 degrees of freedom
Multiple R-squared:  0.4835,   Adjusted R-squared:  0.4825
F-statistic: 471.8 on 1 and 504 DF,  p-value: < 2.2e-16
```

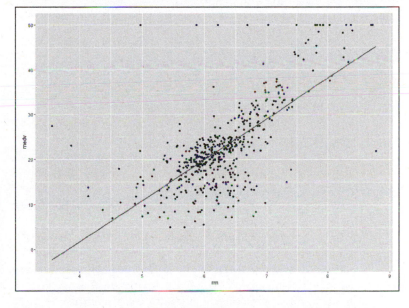

FIGURE 16-12:
Scatterplot of median value (medv) vs rooms (rm) in the Boston data frame, with the regression line.

The F and p-value show that this is a good fit. R-squared tells you that about 48 percent of the SS_{Total} for medv is tied up in the relationship between rm and medv. (Check out Chapter 15 if that last sentence sounds unfamiliar.)

The coefficients tell you that the linear model is

$$medv' = -34.671 + 9.102rm$$

But perhaps a model with a change of direction provides a better fit. To set this up in R, create a new variable `rm2` — which is just `rm` squared:

```
rm2 <- Boston$rm^2
```

Now treat this as a multiple regression analysis with two predictor variables: `rm` and `rm2`:

```
polyfit2 <-lm(medv ~ rm + rm2, data=Boston)
```

TIP

You can't just go ahead and use `rm^2` as the second predictor variable: `lm( )` won't work with it in that form.

After you run the analysis, here are the details:

```
> summary(polyfit2)

Call:
lm(formula = medv ~ rm + rm2, data = Boston)

Residuals:
    Min      1Q  Median      3Q     Max
-35.769  -2.752   0.619   3.003  35.464

Coefficients:
            Estimate Std. Error t value Pr(>|t|)
(Intercept)  66.0588    12.1040   5.458 7.59e-08 ***
rm          -22.6433     3.7542  -6.031 3.15e-09 ***
rm2           2.4701     0.2905   8.502  < 2e-16 ***
---
Signif. codes: 0 '***' 0.001 '**' 0.01 '*' 0.05 '.' 0.1 ' ' 1

Residual standard error: 6.193 on 503 degrees of freedom
Multiple R-squared:  0.5484,   Adjusted R-squared:  0.5466
F-statistic: 305.4 on 2 and 503 DF,  p-value: < 2.2e-16
```

Looks like a better fit than the linear model. The F-statistic here is higher, and this time R-squared tells you that almost 55 percent of the SS_{Total} for `medv` is due to the relationship between `medv` and the combination of `rm` and `rm^2`. The increase in F and in R-squared comes at a cost — the second model has 1 less df (503 versus 504).

The coefficients indicate that the polynomial regression equation is

$$medv' = 66.0588 - 22.6433rm + 2.4701rm^2$$

Is it worth the effort to add `rm^2` to the model? To find out, I use `anova()` to compare the linear model with the polynomial model:

```
> anova(linfit,polyfit2)
Analysis of Variance Table

Model 1: medv ~ rm
Model 2: medv ~ rm + rm2
  Res.Df   RSS Df Sum of Sq      F    Pr(>F)
1    504 22062
2    503 19290  1    2772.3 72.291 < 2.2e-16 ***
---
Signif. codes: 0 '***' 0.001 '**' 0.01 '*' 0.05 '.' 0.1 ' ' 1
```

The high F-ratio (72.291) and extremely low `Pr(>F)` indicate that adding `rm^2` is a good idea.

Here's the code for the scatterplot, along with the curve for the polynomial model:

```
ggplot(Boston, aes(x=rm,y=medv))+
  geom_point()+
  geom_line(aes(y=polyfit2$fitted.values))
```

The predicted values for the polynomial model are in `polyfit2$fitted.values`, which you use in the last statement to position the regression curve in Figure 16-13.

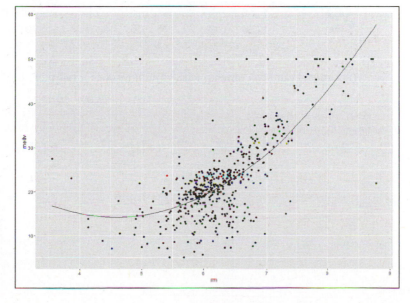

FIGURE 16-13: Scatterplot of median value (medv) versus rooms (rm) in the Boston data frame, with the polynomial regression curve.

The curve in the figure shows a slight downward trend in the dwelling's value as rooms increase from fewer than four to about 4.5, and then the curve trends more sharply upward.

Which Model Should You Use?

I present a variety of regression models in this chapter. Deciding on the one that's right for your data is not necessarily straightforward. One superficial answer might be to try each one and see which one yields the highest F and R-squared.

The operative word in that last sentence is "superficial." The choice of model should depend on your knowledge of the domain from which the data comes and the processes in that domain. Which regression type allows you to formulate a theory about what might be happening in the data?

For instance, in the Boston example, the polynomial model showed that dwelling-value *decreases* slightly as the number of rooms *increases* at the low end, and then value steadily *increases* as the number of rooms increases. The linear model couldn't discern a trend like that. Why would that trend occur? Can you come up with a theory? Does the theory make sense?

I'll leave you with an exercise. Remember the shoelace-tying example at the beginning of this chapter? All I gave you was Figure 16-1, but here are the numbers:

```
trials <-seq(1,18,1)
time.sec <- c(230, 140, 98, 75, 66, 54, 45, 31, 20, 15,
        10, 9, 9, 9, 8, 8, 8, 8)
```

What model can *you* come up with? And how does it help you explain the data?

4

Working with Probability

IN THIS CHAPTER

» **Defining probability**

» **Working with probability**

» **Dealing with random variables and their distributions**

» **Focusing on the binomial distribution**

» **Learning probability-related R functions**

Chapter **17**

Introducing Probability

Probability is the basis of hypothesis testing and inferential statistics, so I use this concept throughout the book. (Seems like a fine time to introduce it!)

Most of the time I represent probability as the proportion of area under part of a distribution. For example, the probability of a Type I error (also known as α) is the area in a tail of the standard normal distribution, or in a tail of the t distribution.

It's time to examine probability in greater detail, including random variables, permutations, and combinations. I show you some fundamentals and applications of probability, and then I focus on a couple of specific probability distributions and also tell you about some probability-related R functions.

What Is Probability?

Most of us have an intuitive idea of probability. Toss a fair coin, and you have a 50–50 chance that it comes up heads. Toss a fair die (one of a pair of dice) and you have a 1–in–6 chance that it comes up displaying a 2.

If you wanted to be more formal in your definition, you'd most likely say something about all the possible things that could happen, and the proportion of those things you care about. Two things can happen when you toss a coin, and if you only care about one of them (heads), the probability of that event happening is one out of two. Six things can happen when you toss a die, and if you only care about one of them (2), the probability of that event happening is one out of six.

Experiments, trials, events, and sample spaces

Statisticians and others who work with probability refer to a process like tossing a coin or throwing a die as an *experiment.* Each time you go through the process, that's a *trial.*

This might not fit your personal definition of an experiment (or of a trial, for that matter), but for a statistician, an *experiment* is any process that produces one of at least two distinct results (like heads or tails).

Here's another piece of the definition of an experiment: You can't predict the result with certainty. Each distinct result is called an *elementary outcome.* Put a bunch of elementary outcomes together and you have an *event.* For example, with a die the elementary outcomes 2, 4, and 6 make up the event "even number."

Put all the possible elementary outcomes together and you've got yourself a *sample space.* The numbers 1, 2, 3, 4, 5, and 6 make up the sample space for a die. Heads and tails make up the sample space for a coin.

Sample spaces and probability

How do events, outcomes, and sample spaces play into probability? If each elementary outcome in a sample space is equally likely, the probability of an event is

$$\text{pr}(\text{Event}) = \frac{\text{Number of Elementary Outcomes in the Event}}{\text{Number of Elementary Outcomes in the Sample Space}}$$

So the probability of tossing a die and getting an even number is

$$\text{pr}(\text{Even Number}) = \frac{\text{Number of Even-Numbered Elementary Outcomes}}{\text{Number of Possible Outcomes of a Die}} = \frac{3}{6} = .5$$

If the elementary outcomes are not equally likely, you find the probability of an event in a different way. First, you have to have some way to assign a probability to each one. Then you add up the probabilities of the elementary outcomes that make up the event.

A couple of things to bear in mind about outcome probabilities:

» Each probability has to be between 0 and 1.

» All the probabilities of elementary outcomes in a sample space have to add up to 1.00.

How do you assign those probabilities? Sometimes you have advance information — such as knowing that a coin is biased toward coming up heads 60 percent of the time. Sometimes you just have to think through the situation to figure out the probability of an outcome.

Here's a quick example of "thinking through the situation." Suppose a die is biased so that the probability of an outcome is proportional to the numerical label of the outcome: A 6 comes up six times as often as a 1, a 5 comes up five times as often as a 1, and so on. What is the probability of each outcome? All the probabilities have to add up to 1.00, and all the numbers on a die add up to 21 ($1+2+3+4+5+6=21$), so the probabilities are: $\mathrm{pr}(1)=1/21$, $\mathrm{pr}(2)=2/21,...$, $\mathrm{pr}(6)=6/21$.

Compound Events

Some rules for dealing with *compound events* help you "think through." A compound event consists of more than one event. It's possible to combine events by either *union* or *intersection* (or both).

Union and intersection

On the toss of a fair die, what's the probability of getting a 1 or a 4? Mathematicians have a symbol for *or*. It's called *union*, and it looks like this: ∪. Using this symbol, the probability of a 1 or a 4 is *pr*(1 ∪ 4).

In approaching this kind of probability, it's helpful to keep track of the elementary outcomes. One elementary outcome is in each event, so the event "1 or 4" has two elementary outcomes. With a sample space of six outcomes, the probability is 2/6, or 1/3. Another way to calculate this is

$$pr(1 \cup 4) = pr(1) + pr(4) = \frac{1}{6} + \frac{1}{6} = \frac{2}{6} = \frac{1}{3}$$

Here's a slightly more involved one: What's the probability of getting a number between 1 and 3 or a number between 2 and 4?

Just adding the elementary outcomes in each event won't get it done this time. Three outcomes are in the event "between 1 and 3" and three are in the event "between 2 and 4." The probability can't be $3 + 3$ divided by the six outcomes in the sample space, because that's 1.00, leaving nothing for $pr(5)$ and $pr(6)$. For the same reason, you can't just add the probabilities.

The challenge arises in the overlap of the two events. The elementary outcomes in "between 1 and 3" are 1, 2, and 3. The elementary outcomes in "between 2 and 4" are 2, 3, and 4. Two outcomes overlap: 2 and 3. In order to not count them twice, the trick is to subtract them from the total.

A couple of things will make life easier as I proceed. I abbreviate "between 1 and 3" as A and "between 2 and 4" as B. Also, I use the mathematical symbol for "overlap." The symbol is $\cap$ and it's called *intersection*.

Using the symbols, the probability of "between 1 and 3" or "between 2 and 4" is

$$pr(A \cup B) = \frac{\text{Number of Outcomes in A} + \text{Number of Outcomes in B} - \text{Number of Outcomes in } (A \cap B)}{\text{Number of Outcomes in the Sample Space}}$$

$$pr(A \cup B) = \frac{3 + 3 - 2}{6} = \frac{4}{6} = \frac{2}{3}$$

You can also work with the probabilities:

$$pr(A \cup B) = \frac{3}{6} + \frac{3}{6} - \frac{2}{6} = \frac{4}{6} = \frac{2}{3}$$

The general formula is

$$pr(A \cup B) = pr(A) + pr(B) - pr(A \cap B)$$

Why was it okay to just add the probabilities together in the earlier example? Because $pr(1 \cap 4)$ is zero: It's impossible to get a 1 and a 4 in the same toss of a die. Whenever $pr(A \cap B) = 0$, A and B are said to be *mutually exclusive*.

Intersection again

Imagine throwing a coin and rolling a die at the same time. These two experiments are *independent*, because the result of one has no influence on the result of the other.

What's the probability of getting heads and a 4? You use the intersection symbol and write this as $pr(\text{heads} \cap 4)$:

$$pr(\text{Heads} \cap 4) = \frac{\text{Number of Elementary Outcomes in Heads} \cap 4}{\text{Number of Elementary Outcomes in the Sample Space}}$$

Start with the sample space. Table 17-1 lists all the elementary outcomes.

TABLE 17-1

The Elementary Outcomes in the Sample Space for Throwing a Coin and Rolling a Die

Heads, 1	Tails, 1
Heads, 2	Tails, 2
Heads, 3	Tails, 3
Heads, 4	Tails, 4
Heads, 5	Tails, 5
Heads, 6	Tails, 6

As the table shows, 12 outcomes are possible. How many outcomes are in the event "heads and 4"? Just one. So

$$pr(\text{Heads} \cap 4) = \frac{\text{Number of Elementary Outcomes in Heads} \cap 4}{\text{Number of Elementary Outcomes in the Sample Space}} = \frac{1}{12}$$

You can also work with the probabilities:

$$pr(\text{Heads} \cap 4) = pr(\text{Heads}) \times pr(4) = \frac{1}{12}$$

In general, if A and B are independent,

$$pr(A \cap B) = pr(A) \times pr(B)$$

Conditional Probability

In some circumstances, you narrow the sample space. For example, suppose I toss a die and I tell you the result is greater than 2. What's the probability that it's a 5?

Ordinarily, the probability of a 5 would be 1/6. In this case, however, the sample space isn't 1, 2, 3, 4, 5, and 6. When you know the result is greater than 2, the sample space becomes 3, 4, 5, and 6. The probability of a 5 is now 1/4.

This is an example of *conditional probability*. It's "conditional" because I've given a "condition" — the toss resulted in a number greater than 2. The notation for this is

$$pr(5 \mid \text{Greater than 2})$$

REMEMBER

The vertical line (|) is shorthand for the word "given," and you read that notation as "the probability of a 5 given greater than 2."

Working with the probabilities

In general, if you have two events A and B,

$$pr(A \mid B) = \frac{pr(A \cap B)}{pr(B)}$$

as long as pr(B) isn't zero.

For the intersection in the numerator on the right, this is *not* a case where you just multiply probabilities together. In fact, if you could do that, you wouldn't have a conditional probability, because that would mean A and B are independent. If they're independent, one event can't be conditional on the other.

You have to think through the probability of the intersection. In a die, how many outcomes are in the event "5 ∩ Greater than 2"? Just one, so pr(5 ∩ Greater than 2) is 1/6, and

$$pr(5 \mid \text{Greater than 2}) = \frac{pr(5 \cap \text{Greater than 2})}{pr(\text{Greater than 2})} = \frac{\frac{1}{6}}{\frac{4}{6}} = \frac{1}{4}$$

The foundation of hypothesis testing

All the hypothesis testing I discuss in previous chapters involves conditional probability. When you calculate a sample statistic, compute a statistical test, and then compare the test statistic against a critical value, you're looking for a conditional probability. Specifically, you're trying to find

$$pr(\text{obtained test statistic or a more extreme value} \mid H_0 \text{ is true})$$

If that conditional probability is low (less than .05 in all the examples I show you in hypothesis-testing chapters), you reject H_0.

Large Sample Spaces

When dealing with probability, it's important to understand the sample space. In the examples I've shown you so far in this chapter, the sample spaces are small. With a coin or a die, it's easy to list all the elementary outcomes.

The world, of course, isn't that simple. In fact, even the probability problems that live in statistics textbooks aren't that simple. Most of the time, sample spaces are large and it's not convenient to list every elementary outcome.

Take, for example, rolling a die twice. How many elementary outcomes are in the sample space consisting of both tosses? You can sit down and list them, but it's better to reason it out: Six possibilities for the first toss, and each of those six can pair up with six possibilities on the second. So the sample space has $6 \times 6 = 36$ possible elementary outcomes.

This is similar to the coin-and-die sample space in Table 17-1, where the sample space consists of $2 \times 6 = 12$ elementary outcomes. With 12 outcomes, it was easy to list them all in a table. With 36 outcomes it starts to get, well, dicey. (Sorry.)

Events often require some thought, too. What's the probability of rolling a die twice and totaling 5? You have to count the number of ways the two tosses can total 5, and then divide by the number of elementary outcomes in the sample space (36). You total a 5 by getting any of these pairs of tosses: 1 and 4, 2 and 3, 3 and 2, or 4 and 1. That totals four ways, and they don't overlap (excuse me — *intersect*), so

$$pr(5) = \frac{\text{Number of Ways of Rolling a 5}}{\text{Number of Possible Outcomes of Two Tosses}} = \frac{4}{36} = .11$$

Listing all the elementary outcomes for the sample space is often a nightmare. Fortunately, shortcuts are available, as I show in the upcoming subsections. Because each shortcut quickly helps you count a number of items, another name for a shortcut is a *counting rule*.

Believe it or not, I just slipped one counting rule past you. A couple of paragraphs ago, I say that in two tosses of a die you have a sample space of $6 \times 6 = 36$ possible outcomes. This is the *product rule*: If N_1 outcomes are possible on the first trial of an experiment, and N_2 outcomes are possible on the second trial, the number of possible outcomes is $N_1 N_2$. Each possible outcome on the first trial can associate with all possible outcomes on the second. What about three trials? That's $N_1 N_2 N_3$.

Now for a couple more counting rules.

Permutations

Suppose you have to arrange five objects into a sequence. How many ways can you do that? For the first position in the sequence, you have five choices. After you make that choice, you have four choices for the second position. Then you have three choices for the third, two for the fourth, and one for the fifth. The number of ways is $(5)(4)(3)(2)(1) = 120$.

In general, the number of sequences of N objects is $N(N-1)(N-2)...(2)(1)$. This kind of computation occurs fairly frequently in the probability world, and it has its own notation: $N!$ You don't read this by screaming out "N" in a loud voice. Instead, it's "N factorial." By definition, $1! = 1$, and $0! = 1$.

Now for the good stuff. If you have to order the 26 letters of the alphabet, the number of possible sequences is 26!, a huge number. But suppose the task is to create five-letter sequences so that no letter repeats in the sequence. How many ways can you do that? You have 26 choices for the first letter, 25 for the second, 24 for the third, 23 for the fourth, 22 for the fifth, and that's it. So that's (26)(25)(24)(23)(22). Here's how that product is related to 26!:

$$\frac{26!}{21!}$$

Each sequence is called a *permutation*. In general, if you take permutations of N things r at a time, the notation is $_NP_r$ (the P stands for *permutation*). The formula is

$$_NP_r = \frac{N!}{(N-r)!}$$

Just for completeness, here's another wrinkle. Suppose that I allow repetitions in these sequences of 5. That is, aabbc is a permissible sequence. In that case, the number of sequences is $26 \times 26 \times 26 \times 26 \times 26$, or as mathematicians would say, "26 raised to the fifth power." Or as mathematicians would write, "26^5."

Combinations

In the preceding example, these sequences are different from one another: *abcde, adbce, dbcae,* and on and on and on. In fact, you could come up with $5! = 120$ of these different sequences just for the letters $a, b, c, d,$ and e.

Suppose I add the restriction that one of these sequences is no different from another, and all I'm concerned about is having sets of five nonrepeating letters in no particular order. Each set is called a *combination*. For this example, the number of combinations is the number of permutations divided by 5!:

$$\frac{26!}{5!(21!)}$$

In general, the notation for combinations of N things taken r at a time is $_NC_r$ (the C stands for *combination*). The formula is

$$_NC_r = \frac{N!}{r!(N-r)!}$$

I touch on this topic in Appendix B. In the context of a statistical test called the Wilcoxon rank sum test, I use as an example the number of combinations of eight things taken four at a time:

$$_8C_4 = \frac{8!}{4!4!} = 70$$

Now for that completeness wrinkle again. Suppose I allow repetitions in these sequences. How many sequences would I have? It turns out to be equivalent to $N+r-1$ things taken $N-1$ at a time, or $_{N+r+1}C_{N-1}$. For this example, that would be $_{30}C_{25}$.

R Functions for Counting Rules

R provides `factorial()` for finding the factorial of a number:

```
> factorial(6)
[1] 720
```

You can also use this function to find the factorial of each number in a vector:

```
> xx <- c(2,3,4,5,6)
> factorial(xx)
[1]    2    6   24  120  720
```

For combinations, R provides a couple of possibilities. The `choose()` function calculates $_NC_r$ — the number of combinations of N things taken r at a time. So, for 8 things taken 4 at a time (refer to the example from Appendix B), that's

```
> choose(8,4)
[1] 70
```

To list all the combinations, use `combn()`. I illustrate with $_4C_2$. I have a vector containing the names of four of the Marx Brothers

```
Marx.Bros <- c("Groucho","Chico","Harpo","Zeppo")
```

and I want to list all possible combinations of them taken two at a time:

```
> combn(Marx.Bros,2)
        [,1]      [,2]      [,3]      [,4]     [,5]     [,6]
[1,] "Groucho" "Groucho" "Groucho" "Chico"  "Chico"  "Harpo"
[2,] "Chico"   "Harpo"   "Zeppo"   "Harpo"  "Zeppo"  "Zeppo"
```

This matrix tells me that six such combinations are possible, and the two rows in each column show the two names in each combination.

In my view, the best functions for dealing with combinations and permutations are in the `gtools` package. On the Packages tab, find `gtools` and select its check box.

Here are the `combinations()` and `permutations()` functions from `gtools` at work:

```
> combinations(4,2,v=Marx.Bros)
      [,1]       [,2]
[1,] "Chico"    "Groucho"
[2,] "Chico"    "Harpo"
[3,] "Chico"    "Zeppo"
[4,] "Groucho"  "Harpo"
[5,] "Groucho"  "Zeppo"
[6,] "Harpo"    "Zeppo"

> permutations(4,2,v=Marx.Bros)
       [,1]       [,2]
 [1,] "Chico"    "Groucho"
 [2,] "Chico"    "Harpo"
 [3,] "Chico"    "Zeppo"
 [4,] "Groucho"  "Chico"
 [5,] "Groucho"  "Harpo"
 [6,] "Groucho"  "Zeppo"
 [7,] "Harpo"    "Chico"
 [8,] "Harpo"    "Groucho"
 [9,] "Harpo"    "Zeppo"
[10,] "Zeppo"    "Chico"
[11,] "Zeppo"    "Groucho"
[12,] "Zeppo"    "Harpo"
```

For each function, the first argument is N, the second is r, and the third is the vector containing the items. Without the vector, here's what happens:

```
> combinations(4,2)
      [,1] [,2]
[1,]    1    2
[2,]    1    3
[3,]    1    4
[4,]    2    3
[5,]    2    4
[6,]    3    4
```

If all you want to do is solve for the number of combinations:

```
> nrow(combinations(4,2))
[1] 6
```

Of course, you can do the same for permutations.

Random Variables: Discrete and Continuous

Let me go back to tosses of a fair die, where six elementary outcomes are possible. If I use *x* to refer to the result of a toss, *x* can be any whole number from 1 to 6. Because *x* can take on a set of values, it's a variable. Because *x*'s possible values correspond to the elementary outcomes of an experiment (meaning you can't predict its values with absolute certainty), *x* is called a *random variable*.

Random variables come in two varieties. One variety is *discrete*, of which die-tossing is a good example. A discrete random variable can only take on what mathematicians like to call a *countable* number of values — like the numbers 1 through 6. Values between the whole numbers 1 through 6 (like 1.25 and 3.1416) are impossible for a random variable that corresponds to the outcomes of die-tosses.

The other kind of random variable is *continuous.* A continuous random variable can take on an infinite number of values. Temperature is an example. Depending on the precision of a thermometer, having temperatures like 34.516 degrees is possible.

Probability Distributions and Density Functions

Back again to die-tossing. Each value of the random variable *x* (1–6, remember) has a probability. If the die is fair, each probability is 1/6. Pair each value of a discrete random variable like *x* with its probability, and you have a *probability distribution.*

Probability distributions are easy enough to represent in graphs. Figure 17-1 shows the probability distribution for *x*.

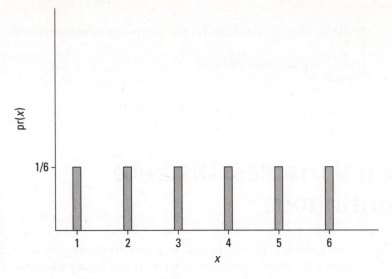

FIGURE 17-1:
The probability
distribution for x,
a random
variable based on
the tosses of a
fair die.

A random variable has a mean, a variance, and a standard deviation. Calculating these parameters is pretty straightforward. In the random-variable world, the mean is called the *expected value*, and the expected value of random variable x is abbreviated as E(x). Here's how you calculate it:

$$E(x) = \sum x\big(pr(x)\big)$$

For the probability distribution in Figure 17-1, that's

$$E(x) = \sum x\big(pr(x)\big) = (1)\left(\frac{1}{6}\right)+(2)\left(\frac{1}{6}\right)+(3)\left(\frac{1}{6}\right)+(4)\left(\frac{1}{6}\right)+(5)\left(\frac{1}{6}\right)+(6)\left(\frac{1}{6}\right) = 3.5$$

The variance of a random variable is often abbreviated as V(x), and the formula is

$$V(x) = \sum x^2\big(pr(x)\big) - \big[E(x)\big]^2$$

Working with the probability distribution in Figure 17-1 once again,

$$V(x) = \left(1^2\right)\left(\frac{1}{6}\right)+\left(2^2\right)\left(\frac{1}{6}\right)+\left(3^2\right)\left(\frac{1}{6}\right)+\left(4^2\right)\left(\frac{1}{6}\right)+\left(5^2\right)\left(\frac{1}{6}\right)+\left(6^2\right)\left(\frac{1}{6}\right) - \left[3.5\right]^2 = 2.917$$

The standard deviation is the square root of the variance, which in this case is 1.708.

For continuous random variables, things get a little trickier. You can't pair a value with a probability, because you can't really pin down a value. Instead, you associate a continuous random variable with a mathematical rule (an equation) that generates *probability density*, and the distribution is called a *probability density function.* To calculate the mean and variance of a continuous random variable, you need calculus.

In Chapter 8, I show you a probability density function — the standard normal distribution. I reproduce it here as Figure 17-2.

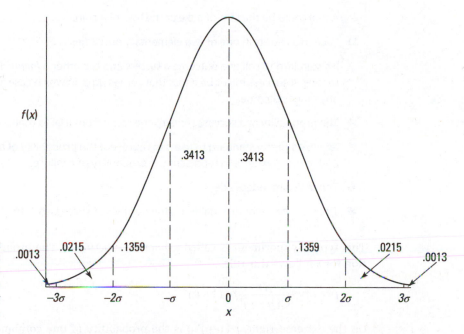

FIGURE 17-2:
The standard
normal
distribution: a
probability
density function.

In the figure, $f(x)$ represents the probability density. Because probability density can involve some heavyweight mathematical concepts, I won't go into it. As I mention in Chapter 8, think of probability density as something that turns the area under the curve into probability.

Although you can't speak of the probability of a specific value of a continuous random variable, you can work with the probability of an interval. To find the probability that the random variable takes on a value within an interval, you find the proportion of the total area under the curve that's inside that interval. Figure 17-2 shows this concept. The probability that x is between 0 and 1σ is .3413.

For the rest of this chapter, I deal just with discrete random variables. A specific one is up next.

The Binomial Distribution

Imagine an experiment that has these five characteristics:

» The experiment consists of *N* identical trials.

A trial could be the toss of a die or the toss of a coin.

» Each trial results in one of two elementary outcomes.

It's standard to call one outcome a *success* and the other a *failure*. For die-tossing, a success might be a toss that comes up 3, in which case a failure is any other outcome.

» The probability of a success remains the same from trial to trial.

Again, it's pretty standard to use *p* to represent the probability of a success and to use *1–p* (or *q*) to represent the probability of a failure.

» The trials are independent.

» The discrete random variable *x* is the number of successes in the *N* trials.

This type of experiment is called a *binomial experiment*. The probability distribution for *x* follows this rule:

$$pr(x) = \frac{N!}{x!(n-x)!} p^x (1-p)^{N-x}$$

On the extreme right, $p^x(1-p)^{N-x}$ is the probability of one combination of *x* successes in *N* trials. The term to its immediate left is $_NC_x$, the number of possible combinations of *x* successes in *N* trials.

This is called the *binomial distribution.* You use it to find probabilities like the probability you'll get four 3s in ten tosses of a die:

$$pr(4) = \frac{10!}{4!(6!)} \left(\frac{1}{6}\right)^4 \left(\frac{5}{6}\right)^6 = .054$$

The *negative binomial distribution* is closely related. In this distribution, the random variable is the number of trials before the *x*th success. For example, you use the negative binomial to find the probability of five tosses that result in anything but a 3 before the fourth time you roll a 3.

For this to happen, in the eight tosses before the fourth 3, you have to get five non–3s and three successes (tosses when a 3 comes up). Then the next toss results in a 3. The probability of a combination of four successes and five failures is

$p^4(1-p)^5$. The number of ways you can have a combination of five failures and four-to-one successes is $_{5+4-1}C_{4-1}$. So the probability is

$$pr(5 \text{ failures before the 4th success}) = \frac{(5+4-1)!}{(4-1)!(5!)}\left(\frac{1}{6}\right)^4\left(\frac{5}{6}\right)^5 = .017$$

In general, the negative binomial distribution (sometimes called the *Pascal distribution*) is

$$pr(f \text{ failures before the } x\text{th success}) = \frac{(f+x-1)!}{(x-1)!(f!)}p^x(1-p)^f$$

The Binomial and Negative Binomial in R

R provides `binom` functions for the binomial distribution, and `nbinom` functions for the negative binomial distribution. For both distributions, I work with die-tosses so that p (the probability of a success) = 1/6.

Binomial distribution

As is the case for other built-in distributions, R provides these functions for the binomial distribution: `dbinom()` (density function), `pbinom()` (cumulative distribution function), `qbinom()` (quantiles), and `rbinom()` (random number generation).

To show you a binomial distribution, I use `dbinon()` to plot the density function for the number of successes in ten tosses of a fair die. I begin by creating a vector for the number of successes:

```
successes <- seq(0,10)
```

and then a vector for the associated probabilities:

```
probability <- dbinom(successes,10,1/6)
```

The first argument, of course, is the vector of successes, the second is the number of trials, and the third (1/6) is the probability of a success with a fair six-sided die.

To plot this density function:

```
ggplot(NULL,aes(x=successes,y=probability))+
  geom_bar(stat="identity",width=1,color="white")
```

The `NULL` argument in `ggplot()` indicates that I haven't created a data frame — I'm just using the `successes` and `probability` vectors. In `geom_bar()`, the `stat="identity"` argument indicates that the values in the `probability` vector set the heights of the bars, `width = 1` widens the bars a bit from the default width, and `color = "white"` adds clarity by putting a white border around each bar. The code creates Figure 17-3.

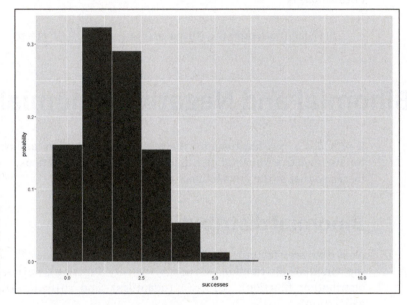

FIGURE 17-3:
Binomial distribution of the number of successes in ten tosses of a fair die.

Next, I use `pbinom()` to show you the cumulative distribution for the number of successes in ten tosses of a fair die:

```
cumulative <-pbinom(successes,10,1/6)
```

And here's the code for the plot:

```
ggplot(NULL,aes(x=successes,y=cumulative))+
  geom_step()
```

The second statement produces the stepwise function you see in Figure 17-4:

Each step represents the probability of getting *x* or fewer successes in ten tosses.

The qbinom() function computes quantile information. For every fifth quantile from the 10th through the 95th in the binomial distribution with $N = 10$ and $p = 1/6$:

```
> qbinom(seq(.10,.95,.05),10,1/6)
 [1] 0 0 1 1 1 1 1 1 2 2 2 2 2 2 2 3 3 3 4
```

To sample 5 random numbers from this binomial distribution

```
> rbinom(5, 10, 1/6)
[1] 4 3 3 0 2
```

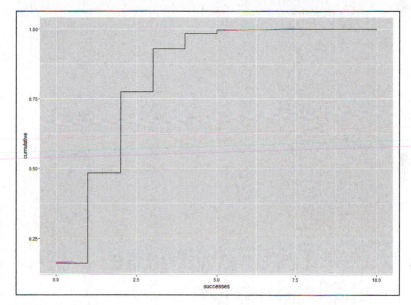

FIGURE 17-4:
Cumulative distribution of the number of successes in ten tosses of a fair die.

Negative binomial distribution

For the negative binomial functions, dnbinom() provides the density function, pnbinom() gives you the cumulative distribution function, qnbinom() gives quantile information, and rnbinom() produces random numbers.

The example I show you earlier involves the number of failures before the fourth success of a die-toss. That case was the probability of 5 failures before the fourth toss, and I use dnbinom() to calculate that probability:

```
> dnbinom(5,4,1/6)
[1] 0.01736508
```

The first argument to dnbinom() is the number of failures, the second is the number of successes, and the third is the probability of a success.

If I want to know the probability of five or fewer failures before the fourth success:

```
> pnbinom(5,4,1/6)
[1] 0.04802149
```

which is the same as

```
> sum(dnbinom(seq(0,5),4,1/6))
[1] 0.04802149
```

For every fifth quantile from the 10th through 95th of the number of failures before four successes (with $p = 1/6$):

```
> qnbinom(seq(.10,.95,.05),4,1/6)
 [1]  8  9 11 12 13 14 16 17 18 20 21 22 24 26 28 31 35 41
```

And to sample five random numbers from the negative binomial with 4 successes and $p = 1/6$:

```
> rnbinom(5, 4, 1/6)
[1] 10  5  4 23  7
```

Hypothesis Testing with the Binomial Distribution

Hypothesis tests sometimes involve the binomial distribution. Typically, you have some idea about the probability of a success, and you put that idea into a null hypothesis. Then you perform N trials and record the number of successes. Finally, you compute the probability of getting that many successes or a more extreme amount if your H_0 is true. If the probability is low, reject H_0.

When you test in this way, you're using sample statistics to make an inference about a population parameter. Here, that parameter is the probability of a success in the population of trials. By convention, Greek letters represent parameters. Statisticians use π (pi), the Greek equivalent of p, to stand for the probability of a success in the population.

Continuing with the die-tossing example, suppose you have a die and you want to test whether or not it's fair. You suspect that if it's not, it's biased toward 3. Define a toss that results in 3 as a success. You toss it ten times. Five tosses are successes. Casting all this into hypothesis-testing terms:

$H_0: \pi \le 1/6$

$H_{1:}\ \pi > 1/6$

As I usually do, I set $\alpha = .05$.

To test these hypotheses, you have to find the probability of getting at least four successes in ten tosses with p = 1/6. That probability is $pr(5) + pr(6) + pr(7) + pr(8) + pr(9) + pr(10)$. If the total is less than .05, reject H_o.

Once upon a time, that would have been a lot of calculating. With R, not so much. The function `binom.test()` does all the work:

```
binom.test(5,10,1/6, alternative="greater")
```

The first argument is the number of successes, the second is the number of tosses, the third is π, and the fourth is the alternative hypothesis. Running this function produces

```
> binom.test(5,10,1/6, alternative="greater")

        Exact binomial test

data:   5 and 10
number of successes = 5, number of trials = 10,
p-value = 0.01546
alternative hypothesis: true probability of success is greater
        than 0.1666667
95 percent confidence interval:
 0.2224411 1.0000000
sample estimates:
probability of success
        0.5
```

The *p*-value (0.01546) is much less than .05, and that tells me to reject the null hypothesis. Also, note the additional information about confidence intervals and the estimated probability of a success (the number of obtained successes divided by number of trials).

If you've been following the discussion about the binomial distribution, you know that two other ways of calculating that p-value are

```
> sum(dbinom(seq(5,10),10,1/6))
[1] 0.01546197
```

and

```
> 1-pbinom(4,10,1/6)
[1] 0.01546197
```

Any way you slice it, the decision is to reject the null hypothesis.

More on Hypothesis Testing: R versus Tradition

When $N\pi \geq 5$ (Number of trials × the hypothesized probability of a success) and $N(1-\pi) \geq 5$ (number of trials × the hypothesized probability of a failure) are both greater than 5, the binomial distribution approximates the standard normal distribution. In those cases, statistics textbooks typically tell you to use the statistics of the normal distribution to answer questions about the binomial distribution. For the sake of tradition, let's carry that through and then compare with `binom.test()`.

Those statistics involve z-scores, which means that you have to know the mean and the standard deviation of the binomial. Fortunately, they're easy to compute. If N is the number of trials and π is the probability of a success, the mean is

$$\mu = N\pi$$

the variance is

$$\sigma^2 = N\pi(1-\pi)$$

and the standard deviation is

$$\sigma = \sqrt{N\pi(1-\pi)}$$

When you test a hypothesis, you're making an inference about π and you have to start with an estimate. You run N trials and get x successes. The estimate is

$$P = \frac{x}{N}$$

To create a z-score, you need one more piece of information — the standard error of P. This sounds harder than it is, because this standard error is just

$$\sigma_P = \sqrt{\frac{\pi(1-\pi)}{N}}$$

Now you're ready for a hypothesis test.

Here's an example. The CEO of FarKlempt Robotics, Inc., believes that 50 percent of FarKlempt robots are purchased for home use. A sample of 1,000 FarKlempt customers indicates that 550 of them use their robots at home. Is this significantly different from what the CEO believes? The hypotheses:

$H_0: \pi = .50$

$H_1: \pi \neq .50$

I set $\alpha = .05$

$N\pi = 500$, and $N(1-\pi) = 500$, so the normal approximation is appropriate.

First, calculate P:

$$P = \frac{x}{N} = \frac{550}{1000} = .55$$

Now create a z-score

$$z = \frac{P - \pi}{\sqrt{\frac{\pi(1-\pi)}{N}}} = \frac{.55 - .50}{\sqrt{\frac{(.50)(1-.50)}{1000}}} = \frac{.05}{\sqrt{\frac{.25}{1000}}} = 3.162$$

With $\alpha = .05$, is 3.162 a large enough z-score to reject H_0?

```
> pnorm(3.162,lower.tail = FALSE)*2
[1] 0.001566896
```

This is much less than .05, so the decision is to reject H_0.

With a little thought, you can see why statisticians recommended this procedure back in the day. To compute the exact probability, you have to calculate the probability of at least 550 successes in 1,000 trials. That would be $pr(550) + pr(551) + \ldots + pr(1000)$, so an approximation based on a well-known distribution was most welcome — particularly in statistics textbooks.

But now

```
> binom.test(550,1000,.5,alternative="two.sided")

          Exact binomial test

data:  550 and 1000
number of successes = 550, number of trials = 1000,
p-value = 0.001731
alternative hypothesis: true probability of success is not
          equal to 0.5
95 percent confidence interval:
 0.5185565 0.5811483
sample estimates:
probability of success
                  0.55
```

Voilà! The `binom.test()` function calculates the exact probability in the blink of an eye. As you can see, the exact probability (0.001731) differs slightly from the normally approximated p-value but the conclusion (reject H_0) is the same.

Chapter **18**

Introducing Modeling

A *model* is something you know and can work with that helps you understand something you know little about. A model is supposed to mimic, in some way, the thing it's modeling. A globe, for example, is a model of the earth. A street map is a model of a neighborhood. A blueprint is a model of a building.

Researchers use models to help them understand natural processes and phenomena. Business analysts use models to help them understand business processes. The models these people use might include concepts from mathematics and statistics — concepts that are so well known they can shed light on the unknown. The idea is to create a model that consists of concepts you understand, put the model through its paces, and see if the results look like real-world results.

In this chapter, I discuss modeling. My goal is to show how you can harness R to help you understand processes in your world.

Modeling a Distribution

In one approach to modeling, you gather data and group them into a distribution. Next, you try to figure out a process that results in that kind of a distribution. Restate that process in statistical terms so that it can generate a distribution, and then see how well the generated distribution matches up with the real one. This "process you figure out and restate in statistical terms" is the model.

If the distribution you generate matches up well with the real data, does this mean your model is "right"? Does it mean that the process you guessed is the process that produces the data?

Unfortunately, no. The logic doesn't work that way. You can show that a model is wrong, but you can't prove that it's right.

Plunging into the Poisson distribution

In this section, I walk you through an example of modeling with the Poisson distribution. I discuss this distribution in Appendix A, where I tell you it seems to characterize an array of processes in the real world. By "characterize a process," I mean that a distribution of real-world data looks a lot like a Poisson distribution. When this happens, it's possible that the kind of process that produces a Poisson distribution is also responsible for producing the data.

What is that process? Start with a random variable x that tracks the number of occurrences of a specific event in an interval. In Appendix A, the "interval" is a sample of 1,000 universal joints, and the specific event is "defective joint." Poisson distributions are also appropriate for events occurring in intervals of time, and the event can be something like "arrival at a toll booth."

Next, I outline the conditions for a *Poisson process* and use both defective joints and toll booth arrivals to illustrate:

>> The numbers of occurrences of the event in two non-overlapping intervals are independent.

    The number of defective joints in one sample is independent of the number of defective joints in another. The number of arrivals at a toll booth during one hour is independent of the number of arrivals during another.

>> The probability of an occurrence of the event is proportional to the size of the interval.

    The chance that you'll find a defective joint is larger in a sample of 10,000 than it is in a sample of 1,000. The chance of an arrival at a toll booth is greater for one hour than it is for a half-hour.

>> The probability of more than one occurrence of the event in a small interval is 0 or close to 0.

In a sample of 1,000 universal joints, you have an extremely low probability of finding two defective ones right next to one another. At any time, two vehicles don't arrive at a toll booth simultaneously.

As I show you in Appendix A, the formula for the Poisson distribution is

$$pr(x) = \frac{\mu^x e^{-\mu}}{x!}$$

In this equation, μ represents the average number of occurrences of the event in the interval you're looking at, and e is the constant 2.781828 (followed by infinitely many more decimal places).

Modeling with the Poisson distribution

Time to use the Poisson in a model. At the FarBlonJet Corporation, web designers track the number of hits per hour on the intranet home page. They monitor the page for 200 consecutive hours and group the data, as listed in Table 18-1.

TABLE 18-1

Hits Per Hour on the FarBlonJet Intranet Home Page

Hits per Hour	Observed Hours	Hits/Hour X Observed Hours
0	10	0
1	30	30
2	44	88
3	44	132
4	36	144
5	18	90
6	10	60
7	8	56
Total	200	600

The first column shows the variable Hits per Hour. The second column, Observed Hours, shows the number of hours in which each value of hits per hour occurred. In the 200 hours observed, 10 of those hours went by with no hits, 30 hours had one hit, 44 had two hits, and so on. These data lead the web designers to use a Poisson distribution to model hits per hour. Here's another way to say this: They believe that a Poisson process produces the number of hits per hour on the web page.

Multiplying the first column by the second column results in the third column. Summing the third column shows that in the 200 observed hours, the intranet page received 600 hits. So the average number of hits per hour is 3.00.

Applying the Poisson distribution to this example,

$$pr(x) = \frac{\mu^x e^{-\mu}}{x!} = \frac{3^x e^{-3}}{x!}$$

Figure 18-1 shows the density function for the Poisson distribution with $\mu = 3$.

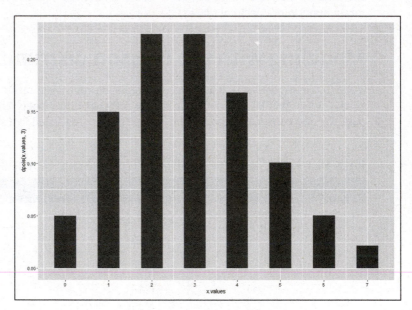

FIGURE 18-1: The Poisson distribution with $\mu = 3$.

The axis labels in the figure hint at how to create it.

Start with a vector of values for the x-axis.

    x.values <- seq(0,7)

Then, work with the density function for the Poisson distribution (see Appendix A):

```
dpois(x.values,3)
```

That's the function to use for the aesthetic mapping of y in ggplot():

```
ggplot(NULL,aes(x=x.values,y=dpois(x.values,3)))+
   geom_bar(stat="identity",width=.5)+
   scale_x_continuous(breaks=seq(0,7))
```

The second statement plots the bars. Its first argument (stat="identity") specifies that the height of each bar is the corresponding density function value mapped to y. The indicated width (.5) in its second argument narrows the bars a bit from the default value (.9). The third statement puts 0–7 on the x-axis.

The purpose of a model is to predict. For this model, you want to use the Poisson distribution to predict the distribution of hits per hour. To do this, multiply each Poisson probability by 200 — the total number of hours:

```
Predicted <- dpois(x.values,3)*200
```

Here are the predictions:

```
> Predicted
[1]   9.957414 29.872241 44.808362 44.808362 33.606271
          20.163763 10.081881  4.320806
```

To work with the observed values (Column 2 in Table 18-1), create a vector:

```
Observed <- c(10,30,44,44,36,18,10,8)
```

You want to use ggplot to show how close the predicted hours are to the observed, so create a data frame. This involves three more vectors:

```
Category <-c(rep("Observed",8),rep("Predicted",8))
Hits.Hr <- c(x.values,x.values)
Hours <- c(Observed,Predicted)
```

And now you can create

```
FBJ.frame <-data.frame(Category,Hits.Hr,Hours)
```

which looks like this

```
> FBJ.frame
     Category Hits.Hr      Hours
1    Observed       0 10.000000
2    Observed       1 30.000000
3    Observed       2 44.000000
```

```
4    Observed      3 44.000000
5    Observed      4 36.000000
6    Observed      5 18.000000
7    Observed      6 10.000000
8    Observed      7  8.000000
9    Predicted     0  9.957414
10 Predicted     1 29.872241
11 Predicted     2 44.808362
12 Predicted     3 44.808362
13 Predicted     4 33.606271
14 Predicted     5 20.163763
15 Predicted     6 10.081881
16 Predicted     7  4.320806
```

To plot it all out:

```
ggplot(FBJ.frame,aes(x=Hits.Hr,y=Hours,fill=Category))+
   geom_bar(stat="identity", position="dodge", color="black",
            width=.6)+
   scale_x_continuous(breaks=x.values)+
   scale_fill_grey()+
   theme_bw()
```

The first statement uses the data frame, with the indicated aesthetic mappings to x, y, and `fill`. The second statement plots the bars. The `position= "dodge"` argument puts the two categories of bars side-by-side, and `color = "black"` draws a black border around the bars (which won't show up on the black-filled bars, of course). As before, the third statement puts the values in the `x.values` vector on the x-axis.

The fourth statement changes the fill-colors of the bars to colors that show up on the page you're reading, and the final statement removes the default gray background. (That makes the bars easier to see.)

Figure 18-2 shows the plot. The observed and the predicted look pretty close, don't they?

Testing the model's fit

Well, "looking pretty close" isn't enough for a statistician. A statistical test is a necessity. As is the case with all statistical tests, this one starts with a null hypothesis and an alternative hypothesis. Here they are:

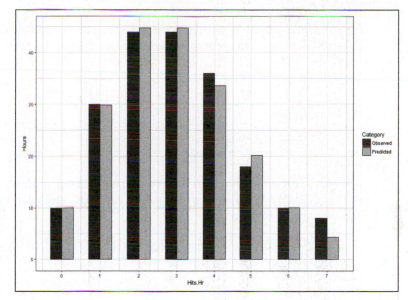

FIGURE 18-2:
FarBlonJet
intranet home
page hits per
hour, observed
and Poisson-
predicted ($\mu = 3$).

H_0: The distribution of observed hits per hour follows a Poisson distribution.

H_1: Not H_0

The appropriate statistical test involves an extension of the binomial distribution. It's called the multinomial distribution — "multi" because it encompasses more categories than just "success" and "failure." This is a difficult distribution to work with.

Fortunately, pioneering statistician Karl Pearson (inventor of the correlation coefficient) noticed that χ^2 ("chi-square"), a distribution I show you in Chapter 10, approximates the multinomial. Originally intended for one-sample hypothesis tests about variances, χ^2 has become much better known for applications like the one I'm about to show you.

Pearson's big idea was this: If you want to know how well a hypothesized distribution (like the Poisson) fits a sample (like the observed hours), use the distribution to generate a hypothesized sample (your predicted hours, for instance), and work with this formula:

$$\chi^2 = \sum \frac{\left(\text{Observed} - \text{Predicted}\right)^2}{\text{Predicted}}$$

Usually, the formula is written with *Expected* rather than *Predicted*, and both Observed and Expected are abbreviated. The usual form of this formula is

$$\chi^2 = \sum \frac{(O-E)^2}{E}$$

For this example,

$$\chi^2 = \sum \frac{(O-E)^2}{E} = \frac{(10-9.9574)^2}{9.9574} + \frac{(30-29.8722)^2}{29.8722} + \ldots + \frac{(8-4.3208)^2}{4.3208}$$

what does that total up to? You can use R as a calculator to figure this out — I've already called the vector of predicted values Predicted, and I don't feel like changing the name to Expected:

```
> chi.squared <- sum(((Observed-Predicted)^2)/Predicted)
> chi.squared
[1] 3.566111
```

Okay. Now what? Is 3.566111 high, or is it low?

To find out, you evaluate chi.squared against the χ^2 distribution. The goal is to find the probability of getting a value at least as high as the calculated value, 3.566111. The trick is to know how many degrees of freedom (df) you have. For a goodness-of-fit application like this one

$$df = k - m - 1$$

where k = the number of categories and m = the number of parameters estimated from the data. The number of categories is 8 (0 Hits per Hour through 7 Hits per Hour). The number of parameters? I used the observed hours to estimate the parameter μ, so m in this example is 1. That means df = 8−1−1 = 6.

To find the probability of obtaining a value of chi.squared (3.566111) or more, I use pchisq() with 6 degrees of freedom:

```
> pchisq(chi.squared,6,lower.tail = FALSE)
[1] 0.7351542
```

The third argument, lower.tail = FALSE, indicates that I want the area to the right of 3.56111 in the distribution (because I'm looking for the probability of a value that extreme or higher). If α = .05, the returned probability (.7351542) tells me to not reject H_0 — meaning you can't reject the hypothesis that the observed data come from a Poisson distribution.

This is one of those infrequent times when it's beneficial to *not* reject H_0 — if you want to make the case that a Poisson process is producing the data. A low value of

χ^2 indicates a close match between the data and the Poisson predictions. If the probability had been just a little greater than .05, not rejecting H_0 would look suspicious. The high probability, however, makes it reasonable to not reject H_0 — and to think that a Poisson process might account for the data.

A word about chisq.test()

R provides the function `chisq.test()`, which by its name suggests that you can use it instead of the calculation I show you in the preceding section. You can, but you have to be careful.

This function can take up to eight arguments, but I discuss only three:

```
chisq.test(Observed,p=dpois(x.values,3),rescale.p=TRUE)
```

The first argument is the vector of data — the observed values. The second is the vector of Poisson-predicted probabilities. I have to include p= because it's not really the second argument in the list of arguments the function takes.

For the same reason, I include `rescale.p=` in the third argument, which tells the function to "rescale" the vector of probabilities. Why is that necessary? One requirement for this function is that the probabilities have to add up to 1.00, and these probabilities do not:

```
> sum(dpois(x.values,3))
[1] 0.9880955
```

"Rescaling" changes the values so that they do add up to 1.00.

When you run that function, this happens:

```
> chisq.test(Observed,p=dpois(x.values,3),rescale.p=TRUE)

        Chi-squared test for given probabilities

data:  Observed
X-squared = 3.4953, df = 7, p-value = 0.8357

Warning message:
In chisq.test(Observed, p = dpois(x.values, 3), rescale.p =
        TRUE) :
  Chi-squared approximation may be incorrect
```

Let's examine the output. In the line preceding the warning message, notice the use of X^2 rather than χ^2. This is because the calculated value approximates χ^2, and the shape and appearance of X approximate the shape and appearance of χ. The X-squared value is pretty close to the value I calculated earlier, but it's off because of the rescaled probabilities.

But another problem lurks. Note that df equals 7 rather than the correct value, 6, and thus the test against the wrong member of the χ^2 family. Why the discrepancy? Because chisq.test() doesn't know how you arrived at the probabilities. It has no idea that you had to use the data to estimate one parameter (μ), and thus lose a degree of freedom. So in addition to the warning message about the chi-squared approximation, you have to also be aware that the degrees of freedom aren't correct for this type of example.

TIP

When would you use chisq.test()? Here's a quick example: You toss a coin 100 times and it comes up Heads 65 times. The null hypothesis is that the coin is fair. Your decision?

```
> chisq.test(c(65,35), p=c(.5,.5))

          Chi-squared test for given probabilities

data:  c(65, 35)
X-squared = 9, df = 1, p-value = 0.0027
```

The low p-value tells you to reject the null hypothesis.

In Chapter 20 I show you another application of chisq.test().

Playing ball with a model

Baseball is a game that generates huge amounts of statistics — and many people study these statistics closely. The Society for American Baseball Research (SABR) has sprung from the efforts of a band of dedicated fan-statisticians (fantasticians?) who delve into the statistical nooks and crannies of the Great American Pastime. They call their work *sabermetrics*. (I made up "fantasticians." They call themselves "sabermetricians.")

The reason I mention this is that sabermetrics supplies a nice example of modeling. It's based on the obvious idea that during a game, a baseball team's objective is to score runs and to keep its opponent from scoring runs. The better a team does at both tasks, the more games it wins. Bill James, who gave sabermetrics its name and is its leading exponent, discovered a neat relationship between the number of runs a team scores, the number of runs the team allows, and its winning percentage. He calls it the *Pythagorean percentage*:

$$\text{Pythagorean Percentage} = \frac{\left(\text{Runs Scored}\right)^2}{\left(\text{Runs Scored}\right)^2 + \left(\text{Runs Allowed}\right)^2}$$

The squares in the expression reminded James of the Pythagorean theorem, hence the name "Pythagorean percentage." Think of it as a model for predicting games won. (This is James' original formula, and I use it throughout. Over the years, sabermetricians have found that 1.83 is more accurate than 2.)

Calculate this percentage and multiply it by the number of games a team plays. Then compare the answer to the team's wins. How well does the model predict the number of games each team won during the 2016 season?

To find out, I found all the relevant data (number of games won and lost, runs scored, and runs allowed) for every National League (NL) team in 2016. (Thank you, www.baseball-reference.com.) I put the data into a data frame called NL2016.

```
> NL2016
   Team Won Lost Runs.scored Runs.allowed
1  ARI   69   93         752          890
2  ATL   68   93         649          779
3  CHC  103   58         808          556
4  CIN   68   94         716          854
5  COL   75   87         845          860
6  LAD   91   71         725          638
7  MIA   79   82         655          682
8  MIL   73   89         671          733
9  NYM   87   75         671          617
10 PHI   71   91         610          796
11 PIT   78   83         729          758
12 SDP   68   94         686          770
13 SFG   87   75         715          631
14 STL   86   76         779          712
15 WSN   95   67         763          612
```

The three-letter abbreviations in the Team column alphabetically order the NL teams from ARI (Arizona Diamondbacks) to WSN (Washington Nationals). (I strongly feel that a much higher number to the immediate right of NYM would make the world a better place, but that's just me.)

The next step is to find the Pythagorean percentage for each team:

```
pythag <- with(NL2016,
            Runs.scored^2/(Runs.scored^2 + Runs.allowed^2))
```

I use `with()`, to avoid having to type expressions like `NL2016$Runs.scored^2`.

Then, I find the predicted numbers of wins:

```
Predicted.wins <- with(NL2016, pythag*(Won + Lost))
```

The expression `Won + Lost`, of course, gives the number of games each team played. Don't they all play the same number of games? Nope. Sometimes a game is rained out and then not rescheduled if the outcome wouldn't affect the final standings.

All that remains is to find χ^2 and test it against a chi-squared distribution:

```
> chi.squared <- with(NL2016,
            sum((Won-Predicted.wins)^2/Predicted.wins))
> chi.squared
[1] 3.402195
```

I didn't use the `Won` data in Column 2 to estimate any parameters, like a mean or a variance, and then apply those parameters to calculate predicted wins. Instead, the predictions came from other data — the Runs Scored and the Runs Allowed. For this reason, df = k−m−1= 15−0−1 = 14. The test is

```
> pchisq(chi.squared,14,lower.tail=FALSE)
[1] 0.9981182
```

As in the previous example, `lower.tail=FALSE` indicates that I want the area to the right of 3.40215 in the distribution (because I'm looking for the probability of a value that extreme or higher).

The very high p-value tells you that with 14 degrees of freedom, you have a huge chance of finding a value of χ^2 at least as high as the X^2 you'd calculate from these observed values and these predicted values. Another way to say this: The calculated value of X^2 is very low, meaning that the predicted wins are close to the actual wins. Bottom line: The model fits the data extremely well.

If you're a baseball fan (as I am), it's fun to match up `Won` with `Predicted.wins` for each team. This gives you an idea of which teams overperformed and which ones underperformed given how many runs they scored and how many they allowed. These two expressions

```
NL2016["Predicted"]<-round(Predicted.wins)
NL2016["W-P"] <- NL2016["Won"]-NL2016["Predicted"]
```

create a column for `Predicted` and a column for `W-P` (Won-Predicted), respectively, in the data frame. These are the sixth and seventh columns.

This expression

```
NL2016 <-NL2016[,c(1,2,6,7,3,4,5)]
```

puts the sixth and seventh columns next to `Won`, for easy comparison. (Don't forget that first comma in the bracketed expression on the right.)

The data frame is now

```
> NL2016
    Team Won Predicted W-P Lost Runs.scored Runs.allowed
1   ARI  69        67   2   93         752          890
2   ATL  68        66   2   93         649          779
3   CHC 103       109  -6   58         808          556
4   CIN  68        67   1   94         716          854
5   COL  75        80  -5   87         845          860
6   LAD  91        91   0   71         725          638
7   MIA  79        77   2   82         655          682
8   MIL  73        74  -1   89         671          733
9   NYM  87        88  -1   75         671          617
10  PHI  71        60  11   91         610          796
11  PIT  78        77   1   83         729          758
12  SDP  68        72  -4   94         686          770
13  SFG  87        91  -4   75         715          631
14  STL  86        88  -2   76         779          712
15  WSN  95        99  -4   67         763          612
```

The `W-P` column shows that `PHI` (the Philadelphia Phillies) outperformed their prediction by 11 games — and that was the biggest overperformance in the National League in 2016.

Who was the biggest *under*performer? Interestingly enough, that would be `CHC` (the Chicago Cubs — six games worse than their prediction). If you followed the 2016 postseason, however, you know they more than made up for this. . . .

A Simulating Discussion

Another approach to modeling is to simulate a process. The idea is to define as much as you can about what a process does and then somehow use numbers to represent that process and carry it out. It's a great way to find out what a process does in case other methods of analysis are very complex.

Taking a chance: The Monte Carlo method

Many processes contain an element of randomness. You just can't predict the outcome with certainty. To simulate this type of process, you have to have some way of simulating the randomness. Simulation methods that incorporate randomness are called *Monte Carlo* simulations. The name comes from the city in Monaco whose main attraction is gambling casinos.

In the next few sections, I show you a couple of examples. These examples aren't so complex that you can't analyze them. I use them for just that reason: You can check the results against analysis.

Loading the dice

In Chapter 17, I talk about a *die* (one member of a pair of dice) that's biased to come up according to the numbers on its faces: A 6 is six times as likely as a 1, a 5 is five times as likely, and so on. On any toss, the probability of getting a number n is $n/21$.

Suppose you have a pair of dice loaded this way. What would the outcomes of 2,000 tosses of these dice look like? What would be the average of those 2,000 tosses? What would be the variance and the standard deviation? You can use R to set up Monte Carlo simulations and answer these questions.

I begin by writing an R function to calculate the probability of each possible outcome. Before I develop the function, I'll trace the reasoning for you. For each outcome (2–12), I have to have all the ways of producing the outcome. For example, to roll a 4, I can have a 1 on the first die and a 3 on the second, 2 on the first die and 2 on the second, or 3 on the first and 1 on the second. The probability (I call it *loaded.pr*) of a 4, then, is

$$loaded.pr(4) = \left(\frac{1}{21} \times \frac{3}{21}\right) + \left(\frac{2}{21} \times \frac{2}{21}\right) + \left(\frac{3}{21} \times \frac{1}{21}\right) = \frac{(1 \times 3) + (2 \times 2) + (3 \times 1)}{21^2} = .02267574$$

Rather than enumerate all possibilities for each outcome and then calculate the probability, I create a function called loaded.pr() to do the work. I want it to work like this:

```
> loaded.pr(4)
[1] 0.02267574
```

First, I set up the function:

```
loaded.pr <-function(x){
```

Next, I want to stop the whole thing and print a warning if x is less than 2 or greater than 12:

```
if(x <2 | x >12) warning("x must be between 2 and 12,
          inclusive")
```

Then I set a variable called first that tracks the value of the first die, depending on the value of x. If x is less than 7, I set first to 1. If x is 7 or more, I set first to 6 (the maximum value of a die-toss):

```
if(x < 7) first=1
      else first=6
```

The variable second (the value of the second die), of course, is x–first:

```
second = x-first
```

I'll want to keep track of the sum for the numerator (as in the equation I just showed you), so I start the value at zero:

```
sum = 0
```

Now comes the business end: a for loop that does the calculating given the values of first (the toss of the first die) and second (the toss of the second die):

```
for(first in first:second){
    second = x-first
    sum = sum + (first*second)
 }
```

Because of the preceding if statement, if x is less than 7, first increases from 1 to x–1 with each iteration of the for loop (and second decreases). If x is 7 or greater, first decreases from 6 to x–6 with each iteration (and second increases).

Finally, when the loop is finished, the function returns the sum divided by 21²:

```
}
  return(sum/21^2)
}
```

Here it is all together:

```
loaded.pr <- function(x){
  if(x < 2 | x > 12) warning("x must be between 2 and 12,
       inclusive")
  if(x < 7) first=1
    else first=6
  second = x-first
  sum = 0
  for(first in first:second){
    second = x-first
    sum=sum + (first*second)
  }
  return(sum/21^2)
}
```

To set up the probability distribution, I create a vector for the outcomes

```
outcome <- seq(2,12)
```

and use a `for` loop to create a vector `pr.outcome` to hold the corresponding probabilities:

```
pr.outcome <- NULL
for(x in outcome){pr.outcome <- c(pr.outcome,loaded.pr(x))}
```

In each iteration of the loop, the curly-bracketed statement on the right appends a calculated probability to the vector.

Here are the probabilities rounded to three decimal places so that they look good on the page:

```
> round(pr.outcome,3)
 [1] 0.002 0.009 0.023 0.045 0.079 0.127 0.159 0.172 0.166
       0.136 0.082
```

And now I'm ready to randomly sample 2,000 times from this discrete probability distribution — the equivalent of 2,000 tosses of a pair of loaded dice.

Randomization functions in R are really "pseudorandom." They start from a "seed" number and work from there. If you set the seed, you can determine the course of the randomization; if you don't set it, the randomization takes off on its own each time you run it.

So I start by setting a seed:

```
set.seed(123)
```

This isn't necessary, but if you want to reproduce my results, start with that function and that seed number. If you don't, your results won't look exactly like mine (which is not necessarily a bad thing).

For the random sampling, I use the `sample()` function and assign the results to `results`:

```
results <- sample(outcome,size = 2000,replace = TRUE,
           prob=pr.outcome)
```

The first argument, of course, is the set of values for the variable (the possible dice-tosses), the second is the number of samples, the third specifies sampling with replacement, and the fourth is the vector of probabilities I just calculated.

TIP

To reproduce the exact results, remember to set that seed before every time you use `sample()`.

Here's a quick look at the distribution of the results:

```
> table(results)
results
   2    3    4    5    6    7    8    9   10   11   12
   3   28   39   79  154  246  335  356  311  284  165
```

The first row is the possible outcomes, and the second is the frequencies of the outcomes. So 39 of the 2,000 tosses resulted in 4, and 165 of them came up 12. I leave it as an exercise for you to graph these results.

What about the statistics for these simulated tosses?

```
> mean(results)
[1] 8.6925
> var(results)
[1] 4.423155
> sd(results)
[1] 2.10313
```

How do these values match up with the parameters of the random variable? This is what I meant earlier by "checking against analysis." In Chapter 17, I show how to calculate the expected value (the mean), the variance, and the standard deviation for a discrete random variable.

The expected value is

$$E(x) = \sum x \left(pr(x) \right)$$

I can calculate that easily enough in R:

```
> E.outcome = sum(outcome*pr.outcome)
> E.outcome
[1] 8.666667
```

The variance is

$$V(x) = \sum x^2 \left(pr(x) \right) - \left[E(x) \right]^2$$

In R, that's

```
> Var.outcome <- sum(outcome^2*pr.outcome)-E.outcome^2
> Var.outcome
[1] 4.444444
```

The standard deviation is, of course

```
> sd.outcome <- sqrt(Var.outcome)
> sd.outcome
[1] 2.108185
```

Table 18-2 shows that the results from the simulation match up closely with the parameters of the random variable. You might try repeating the simulation with a lot more simulated tosses — 10,000, perhaps. Will increased tosses pull the simulation statistics closer to the distribution parameters?

TABLE 18-2 | **Statistics from the Loaded-Dice-Tossing Simulation and the Parameters of the Discrete Distribution**

	Simulation Statistic	Distribution Parameter
Mean	8.6925	8.666667
Variance	4.423155	4.444444
Standard Deviation	2.10313	2.108185

Simulating the central limit theorem

This might surprise you, but statisticians often use simulations to make determinations about some of their statistics. They do this when mathematical analysis becomes very difficult.

For example, some statistical tests depend on normally distributed populations. If the populations aren't normal, what happens to those tests? Do they still do what they're supposed to? To answer that question, statisticians might create non-normally distributed populations of numbers, simulate experiments with them, and apply the statistical tests to the simulated results.

In this section, I use simulation to examine an important statistical item: the central limit theorem. In Chapter 9, I introduce this theorem in connection with the sampling distribution of the mean. In fact, I simulate sampling from a population with only three possible values to show you that even with a small sample size, the sampling distribution starts to look normally distributed.

Here, I set up a normally distributed population and draw 10,000 samples of 25 scores each. I calculate the mean of each sample and then set up a distribution of those 10,000 means. The idea is to see how that distribution's statistics match up with the central limit theorem's predictions.

The population for this example has the parameters of the population of scores on the IQ test, a distribution I use for examples in several chapters. It's a normal distribution with $\mu = 100$ and $\sigma = 15$. According to the central limit theorem, the mean of the distribution of means (the sampling distribution of the mean) should be 100, and the standard deviation (the standard error of the mean) should be 3 — the population standard deviation (15) divided by the square root of the sample size (5). The central limit theorem also predicts that the sampling distribution of the mean is normally distributed.

The `rnorm()` function does the sampling. For one sample of 25 numbers from a normally distributed population with a mean of 100 and a standard deviation of 15, the function is

```
rnorm(25,100,15)
```

and if I want the sample mean, it's

```
mean(rnorm(25,100,15))
```

I'll put that function inside a `for` loop that repeats 10,000 times and appends each newly calculated sample mean to a vector called `sampling.distribution`, which I initialize:

```
sampling.distribution <- NULL
```

The `for` loop is

```
for(sample.count in 1:10000){
  set.seed(sample.count)
  sample.mean <- mean(rnorm(25,100,15))
  sampling.distribution <- c(sampling.distribution,sample.mean)
}
```

Again, the `set.seed()` statement is necessary only if you want to reproduce my results.

How about the statistics of the sampling distribution?

```
> mean(sampling.distribution)
[1] 100.029
> sd(sampling.distribution)
[1] 3.005007
```

Pretty close to the predicted values!

TIP

Be sure to reset `sampling.distribution` to NULL before each time you run the `for` loop.

What does the sampling distribution look like? To keep things looking clean, I round off the sample means in `sampling.distribution` and then create a table:

```
table(round(sampling.distribution))
```

I'd show you the table, but the numbers get all scrambled up on the page. Instead, I'll go ahead and use `ggplot()` to graph the sampling distribution.

First, I create a data frame

```
sampling.frame <- data.frame(table(round(sampling.
        distribution)))
```

and specify its column names:

```
colnames(sampling.frame) <- c("Sample.Mean","Frequency")
```

Now for the plot:

```
ggplot(sampling.frame,aes(x=Sample.Mean,y=Frequency))+
    geom_bar(stat="identity")
```

The result is shown in Figure 18-3, a plot that closely approximates the shape and symmetry of a normal distribution.

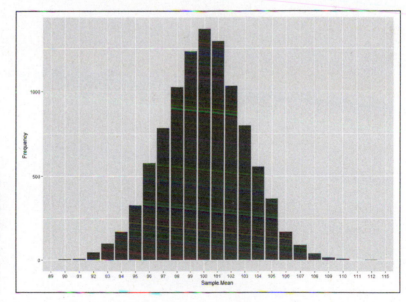

FIGURE 18-3:
Sampling distribution of the mean (N = 25) based on 10,000 samples from a normal distribution with μ = 100 and σ = 15.

5

The Part of Tens

IN THIS PART . . .

Learn similarities and differences between R and Excel

Use the clipboard to import data from Excel into R

Explore online resources for learning R

Chapter **19**

Ten Tips for Excel Emigrés

Excel, the most widely used spreadsheet program, has an impressive array of statistical analysis tools. Although some have characterized Excel as the Rodney Dangerfield of analysis software ("don't get no respect!"), a lot of people use Excel's analysis tools. (And believe me, no one is happier about that than I am!)

If you're one of those people and you need a bit of help transitioning to R, this chapter is for you. I point out similarities and differences that might help you make the leap.

Defining a Vector in R Is Like Naming a Range in Excel

Here's a standard, everyday garden-variety vector in R:

```
x <- c(15,16,17,18,19,20)
```

If you're used to naming arrays in Excel, you've already done something like this. Figure 19-1 shows a spreadsheet with these numbers in cells F2 through F7 and headed by x in F1. The figure also shows the New Name dialog box that opens when I highlight that range, right-click, and select Define Name from the menu that pops up. Clicking OK defines x as the name of that range, just as the R statement creates the vector x.

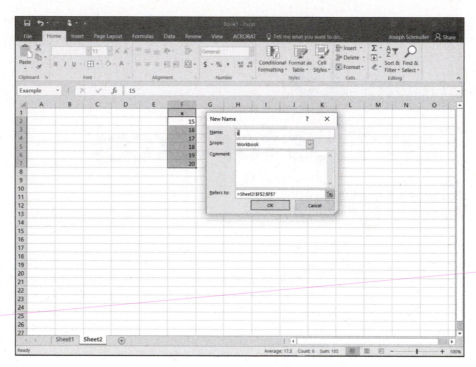

FIGURE 19-1:
A range in Excel, about to be named x.

TIP

What? You don't name ranges in Excel? Don't make me shamelessly plug that other book again. . . . I mean it!

Operating on Vectors Is Like Operating on Named Ranges

I can multiply the vector x by a constant:

```
> 5*x
[1]  75  80  85  90  95 100
```

Back to the spreadsheet with the named range x. I select a range of cells with the same length as x — say, G2 through G —, and type

= 5*x

in G2. Figure 19-2 shows this.

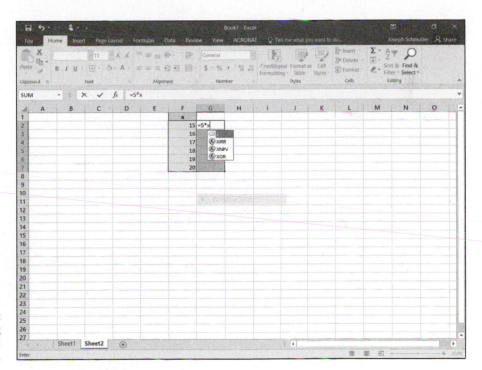

FIGURE 19-2:
Multiplying
the named
range *x* by 5.

Pressing the key-combination Ctrl+Shift+Enter puts the results in G2 through G7, as Figure 19-3 shows. That key combination is for an *array function* in Excel — a function that returns answers in an array of cells rather than in a single cell.

Of course, another way to do the multiplication is to type =5*x into G2, press Enter, and then autofill to G7.

The similarities abound. In R,

```
> sum(x)
[1] 105
```

adds up the numbers in x, as does =SUM(x) typed into a selected cell.

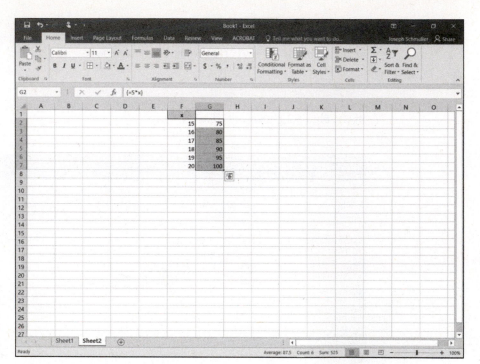

FIGURE 19-3:
The results of the
multiplication
come back in
an array.

To sum the squares of the numbers in x:

```
> sum(x^2)
[1] 1855
```

In the spreadsheet, select a cell and type **=SUMSQ(x)**.

If I have another vector y

```
y <- c(42,37,28,44,51,49)
```

then

```
> x*y
[1] 630 592 476 792 969 980
```

On the spreadsheet, I can have another named range called y in cells G2 through G7, as in Figure 19-4.

Selecting a range like H2 through H7, typing **=x*y**, and pressing Ctrl+Shift+Enter puts the answers in the selected array, as Figure 19-5 shows.

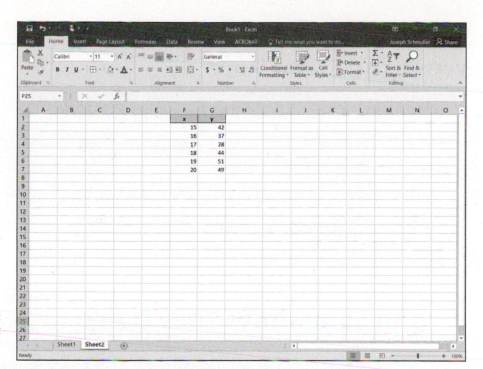

FIGURE 19-4:
A spreadsheet with two named arrays, x and y.

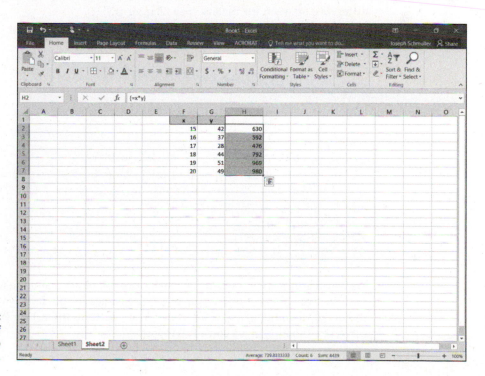

FIGURE 19-5:
The result of multiplying two named arrays.

Sometimes Statistical Functions Work the Same Way . . .

To find the correlation between the vectors x and y in R:

```
> cor(x,y)
[1] 0.5900947
```

For the named ranges x and y in the spreadsheet, select a cell and enter

```
=CORREL(x,y)
```

The answer appears in the selected cell.

. . . And Sometimes They Don't

If x and y represent data from two groups, a *t*-test is appropriate for testing the difference between the means. (See Chapter 11.)

If I carry out that test in R:

```
> t.test(x,y,alternative="two.sided",var.equal=FALSE)

        Welch Two Sample t-test

data:  x and y
t = -6.9071, df = 5.492, p-value = 0.000663
alternative hypothesis: true difference in means is not equal to 0
95 percent confidence interval:
 -33.15068 -15.51598
sample estimates:
mean of x mean of y
 17.50000  41.83333
```

The third argument to t.test specifies a two-tailed test, and the fourth indicates that the two variances are not equal. (Those values for the last two arguments are the default conditions, so it's not necessary to state them.) As you can see, R's t.test() function gives you a full report.

Not so in Excel. Select a cell and enter

```
=T.TEST(x,y,2,3)
```

The third argument, 2, means this is a two-tailed test. The fourth argument, 3, specifies unequal variances. Press Enter and all you get is the *p*-value.

Contrast: Excel and R Work with Different Data Formats

Throughout the book, I differentiate between wide format

```
> wide.format
   x   y
1 15 42
2 16 37
3 17 28
4 18 44
5 19 51
6 20 49
```

and long format

```
> long.format
   Group Score
1      x    15
2      x    16
3      x    17
4      x    18
5      x    19
6      x    20
7      y    42
8      y    37
9      y    28
10     y    44
11     y    51
12     y    49
```

Excel works with wide format.

TIP

If you worked with Excel 2011 for the Mac (or earlier Mac versions), you might have installed StatPlus:mac LE, a third party add-in that provides numerous statistical analysis tools for the Mac version of Excel. StatPlus works with long-format data.

R, for the most part, uses long format. For example, the t.test() function I just showed you can also work like this:

```
> t.test(Score ~ Group, alternative="two.sided", var.
  equal=FALSE, data=long.format)


         Welch Two Sample t-test

data:  Score by Group
t = -6.9071, df = 5.492, p-value = 0.000663
alternative hypothesis: true difference in means is not equal to 0
95 percent confidence interval:
 -33.15068 -15.51598
sample estimates:
mean in group x mean in group y
       17.50000        41.83333
```

Notice that the output is the same except for data: Score by Group rather than data: x and y as in the earlier example. The next-to-last line is also slightly different.

Distribution Functions Are (Somewhat) Similar

Both Excel and R have built-in functions that work with distribution families (like the normal and the binomial). Because R is specialized for statistical work, it has functions for more distribution families than Excel does.

I'll show you how both work with the normal family, and you'll see the similarities.

In a normal distribution with mean = 100 and standard deviation = 15, if I want to find the density associated with 110 in Excel, that's

=NORM.DIST(110,100,15,FALSE)

The fourth argument, FALSE, indicates the density function.

In R, you'd use

```
> dnorm(110,100,15)
[1] 0.02129653
```

For the cumulative probability of 110 in that distribution

=NORM.DIST(110,100,15,TRUE)

Here, TRUE indicates the cumulative distribution function.

The R version is

```
> pnorm(110,100,15)
[1] 0.7475075
```

To find the score at the 25th percentile in Excel, I use the NORM.INV function:

=NORM.INV(0.25,100,15)

And in R:

```
> qnorm(.25,100,15)
[1] 89.88265
```

One difference: R has a function for generating random numbers from this distribution:

```
> rnorm(5,100,15)
[1] 85.06302 84.40067 99.73030 98.01737 61.75986
```

To do this in Excel, you have to use the Random Number Generation tool in an add-in called the Data Analysis ToolPak.

A Data Frame Is (Something) Like a Multicolumn Named Range

For this section and the next, I use a spreadsheet that holds a multicolumn array corresponding to the NL2016 data frame in Chapter 20. Here's the data frame:

```
> NL2016
   Team Won Lost Runs.scored Runs.allowed
1   ARI  69   93         752          890
2   ATL  68   93         649          779
3   CHC 103   58         808          556
4   CIN  68   94         716          854
5   COL  75   87         845          860
6   LAD  91   71         725          638
7   MIA  79   82         655          682
8   MIL  73   89         671          733
9   NYM  87   75         671          617
10  PHI  71   91         610          796
11  PIT  78   83         729          758
12  SDP  68   94         686          770
13  SFG  87   75         715          631
14  STL  86   76         779          712
15  WSN  95   67         763          612
```

Figure 19-6 shows the spreadsheet. I've defined NL_2016 as the name for the entire table (cells A2 through E16).

In R, I can find the average of Runs.scored this way

```
> mean(NL2016[,4])
[1] 718.2667
```

Runs.scored is in column 4, and the comma in the square brackets specifies all the rows in that column.

On the spreadsheet, I select a cell and enter

```
=AVERAGE(INDEX(NL_2016,,4))
```

The two commas in the parentheses specifies all the rows in column 4.

I know, I know. You can do that in several other ways in both R and Excel. I'm just trying to show you the commonalities.

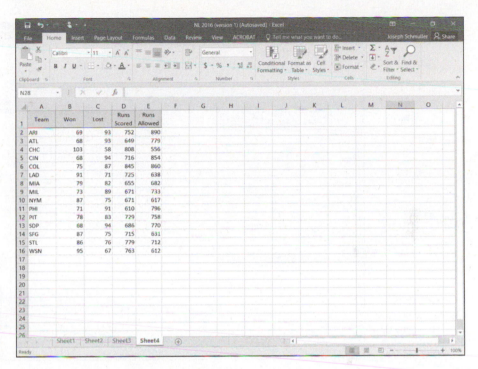

FIGURE 19-6:
The NL2016 data frame in a spreadsheet. Its Excel name is NL_2016.

The "several other ways" make things fall apart. For example, Excel has nothing analogous to

```
> mean(NL2016$Runs.scored)
[1] 718.2667
```

The sapply() Function Is Like Dragging

To find all the column means in NL_2016 in Excel, I can select cell B17 at the bottom of the second column and enter

```
=AVERAGE(B2:B16)
```

and then drag through the third, fourth, and fifth columns. Figure 19-7 shows the results of dragging.

To calculate those column means in R:

```
> sapply(NL2016[,2:5],mean)
        Won         Lost  Runs.scored Runs.allowed
   79.86667     81.86667     718.26667    725.86667
```

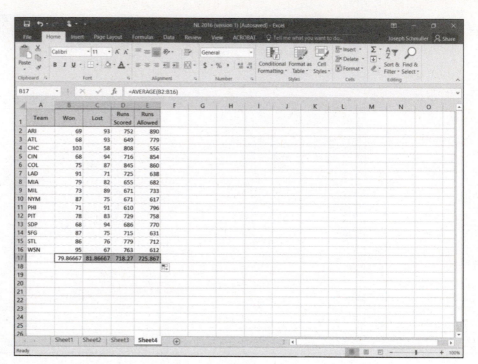

FIGURE 19-7:
Averaging across columns by dragging from the first column.

Using edit() Is (Almost) Like Editing a Spreadsheet

In Chapter 2, I mention that edit() opens a spreadsheet-like ("spreadshee-tesque"?) view of a data frame. This seems like a good place to bring that up again, particularly if you're used to spreadsheets and you're finding it hard to make changes to data frames in R.

To change a data frame, I assign it another name and open it with edit():

```
> NL2016.changed <- edit(NL2016)
```

This opens up the Data Editor window in Figure 19-8.

Now I can make changes. For example, to indulge my wishful thinking, I change NYM's Won from 87 to 107, and Lost from 75 to 55. To do that, I double-click the appropriate cells, make the changes, and choose File ⇨ Close from the main menu.

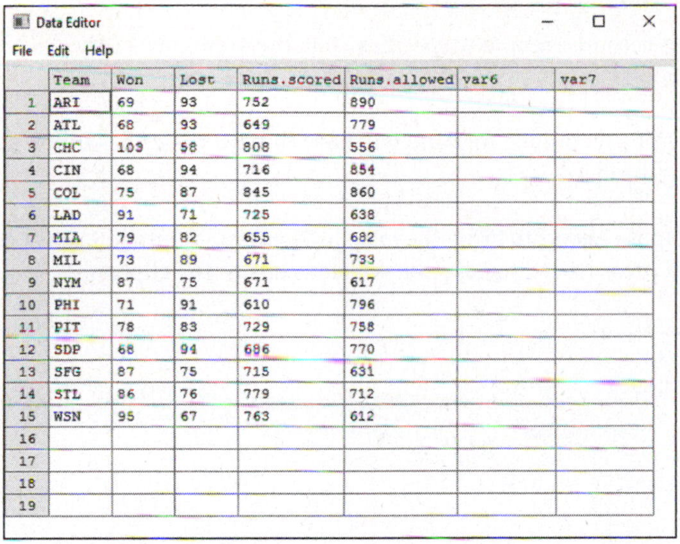

	Team	Won	Lost	Runs.scored	Runs.allowed	var6	var7
1	ARI	69	93	752	890		
2	ATL	68	93	649	779		
3	CHC	103	58	808	556		
4	CIN	68	94	716	854		
5	COL	75	87	845	860		
6	LAD	91	71	725	638		
7	MIA	79	82	655	682		
8	MIL	73	89	671	733		
9	NYM	87	75	671	617		
10	PHI	71	91	610	796		
11	PIT	78	83	729	758		
12	SDP	68	94	686	770		
13	SFG	87	75	715	631		
14	STL	86	76	779	712		
15	WSN	95	67	763	612		
16							
17							
18							
19							

FIGURE 19-8: R's Data Editor window.

When I open the ninth row of the newly named data frame, I see data that is eminently more palatable, although regrettably unrealistic:

```
> NL2016.changed[9,]
  Team Won Lost Runs.scored Runs.allowed
9  NYM 107   55         671          617
```

Use the Clipboard to Import a Table from Excel into R

So you want to use R to analyze your data, but your data resides mostly in spreadsheets. What do you do?

In Chapter 2, I describe the `xlsx` package. This package provides `read.xlsx()`, which enables you to read a spreadsheet into R. To use this function, you have to know which directory the spreadsheet is in and which page of the spreadsheet you want to import.

But here's the easiest way to import an Excel table into an R data frame: Copy the table (onto the clipboard) and then use

```
read.table("clipboard", header = TRUE)
```

The second argument specifies that the first row of the table contains column headers.

TIP

For this technique to work, you have to have no spaces in the names in your column headers.

Suppose I want to bring the table in Figure 19-4 into R. I select cells F1 through G7 and press Ctrl+C to copy the selected cells to the clipboard.

Then in R:

```
> clip.frame <-read.table("clipboard", header = TRUE)
> clip.frame
   x  y
1 15 42
2 16 37
3 17 28
4 18 44
5 19 51
6 20 49
```

and you have yourself a data frame.

TIP

How can you be sure it's a data frame? The function is.data.frame() returns TRUE if its argument is a data frame; FALSE, if not:

```
> is.data.frame(clip.frame)
[1] TRUE
```

Chapter **20**

Ten Valuable Online R Resources

O ne reason for the rapid rise of R is the supportive R community. It seems that as soon as someone becomes proficient in R, they immediately want to share their knowledge with others — and the web is the place to do it. This chapter points you to some of the helpful web-based resources the R community has created.

Websites for R Users

As you work with R, you might run into a situation or two that requires some expert help. The websites in this section can provide the assistance you need.

R-bloggers

As I write this, the R-bloggers website comprises the efforts of 750 R bloggers. By the time you visit `www.r-bloggers.com/`, this number will surely be larger.

Statistics Ph.D. candidate Tal Galili runs the show. As he says, his objective is to empower R bloggers to empower R users. In addition to the blogs, you'll find links to courses, conferences, and job opportunities.

Microsoft R Application Network

Once upon a time, a terrific site called Inside-R provided a variety of resources for R users. Recently, Microsoft acquired Inside-R's parent company Revolution Analytics.

One result of this acquisition is the Microsoft R Application Network, (MRAN) which is where you'll find all the blogs and links that used to reside on Inside-R.

To visit the MRAN, point your browser to `https://mran.microsoft.com/`.

Another result of the acquisition is Microsoft R Open, which Microsoft bills as an "enhanced" distribution of R. You can download Microsoft R Open from the MRAN website.

Quick-R

Wesleyan University professor Rob Kabacoff created this website to introduce you to R and its application to statistical concepts, both introductory and advanced. You'll find the extremely well-written content (and neat graphics!) at `www.statmethods.net/`.

RStudio Online Learning

The great folks behind RStudio have created an online learning page that links to tutorials and examples to help you master R and related tools — and you get to learn the basics of data science as well. The URL is `www.rstudio.com/online-learning/`.

Stack Overflow

Not limited to R, Stack Overflow is a multimillion-member community of programmers dedicated to helping each other. You can search their Q&A base for help with a problem, or you can ask a question. To ask a question, however, you have to be a member (it's free) and log in.

The site also provides links to jobs, documentation, and more. Unsurprisingly, the website is at `http://stackoverflow.com/`.

Online Books and Documentation

The web has a wealth of books and documents that will help get you up to speed when it comes to R. One way to link to them is to click the Home button of the Help tab in RStudio.

Here are a few more resources.

R manuals

If you want to go directly to the source, visit the R manuals page at `https://cran.r-project.org/manuals.html`.

That's where you'll find links to the R Language Definition and other documentation.

R documentation

For links to even more R documentation, try `https://www.r-project.org/other-docs.html`.

RDocumentation

Wait. Didn't I just use this title? Yes, well . . . the Canadian Football League once had a team named the Rough Riders and another named the Roughriders. It's something like that.

The RDocumentation page at `www.rdocumentation.org/` is quite a bit different from the web page in the previous section. This one doesn't link to manuals and other documents. Instead, this website enables you to search for R packages and functions that suit your needs.

How many packages are available? Over 12,000!

YOU CANanalytics

The brainchild of Roopham Upadhyay, the YOU CANanalytics website provides a number of helpful blogs and case studies, and could have gone into the first main section.

Why is it in this one? Because this page

```
http://ucanalytics.com/blogs/learn-r-12-books-and-online-resources/
```

enables you to download classic R books in PDF format. Some of the titles are at the introductory level, some are advanced, and all of them are free!

TIP

A book in PDF format is a very long document. If you're reading it on a tablet, it's user-friendlier to turn the PDF file into an e-book. To do this, upload your PDF document into an e-reader like Google Playbooks, and voilà — your PDF file becomes an e-book.

The R Journal

I saved this one for last, because it's at an advanced level. Like academic publications, The *R Journal* is refereed — experts in the field decide whether a submitted article is worthy of publication.

Take a look at the articles at `https://journal.r-project.org/` and you'll see what's in store for you when you become one of those experts!

Index

D

data
  exploring, 95–96
  extracting from data frames, 38–39
  formats for, 413–414
  missing, 26
  types of, 12
data frames
  about, 36–39, 416–417
  editing, 37–38
  extracting data from, 38–39
  summarizing, 139–142
  working with, 215–216
datadensity() function, 141–142
data.frame() function, 36–37
dbeta() function, A2
dbinom() function, 375
dchisq() function, 201, 202–203
de Vries, Andrie (author)
  R For Dummies, 29
degrees of freedom (df), 107, 175–177, 187–188, 212, 233, 283
density functions, 371–373
density plot, 59
dependent variables, 11–12, 278
describe.data.frame() function, 140
descriptive statistics
  about, 10, 123
  frequency, 131–139
  kurtosis, 130–131
  maximum value, 125
  minimum value, 125
  moments, 125–131
  nominal variables, 131–132
  numerical variables, 132–139
  quantity, 123–125
  skewness, 127–130
  summarizing data frames, 139–142
dexp() function, A9
df (degrees of freedom), 107, 175–177, 187–188, 212, 233, 283
df() function, 226, 227
dgamma() function, A8

dim() function, 32
discordant pairs, B18
discrete random variables, 171, 371
distribution functions, 414–415
distributions
  binomial, 374–377
  chi-square, 201–204
  graphing, 52–53
  modeling, 383–395
  normal, 145–157
  Poisson, 384–388, A4–A6
  probability, 371–373
  sampling, 164–165, 181–183, 206–212
  standard normal, 130, 158, 159, 160
  t-distributions, 175–177, 189–198
dnbinom() function, 377
dnorm() function, 147, 148, 153–154, 160
dollar sign ($), 35
dot charts, 62–63
double equal-sign (a==b), 38
downloading
  R, 18–21
  RStudio, 18–21
dplyr package, C16–C17
dpois() function, A5–A6
dt() function, 176, 189–190
Dummies (website), 5
dummy variables, 304

E

e, 338–341
ecdf (empirical cumulative distribution function), 134–135
edit() function, 37–38, 418–419
elementary outcome, 362
element_blank() function, 83
empirical cumulative distribution function (ecdf), 134–135
epsilon, 285
equal variances, two-sample hypothesis testing and, 212–214
Erlang distribution, A7
error term, 236, 246

K

Kendall's Tau, B18–B21
Kruskal-Wallis One-Way ANOVA, B5–B8
kurtosis, 126, 130–131
kurtosis() function, 131

L

labels argument, 137
labs() function, 74, 78, 83
lattice package, C19
legend() function, 66–67
length() function, 38, 98, 107, 123–124
leptokurtic, 130
line plot, 191
linear equation, 280
linear regression, 290–295
lines, graphing, 279–281
lines() function, 59
list() function, 34–35
lists, 34–36
lm() function, 291, 292, 297, 309, 327–328, 343–345, 347, 349, 356
loaded.pr() function, 397
logarithm, 336–338
logarithmic regression, 350–353
logical vector, 30
lower tail, 184

M

manova() function, 272
map_data() function, C11
maps, drawing, C10–C13
margin.table() function, 132
matched samples, B8–B16
matrices, 31–33
matrix() function, 33, 242–243
maximum value, 125
mean
  about, 91–93
  arithmetic, 97
  finding confidence limits for a, 173–175

geometric, 97–98
harmonic, 98–99
trimming the, 96
mean() function
  about, 26, 93, 120–121, 308
  arithmetic mean, 97
  conditions, 93–94
  exploring data, 95–96
  geometric mean, 97–98
  harmonic mean, 98–99
  outliers, 96–97
  $-sign, 94–95
median, 99–100
median() function, 100
melt() function, 80, 227
melting data, 193, 227
Meys, Joris (author)
  R For Dummies, 29
mfv() function, 101
Microsoft Excel, 407–420
Microsoft R Application Network, 422
minimum value, 125
minus sign (-), 117
missing data, 26
mixed ANOVA, 264–269
mode, 101
mode() function, 101
modeling
  about, 383
  distributions, 383–395
  simulating a process, 396–403
moment() function, 131
moments
  about, 125–126
  kurtosis, 130–131
  skewness, 127–130
Monte Carlo method, 396
mtext() function, 202
multiple correlation, 326–329
multiple regression, 295–301
multivariate analysis of variance (MANOVA), 270–276

N

Napier, John (mathematician), 337

natural logarithm, 340

nbinom function, 375

ncol() function, 124

negative binomial distribution, 377–378

nominal data, 12

nominal variables
margin.table() function, 132
prop.table() function, 131–132
table() function, 131

noncentrality, C8–C10

non-parametric statistics
about, B1
independent samples, B2–B8
Kendall's Tau, B18–B21
matched samples, B8–B16
Spearman's correlation coefficient, B16–B18

norm() function, 147, 159

normal
bell curve, 143–147
distributions, 147–157
standardizing scores, 158–160

normal curves, plotting, 148–152

normal density function, 147–152

normal distributions
about, 145
parameters of, 145–147
quantiles of, 155–156
working with, 147–157

nrow() function, 124

null hypothesis, 14–15, 180

numerical variables
hist() function, 132–138
stem() function, 138–139

numerical vectors, 30–31

O

one-sample hypothesis testing
about, 179
chi-square distributions, 201
degrees of freedom (df), 187–188
hypothesis tests and sampling distributions, 181–183

t-distributions, 189–190
testing variances, 198–200
t.test() function, 188–189
visualizing chi-square distributions, 201–204
visualizing t-distributions, 190–198
z-scores, 183–185
z.test() function, 185–187

one-tailed hypothesis testing, 184–185, 205–206

online resources, 421–424

ordinal data, 12

outliers, 96–97

overplotting, 87

P

packages, 19, 39–43

Packages dialog box, 42

Packages tab (RStudio), 19, 20

paired sample *t*-tests, two-sample hypothesis testing and, 222

paired samples, two-sample hypothesis testing for, 220–221

pairs() function, 69, 71, 84, 85

parameters
defined, 10
of normal distribution, 145–147

partial correlation, 329–331

Pascal distribution, 375

patterns, finding, 51–57

pbeta() function, A4

pbinom() function, 375, 376

pchisq() function, 201, 390, B6, B14

pcor() function, 331, 333

pcor.test() function, 330–331

Pearson, Karl (statistician), 315, 389

Pearson product-moment correlation coefficient, 315–316, 322

percent ranks, 120

percentiles, 118–120

permutations, 367–368

permutations() function, 370

pexp() function, A9, A10

pf() function, 226

pgamma() function, A8

phyper() function, C4–C5

R

R. *See also specific topics*
  about, 17
  comments, 29
  defining vectors in, 407–408
  distributions in, 147
  documentation for, 423
  downloading, 18–21
  formulas, 43–44
  functions, 26–28, 369–371
  manuals for, 423
  packages, 39–43
  ranking in, 117
  sessions in, 21–26
  standard normal distribution in, 159
  standard scores in, 114–115
  structures, 29–39
  user-defined functions, 28–29
  website, 18
  working directory, 21–22
R For Dummies (de Vries and Meys), 29
R Journal, 424
random sampling, 156–157
random variables, 371
randomized blocks. *See* repeated measures
randomiztion, 157
`rank()` function, 117
ranking
  percent ranks, 120
  percentiles, 118–120
  in R, 117
  `sort()` function, 118
  tied scores, 117–118
ratio data, 12
raw moment, 125
`rbinom()` function, 375
R-bloggers, 421–422
`rchisq()` function, 201
RDocumentation, 423
`read.table()` function, 47
reciprocal, of a number, 98
regression. *See also* curvilinear regression
  about, 277

analysis of covariance (ANCOVA), 305–312
analysis of variance (ANOVA), 301–305
correlation and, 316–319
exponential, 346–350
graphing lines, 279–281
linear, 290–295
logarithmic, 350–353
multiple, 295–301
polynomial, 354–358
power, 341–346
regression line, 281–290
scatterplots, 277–279
regression coefficients, 281
regression line
  about, 281–290
  correlation and, 316
  variation around, 283–285
  visualizing, 293–294
regression plane, visualizing, 298–301
Remember icon, 4
`rep()` function, 30–31
repeated measures
  about, 244
  in R, 247–249
  visualizing results, 249–250
  working with, 245–246
residuals, 239, 283, 294–295, 317
resources, online, 421–424. *See also* websites
`rexp()` function, A9
`rf()` function, 226
`rhyper()` function, C4–C5
`rnbinom()` function, 377
`rnorm()` function, 147, 156–157, 402
`rolldie()` function, C18
`round()` function, 120, 139
row factor, 256
RStudio
  about, 17
  downloading, 18–21
  website, 18
RStudio Online Learning, 422
`rt()` function, 176, 189–190
`r.test()` function, 323

S

sabermetrics, 392
sample( ) function, 399
sample space, 362–363, 366–369
sample standard deviation, 109
sample variance, 106
sample_n( ) function, C18
samples
  about, 10–11
  defined, 163
  independent, B2–B8
  matched, B8–B16
  testing more than two, 231–254
sampling distribution of the mean, 164
sampling distributions
  about, 164–165
  hypothesis tests and, 181–183
  two-sample hypothesis testing and, 206–212
sapply( ) function, 417–418
scale( ) function, 114–115
scale_x_continuous( ) function, 137, 149, 151, 156, 160
scatter plot matrix, 69–71, 84–86
scatter3d( ) function, 300
scatterplots
  about, 55–56, 67–71, 82–84
  correlation and, 313–314
  regression and, 277–279
  visualizing, 293–294
Schmuller, Joseph (author)
  Statistical Analysis with Excel For Dummies, 2, 44
scores, standardizing, 158–160
sd( ) function, 109–110
seed, 157
segments, 150
select( ) function, C16–C17
semipartial correlation, 331–333
seq( ) function, 30–31
set.seed( ) function, 157, 402
$-sign, 94–95
significant linear component, 252
simple main effects, 269
skewness, 127–130

skewness( ) function, 128, 131
slice( ) function, C17
slope, testing, 289
sort( ) function, 118
spcor( ) function, 332
spcor.test( ) function, 332
Spearman's correlation coefficient, B16–B18
spreadsheets, 44–46
squaring a deviation, 105
Stack Overflow, 422
standard deviation
  about, 107, 199
  population, 107–109
  sample, 109
standard error, 164
standard error of the mean, 164
standard normal distribution, 130, 158, 159, 160
standard score. *See* z-score
standards
  about, 111
  ranking, 117–121
  scale( ) function, 114–115
  summarizing, 121–122
  z-score, 112–114, 116
Stanford-Binet score, 158
stat function, 216, 228
stat_boxplot( ) function, 216, 274
stat_function( ) function, C5–C8, C10
Statistical Analysis with Excel For Dummies (Schmuller), 2, 44
statistical functions, 412–413, C5–C8
statistically significant, 184
statistics
  about, 9
  data types, 12
  descriptive. *See* descriptive statistics
  error types, 15–16
  inferential, 10, 14–16
  lists and, 35–36
  non-parametric, B1–B21
  populations, 10–11
  probability, 13–14
  samples, 10–11
  variables, 11–12

W

X

Y

Z

About the Author

Joseph Schmuller, PhD is a veteran of academia and corporate Information Technology. He is the author of several books on computing, including the three editions of *Teach Yourself UML in 24 Hours* (SAMS), and the four editions of *Statistical Analysis with Excel For Dummies* (Wiley). He has created online coursework for Lynda.com, and he has written numerous articles on advanced technology. From 1991 through 1997, he was Editor-in-Chief of *PC AI* magazine.

He is a former member of the American Statistical Association, and he has taught statistics at the undergraduate and graduate levels. He holds a B.S. from Brooklyn College, an M.A. from the University of Missouri-Kansas City, and a Ph.D. from the University of Wisconsin, all in psychology. He and his family live in Jacksonville, Florida, where he is a Research Scholar at the University of North Florida.

Dedication

For my wonderful mentor, Al Hillix — with eternal thanks for his timeless wisdom, his sage guidance, and his lasting friendship.

Author's Acknowledgments

Writing a *For Dummies* book is one of the most fun things an author can do. You get to express yourself in a friendly, conversational way, and you get to throw in some humor, too.

As a former magazine editor, I appreciate what editors do, but never more so than on this project. The Wiley team was terrific from start to finish. Acquisitions Editor Katie Mohr initiated this effort. Project Editor Paul Levesque tightened up my writing and did a marvelous job coordinating all the myriad things that go into a book like this. Copy Editor Becky Whitney also contributed valuable insights that make the book you're holding easier to read. Technical Editor Russ Mullen made sure the code and other technical aspects were correct. Any errors that remain are under the ownership and sole proprietorship of the author.

My thanks to David Fugate of Launchbooks.com for representing me in this effort.

I could never have written this book without the mentors in college and graduate school who helped shape my statistical knowledge: Mitch Grossberg (Brooklyn College); Al Hillix, Jerry Sheridan, the late Mort Goldman, and the late Larry Simkins (University of Missouri-Kansas City); and Cliff Gillman and the late John Theios (University of Wisconsin-Madison). I hope this book is an appropriate testament to my mentors who have passed on.

As always, my thanks to Kathryn for her inspiration and support.

Publisher's Acknowledgments

Acquisitions Editor: Katie Mohr

Senior Project Editor: Paul Levesque

Copy Editor: Becky Whitney

Technical Editor: Russ Mullen

Editorial Assistant: Serena Novosel

Sr. Editorial Assistant: Cherie Case

Production Editor: Tamilmani Varadharaj

Cover Image: © jastrijebphoto/iStockphoto